THE ALLIED AIR CAMPAIGN AGAINST HITLER'S U-BOATS

THE ALLIED AIR CAMPAIGN AGAINST HITLER'S U-BOATS

VICTORY IN THE BATTLE OF THE ATLANTIC

By Timothy S. Good

FRONTLINE BOOKS

The Allied Air Campaign Against Hitler's U-boats

This edition published in 2021 by Frontline Books,
an imprint of Pen & Sword Books Ltd, Yorkshire – Philadelphia

Copyright © Timothy S. Good.
ISBN: 9781 3990 96492

No part of this book may be reproduced or transmitted in any form or by any means, electronic or mechanical including photocopying, recording or by any information storage and retrieval system, without permission from the Publisher in writing.

Typeset in by Printed and bound by CPI UK

Pen & Sword Books Ltd incorporates the imprints of Pen & Sword Archaeology, Air World Books, Atlas, Aviation, Battleground, Discovery, Family History, History, Maritime, Military, Naval, Politics, Social History, Transport, True Crime, Claymore Press, Frontline Books, Praetorian Press, Seaforth Publishing and White Owl

For a complete list of Pen & Sword titles please contact:

PEN & SWORD BOOKS LTD
47 Church Street, Barnsley, South Yorkshire, S70 2AS, UK.
E-mail: enquiries@pen-and-sword.co.uk
Website: www.pen-and-sword.co.uk

Or

PEN AND SWORD BOOKS,
1950 Lawrence Roadd, Havertown, PA 19083, USA
E-mail: Uspen-and-sword@casematepublishers.com
Website: www.penandswordbooks.com

To my brother, Travis

Thanks for all the Second World War 'discussions'

And to the P-8 Poseidon crews, the direct descendants of the B-24 Liberator crews

Acknowledgements

I would to thank Dr Axel Niestle for his constant and outstanding expertise, Gene Finke and my dad for input, and to the great staff at the National Archives for all of their assistance and guidance.

Table of Contents

Preface		xi
Chapter 1	The Second Happy Time	1
Chapter 2	1939–1941	15
Chapter 3	1942	27
Chapter 4	The B-24 Arrives	41
Chapter 5	The Casablanca Conference	53
Chapter 6	The B-24s in the North Atlantic: January–May 1943	65
Chapter 7	The Allies' Other Aircraft in the North Atlantic: January–May 1943	75
Chapter 8	Outside the North Atlantic: January–May 1943	85
Chapter 9	B-24s: June–July 1943	97
Chapter 10	United States Navy: June–July 1943	105
Chapter 11	The B-24s: August–October 1943	117
Chapter 12	The United States Navy: August–October 1943	125
Chapter 13	November–December 1943	137
Chapter 14	B-24s: January–May 1944	149
Chapter 15	Swordfish, Catalinas, Avengers and Wellingtons: January–May 1944	159
Chapter 16	June 1944	175
Chapter 17	July–December 1944	189
Chapter 18	1945	203
Chapter 19	Conclusion	213

Endnotes	221
Bibliography	251
Index	259

Preface

This is the first book-length study of the Allied air campaign against the German U-boats in the Second World War. The Battle of the Atlantic has received attention from historians in countless publications. However, the attention has been focused on either the overall story of the battle – such as Clay Blair's two-volume work entitled *Hitler's U-Boat War*, S.W. Roskill's multi-volume *The War at Sea: 1939–1945* and Dan Van der Vat's *The Atlantic Campaign: The Great Struggle at Sea* – or centred on limited aspects of the campaign such as U-boat operations, escort carrier operations or specific geographic areas. The Allied air campaign receives compartmentalised coverage, as evidenced in Alan C. Carey's *Sighted Sub: The United States Navy's Air Campaign against the U-Boat*, William T. Y'Blood's *Hunter Killer: U.S. Navy Escort Carriers in Gallant Battle Against the Nazi U-Boat Menace*, Andrew Hendrie's *The Cinderella Service: RAF Coastal Command, 1939–1945*, and Marc Milner's *The U-Boat Hunters: The Royal Canadian Navy and the Offensive against Germany's Submarines*. No previous studies have comprehensively studied the Allied aircrafts' critical importance through the evaluation of all Allied anti-submarine air operations.

No weapon platform sank more U-boats than aircraft. Whether it was American aircraft from American escort carriers, American aircraft from Royal Air Force bases, or British aircraft from bases throughout the world, these officers and men became the most decisive factor in turning the tide against the U-boat threat. While German crews could threaten escort vessels with torpedoes, or successfully avoid them by remaining submerged, their leaders never developed an effective strategy against aircraft. A surfaced U-boat discovered by a depth-charge-laden aircraft had little recourse besides crash diving or employing flak guns.

However, the Allied aircraft effort did not commence with success. British, Canadian and Australian air crews that fought the U-boats from 1939–1941 achieved few triumphs. They possessed neither the aircraft nor the bases necessary to deliver consistent lethal attacks against German submarines. While radar, the breaking of the Nazi code, and improved depth charges all contributed to Allied victory, the aircraft is the one platform that brought all the technological advances together. And in 1941 the RAF finally began implementing an effective aircraft response when it initiated training on American-built B-24 Liberators. These aircraft would prove to be decisive.

With America's entry into the war, the United States Navy and the United States Army Air Forces also began employing the four-engine Liberators against U-boats so that by mid–1943, the German Admiral Karl Dönitz, commander of U-boat forces, withdrew his submarines from the North Atlantic in recognition of the Allied aircraft's new dominance. The B-24s, flown by American, British, Canadian and Czechoslovakian crews, could cruise for over twelve hours, could carry a significant payload of depth charges, and with their speed, they could surprise and attack a surfaced U-boat before a crash dive. The German's only defence – flak guns – proved to be of limited success against a fast, large aircraft such as the Liberator, which could absorb significant punishment while delivering its fatal payload. The B-24s would sink more U-boats than any other Allied aircraft.

From Dönitz's retreat to the end of the war, Allied aircraft continued to dominate the U-boat battle as it shifted to other areas including the Bay of Biscay. Dönitz eventually ordered his U-boats to remain on the surface and engage Allied aircraft as opposed to submerging. This failed approach did lead to the demise of some Allied aircraft, but it also resulted in more U-boat sinkings. Most critically, Dönitz acknowledged with his new policy that he knew of no tactics or weapons that would defend his U-boats from Allied aircraft. In the end, it was a matter of choosing whether his submariners would die submerged or die surfaced. Either way, Allied aircraft had prevailed.

Chapter 1

The Second Happy Time

On 14 April 1939, President Franklin D. Roosevelt dispatched a letter to Nazi Chancellor Adolf Hitler. The American leader reminded the German leader that: 'On a previous occasion I have addressed you on behalf of the settlement of political, economic, and social problems by peaceful methods and without resort to arms.' Roosevelt noted that 'the tide of events seems to have reverted to the threat of arms' and warned the dictator that 'If such threats continue, it seems inevitable that much of the world must become involved in common ruin. All the world,' he predicted, 'victor nations, vanquished nations, and neutral nations, will suffer. I refuse to believe that the world is, of necessity, such a prisoner of destiny. On the contrary, it is clear that the leaders of great nations have it in their power to liberate their peoples from the disaster that impends. It is equally clear that in their own minds and in their own hearts the peoples themselves desire that their fears be ended.'

The president further requested that Hitler respect the boundaries of thirty-one nations for the next decade. Two weeks later, Hitler publicly responded to Roosevelt's request before the Reichstag in a two-hour speech in which he mocked and ridiculed the American's requests. And the assembled Nazis laughed. Again and again, they laughed. The moment served as a prime example of Hitler's and the Nazi Party's contempt for the American people and their president.[1]

Two years later, when the Japanese assaulted Pearl Harbor, both the British Prime Minister Winston Churchill and Roosevelt faced a quandary. They both considered Nazi Germany as the main aggressor, but the Japanese attack failed to provide the president with justification to declare war on Hitler's empire. The German Chancellor though, solved the Allies' predicament by declaring war against the United States, an action that Roosevelt quickly reciprocated.

Hitler's declaration is most easily explained by his growing anger at the Americans. His bitterness as displayed in 1939 had only increased over time, and now he had the opportunity to bring the war to America. While his forces had ravaged much of Europe, the continental United States remained untouched, a fact that Hitler now sought to change. And, he had the ideal weapon with which to accomplish his terror: the U-boat. He unleashed his forces on the unprepared Americans for eight months, from January to August 1942, a period that German submariners referred to as the 'Second Happy Time'.[2]

If the Americans sought to anticipate what disaster to which Hitler intended to subject them, they had only to study the 'First Happy Time', as the U-boat commanders referred to the period from the commencement of war in September 1939 until the end of 1940. During those months, Nazi submarines terrorised British shipping and sank over 215 merchant vessels and two warships. In response, the Allies destroyed only twenty-four U-boats. Admiral Karl Dönitz began this campaign with fifty-seven U-boats and ended with fifty-one of them. By all calculations, his men devastated Allied shipping. Of especial note, 195 of the ships – 90 per cent – sunk by U-boats during this multi-month assault had been unescorted. The British did not possess the escort vessels or aircraft necessary to protect their merchantmen, and neither did the Americans. When Hitler now focused on the United States, his U-boat commanders would encounter dozens of American ships traversing the Atlantic waters unescorted and unarmed, hence their phrase, 'Second Happy Time'.[3]

Two days after Pearl Harbor, Admiral Dönitz, recorded in his diary: 'The attempt must be made to exploit these advantages, which will disappear in the foreseeable future, and to strike a blow at the American coast with a drumbeat.' This was Operation Paukenschlag, translated as either 'drumbeat' or 'thunderbolt'. Either way, it would prove to be a disastrous period for the Allies.[4] Dönitz unleashed five of his Type IX U-boats on the Americans. The Germans designed these larger boats to operate over greater distances and for longer patrols. Slower than other designs, they nevertheless proved to be ideal for the task at hand. Additionally, these boats were well commanded; all five commanders had already achieved numerous successes. For example, Reinhard Hardegen, *U-123*'s commander, had sunk five Allied vessels prior to his mission to America.[5]

From 16 December to 25 December, these massive Nazi submarines departed their French Bay of Biscay ports. Dönitz noted the distances from their home ports to Western Hemisphere targets: Sydney, Nova Scotia, 2,200 miles; Halifax, Nova Scotia, 2,400 miles; New York, 3,000 miles; Trinidad, 3,800 miles; Key West 4,000 miles; and Aruba 4,000 miles. The German admiral realised that the 'big Type IX boats could reach all these places and still have enough fuel in hand to operate for two or three weeks'. To achieve surprise, he 'selected as the site of our first offensive the area between St Lawrence and Cape Hatteras' and, to ensure that they arrived safely at his intended destination, he ordered the boats 'to keep out of sight between Newfoundland and the east coast of America'. Regarding the transatlantic passage, he further stipulated that 'en route they were to restrict their attack to really worth-while targets – ships of 10,000 tons and over'. His strategy would serve his Führer well.[6]

The first U-boat sinking illustrated the Allies' vast unpreparedness. On 12 January, *U-123* discovered the large British steamship *Cyclops* of over 9,000 tons, just a little over 100 miles south of Nova Scotia, and most critically, unescorted.[7] At almost two hours after midnight, the German U-boat hit the merchant vessel with a single torpedo and then, about twenty minutes later, fired a second one that also struck the doomed ship, causing it to sink in minutes. Despite the report of the attack having been sent and received at the time of the sinking, an Allied Catalina aircraft did not sight the survivors until the next day, followed by retrieval by a minesweeper. Nearly 100 of the 181 crew members died due to exposure. The lengthy time for rescue well demonstrated the complete lack of forces available to respond to U-boat attacks.[8]

Dönitz did not consider the five Type IX boats sufficient for his American operations. He contemplated the 'possibility of making use of the medium Type VIIC boats (517 tons), whose radius of action was considerably smaller' than the Type IX 'for operations in these distant areas'. Yet, the German 'calculations' proved that the Type VIIC boats 'could reach the shipping lanes of Nova Scotia and still have enough fuel to remain there for a reasonable period'. However, Dönitz realised that 'their radius of action' would not allow them to operate 'farther to the south and west, off the coast of the United States'. Dönitz recalled, 'when Naval High Command's order of January 2, 1942, released for operations in the Atlantic all the new Type VIIC boats which had been originally earmarked for the Mediterranean, I at once diverted seven of them ... and sent them to the Nova Scotia-Newfoundland area'. The Allies would now face twelve U-boats along the Atlantic seaboard.[9]

The large Type IX Nazi submarines sank sixteen other Allied merchant vessels in January in the American eastern seaboard vicinity.[10] After the destruction of the *Cyclops*, Reinhard Hardegen in Type IXB *U-123* achieved his second sinking, that of the Panamanian tanker *Norness*, on the 14th.[11] Fortunately, all but one of the forty-one crew members survived. Five days later, Hardegen's *U-123* struck again by sinking the unarmed American steamship *City of Atlanta* off the North Carolina coast, bringing his total of merchantmen sunk to three in just a week. The railroad ferry *Seatrain Texas* saved three men from the forty-six-man crew. Remaining off the North Carolina coast, *U-123* completed its fourth sinking for January when it encountered the unarmed American freighter *Norvana*. None of her crew survived Hardegen's assault. Type IXC boat *U-130*, commanded by the highly capable commander Ernst Kals, also devastated Allied shipping this month. He sank the Norwegian *Frisco* on the 12th and the Panamanian *Friar Rock* the next day. After an eight-day lull, Kals delivered one successful assault after another. He destroyed the Norwegian *Alexandra Hoegh* on the 21st, the Panamanian *Olympic* on the 22nd, and the Norwegian *Varanger* on the 25th. Then, on 27 January, Kals sank the unarmed American tanker *Francis E. Powell* just 8 miles from the Winter Quarter Lightship off New Jersey. Of the thirty-two-man crew, a Coast Guard boat and an American tanker, the *W.C. Fairbanks*, saved twenty-eight. Richard Zapp, having already sunk five Allied vessels before Dönitz sent him to the American coast, continued his successful career. In *U-66*, he commenced his assault along the American seaboard by sinking the unarmed American tanker *Allan Jackson* only 50 miles east of Cape Hatteras, North Carolina. The American destroyer USS *Roe* rescued thirteen men of the thirty-five-man crew. Zapp then destroyed the Canadian *Lady Hawkins* on the 19th, the British *Empire Gem* on the 24th before his last victory, the fatal torpedoing of the unarmed American collier *Venore*. *U-125* inaugurated its highly successful career with the sinking of the American freighter *West Ivis* on the 26th and no one heard from the vessel's forty-five crew members again.[12]

Dönitz's Type VIIC boats also terrorised Allied shipping in January. On the 15th, *U-552*, commanded by Erich Topp, sank the British vessel *Dayrose* and three days later Topp found the American freighter *Frances Salman* off St John's, Newfoundland, and fatally torpedoed her. All twenty-eight crew members died in the attack. This sinking did not mark Topp's first encounter with an American vessel; he had previously sunk the American destroyer *Reuben James* on 30 October 1941, the first US Navy vessel lost in the Second World War.[13] *U-106* completed the Nazi terror for January by using gun fire and torpedoes to sink the unarmed American tanker *Rochester*. The American destroyer USS *Roe* (DD-418) saved twenty-nine of the thirty-two crew members.

The news thrilled Hitler. In late January, a German official recorded in the Naval Command War Diary that: 'Captain von Puttkamer telephoned to say that the Fuehrer had noted with great satisfaction the rising figures of sinkings off the American coast.' When Hitler had been informed about the number of U-boats operating there, 'he expressed the desire that these boats should remain thus employed'. And the sinkings continued.[14]

U-boats destroyed twenty Allied vessels in February with the large Type IX boats continuing their depredations. Werner Winter, commanding the Type IXB boat *U-103*, claimed four in just four days. He sighted and sank the unarmed American tanker *W.L. Steed* on 2 February less than 100 miles east of the Delaware River. The freezing temperatures killed thirty-four of the thirty-eight-man crew. The next day, Winter attacked the Panamanian freighter *San Gil* with torpedoes and shells to sink her. This attack occurred just 15 miles south of the Delaware coast. The German assault killed two crew members while the Coast Guard cutter *Nike* (WPC-112) rescued the remaining thirty-eight. The same day, Werner found the unarmed American tanker *India Arrow* just 20 miles off the New Jersey shoreline. He torpedoed, shelled and sank the merchant vessel. The shelling killed two crew members, while twenty-four drowned when their lifeboats swamped. Twelve miles from the New Jersey coastline, the fishing skiff *Gitana* found and rescued the twelve remaining crew. Werner completed his shocking and successful patrol the following day with the destruction of the unarmed American tanker *China Arrow*.

Four other Type IX boats combined for seven sinkings in February. Hans-Georg Friedrich Poske, commanding Type IXC *U-504*, sank three Allied merchantmen. On 21 February, he torpedoed unarmed American tanker *Republic* just 3 miles off the Florida coast. The following day, Poske sank the unarmed American tanker *W.D. Anderson*. One crew member survived and successfully swam to the Florida shoreline. Five days later, he sank the Dutch merchantmen *Mamura*.[15] On the 19th, commander Ulrich Heyse achieved his first victory when Type IXC *U-128* fatally torpedoed the unarmed American tanker *Pan Massachusetts* 20 miles off Cape Canaveral, Florida. Fortunately, Coast Guard lighthouse tender *Forward* (WAGL-160) and British tanker *Elizabeth Massey* rescued eighteen members of the thirty-eight-man crew. Three days later, Heyse struck again by sinking the American tanker *Cities Service Empire*. On the sixth day of the month, Type IXB *U-107* torpedoed and sank unarmed American freighter *Major Wheeler*. None of the thirty-five-man crew survived. On the 20th, Type IXC *U-156* destroyed American freighter *Delplata* but fortunately the flying boat tender *Lapwing* (AVP-1) saved all fifty-two crew members.[16]

The smaller Type VIIC boats contributed to the Nazi cause as well. Heinz-Otto Schultze, commander of Type VIIC *U-432*, could not claim to have matched Winter's four sinkings in four days, but he did destroy six Allied merchant vessels in February. On the 15th, he torpedoed Brazilian steamship *Buarque* 30 miles from the North Carolina coast. Three days later Schultze struck another Brazilian vessel, the tanker *Olinda*. The next day, he sank British merchant vessel *Miraflores* and on the 20th, Schultze torpedoed the American freighter *Azalea City* a little over 100 miles from the Maryland shoreline. None of the thirty-eight-man crew survived. He then destroyed the American merchant vessel *Norlavore* four days later. On the 26th, he shelled and torpedoed the unarmed American bulk carrier *Marore*.[17]

Ernst-August Rehwinkel, in Type VIIC *U-578*, achieved his first sinking in February. On the 26th, he fatally torpedoed American tanker *R.P. Resor* only 5 miles from the Delaware coastline. Most critically, *U-578* also demonstrated to the Americans the vulnerability of their naval vessels when the destroyer *Jacob Jones*, DD-130, entered the hunting ground. The warship departed New York harbour a day after the strike on *Resor* and found the tanker's burning remains. The American destroyer remained in the area for a couple of hours hoping to locate survivors before turning south again. As sunlight emerged on the morning of the 28th, Rehwinkel fired multiple torpedoes. The destroyer crew noticed neither the U-boat nor the wakes of the oncoming threat. Rehwinkel's first hits struck the ship's magazine and fuelled an explosion that eviscerated 'the bridge, the chart room, and the officers' and petty officers' quarters'. The destroyer lost all speed. Rehwinkel launched another torpedo. This strike wrecked the rear 'part of the ship above the keel plates and shafts and destroyed' the rear crew's quarters. Approximately two dozen men survived at this point. An aircraft spotted the destroyer's life rafts but once rescued, only eleven returned to shore. A total of 102 Americans perished.[18]

Three other U-boat commanders each sank a single Allied vessel in Type VIIC boats in February. On the 11th, *U-564* destroyed the Canadian motor tanker *Victolite*, while on the 19th, *U-96* torpedoed the American freighter *Lake Osweya*. The Germans recorded witnessing multiple lifeboats from this sinking but the Americans found none of the thirty-man crew. Then, on the 28th, *U-653* sank the Norwegian merchant vessel *Leif*. After two months of attacks, the Americans had initiated no successful responses to the German assaults.[19]

In March, Dönitz's U-boats continued their terror off the Atlantic seaboard by sinking eleven Allied merchant vessels, with two U-boats claiming multiple sinkings. On the fifth of the month, Type VIIC *U-404* fatally torpedoed the unarmed United States freighter *Collamer*, which had fallen behind its convoy, HX 178. British freighter *Empire Woodcock* rescued twenty-four survivors from the thirty-one-man crew.²⁰ For *U-404*'s commander, Otto von Bülow, the *Collamer* would mark the first of many destroyed Allied ships. Later that month, he sank the Chilean freighter *Tolten* off the New Jersey coast. Of over a dozen crew members, only one survived.

On 10 March, Type VIIC *U-588* sank American tanker *Gulftrade* within sight of the New Jersey shore and a day later, 14 miles off the North Carolina coast, *U-158* fatally torpedoed the unarmed American freighter *Caribsea* and then, twenty-four hours later, severely damaged the American tanker *John D. Gill*.²¹

A variety of U-boats destroyed the remainder of Allied vessels. Another of Dönitz's large U-boats, Type IXC *U-155*, made its presence known to the Americans on 7 March. Cruising off the Virginia coast, Adolf Piening, one of the most successful U-boat commanders, having sunk two Allied vessels when transiting the Atlantic on his mission to the American seaboard, added to his total when he fatally torpedoed the Brazilian steamship *Arabutan*.²² On 9 March, Type VIIC *U-94* struck the Brazilian steamship *Cayru*. Type VIIC *U-332* sank the unarmed American schooner *Albert F. Paul* and none of the crew survived. On 25 March, Type VIIC *U-552* fatally torpedoed the Dutch tanker *Ocana*. The American destroyer *Mayo* (DD-422) located four survivors. One of America's two Q-ships, anti-submarine armed vessels disguised as merchantmen, engaged Type IXB *U-123* in battle. While sustaining some damage, the U-boat sank her and the Americans found no crew members. Three days later, less than 50 miles from the North Carolina coast, Type IXC *U-160* destroyed the American steamship *City of New York*.

Finally, on the last day of the month, Dönitz's commanders attacked multiple targets. Just 50 miles from the American naval base at Norfolk, Virginia, Type VIIC *U-753* assaulted the unarmed American tug *Menominee* with gun fire, killing sixteen of her eighteen crew, and also fired on her three barges: *Allegheny*, *Barnegat*, and *Ontario*. Type VIIC *U-754* fatally torpedoed the unarmed American tanker *Tiger*, resulting in the death of one crew member.²³

U-boats continued their depredations in April with the destruction of nine Allied merchant vessels. Type IXB *U-123*'s commander Hardegen continued his successful patrol by claiming four American vessels, the first three of which he torpedoed within 15 miles of the Georgia coast. He commenced his successful month by attacking two American tankers. The U-boat torpedoed and shelled the unarmed tanker *Oklahoma*, then targeted the unarmed tanker *Esso Baton Rouge*. From both vessels, fifty-four were rescued and twenty-two died. The tankers though, survived. The Americans refloated and repaired both of them so that they would sail again. *U-123* also fatally torpedoed the unarmed American freighter *Esparta*, en route from Honduras to New York. By 10 April, the U-boat had moved to the Florida coast where, with the lights of Jacksonville illuminating the area, it assaulted the American tanker *Gulfamerica* with torpedoes and shells that killed dozens of the crew. Many also drowned and only twenty-two of the forty-one-man crew survived.[24]

Topp, in Type VIIC *U-552*, continued to terrorise American shipping in April by sinking multiple vessels. On the second day of the month, surfaced *U-552*, just 10 miles off the Virginia coastline, fired on the unarmed American freighter *David H. Atwater*. Coast Guard cutter *Legare* (WPC-144) located only three members of the twenty-five-man crew. The US Navy ordered two destroyers – *Noa* (DD-343) and *Herbert* (DD-160) – to the *Atwater*'s location but both arrived after *U-552* had disappeared. Two days later, Topp also sank the unarmed American tanker *Byron D. Benson* 8 miles off the North Carolina coast. Nine of the thirty-seven-man crew perished in the resulting blaze and *Hamilton* (DMS-18), an American minesweeper, brought twenty-seven men aboard, while a British vessel rescued another one. Topp lingered off the North Carolina coast and fatally torpedoed the unarmed American tanker *Atlas*. Coast Guard cutter *CG 462* saved thirty-two of the thirty-four-man crew from the tanker's gasoline-fuelled fire. Hours later, he attacked tanker *Tamaulipas*, which sank the next morning due to the intensity of the fire on board.[25]

Type IXCs *U-160* and *U-154* also sank multiple Allied vessels in April. *U-160* fatally torpedoed the British steamship *Rio Blanco* on the 1st, and attacked the unarmed *Bidwell*, 30 miles east of the North Carolina coastline three days later. *Bidwell*, though, arrived at Hampton Roads. Then, on the 9th, only 50 miles off the Cape Hatteras coast, *U-160* sank the unarmed American freighter *Malchace*, followed by the British steamship *Ulysses* on the 11th. On 4 April, *U-154* destroyed American tanker *Comol Rico* and the next day this U-boat fatally attacked another American tanker, the *Catahoula*.[26]

While the U-boat sinkings through April only involved merchant vessels, Nazi commanders also targeted passenger vessels, which often carried hundreds of people. *U-160* found one, the British steamship *Ulysses*, carrying 195 crew members and 95 passengers, and torpedoed her. Remarkably, the high-speed transport *Manley* (APD-1) arrived and saved all hands.[27]

In May, six merchantmen fell victim to German assaults, one by Type VIIC *U-404*, one by Type VIIC *U-656*, and the other four by Type

VIIC *U-588*. *U-404* sank the American *Alcoa Shipper*,[28] while *U-588*, commanded by Victor Vogel, destroyed the British merchant vessel *Kittys Kitty's Brook* on 10 May and the Norwegian *Skottland* on 15 May. Two days later, *U-656* fatally torpedoed the British merchant vessel *Peisander*. On the 21st, crew members on the American freighter *Plow City* misidentified a lifeboat from the *Peisander* as a U-boat and increased speed to escape. *U-588*'s crew spotted the exhaust smoke from the fleeing freighter and pursued, torpedoed and sank her. The attack killed one of *Plow City*'s crew members outright, while the U-boat crew captured and interrogated another on *U-588*. Vogel returned the crew member to his shipmates with 'rum and cigarettes' and assisted the Americans in righting a capsized lifeboat.[29] *U-588* concluded its patrol in American hunting grounds with the sinking of the British merchant vessel *Margot* two days later. Vogel safely returned to France after this patrol but his next foray into the North Atlantic proved to be more challenging. On 19 July, the Royal Canadian Navy delivered a fatal depth charge attack with the destroyer HMCS *Skeena* and the corvette HMCS *Wetaskiwin*. All hands perished in the sinking.[30]

During June, U-boats sank six American vessels near the Atlantic seaboard. On the first day of the month, the commander of *U-404*, so confident of the ineptness of the American defences, actually assaulted the American freighter *West Notus* with shellfire while surfaced off Cape Hatteras, North Carolina. The following day, the U-boat crew boarded the freighter and sank her with explosive charges.[31] On 1 June, in the Gulf of Mexico, Type IXB *U-106* fatally torpedoed the unarmed American freighter *Hampton Roads*. Type IXC *U-502*, cruising about the Florida Keys on 3 June, struck the American tanker *M.F. Elliott*. The Germans seized two crew members but during interrogation the U-boat had to crash dive upon sight of a US Navy aircraft. Later, the crew returned the captured crew members with supplies and a life raft. On the 7th, Type VIIC *U-653* destroyed the American patrol vessel *Gannet*, while three days later Type IXC *U-157* torpedoed American tanker *Hagan*, killing six crew members. The remaining twenty-nine men arrived in Cuba via lifeboat the next day.[32]

U-boats even targeted vessels transiting along the American Gulf of Mexico shoreline. On 12 June, Type IXC *U-158* sighted the unescorted United States tanker *Cities Service Toledo* just off the Louisiana coast. The American vessel carried 84,000 barrels of crude oil. *U-158*'s torpedoes struck the tanker and a massive explosion erupted. Eleven of the thirty-six-man crew died in the fire, along with four of the nine-man Armed Guard. Three vessels came to the survivors' aid: the Norwegian tanker *Belinda*, the American tanker *Gulf King*, and the American steamship *San Antonio*. These three vessels saved thirty men.[33]

Dönitz considered this period highly successful, as he attested in his war diary for 15 April. 'What counts in the long run,' he argued, 'is the preponderance of sinkings over new construction.' The German admiral fully recognised that 'shipbuilding and arms production are centred in the United States, while England is the European outpost and sally-port. By attacking the supply-traffic – particularly the oil – in the US zone, I am striking at the root of the evil, for here,' Dönitz insisted, 'the sinking of each ship is not only a loss to the enemy but also deals a blow at the source of his shipbuilding and war production. Without shipping,' he believed, 'the sally-port cannot be used for an attack on Europe.' He argued that Nazi Germany 'should continue to operate the U-boats where they can sink the greatest tonnage with the smallest losses, which at present is in American waters'.[34] Dönitz rightly recognised the critical importance of petroleum and America's vulnerability. When he unleashed his U-boats on the American coastline, 95 per cent of petroleum destined for east coast ports arrived by ship.[35]

American General George C. Marshall, in considering the necessity of winning the war in Europe by having to transit the Atlantic, agreed with Dönitz's assessment and expressed his frustration to the commander of the US Navy, Admiral Ernest King, to whose responsibility the Battle of Atlantic fell. On 19 June, two months after Dönitz's diary entry, Marshall wrote: 'The losses by submarines off our Atlantic seaboard and in the Caribbean now threaten our entire war effort. The following statistics bearing on the subject have been brought to my attention.'

The general noted that 'of the seventy-four ships allocated to the Army for July by the War Shipping Administration, seventeen have already been sunk. Twenty-two percent of the bauxite fleet has already been destroyed. Twenty percent of the Puerto Rican fleet has been lost' Referring to the issue that Dönitz considered most crucial, he also related that 'tanker sinkings have been 3.5 percent per month of tonnage in use'.

Marshall understood that 'we are all aware of the limited number of escort craft available but has every conceivable improvised means been brought to bear on this situation? I am fearful that another month or two of this will so cripple our means of transport that we will be unable to bring sufficient men and planes to bear against the enemy in critical theatres to exercise a determining influence on the war.'

In response, on 21 June, King confessed that he had 'long been aware, of course, of the implications of the submarine situation as pointed out in your memorandum'. He claimed to 'have employed – and will continue to employ – not only regular forces but also such improvised means to give any promise of usefulness'. After this statement, he blamed the British for not destroying the European U-boat infrastructure such as submarine bases and construction yards. The admiral contended that 'if all shipping can be brought under escort and air-cover our losses will be reduced to an acceptable figure'. King further asserted, in ignoring the benefit of air cover, that 'escort is not just *one* way of handling the submarine menace; it is the *only* way that gives any promise of success'. The two words emphasized by the admiral further demonstrate his bias toward surface vessels. He dismissed 'the so-called patrol and hunting operations' as 'futile' and concluded with the statement that 'we must get every ship that sails the seas under constant protection'.[36]

The official US Navy historian, Admiral Samuel Eliot Morison, arrived at a different conclusion by admitting that 'the writer cannot avoid the conclusion that the US Navy was woefully unprepared, materially and mentally, for the U-boat blitz on the Atlantic coast'. The situation could only be explained as 'largely the Navy's own fault' because 'it had no plans ready for a reasonable protection to shipping' and 'was unable to improvise them for several months'.[37]

By July, the Americans finally commenced convoy operations, which brought the 'Second Happy Time' to a conclusion, but Dönitz considered the first half of 1942 a stunning success.[38] 'A review of the first six months of the year,' he wrote, 'shows that the results obtained had by far exceeded the high expectations held by U-boat Command in January, when operations in American waters had started. At the beginning the enemy's defensive measures had been less effective than had been anticipated,' Dönitz recalled, 'and he took longer than I had expected to strengthen his defences and to organise a controlled routing of his shipping'. But overall, the German admiral described 'the successes achieved by a small number of U-boats' as 'extraordinary'.[39]

During this U-boat onslaught, the Allies achieved minimal success in combating the U-boat menace along the Atlantic seaboard, destroying only twelve. However, these sinkings offered the Allies great insight as to the means by which they could defeat this enemy. These incidents proved the effectiveness of aircraft over surface vessels. In nine of the twelve submarine sinkings, Allied forces detected the U-boats, not submerged, but on the surface, and in seven of these nine sinkings, aircraft, not surface vessels, delivered the fatal attack. A US Navy VP-82 Squadron crew flying twin-engine Lockheed Hudson P-8 on 1 March, while escorting a convoy south of Newfoundland, discovered the surfaced Type VIIC *U-656* and delivered a lethal assault with depth charges.⁴⁰ VP-82 followed this success two weeks later, with another Hudson attacking and sinking surfaced Type IXC *U-503*.⁴¹ On 30 June, a VP-74 PBM Mariner P-1 caught Type IXC *U-158* on the surface and sank her with multiple depth charges. A USAAF 59th Squadron crew sighted and sank the surfaced Type IXC *U-153* with A-20A Havoc 40-106 on 6 July, and the following day USAAF 396th Squadron Hudson 9-29 found Type VIIC *U-701* moving on the surface and fatally attacked with two bombs.⁴² Type VIIC *U-576* surfaced, apparently accidentally, amidst convoy KS 520 on 15 July, and two US Navy Vought OS2U Kingfisher aircraft immediately fatally struck the U-boat with depth charges.⁴³ On July's last day, 113 Squadron Royal Canadian Air Force Hudson 625 successfully depth charged surfaced Type VIIC *U-754* just south of Newfoundland.⁴⁴

Two U-boat sinkings that involved surface sightings included attacks by a US destroyer and a patrol craft. On 14 April, the USS *Roper* engaged the surfaced Type VIIB *U-85* with gun fire before attacking and sinking the then submerged boat with depth charges.⁴⁵ Type IXC *U-166* torpedoed steam passenger ship SS *Robert E. Lee*, and its escort, US Navy patrol craft *PC-566*, engaged. Lieutenant Commander Herbert G. Claudius headed for the U-boat's position by sighting the periscope protruding from the surface and delivered a successful fatal attack.⁴⁶

The three sinkings that involved sonar and no surface sightings were: the United States Coast Guard Cutter *Icarus* depth charged the submerged Type VIIC *U-352* before completing the combat with gun fire on the surfaced craft;⁴⁷ the United States Coast Guard Cutter *Thetis* sank Type IXC *U-157* with depth charges and HMS *Le Tiger* fatally depth charged Type VIID *U-215*.

Of these twelve Allied U-boat victories, experienced U-boat crews manned four of them. Johannes Ostermann commanding *U-754* had completed two war patrols and had sunk thirteen merchant vessels. *U-158*'s commander, Erwin Rostin, although only on his second war patrol, had destroyed sixteen Allied vessels. Horst Degen, in *U-701*, completed two war patrols and sank eight merchant vessels before the USAAF aircraft destroyed his boat. Hans-Dieter Heinicke's *U-576* managed four war patrols and sank five Allied vessels before his demise.

The other eight U-boats sinkings ensnarled the novice. The Allies fatally depth charged *U-503* and *U-215* on their first war patrols, having no sinkings to their credit. *U-656*, the first U-boat sunk by the US Navy, and *U-352* had ended their careers on only their second war patrol, having destroyed no ships. *U-157* fared marginally better with one sinking in two war patrols, while *U-153*, on its second outing, had sunk only three vessels when destroyed by USAAF aircraft. *U-85* and *U-166* tallied only four vessels sunk when destroyed by US navy ships. In total, eight of the U-boats sunk by Allied forces during Dönitz's 1942 assault along the American coastline had minimal experience and minimal success.

The early lesson for the Americans specifically, but for the Allies as a whole, lay in the fact that German commanders placed their U-boats in the most vulnerable situation when surfaced, and that aircraft proved to be the weapon platform most effective in discovering and sinking surfaced U-boats. After all, seven of the nine successful sinkings that involved surface sightings during the 'Second Happy Time' had commenced with an aircraft sighting.

One would expect that the British had previously learned that lesson and, had in turn, emphasized anti-submarine aircraft. They had, prior to America's entry in the war, battled the U-boat menace from September 1939 until the end of 1941, for nearly twenty months. And yet, after fighting for their very survival during the first period of the Second World War, Allied aircraft had only sunk five German U-boats. The British could be accused of facing the U-boat menace 'woefully unprepared, materially and mentally', as Admiral Morison had so stated of the Americans.

Chapter 2

1939–1941

German U-boats devastated Allied shipping in the First World War. During that conflict, the United States and Britain co-operated on a variety of measures in order to blunt the U-boat threat including escorts and convoys, measures which successfully thwarted attacks. Despite these successes though, some Britons, such as Winston Churchill, recognised the U-boats as a formidable future danger to Atlantic shipping. During the 1930s as a Member of Parliament but not yet Prime Minister, he warned of Nazi Germany's industrial rise in speeches intended for the English-speaking people on both sides of the Atlantic.

On 16 October 1938, over a year before the Second World War would erupt, Churchill, in a speech carried in Britain and America, pleaded: 'We must arm. Britain must arm. America must arm.' He recognised that some had advocated for less military preparedness as the best means by which to preserve peace, but now, having pursued that course, and placing 'ourselves at a disadvantage, we must make up for it by redoubled exertions'. He later declared: 'Is this a call for war? Does anyone pretend that preparation for resistance to aggression is unleashing war? I declare it to be the sole guarantee of peace.'[1] Six months later, on 16 March 1939, in addressing Parliament, he asserted that 'last year, when we looked at the programme of new construction' Britain had included 'no destroyers'. The former Minister of Munitions said 'perhaps it was due to a misprint, for nothing could be more necessary and obvious than the construction of destroyers', especially since the Anglo-German Naval Treaty had permitted the development of German U-boats. The future First Lord of the Admiralty warned that 'the perils which will be run by submarines in a future war are incomparably greater than the perils to which, let us not forget, the submarine succumbed in 1918'. However, Britain would only possess the superiority over U-boats, he contended, 'if there is an abundance, a super-abundance, of destroyers, and other small craft available'. Although the government had now authorised destroyer construction, Churchill lamented that 'it seems a great pity that the usual flotilla was dropped last year because we should have had all the hulls built by now'.[2]

Discussions within the Third Reich justified Churchill's fears. On 28 September, six months after his March speech and less than a month into the war, Admiral Dönitz met with the Führer. At that meeting he conveyed to the Nazi Chancellor that, in reference to the deadly wolf packs of U-boats that he would develop, new communication abilities between U-boats now permitted the Germans to 'co-ordinate the movements of U-boats spread over the widest sea areas'. The convoys, which the Allies employed as a means of protection, would become, under Dönitz's plans, a weakness that would allow him to focus the U-boats at a 'rallying point' for attacks. Dönitz's unbridled confidence led him to assert that this strategy would deliver 'a mortal blow' to Britain 'at her most vulnerable spot.'[3]

And yet despite Churchill's warnings and Nazi Germany's obvious emphasis on U-boats, Britain remained wholly unprepared for the coming Nazi onslaught. Completely disregarding past history, the Royal Navy considered U-boats a passing threat. A 1937 naval staff report captured the British perspective: 'The submarine should never again be able to present us with the problem we were faced with in 1917.' The Royal Navy rested their confidence in their new submarine detection system as the means by which the British would vanquish the U-boats. In recognition of this new technology, Dönitz in 1939, knowing that the Royal Navy now considered itself invulnerable to his force because of advances in detection equipment, concluded: 'Our goal must under all circumstances to leave England in this belief.' To the German admiral's credit, while certainly an advance in anti-submarine warfare, the systems for detecting submerged submarines would not contribute to a majority of U-boats destroyed, especially those sunk by Allied aircraft, the chief means by which they destroyed German U-boats.[4]

However, at the war's commencement, Allied aircraft, specifically those of the RAF, had, prior to America's entry into the war, failed miserably against Dönitz's U-boats. The British aircraft achieved only five fatal sinkings. Considering that, during the 1939–41 period, Allied forces sank sixty U-boats, and that Allied aircraft would destroy more of them than any other means during the whole conflict, the early part of the war represented an extraordinary nadir for aerial anti-submarine efforts.[5]

Allied aircraft failed during this time because Britain failed to prepare for another U-boat war. In lacking the necessary pre-war planning, the

British fought the U-boat menace in the 1939–41 period with unsuitable aircraft. Of the three RAF branches – Fighter Command, Bomber Command and Coastal Command – the latter led the anti-submarine effort and on 10 September 1939, nine days into the war, it possessed twenty-two squadrons. Of these, thirteen, well over half, flew the Avro Anson.

The Anson possessed no significant anti-submarine capabilities. First, the aircraft deserved, in aircraft terms, the description 'ancient', having been introduced in 1935. It lacked significant range at less than 800 miles, it lacked significant speed with a patrol speed of only 103mph, and it had an endurance of just five-and-half hours. An aircraft that could provide reconnaissance over a limited area for a few hours would only have the opportunity to discover and sink an enemy U-boat by accidental fortune. For example, later Allied anti-submarine aircraft ranged for over 1,000 miles, had a patrol speed of 150mph, and flew for over twelve hours at a time. For the entire conflict, Ansons would not sink a single U-boat, and yet Coastal Command commenced the war with a majority of them in its squadrons.[6]

Beyond the thirteen Anson squadrons, Coastal Command possessed an additional three aircraft unfit for anti-submarine service. The Saro London, a flying boat, could haul an impressive 2,000lb of bombs and depth charges but managed only 86 knots per hour patrol speed and an endurance of just over five hours. Another flying boat, the Supermarine Stranraer, attained a 92 knots per hour patrol speed and had an endurance of just over seven hours, but carried half the ordnance of the London. And finally, the Vickers Vildebeest, a land-based biplane, had nearly an identical patrol speed to the London and the Stranraer, the same carrying capacity as a Stranraer, and an endurance of just over four hours. Five Coastal Command squadrons flew one of these types, but none of these aircraft would ever sink a single U-boat in the Second World War.[7]

Of the remaining four squadrons, one flew the American-built Lockheed Hudson and three flew Short Sunderlands. The twin-engine Hudson could reach over 250mph, and had an impressive patrol speed of 125–140 knots per hour with an endurance of five to six hours. Furthermore, the aircraft could haul 750 to 1,000lb of depth charges or bombs. The Sunderland, a flying boat, possessed two critical characteristics that enabled this aircraft to serve as a lethal U-boat hunter. The Sunderland's endurance allowed crews to remain airborne for up to twelve to thirteen hours and it could haul 2,000lb of depth charges or bombs. Its slow patrol speed of 110–115 knots per hour represented its only significant weakness. Three Coastal Command squadrons flew the Sunderland at the war's commencement.[8]

It should come as no surprise that a Sunderland crew achieved the first U-boat fatality by an Allied aircraft. As would be experienced several times by the Americans in 1942 off their Atlantic seaboard, a U-boat's demise commenced with an aircraft sighting. On 30 January 1940, Flight Lieutenant E.J. Brooks of the RAF's 228 Squadron departed RAF Pembroke Dock in South Wales, in his Sunderland and arrived at the most recent position of U-boat activity an hour after take-off; he discovered no U-boat. Half an hour later, Brooks did sight HMS *Fowey*, an escort vessel, and a French destroyer rescuing survivors from a torpedoed vessel. The Sunderland pilot 'exchanged recognition signals' and flew north to rendezvous with two other destroyers.

Brooks's target, Warren Heidel, *U-55*'s commander, had already experienced a highly successful day against Allied shipping. He had sunk the Greek merchant vessel *Kerimiai* and the British merchant vessel *Vaclite*, both over 5,000 tons. Yet his U-boat had been damaged in the *Vaclite* engagement and could not submerge. *U-55*, a Type VIIB boat, had a decent chance of surviving against any surface vessels, as long as no aircraft spotted it.[9]

No vessels sighted *U-55* but Brooks, thirty minutes after his last contact with the Allied vessels, discovered *U-55* 'slightly on the port bow proceeding towards him on the surface'. Moving at 10 knots with numerous crew members on deck, the Sunderland crew had clearly caught the Germans by surprise. The British crew dropped a single bomb from 700ft, which the crew observed fall 20ft from the U-boat on its starboard side. The Sunderland crew threw out a flame float as Brooks began circling the wounded target. This situation represented a worst-case scenario for a U-boat commander: caught on the surface and battling an aircraft.

Brooks observed the U-boat continuing on the surface without any course alteration. Crew members began pouring from the conning tower while the Germans displayed no intention of submerging. Instead, the Germans responded by firing on the Sunderland, whose crew fired back. The extreme range and the fog prevented any opportunity to observe results and the British aircraft received no damage.

After circling multiple times, Brooks concluded that the U-boat could not submerge. With Royal Navy vessels only 5 miles away, he decided to contact those ships with the hope that the U-boat could be captured with prisoners. The Sunderland departed the scene and set course for the destroyers. Upon arriving in sight of the surface vessels, he conveyed the message 'U-boat follow me' with the Sunderland's Aldis lamp, and the destroyers acknowledged. When returning to the U-boat's previous position, one Sunderland crew member spotted the target about a mile away, but as he observed it, he also witnessed an explosion at the stern. The Sunderland crew spotted 'a rubber boat and some survivors swimming about in the water'. After extensive searching by both aircraft and the vessels, one of the destroyers informed the Sunderland crew 'U-boat apparently sunk, have picked up eleven survivors.' In total, forty-one survived and one perished. This sinking displayed the key aircraft advantages of speed and visibility over surface vessels.[10]

No. 228 Squadron's records bear evidence as to one of the critical problems for Britain's anti-submarine efforts during the month in which Brooks' crew achieved the Allies' first U-boat sinking by aircraft: no other flights besides Brooks's even spotted a U-boat. While the Sunderland represented the RAF's best anti-submarine aircraft in 1940, operating from Pembroke Dock at this time, did not prove to be the ideal base from which to interdict U-boats. The Allies required, for their anti-submarine aircraft, a base closer to the mid-Atlantic – an area with high likelihood of ambushing surfaced U-boats – as opposed to the area around the British Isles where the U-boat commanders anticipated Allied aircraft activity.[11]

Furthermore, while the Sunderland marked a vast improvement over other aircraft, the RAF could not expect a fatal attack with every U-boat encounter. No. 204 Squadron, flying Sunderlands, attacked five U-boats in September 1939 but succeeded in sinking none. No. 210 Squadron, which also flew Sunderlands, participated in two U-boat assaults in August 1940. In those two instances, while the British had the clear advantage of surprise against surfaced U-boats, both attacks failed to deliver a fatal assault. Even when Allied aircraft achieved their zenith in fighting U-boats in the Second World War, fatal attacks were never guaranteed.

After the first Allied aircraft U-boat sinking in January 1940, another five months passed before another aircraft delivered a fatal attack. On 1 July, a 10 Squadron, Royal Australian Air Force, Sunderland commenced an anti-submarine patrol at 0200 hours. Four hours later, the crew sighted the SS *Zarian*, down in the stern and listing to port, having 'been torpedoed aft'. After twelve minutes, the Australians spotted Type IA *U-26* in the western Bay of Biscay, and attacked. The Germans dived immediately as the Sunderland dropped four bombs onto the U-boat, which had submerged to periscope depth. After this assault, the U-boat surfaced suddenly and at 0615 hours, just three minutes after the first attack, the Australians released another four bombs. The Germans leapt into the water after this assault and two minutes after the second attack, the U-boat disappeared from the surface stern first. The British escort vessel HMS *Rochester* rescued all forty-one crew members. The Sunderland landed in the water at base at 1100 hours, a nine-hour mission.[12]

As opposed to Coastal Command's two sinkings, Royal Navy aircraft achieved only one anti-submarine success in 1940. A British Fairey Swordfish Mk. I, a biplane that appeared more similar to a First World War aircraft than a Second World War one with less than a 150mph top speed, took off from the British battleship HMS *Warspite* off the Norwegian coast on 13 April during the Second Battle of Narvik. The crew of this floatplane version spotted long-range Type IXB *U-64* at anchor, the most ideal of situations for a U-boat attacker, and dropped two bombs that struck the vessel, while also attacking with prodigious machine gun fire. *U-64* sank, eight died, and thirty-eight crew members escaped.[13]

With only three U-boat sinkings, 1940 had been an inauspicious year for Allied air anti-submarine operations, and for their anti-submarine efforts in general. In March 1941, Churchill, who was frustrated with Dönitz's continued success, issued his Battle of the Atlantic directive. Unfortunately, this directive demonstrated the Prime Minister's total lack of commitment for long-range, land-based Allied anti-submarine aircraft. The directive opened with the sentence: 'In view of various German statements, we must assume that the Battle of the Atlantic has begun.' Churchill believed that 'the next four months should enable us to defeat the attempt to strangle our food supplies and our connections with the United States' and he called for immediate steps. Churchill insisted that Britain take offensive action against U-boats and the German aircraft that assaulted Allied merchant vessels. He called for hunting the U-boats as they were being constructed, when they were docked at their home ports, and when they were at sea. The Prime Minister also called for aircraft launched at sea. Churchill asked for 'ships to catapult, or otherwise launch, fighter aircraft against bombers attacking our shipping'. He especially insisted upon increasing Coastal Command's strength in the area of the Northwest approaches to Britain with support from Fighter and Bomber Command. The former First Lord of the Admiralty also demanded more destroyers, an examination of new convoy tactics and the further arming of merchant vessels against aircraft.[14] Yet, in regards to the Allied aircraft anti-submarine effort, Churchill placed no emphasis on long-range anti-submarine aircraft. The Allies' aircraft failure against U-boats in 1941, destroying only four U-boats that year, demonstrated the directive's shortcomings. An RAF Lockheed Hudson and a Catalina each claimed one, while a

Royal Navy Martlet fighter – the British name for the US Wildcat –and a Swordfish each sank one as well. However, one of these incidents deserves attention as it involved one of the war's great captures.

On 27 August, 269 Squadron's Hudson 'S' spotted and attacked surfaced Type VIIC *U-570*, dropping four 250lb depth charges at 50ft. The British crew successfully straddled the U-boat with depth charges. The U-boat had been preparing to dive but after the attack it reappeared with its bow down as crew members appeared on deck. The Hudson crew fired machine guns until the Germans waved a white flag from the conning tower. Thirty to forty of the crew then appeared 'on deck holding up large white board'. The British successfully captured the boat and rescued all forty-four of the crew, and although the Germans tossed their Enigma coding machine and other sensitive material into the sea, *U-570* served as a significant intelligence coup for the Allies.[15]

However, this Hudson's success proved to be atypical. This aircraft provided numerous anti-submarine advantages, but its speed and inadequate payload limited its effectiveness in delivering lethal attacks. Two days after *U-570*'s capture, 269 Squadron Hudson 'P' sighted a U-boat at 8 miles and 'turned to intercept'. The U-boat managed to submerge during the three minutes that the Hudson approached, so that the British crew dropped four 250lb depth charges from 50ft on a U-boat at periscope depth. The Hudson remained in the area for three hours after the attack and observed an oil patch, but the U-boat, despite being surprised on the surface, escaped.[16]

That same day another 269 Squadron Hudson spotted a surfaced U-boat at 7 miles distance. The Germans, apparently aware of the RAF aircraft, began to submerge and thirty seconds passed before the British arrived. The Hudson dropped four 250lb depth charges from an altitude of 100 to 150ft. The British remained in the area for an hour after the attack but witnessed no evidence of a sinking. The U-boat had escaped, greatly aided by the time required for the Hudson to initiate its attack, time that permitted the U-boat to submerge safely.[17]

That same month, one of the Allies' more effective anti-submarine aircraft conducted its first successful patrol: the Consolidated PBY Catalina. This twin-engine flying boat provided RAF Coastal Command with two critical capabilities. First, it could patrol for seventeen and half hours over 4,000 miles, a significant increase compared with almost all other British aircraft. Secondly, its payload could reach 2,000lb. The weakness, as compared to later aircraft, lay in its patrol speed of around 100mph. Speed proved to be a key factor when attacking a U-boat attempting to crash dive. Nevertheless, in 1941, the British welcomed this American-built flying boat and 209 Squadron received some of the first Catalinas.[18]

No. 209 Squadron Catalinas based in Reykjavik, Iceland, battled U-boats throughout August. The squadron's only success occurred on the 25th of that month after Catalina 'J' took off at 1630 hours. Over ten hours later, the crew sighted Type VIIC *U-452* on the surface and less than a mile from the flying boat. The Catalina immediately dived and released four depth charges. The resulting explosion blew the boat to the surface and it sank, with its entire forty-two crew members, stern first.[19]

However, 209, like other RAF squadrons, struggled to deliver fatal assaults even after discovering surfaced U-boats. On 19 August, Catalina AH565 took off at 0435 hours and at 1404 observed a periscope swirl less than a mile off the port bow. The flying boat turned, descended to 50ft altitude, and headed for the target. The Catalina pilot noticed 'oil and air bubbles' and released his ordnance 30yd before the U-boat's last observed location in the direction that the boat had been heading. Three depth charges dropped and exploded but one did not. The aircraft circled around and delivered four more depth charges, which failed to explode. The crew remained in the area for over half an hour but observed no signs of damage. All information suggests that the U-boat escaped.

Attacks in September also highlighted the flying boat's weaknesses. On 11 September, 209 Squadron Catalina AH542 became airborne at 1320 hours to escort convoy SC 42. The crew discovered three destroyers performing a sweep for a U-boat and observed one dropping depth charges. When the Catalina met the convoy, the Senior Naval Officer ordered the aircraft to search for a U-boat 30 miles behind it. At 0350 hours the crew spotted a fully surfaced U-boat at less than 2 miles distance. The Catalina dived on the U-boat, which remained on the surface as the flying boat dropped its depth charges. Unfortunately for the British crew, one depth charge failed to release, the second exploded 20ft from the U-boat, and the other two, instead of falling separately in order to maximise the impact of the explosions, dropped together. The U-boat responded to this attack by crash diving and the Catalina crew acknowledged that they observed no damage from the attack; the depth charges failed to sink the U-boat.[20]

The Catalina crew possessed every tactical advantage in this encounter. They had surprised the U-boat and had attacked it on the surface. And yet the attack failed. As depth charges malfunctioned throughout the war, and aircraft crews struggled continually with aiming, the Allies could not expect their aircraft to sink every U-boat at every encounter using a single charge. The Allies required a large aircraft that could drop more than four depth charges in a single pass. Their aircrews had not yet been provided with that ideal weapon platform.

Even when another aircraft accompanied a Catalina, thereby increasing the number of depth charges available for an attack, these additional munitions proved to be insufficient. On 30 October, the crew of 209 Squadron Catalina AH545 observed a surfaced U-boat proceeding at a speed of 15 knots. The U-boat crew responded by firing multiple 'green pyrotechnics' and turned to port. The Catalina, while circling, fired its machine guns. The Germans struck the flying boat's tail with a shell but fortunately at this point the Catalina crew spotted a Hudson. The Germans responded by diving and the Hudson released three bombs, while the Catalina followed with four depth charges, of which one failed to release. The U-boat had submerged just prior to the attacks. The Catalina remained for fifteen minutes and did observe a large oil patch and air bubbles. However, the U-boat survived. The speed of the U-boat's diving, the lack of speed of the Allied aircraft, and the lack of significant dropped ordnance all contributed to the U-boat's escape. As British Air Marshal Sholto Douglas, who became Commander-in-Chief of Coastal Command in 1944, reflected in his autobiography: 'In 1940 ... Coastal Command had to make do with aircraft that were both outdated and insufficient numbers.' This issue had continued into 1941 as well.[21]

Royal Navy aircraft delivered the last two Allied aircraft U-boat sinkings of 1941. In September in the Mediterranean, the British suffered a devastating setback while the Germans celebrated one of their most significant U-boat victories. Type VIIC *U-81*'s torpedoes struck one of Britain's prized vessels, the aircraft carrier *Ark Royal*, which disappeared under the water fifteen hours later on 14 November. Fortunately for the Royal Navy, many of the stricken ship's aircraft, airborne at the time, landed at Gibraltar, from where they operated for several months. From that strategic base, towards year's end on 21 December, one of the surviving Fairey Swordfish departed to search for German U-boats and discovered Type VIIC *U-451* on the surface. The Fleet Air Arm crew attacked with three depth charges and sank the boat. Later, the British corvette, *HMS Myosotis*, rescued one man; all the other forty-four crew members perished.[22]

Escort carriers, smaller versions of the larger fleet carriers, contributed to winning the Battle of the Atlantic. The Royal Navy commissioned *HMS Audacity* as the first such carrier in July 1941, a vessel that the British converted from a captured German merchantman, and which operated only six aircraft. Yet, throughout the conflict, despite their limited capabilities and their lighter aircraft, escort carriers contributed to numerous sinkings not only through direct attack but also by providing reconnaissance over a far larger area than any surface vessel could manage.[23]

The American Wildcat or Martlet served in a vital reconnaissance role. The US Navy employed these single-engine aircraft as its front-line fighter in the early years of the Pacific war. In the Atlantic, the Allies did not require the Wildcats to engage enemy aircraft, but rather enemy U-boats. And while these small aircraft could not carry anti-submarine ordnance, and their machine gun fire proved to be of little threat to the U-boats, their ability to direct surface vessels with their substantial firepower proved to be their most significant contribution.

On 17 December, a British Martlet from the Fleet Air Arm's 802 Squadron took off from escort carrier HMS *Audacity* and at 0918 hours approximately 400 miles west of Gibraltar spotted long-range Type IXC *U-131*. The pilot radioed the contact information, the U-boat dived, and five Royal Navy escort vessels turned towards the location. A cat-and-mouse game ensued until another Martlet located the U-boat on the surface again and fired upon it, only to be hit and downed by the U-boat's gun fire. The British vessels then engaged with their guns, mortally damaging the boat, which the German commander in turn scuttled. The Royal Navy rescued all forty-seven men. Although Allied aircraft had not struck the U-boat, the two Martlets had served a vital role in finding the surfaced craft on two occasions. *U-131*'s downing of the Martlet marked the first time in the war that a U-boat had shot down an Allied aircraft.[24]

Four days later though, a U-boat exacted revenge when *U-751* discovered HMS *Audacity* as she escorted an Allied convoy. One German torpedo struck the escort carrier, but she maintained speed. The next two hits proved to be fatal and she sank in less than fifteen minutes, with 802 Squadron's aircraft lost with her. This attack occurred less than a month after the U-boat sinking of *Ark Royal* and a year after the Royal Navy had lost another aircraft carrier – *Courageous* – again, due to an attack by one of Dönitz's U-boats.[25]

The sinkings of the *Courageous*, *Ark Royal* and *Audacity* all demonstrated a fundamental weakness of naval aircraft, and a strength of land-based aircraft. The U-boats had no means to attack land air bases, while they possessed significant capability to attack and sink aircraft carriers. Of course, the escort carriers could remain with the convoys throughout their passage. With the addition of long-range aircraft though, the Allies could bring to the convoys all the advantages of naval aircraft without the vulnerability of a naval vessel.

Allied aircraft would not sink another U-boat until March 1942, during the 'Second Happy Time'. The British did not yet have the proper aircraft for the Battle of the Atlantic. They required a long-range aircraft with speed and large payload. And in 1942, that type of aircraft would finally be deployed.

Chapter 3

1942

The year 1942 marked the beginning of the turning point in the Allied air war against the U-boats. Several factors contributed to this watershed. First of all, the Americans had fully arrived in the war. American-built aircraft, especially four-engine ones, would sink more U-boats than any other type. Additionally, the US Navy and USAAF aircraft began contributing to U-boat sinkings. And finally, British resources, specifically, Coastal Command, would incorporate the most successful anti-submarine aircraft of the war, the B-24.

The British continued to debate whether Coastal Command required four-engine aircraft in 1942, though. RAF Bomber Command, led by Chief Marshal Arthur Harris, insisted on more and more bombers, thus competing directly with Coastal Command for these valuable aircraft. This debate involved not only military officers, but also included those scientists advising the British government. One of the most prominent, Oxford physical chemist, Henry Tizard, engaged in this debate and on 17 February penned a note to the British minister of aircraft production. He not only sought to advocate for four-engine aircraft for Coastal Command but to also attack Bomber Command. 'I say emphatically as a conclusion,' Tizard wrote, 'that a calm dispassionate review of the facts will reveal that the present policy of bombing Germany is wrong; that we must put our maximum effort first in destroying the enemy's sea communications and preserving our own.' The advisor argued that this goal could only be accomplished 'by operating aircraft over sea on a very much larger scale than we have done hitherto, and that we shall be forced to use much longer-range aircraft'.

Tizard asserted that the 'heavy scale [of strategic bombing] will only be justified and economic at the concluding stages of the war when (or if) we are fortunate enough to have defeated the enemy at sea and to have command of it. Until that time is ripe,' he argued, 'everything is to be lost by concentrating on this bombing offensive instead of by concentrating on the sea problem.'[1]

In April, the debate continued with one of Britain's leading physicists, Frederick Lindemann, also known as Lord Cherwell, asserting that Bomber Command could render the majority of Germans in their fifty-eight cities homeless. Tizard disagreed. On 30 April, he confessed 'trouble' with the bombing argument because he could not 'see a decisive effect being caused by this wholesale bombing before the middle of 1943'. Instead, he asserted that 'in the meantime, we must preserve command of the seas, and it is difficult for me to see how we are going to do this without strong support of the Navy by long-range bombers'. As Tizard's biographer concluded, in regard to his calculations 'he was right' and his adversary 'was wrong, as events were to prove'.[2]

Tizard and his other loyal scientists, such as British physicist Patrick Blackett, considered their efforts in this respect as a failure. Three years after the war, Blackett received the Nobel Prize for Physics and in 1961 admitted that Bomber Command's approach 'was the first time a modern nation had deliberately planned a major military campaign against the enemy's civilian population rather than against his armed forces'. Blackett believed that 'if the Allied air effort had been used more intelligently, if more aircraft had been supplied for the Battle of the Atlantic and to support the land fighting in Africa and later in France, if the bombing of Germany had been carried out with the attrition of enemy defences in mind rather than the razing of cities to the ground, I believe the war could have been won half a year or even a year earlier'. He considered Bomber Command's approach 'in which the traditional military doctrine of waging war against the enemy's armed forces was abandoned for a planned attack on its civilian life was a disastrous flop, and I am sure that Tizard felt the same way'. Blackett concluded that 'if we had only been more persuasive and had forced people to believe our simple arithmetic, if we had fought officialdom more cleverly and lobbied ministers more vigorously, might we not have changed the decision?'[3]

Tizard and Blackett, and those who agreed with them, had not been persuasive. Besides the before-mentioned attacks along and near the North Atlantic seaboard during the 'Second Happy Time', and before the emergence of the four-engine B-24 as the Allies' key anti-submarine aircraft, the Allies battled the U-boat threat with inferior aircraft, and achieved limited success in 1942. Allied single-engine and twin-engine aircraft destroyed thirty-three U-boats that year, four-engine aircraft claimed five, while all Allied attacks totalled seventy-four sinkings.

Aircraft contributed to 51 per cent of the U-boats destroyed in 1942, with the RAF contributing the most of any entity at nineteen, US Navy with eight, followed by the Royal Navy and the USAAF both with four each, while Royal Canadian Air Force participated in three fatal sinkings.

Hudsons achieved the most sinkings by an aircraft with twelve fatal attacks, with RAF Hudsons contributing to the destruction of six U-boats in the Mediterranean. On 1 May, 233 Squadron Hudson 'M' found the surfaced Type VIIC *U-573*. The British aircraft dived from 1,700ft to 30ft and assaulted the U-boat with three 250lb depth charges, catching the German still on the surface. Two of the depth charges struck the starboard side and the Germans submerged, leaving a large oil patch on the surface. Sixty seconds later, 10ft of the bow emerged perpendicularly and then disappeared. The U-boat then surfaced, 'on an even keel', with the crew in the conning tower raising hands. Remarkably, after the aircraft departed, the German crew managed to manoeuvre the boat into Spanish territory, where the authorities subsequently interned forty-three crew members; one having perished in the battle. Thus ended its fourth patrol and its career, having destroyed only one Allied vessel.[4]

In November, Gibraltar-based Hudsons fought U-boats on six notable occasions. In the western Mediterranean, on 1 November, two 233 Squadron Hudsons assaulted Type VIIC *U-565*, delivering multiple attacks that damaged the boat. However, Hudson AE591 suffered fatal damage from anti-aircraft fire and crashed into the sea, killing all four crew members: *U-565* escaped.[5] Type VIIC *U-411* would not prove to be so fortunate. On 13 November, 500 Squadron Hudson 'D', which, with four other Hudsons, was conducting a wide-ranging patrol from Gibraltar, discovered it on the surface at 5 miles distance. The British aircraft dived, as did the U-boat, and when the Hudson arrived above it, the German had been submerged for forty seconds. Nevertheless, the pilot released four depth charges from 50ft 'a hundred and fifty yards ahead of the swirl made by the U-boat'. The crew reported observing no results but they had, in fact, sunk *U-411*. All forty-six hands went down with the boat, which was on its first war patrol.[6]

In mid-November, Hudsons sank two U-boats, both Type VIIC designs. On the 14th, 233 Squadron Hudson 'B' found *U-605* on the surface and dropped three depth charges that all struck the U-boat, lifting it from the sea. *U-605* disappeared stern first, taking its forty-six crew members with it, and the British crew observed the telltale oil patch and debris. The following day 500 Squadron Hudson 'S' spotted the surfaced *U-259* from 7,000ft and the pilot dived and attacked from 50ft. The crew believed that their second depth charge struck the U-boat because they observed an 'enormous explosion' that threw the gun into the air and ripped the conning tower open. All forty-eight crew members went down with the boat. The explosion though, also damaged the Hudson, but the pilot managed to remain airborne for fifteen minutes until the port engine stopped at an altitude of 1,500ft and the aircraft then commenced an uncontrollable spiral dive. All of the crew bailed out, although only two survived.[7]

However, while the Hudsons had achieved successes, two other instances highlight their weakness as an effective anti-submarine aircraft. Jürgen Quaet-Faslem, commander of Type VIIC *U-595*, had achieved minimal success in his first two patrols, with only one Allied merchant vessel sunk. On his third patrol, he would face multiple Allied aircraft, however, he would be fortunate that they were Hudsons. These attacks would demonstrate the limited lethal ability of the smaller aircraft, which lacked the necessary speed required to assault a surfaced U-boat before submerging, and also lacked the necessary ordnance to deliver a fatal attack. In this instance, six Hudsons participated. No. 608 Squadron Hudson 'C' found the surfaced *U-595* on 14 November but the U-boat submerged before an attack could be conducted. Later, 'D' from the same squadron discovered *U-595* back on the surface. This Hudson's attack caused explosions on both sides of the U-boat. *U-595* then submerged, and 'a large oil patch' appeared. Five to six minutes later, *U-595* surfaced again and the Hudson assaulted it with gun fire. Four 500 Squadron Hudsons now engaged the damaged submarine, with an aircraft carrying the code 'X' dropping depth charges that exploded across the U-boat's stern. 'F' attacked next but the depth charges hung up as the aircraft passed over the U-boat, while the Germans struck the Hudson with numerous shells. 'X' then followed but its depth charges fell 25yd short of the target. 'F' engaged again and its depth charges dropped about 50yd ahead of the U-boat. By this time Quaet-Faslem had had enough and set course slowly for the beach. About this time 'U', on an anti-submarine sweep from Gibraltar, sighted the U-boat and dropped its depth charges. Then 'W' delivered two attacks, one with depth charges and a second with an anti-submarine bomb, just as Quaet-Faslem beached the boat. The U-boat crew maintained continuous and accurate fire throughout the engagement, which contributed to its survival. Most critically, the numerous Hudsons had failed to sink the U-boat. Quaet-Faslem beached the boat on the North African coast, where the French captured all forty-five crew members.[8]

Three days later, the British required three aircraft to disable a surfaced U-boat, but, tragically, this assault again not only demonstrated the

Hudson's weakness against U-boats but a lack of communication between Coastal Command and the Royal Navy's Fleet Air Arm. The capture of Type VIIC *U-331* could have been one of the great Allied victories in the U-boat war. Instead, it marked a lost opportunity and needless loss of life. On 17 November, four Hudsons took off from Gibraltar while five Hudsons became airborne from Tafaouri, near Oran on the north Algerian coast. No. 500 Squadron's 'Z' discovered a surfaced U-boat and attacked with three depth charges. The subsequent explosion blew the U-boat's bow from the water and numerous German crew members appeared in the conning tower. The Hudson commenced to machine gun that area and then dropped an anti-submarine bomb from 600ft. Yet, despite three depth charges and a dropped bomb, *U-331* remained afloat. 'C' 'then arrived, released three depth charges and machine-gunned the German crew as a dozen fell into the water'. Again, the U-boat remained afloat. 'L' now released four additional depth charges as more crew members leapt into the water. Three Hudsons had attacked the surfaced U-boat but had failed to deliver a fatal blow. 'C' and 'L' departed, while 'Z' remained and maintained heavy machine gun fire. Black smoke began emitting from the U-boat's stern, and German crew members now commenced 'waving white objects as a token of surrender'. 'Z' proceeded to Maison Blanche, where the naval authorities promised to send a destroyer to the scene. A Hurricane arrived and reported that 'the remaining crew were seen sitting on deck on boxes, obviously waiting to be rescued'. At this point and in this particular instance, the Hudson's weakness in delivering a fatal blow offered the Allies a grand opportunity. However, an inability to communicate with the the Fleet Air Arm resulted in an unnecessary loss of life and a significant intelligence loss as well. Three FAA aircraft arrived on the scene – 'a Martlet Fighter, a Swordfish and an Albacore' but 'in spite of frantic signals' the Martlet commenced machine gun fire and tragically, the Albacore launched a torpedo that 'completely destroyed' the U-boat and killed thirty-two crew members. A Walrus, a sea rescue plane, saved seventeen Germans.[9]

The last U-boat-Hudson battle of 1942 in the Mediterranean proved victorious for the Germans. On 27 December, 500 Squadron Hudson 'M' discovered surfaced Type VIIB *U-73* just north of the Algerian coast. The British pilot dived, while the Germans fired at the approaching target. The U-boat's shells penetrated the plane, wounding the observer and striking the 'starboard engine and wing', causing the engine to fail just as the Hudson arrived over its target. The aircraft's four depth charges fell on the U-boat's stern, and the Hudson then lost altitude and crashed into the sea. The four crew members scrambled into the dinghy 'just before the aircraft sank' and a Walrus rescue flying boat rescued all of them. *U-73* escaped.[10]

Especially sobering to the RAF though, in the mid-Atlantic, the critical area of U-boat activity, its single and twin-engine aircraft, which constituted the bulk of Coastal Command's squadrons, achieved only one sinking. On 5 October, 269 Squadron's Hudson 'N' departed Iceland on an anti-submarine patrol and when approximately 350 miles south of their home base, the two-man crew sighted a 'glint of metal' that they quickly identified as a U-boat, 5 miles away, moving at 6 knots. The British had discovered Type VIIC *U-619*, on its maiden patrol, having sunk two Allied vessels. The RAF captain dived towards the target, apparently achieving full surprise as the U-boat remained fully surfaced. The Hudson crew released four 250lb Torpex depth charges from 20ft. The explosions straddled the U-boat and after thirty seconds, the crew noticed oil on the surface, along with air bubbles. Ten minutes later, wreckage appeared including wood strips. In thirty minutes, the oil and wreckage amount had increased significantly. All forty-four crew members died.[11]

Along the Atlantic seaboard, besides the before-mentioned fatal attacks during the 'Second Happy Time' by US Navy Hudsons on Type VIIC *U-656* and Type IXC *U-503*, and a USAAF Hudson's sinking of Type VIIC *U-701*, Royal Canadian Air Force Hudsons also fatally struck two U-boats in 1942, both attacks occurring off the Newfoundland coast. On 31 July, a 113 Squadron Hudson sank Type VIIC *U-754*. Forty-three perished. Three months later, on 30 October, two 145 Squadron Hudsons, while escorting a convoy, destroyed Type VIIC *U-658*. All forty-eight crew members perished. Additionally, on 30 October, a RCAF 10 Squadron Douglas Digby bomber sank Type IXC *U-520* and its fifty-three crew members east of Newfoundland, bringing the Canadians' total sinkings in 1942 to three.[12]

US Navy aircraft contributed to eight fatal U-boat attacks in 1942, two by Hudsons and one each by a Kingfisher and Mariner during the 'Second Happy Time'. Catalinas delivered the other four fatal attacks. On 20 August, a VP-73 Catalina found the surfaced Type XIV *U-464* south of Iceland but the attack demonstrated the type's limited lethality. The aircraft struck with five bombs from 100ft altitude but after several further strafing attacks, the Catalina withdrew with the U-boat still afloat. Unable to dive due to the damage though, the Germans scuttled the boat. Two crew members perished. A nearby Icelandic vessel – the *Skatefellingur* – rescued fifty-two crew members and delivered them to British destroyers *Castleton* and *Newark*, which received them as prisoners of war. This U-boat type, often referred to as *milchkuh* (milk cow) possessed no torpedo tubes as the Germans had designed it to provide provisions including fuel and food for other U-boats at sea.[13]

While the Catalina's lack of ordnance highlighted its limitations, the subsequent interview with *U-464* commander Otto Harms demonstrated the inherent advantages of anti-submarine aircraft. Even at this early stage in the war, he claimed that U-boat commanders only 'feel really safe' in the absence of clouds, which permitted aircraft detection up to 16 to 19 miles, a distance that provided sufficient time to dive. At 4 to 5 miles, the commander considered there was still a 'reasonable time to crash dive' but a cloud base ranging from 3,000 to 4,000ft raised concern. In support of these assertions, Harms complimented the American Catalina captain, Lieutenant (jg) R.B. Hopgood, for the 'intelligent use of cloud' that had prevented him from noticing the approaching aircraft. It would become a standard tactic by Allied pilots as the war progressed.[14]

For the remainder of 1942, Catalina attacks occurred over a wide geographic range from the Caribbean to the North Atlantic. In the Caribbean, just off the Haitian coast, on 28 August, the US Navy continued its success when a VP-92 Catalina discovered surfaced Type VIIC *U-94* and assaulted it with four depth charges from 50 to 75ft. Like, *U-464*, while *U-94* dived, the explosion brought it to the surface. The Catalina crew radioed for HMCS *Oakville*, a Canadian Navy corvette, which delivered the final, fatal blow by ramming. Nineteen died; the *Oakville* and USS *Lea* rescued twenty-six.[15] On 5 October, south of Iceland, a US Navy VP-73 Catalina fatally struck Type VIIC *U-582* with multiple bombs. All forty-six crew members perished. The following month, on 5 November, just north of Iceland, a Catalina from VP-84 sank Type VIIC *U-408* and its forty-five crew members.

Catalinas did not prevail in all U-boat battles. On 21 September, the RAF's 330 Squadron Catalina 'Z' departed Iceland and found the surfaced Type VIIC *U-606*, attacking with four bombs. None caused damage but the German flak penetrated the flying boat's petrol tanks, which resulted in a water landing in proximity to the convoy had been escorting. British destroyer *Marne* rescued all crew members, while *U-606* slipped away.[16]

As 1942 proceeded, Admiral Dönitz became continually frustrated with the RAF, especially in a particular area. He became so furious with Allied attacks in the 'murderous area west of Gibraltar' that in November he requested that U-boats not operate in it. Instead he recommended to the German Naval High Command that they should engage Allied shipping 'well out to sea, west of the Azores', an area where Dönitz well knew that Allied anti-submarine aircraft could not patrol because they lacked the necessary range. The RAF successes in the months prior to the admiral's request well illustrate the dangers to U-boats west of Gibraltar – an area comprising the Bay of Biscay and off the Portuguese coast where the RAF aircraft could patrol from bases such as Gibraltar and even southern England.[17]

On 6 July, the RAF defeated one of the most successful U-boat commanders, Jürgen von Rosenstiel. This U-boat commander, in Type IXC *U-502*, had a brilliant career, sinking sixteen Allied merchant ships beginning in October 1941. In June 1942 alone, his crew destroyed seven vessels, including four American ones, two of which exceeded 7,000 tons.[18] A little over two weeks after Rosenstiel's last sinking, a Coastal Command Vickers Wellington began the hunt. These British-built twin-engine bombers had a patrol speed of 125–140km per hour, and a decent endurance of ten hours with 1,500lb of bombs or depth charges. This day would mark the first sinking by such an aircraft. At 2130 hours, on 5 July, 172 Squadron Wellington 'H' took off from RAF Chivenor in Devon. A little over five hours later, at 0455 hours, the British crew used homing aerials to detect the U-boat at 7 miles distance in the Bay of Biscay. At one-mile range, the aircraft illuminated the surfaced *U-502* and attacked. The aircrew dropped four Torpex depth charges across the U-boat from starboard to port as Rosenstiel dived. The subsequent spray from the explosions prevented the British from observing any damage, although they believed that the depth charges had exploded 'well within lethal range'. As the aircraft flew over the U-boat, the rear gunner expended 400 rounds of machine gun fire. The Wellington returned to the area, dropped a flame float and reported that the area of the explosions appeared 'much darker than the rest of sea' but observed no other evidence. Nevertheless, they had sunk *U-502* and its fifty-two crew members, including its formidable commander.[19]

Later that month, a Wellington struck against a noted German officer, Eberhard Hoffmann, who had proven to be, on his first patrol, an effective, dangerous U-boat commander. In August and September 1942, operating off the Canadian coast, he destroyed three Allied vessels and damaged another four. His return journey though, proved to be fatal. On 27 September, after transiting the Atlantic, Type IXC *U-165* cruised on the surface approximately 1,000 miles from the French coastline within the dangerous Bay of Biscay. That day, 311 Squadron Wellington 'Q' took off in the afternoon from RAF Talbenny, South Wales, for a six-hour flight. While searching off the French coast, the Czechoslovakian crew sighted the surfaced U-boat from a distance of 2 miles and, from a height of 1,200ft, dived. Hoffmann's crew, choosing to fight rather than submerge, responded with machine gun and cannon. The Wellington suffered hits to its fuselage and the Nazi fire injured most crew members. The RAF captain continued the attack and dropped six depth charges from 70ft, successfully straddling the conning tower. The U-boat rose briefly due to the depth charge explosions and then slowly dived for the last time. All fifty-one crew members perished. However, due to the extensive injuries to his crew, the Wellington's captain departed the scene and headed home. The German fire had injured the navigator in both legs and had 'shot away' the front gunner's small fingers in his left hand. The wireless operator suffered 'splinter wounds' in his right arm and the co-pilot received 'splinter wounds in leg'. The British aircraft's hydraulics failed and it crash-landed at RAF St Eval in Cornwall, but all the crew members survived.[20]

The third and last Wellington sinking occurred far from the Bay of Biscay. Off the Norwegian coast, on the night of 21 October, at 2300 hours, 179 Squadron Wellington 'B' kept obtaining an intermittent radar contact, which finally became consistent at 5 miles away. The pilot closed the distance and when 1½ miles away, the crew illuminated the searchlight and spied, at 0108 hours, a 'fully surfaced camouflaged U-boat green and white or light grey zig zag pattern' travelling at 12 knots. The Wellington crew dropped four 250lb Torpex depth charges and witnessed four explosions, with two occurring on each side of the U-boat. The crew observed nothing else besides an ever-increasing oil patch and associated air bubbles. The Wellington crew had sunk Type VIIC *U-412* with its forty-seven crew members. It had been on its maiden patrol, having sunk no vessels.[21]

Like the Wellingtons, the twin-engine British Armstrong Whitworth Whitley contributed to three fatal sinkings in 1942, two in the Bay of Biscay area. These aircraft, with a slow 110km per hour patrol speed, would never prove to be a popular U-boat killer. In June 1942 they operated in only five of the fifty Coastal Command squadrons and would participate in only four U-boat sinkings in the entire war. On 17 July though, this aircraft type would engage one of most famous U-boat commanders to date, especially to the British. Gerhard Bigalk had proven to be a lethal combatant in Type VIIC *U-751*, having sunk seven Allied vessels including one of the Royal Navy's most famous vessels of 1940, the first British escort carrier, HMS *Audacity*. Nazi Germany's leadership, recognising the great victory, awarded Bigalk the prestigious Knight's Cross. On 14 July 1942, he departed on his seventh cruise. Three days later, 502 Squadron Whitley Mk. VII 'H' took off from St Eval.

After numerous mundane sightings of Spanish trawlers, they spotted, off their starboard side, the surfaced *U-751*, just west of the Bay of Biscay. The pilot altered to port immediately and descended on the boat, releasing six Torpex depth charges from 50ft. Following the attack, the RAF crew saw *U-751* circling slowly to port with the bow and conning tower visible and surrounded by an oil patch. The crew then dropped two 100lb anti-submarine bombs from 600ft but believed that these had missed the target by 75ft. The Germans fired machine guns at the Whitley but in fourteen minutes, the U-boat slid backwards, stern first, into the sea. While the Whitley departed, the German crew managed to resurface, only to be detected, an hour later, by Lancaster 'F' of Bomber Command's 61 Squadron, flying from RAF Syerston in Nottinghamshire, almost 400 miles north of St Eval. The bomber crew released depth charges that failed to deliver a fatal blow. However, the British realised that *U-751* could not dive and prepared another attack. From 700ft, the Lancaster crew released anti-submarine bombs while gunners fired at U-boat crew members attempting to man and fire the submarine's guns. The bombs proved to be effective as the U-boat disappeared a second and final time, stern first, taking its famous commander with it and all forty-eight crew members.[22]

Two months later, Whitleys achieved two more fatal attacks, including an assault in the region Dönitz described as the 'murderous area'. On 3 September, 77 Squadron Whitley 'P' took off from RAF Chivenor at 1135 hours. Over six hours after take-off, at 1750 hours, from a distance of 5 miles, the British crew discovered Type VIIC *U-705*, on its maiden war patrol, on the surface and cruising at 10 knots just west of the Bay of Biscay. The aircraft descended from 2,500ft to 15ft to release depth charges, with the crew reporting that the U-boat 'appeared taken completely by surprise'. The British believed that one depth charge fell near the starboard side, while two crew members observed a definitive hit on the conning tower as a third depth charge exploded approximately 20ft on the port side. The Whitley's front gunner expended fifty rounds at the Germans on the decks and the conning tower at point-blank range, while the rear gunner expended 450 rounds as the Whitley flew over the boat. The pilot turned the aircraft around for another attack on the now stationary target. Four minutes after the attack though, the U-boat sank horizontally. The Whitley remained in the area for another six minutes but observed no further evidence. Nevertheless, U-boat Command never heard from *U-705* and its forty-five crew members again.[23]

That same month, on the 15th, a Whitley achieved another sinking after its crew discovered Type VIIC *U-261* in the Atlantic north-west of

Scotland. The 58 Squadron aircraft fatally depth charged *U-261*, which had just commenced its first patrol and had never sunk a single Allied vessel. None of its forty-three crew members survived.[24]

The RAF also contributed to a U-boat sinking in the Mediterranean with the outdated Vickers Wellesley. This single-engine aircraft, designed as a medium bomber, had limited utility due to its relative low speed and unimpressive load capacity. However, it could fly faster than any U-boat or surface vessel, which provided some applicability for anti-submarine and anti-ship actions. On 30 October 1942, 47 Squadron Wellesley K8531 departed North Africa at 1051 hours. The crew soon encountered and exchanged communication with four Royal Navy destroyers. At 1234 hours, the crew discovered a U-boat 'directly below' the aircraft with its 'outline' seen just 'below the surface'. The Type VIIC U-boat, at periscope depth, appeared headed for the destroyers. The Wellesley assaulted with three Torpex depth charges that dropped twenty seconds after the U-boat crash dived. The crew noticed no signs of damage but did notify the destroyers by 'white cartridges'. The four vessels – HMS *Pakenham, Petard, Dulverton,* and *Hurworth* – arrived and then with a fifth one, *Hero,* pummelled the area with depth charges. *U-559* later surfaced in sight of the vessels. Seven crew members perished while the British rescued and interred thirty-eight as prisoners of war. *Petard* crew members boarded the U-boat and retrieved a variety of sensitive material, but two Royal Navy crew members failed to evacuate in time and died when it sank. *U-559* had sunk five Allied vessels and damaged another on ten patrols.[25]

This year, the RAF achieved its first victory with a strategy that held great promise but, in the end, delivered few sinkings. The British engaged in aerial sea mine laying throughout the war. On 21 September, in Danzig Bay off the Polish coast, Type VIIC *U-446* became the first U-boat sunk by one of these mines in the minefield 'Privet II'. Twenty-three men perished in the sinking, while the Germans managed to rescue eighteen. Aerial laid mines would not destroy another U-boat until 1944.[26]

Royal Navy aircraft destroyed four U-boats in 1942, with three achieved by Swordfish Mk. Is. One of 815 Squadron's two Fuka, Egypt-based Swordfish, 'G', sank Type VIIC *U-577* and its forty-three crew members on 15 January just off the North African coast. The squadron struck again on 2 June when Swordfish 'L' fatally damaged Type VIIC *U-652,* also off the Egyptian coast. The U-boat crew radioed for assistance and Type VIIC *U-81* arrived, rescued the crew, and completed the Swordfish's work by sinking *U-652* with a single torpedo from one of its stern tubes. On 14 September, HMS *Avenger*'s Swordfish flying south of Norway's Svalbard in the North Atlantic sighted and attacked Type VIIC *U-589,* but due to rare Luftwaffe aircraft interference they failed to deliver the fatal assault. The aircraft's information though led destroyer HMS *Onslow* to the location and it destroyed the surfaced U-boat. All forty-four crew members perished. However, just two months later on 15 November, Type IXC *U-155* exacted revenge by striking the escort carrier HMS *Avenger* with a single torpedo that led to its sinking and the loss of 516 men. Only a dozen survived. Six days later, on 21 November, in the western Atlantic, an HMS *Victorious* Albacore found Type IXC *U-517* on the surface. The U-boat commander immediately began a crash dive but the depth charges from the Fleet Air Arm aircraft brought the U-boat to the surface. The explosion had destroyed the bridge, heavily damaged the conning tower, and sank the boat. One man perished while the British rescued fifty-two of its crew.[27] However, Dönitz's U-boats did strike another Allied carrier during this time. On 11 August, Type VIIB *U-73* discovered HMS *Eagle* in the Mediterranean and fatally hit the vessel with four torpedoes, resulting in a rapid sinking in only four minutes. Some 260 men perished, while 900 survived.[28]

Including the before-mentioned assaults by a Hudson and a Havoc, the USAAF destroyed two other U-boats in 1942 with Douglas B-18 Bolos. The Americans, due to fears of U-boat activity on the approaches to the Panama Canal, based a bomber squadron in Suriname, on the northern coast of South America, to conduct anti-submarine patrols. On 22 August, one of these bombers, a 45th Bomb Squadron Bolo, attacked Type VIIC *U-654* in the Caribbean just 100 miles north of the Canal's Atlantic entrance. The Americans dropped four depth charges that sank the U-boat and all forty-four hands. A 99th Bombardment Squadron Bolo flying off the French Guiana coast on 2 October, discovered Type IXC *U-512* at 15 miles distance. From 50ft, the air crew released four bombs and witnessed two of them striking the U-boat prior to diving. Oil, air and a crew member on the surface proved the U-boat's sinking. Ten days after the attack, the destroyer USS *Ellis* retrieved the lone survivor from the ocean; the other fifty-one crew members perished.[29]

Despite these setbacks, the German U-boat commanders ended 1942 in optimistic spirits. 'The greatest success,' Dönitz asserted, 'then, was achieved in November, during which month the potential was also the highest achieved during the last quarter of the war. And that was in spite of the fact that a large number of U-boats were withdrawn from the war on shipping in order to oppose the enemy's North African operations …' The German admiral boasted that Axis submarines' success in 1942 'was very great' with the destruction of '1,160 ships with a total tonnage of 6,266,215 tons' and proudly noting that German U-boats contributed to the 'greater portion'. He brushed aside the U-boat sinkings during this time by claiming that those losses 'gave rise to no anxiety'. Dönitz recalled that 'in 1941 our losses had been 11.4 per cent of the monthly total number of U-boats at sea', while during the first six months of 1942, 'the propitious months of the operations in American waters, the figure sank to 3.9 per cent'. He asserted that during the latter half of 1942, 'when the favourable conditions due to the elementary state of American anti-submarine defences came to an end, the figure rose again to bring the average for the year up to 8.9 per cent'.

The German admiral scoffed at Allied improvements. 'In spite of a very considerable strengthening of the enemy defensive resources, due primarily to air cover and the introduction of radar, the percentage of losses was lower in 1942 than it had been in 1941,' he contended. Dönitz further boasted that, despite these Allied developments, 'the number of operational U-boats had increased, although the average number of new boats per month was only seventeen instead of twenty as had been anticipated'.

Dönitz, in his memoirs, to demonstrate what he considered the Allied perspective in December 1942, quoted from the standard work on the U-boat war at the time of his writing, S.W. Roskill's *The War At Sea, Volume II*. 'During the closing days of 1942,' the Royal Navy's official historian wrote, 'the Admiralty reviewed yet again the problems and prospects of the Atlantic battle.' A senior British Naval Staff member concluded that: 'Our shipping situation has never been tighter.' Roskill acknowledged that British 'surface and air escorts were still far too few ... grave anxiety was felt that future offensive plans might be delayed or even frustrated for lack of shipping. In particular, fuel stocks had fallen to a very low figure.' In fact, the historian noted, that by the middle of December Britain possessed 'only 300,000 tons of commercial bunker fuel' and the nation consumed an average of 130,000 tons per month.[30]

Regarding the U-boats' ability to sink more vessels than could be adequately replaced, Dönitz again referred to Roskill's narrative. 'As to the losses we had suffered during the year,' Roskill admitted that 'it was beyond question that the enemy had done us great damage' and 'British imports fell below thirty-four million tons – one-third less than the 1939 figure.' The British historian further recognised that Allied forces' U-boat sinkings in 1942 did not 'offset the new construction' – with Roskill claiming that Allied shore-based aircraft had destroyed more than all other means. Nevertheless, Roskill concluded, 'to the British Admiralty it was plain that the Battle of the Convoy Routes was still to be decided, that the enemy had greater strength than ever before, and that the crisis in the long-drawn struggle was near'.[31]

Fortunately for the Allies, B-24s began flying over the Atlantic in 1942 just before the crisis of 1943.

Chapter 4

The B-24 Arrives

U-boat leader Karl Dönitz prized the area 'well out to sea, west of the Azores', where the German admiral knew that Allied anti-submarine aircraft, lacking the necessary range, could not patrol. This gap in the mid-North Atlantic terrified Allied escorts and merchantmen alike. From the outer reaches of Allied aircraft operating from Canada to the outer reaches of aircraft flying from the British Isles, the men on the surface vessels and the men in the U-boats recognised this area as prime hunting ground for the U-boats. Without air cover, the Germans held the advantage.[1]

RAF Coastal Command required an aircraft, such as the American-built B-24 Liberator, that could close this gap. And, it received its first allotment in 1941, by accident. France had originally ordered these bombers, but when conquered by Nazi Germany, the Americans redirected the four-engine aircraft to Britain. Unfortunately, for Coastal Command, they fared poorly when competing against Bomber Command. Of the 120 B-24s in that order, Coastal Command received only seventeen.[2]

Coastal Command though, recognising the Liberators anti-submarine capabilities, prized each one. The B-24s far outshone all the other British anti-submarine aircraft with their combination of speed, endurance and load. Only one Coastal Command aircraft possessed a higher patrol speed – the twin-engine Beaufighter at 180 knots per hour, versus 150 knots per hour for the Liberators. The Beaufighters though, carried no bombs or depth charges. Only the four-engine Halifax, at 2,250lb, could haul more than the 2,000lb of the B-24s, but the Halifaxes flew slower with only two-thirds the endurance. Only the Catalinas maintained a higher endurance at seventeen-and-a-half hours versus the sixteen hours for the Liberators, but they flew at only two-thirds the B-24s' patrol speed.[3] The B-24s, once deployed, would destroy dozens of U-boats, more than any other aircraft.

For 120 Squadron, the most successful Allied anti-submarine unit of the war,[4] 1 June 1941 marked the beginning of the Allied quest to close that gap. On that day, at RAF station Nutts Corner, Northern Ireland, the squadron formed with an 'initial issue of 9 Liberator aircraft'; all Mk. Is, and commenced training on 8 June.[5] Four months later, on 22 October, 120 Squadron attacked its first U-boat. At 0500 hours, Liberator 'F' took off and headed to sea. At 0825 hours, the crew rendezvoused with a convoy of sixteen merchant vessels and two escort vessels. The B-24 tangled with a Luftwaffe Condor, a four-engine aircraft, that the British easily repelled. Then, at 1445 hours, Liberator 'F' spotted a U-boat with 'Conning Tower awash 3 miles away on port bow'. The aircraft, flying at 1,500ft, 'dived steeply and dropped 3 depth charges which exploded across' the U-boat's 'track'. The British believed that the third depth charge hit and further reported that after this explosion they observed an underwater explosion that caused 'considerable disturbance to surface over 50–70ft'. However, no debris appeared and no information then or later suggests a U-boat sinking.[6]

Two months later, on 22 December, 120 Squadron delivered its second assault. Liberator Mk. I 'L', while cruising at 4,500ft, discovered a U-boat and descended rapidly in order to attack two minutes after sighting. The British crew released five 250lb depth charges 'along track' of the target. Five seconds after the last depth charge explosion, the crew observed 'a considerable upheaval of water' and 'oil appeared which eventually' extended to an area of one hundred yards by ten yards. This attack, like the previous one, failed to sink the U-boat. That same day, a Liberator crew spotted two other U-boats but both submerged before the depth charges could be dropped.[7]

The Liberators continued their assaults into 1942. On 11 January, Mk. I 'D' attacked a German aircraft, merchant vessel and a U-boat. Flying from St Eval, the aircraft spotted and assaulted a German He 115 aircraft that had taken 'position immediately below and behind' the Liberator. The British pilot, 'unable to get front guns to bear, banked steeply enabling side and rear gunners to open fire at ranges 200–600 yards'. The RAF crew reported multiple strikes while observing fragments fall from the German twin-engine aircraft. The Luftwaffe sought cover in a rain squall after the B-24 crew had fired 300 rounds from the tail gun and 200 from the side gun. Eleven minutes later, the crew discovered a German merchant vessel and a U-boat at 5 miles distance. The pilot 'altered course and identified M/V as ELSA ESSBERGER', which was 'hardly under way' while the U-boat appeared 'stationary'. The Liberator 'circled, lost height, dived from 1000 ft. to attack U-Boat'.

The RAF crew opened 'fire with 4 Cannons at 800 yards' and released four 250lb depth charges, which straddled the surfaced U-boat. The pilot reported that the U-boat's stern rose from the surface and an extensive oil patch appeared. The Liberator then attacked the merchant vessel without success and engaged an He 115, which fired unsuccessfully on the B-24. The British returned fire and they last observed the German aircraft flying at sea level 'with smoke streaming from starboard engine'. The *Elsa Essberger*, operated as a U-boat supply vessel, escaped damage and no information suggests a U-boat sinking on these two days.[8]

The crews also experienced the general dangers of operating military aircraft. On 18 February, 120 Squadron Liberator Mk. I 'X' took off but immediately crashed. Fire engulfed the B-24 and the British reported the aircraft to be 'completely burnt out'. Of the nine-man crew, the captain, second pilot, the two navigators, and two of the air gunners suffered injuries in the accident. The engineer and two of the air gunners died, and one of the navigators who initially survived the crash perished days later.[9]

Flying from Predannack, Cornwall, three B-24s initiated attacks on U-boats on 15 June. In both instances, the alert Germans dived before the attack. B-24 Mk. I 'W' found a surfaced U-boat and attacked. The U-boat immediately submerged so that the Liberator crew released the depth charges from 70ft five seconds after the conning tower disappeared. The crew witnessed an explosion 20 to 30yd 'in front of swirl' as they could observe the U-boat underwater. Then a 'patch of oil bubbles' appeared. The B-24 crew released anti-submarine bombs but observed no wreckage.[10] The same day, Liberator 'K' spotted a surfaced U-boat and descended rapidly. The boat crash dived fifteen to twenty seconds before the crew could drop depth charges. Nevertheless, they observed two explosions 5 to 10yd ahead of the swirl and reported 'brown oily scum'. A third B-24 crew found a surfaced U-boat and assaulted with depth charges. The U-boat responded by diving 'at speed'. The RAF crew saw explosions 'straddling 50 yds ahead of swirl' and a 'patch of brown oily scum'. In all three instances, no records indicate that any of these attacks sank a U-boat.[11]

The next month, on 26 July, Liberator Mk. II 'Y', flying from Ballykelly, Northern Ireland, spotted a surfaced U-boat only ¾ mile away and dived to assault. With the aircraft in a 30-degree dive, at 400ft, the crew dropped six Torpex depth charges as the U-boat crash dived. The British saw both the 'top of bridge and conning tower' when dropping the depth charges but 'only result observed was column of water about 50 ft high'. The historical records indicate no sinking though.[12]

In August, the Liberators continued attacks, but achieved no sinkings. On the 9th, Mk. I 'W' found a U-boat on the surface and assaulted with six depth charges. Mk. III 'X', on the next day, sighted a U-boat but the German crew submerged and the 'swirl' was lost in 'rough sea' so the RAF crew did not attack. Liberator Mk. I 'F', on the same day, dived on a surfaced U-boat and, four seconds after it submerged, dropped six depth charges that 'straddled wake centre'. Liberator Mk. III 'Z' spotted a periscope on the 13th and released depth charges. Three days later, 'F' dropped six depth charges across a U-boat's bows as it submerged. The crew reported that the 'conning tower lifted out of water' and 'wreckage seen afterwards'. But none of these attacks proved to be fatal.

No. 120 Squadron did not escape August without loss, losing two B-24s this month. On 12 August, Liberator Mk. I 'H', while approaching its assigned convoy, observed thirty-one merchant vessels, one destroyer and four corvettes, and received the following message from convoy ONS 120: 'Our A/C was flying at 300' lost height slowly banked to port' and its 'wing tip touched sea'. The Allied vessels reported that an explosion followed the crash as the aircraft 'burst into fragments' at 0930 hours. They had observed the end of Liberator 'N', which commenced its patrol at 0216 hours. The squadron operational records concluded, 'There were no survivors' of the eight-man crew. The following day, the 13th, Liberator Mk. III 'Z' took off at 0533 hours from Ballykelly. At 1125 hours, the crew reported a periscope sighting and at 1138 hours sent 'Have attacked with DC's results unobserved'. At 1220 hours they reported, 'Expect to arrive 16.27'. The Liberator never did. The Aberdeen trawler *Glenagill* retrieved four survivors – all sergeants – about 20 miles from the Irish coast.[13]

The Liberators, as these engagements demonstrate, had failed to deliver a fatal attack. This failure cannot be assigned to the skill of the RAF crews. Allied aircraft would, throughout the war, deliver lethal results in only a minority of attacks. The B-24s would not encounter a substantial number of U-boats when operating only from the British Isles. The runways at these locations proved to be too far east for the Liberators. Coastal Command required a base that would permit them to engage U-boats in the mid-Atlantic, where the Allies lacked significant air cover, where the U-boat commanders operated predominantly, and most importantly, where the U-boat commanders did not regularly anticipate aerial attacks.

The Germans recognised these limitations, and their reaction to the first mid-Atlantic B-24 sighting illustrated their concern with long-range Allied aircraft. On 17 July 1942, Lieutenant-Commander Suhren of Type VIIC *U-564*, cruising in the North Atlantic, 'crash dived on appearance of four-engined aircraft', an aircraft 800 miles from any Allied airbase. This distance represented an extraordinary increase in aircraft range. Historian Andrew Hendrie noted that Dönitz, considering this event of high significance and concern, recorded it in his memoirs and it appeared in Gunther Hessler's diaries of the U-boats. But the Germans misidentified this plane as a Short Sunderland; in fact, the U-boat commander had observed one of 120 Squadron's B-24s. Dönitz recalled that 'this report, which for the first time established the provision of air cover by land-based aircraft at so great a distance, came as an unpleasant surprise to U-boat Command'. The admiral noted though, that 'we did not, however jump to any conclusions in the face of this isolated case and refrained from disposing the U-boat groups further out into the North Atlantic'. But that would change with a new Liberator base.[14]

Beginning on 6 September 1942, 120 Squadron B-24s took off from Northern Ireland and landed at Reykjavik, Iceland. The Liberators now maintained a presence there and began prowling over the ideal U-boat hunting ground. The following month, 120 Squadron began to turn the tide as the RAF crews, now flying over the mid-Atlantic, significantly increased their U-boat sightings and attacks. On just the third day of operations from Iceland, Liberator Mk. I 'H' dived to assault a surfaced U-boat but at the point of release, the depth charges failed to drop. On the 21st, Liberator 'H''s crew discovered a surfaced U-boat and one at periscope depth. Both U-boats dived before the B-24 could engage. Liberator Mk. II 'K' attacked a surfaced U-boat on the 24th and thirty-seven minutes later initiated another assault on a surfaced U-boat; it sighted two more of them on the same flight. Four days later, Liberator Mk. I 'B' assaulted a U-boat with six depth charges that straddled the boat forward of the conning tower and followed with 200 rounds of cannon fire. On the 29th, 'K' released six depth charges from 50 to 70ft on a U-boat and the crew witnessed a 'large air bubble' rise to the surface along with 'iridescent oil and black objects like barrels'. None of these attacks resulted in a U-boat sinking, but the rapid increase in sightings demonstrated that their new base offered far more opportunities than previous ones. The odds of fatal sinkings had improved dramatically and the following month, the most successful Second World War anti-submarine aircraft, commenced its deadly record.

In October 1942, for the first time in the war, an American-built B-24 Liberator, with an RAF crew, struck fatally. On the 12th, 120 Squadron Liberator Mk. I 'H' departed Reykjavik at 0842 hours to escort convoy ONS 136. Less than three hours later, the crew spotted Type VIIC

U-597 on the surface travelling at 10 knots, 8 miles away. This U-boat had completed only one other patrol, and had not sunk a single Allied vessel. The pilot turned to starboard and, with the sun at his back, descended from 2,000ft to 70ft, releasing six Torpex depth charges above the target. The U-boat shuddered amidst the explosions, which lifted it from the water and fully exposed its deck. It then sank vertically with no forward momentum. All forty-nine U-boat crew members perished. The British crew noticed some debris among the oil. For the first time in the war, the B-24 had destroyed a U-boat. The crew's experience on this flight after the successful attack highlighted one of the consistent challenges for British Liberator pilots: malfunctioning equipment. The crew sighted another U-boat and attacked but six of the seven depth charges failed to release.[15]

The squadron's next victory occurred two months later. Six U-boats had attacked convoy HX 217 on the evening of 7 December and the early morning of 8 December 1942. Multiple RAF Liberators commenced escort service for the convoy's twenty-four merchant vessels and six escorts. One of these, 120 Squadron's Liberator Mk. I 'B', departed Reykjavik 8 December at 0526 hours, and rendezvoused with HX217 at 0900 hours. Twenty-nine minutes later, the crew spotted Type VIIC *U-611* travelling on the surface. It was a U-boat just one month into its first patrol, having achieved no sinkings. The Liberator attacked with six depth charges, which straddled the boat. The British saw '10ft eruption of water', 'oil streak, numerous pieces of yellow wood' and 'many seagulls collected on and over the oil patch'. They guided a corvette to the location and the naval crew reported to the aircraft, 'You killed him' as 'parts of dead-bodies were seen'. The convoy's Senior Naval Officer reported to the air crew that 'Large quantities of oil and wreckage of German origin reported' in the position of 'your attack'. None of *U-611*'s forty-five crew members survived.[16]

This crew's remaining engagements of this day demonstrated the plethora of U-boats in the mid-Atlantic. At 1245 hours, they discovered two 'on surface; neither one submerged', so they attacked one of them with two depth charges, which straddled 'about 200ft ahead of swirl'. After the explosions, 'a 30ft upheaval of water occurred'. The convoy's Senior Naval Officer reported numerous U-boat contacts and at 1426 hours the crew 'sighted and attacked U-boat with cannon fire; bursts were seen round the conning tower as the boat submerged'. Just over twenty minutes later, at 1449 hours, the British assaulted another U-boat 'with 60 rounds cannon fire; damage not observed as U-boat submerged'. About half hour later, at 1524 hours, the Liberator 'attacked with cannon fire another U-boat which submerged quickly'. Then, at 1619 hours this crew targeted a U-boat with sixty rounds of cannon fire from a distance of 600yd but the U-boat escaped by diving. Another sighting and attack followed at 1643 hours, when the Liberator assaulted a U-boat with 'cannon fire at 1000 yards. After 60 rounds cannons jammed' while the 'rear gunner fired 100 rounds' into the conning tower as the U-boat disappeared just fifty seconds after the Liberator overflew the boat.[17]

While these attacks failed to sink any U-boats, the British considered these assaults of great value. The RAF Chief of the Air Staff, Charles Portal, noted in January 1943 that: 'Air patrols over the U-boat routes to the hunting grounds were very costly in aircraft since it was calculated that there was only one sighting for 250 hours flying time.' However, he contended that 'even if a large number of U-boats were not actually destroyed by this means, aircraft patrols had a good effect in compelling U-boats to remain submerged and thereby reducing their time on the hunting grounds.'

The U-boats required time to recharge their batteries on the surface, and they could best discover, track and co-ordinate attacks on convoys while on the surface. Additionally, the German commanders could loiter on the surface knowing that hunting escort vessels would be visually observed from miles away before necessitating a dive. Air attacks though, required the U-boat crews to submerge in thirty seconds or less before ordnance delivery, which explains why German U-boat commanders feared Allied aircraft more than any other weapon.[18]

Other 120 Squadron crews delivered additional attacks this month. On 8 December, the same day that 'B' sank *U-611*, Mk. III 'M' took off from Reykjavik at 1151 hours and over the ten-hour flight carried out four U-boat attacks. While flying 30 miles astern of the assigned convoy, the Liberator crew discovered two U-boats and dropped seven depth charges. In their hurry to submerge, the U-boat disappeared under the surface while two crew members remained in the conning tower. Unfortunately for the British, the attack resulted in 'no debris observed'. Twenty minutes later, they found a U-boat 8 miles from their position and assaulted with a single depth charge. In the official report, the crew noted that 'Brownish colour column of water shot up 100!' But again, 'no debris seen'. Just eight minutes after this engagement, the crew assaulted a U-boat with machine gun fire. And finally, half hour later, again attacked a U-boat with machine gun fire. However, none of these attacks resulted in a sinking.[19]

On 14 December, the crew of Liberator Mk. I 'H' stretched their flight to nearly seventeen hours and reported two U-boat sightings. They attacked the first U-boat with six depth charges, with both the stern and conning tower visible. The crew observed blue-green oil on the surface ninety seconds after the attack but the pilot also confessed that 'nothing else seen'. 'H' returned to convoy but, one hour later, discovered another U-boat and engaged. The U-boat successfully submerged eighteen to twenty seconds before the Liberator arrived at the scene. Nevertheless, the captain used the 'trail of moving air bubbles' as a 'bombing point' to drop two depth charges. Yet, the crew reported that 'nothing further seen'. The following day Liberator 'B' performed a 15-mile sweep around the convoy and, in the process, found another U-boat and released six depth charges on it. The British witnessed 'several black object[s] blown into air' by the explosion. The U-boats escaped in all three of these instances.[20]

No. 120 Squadron continued with U-boat sightings and attacks into December, despite poor weather that forced the aircraft to rotate back to Northern Ireland. On 26 December, Liberator Mk. I 'F', flying from Ballykelly, spotted a U-boat at 7 miles distance and the German crew noticed the approaching four-engine plane and dived. The British crew, nevertheless, dropped six depth charges thirty seconds after submerging 'in track about 100 yards ahead'. They reported 'some oil' and a 'black cylindrical object 1 foot in diameter'. The convoy then signalled the Liberator that another U-boat had been sighted at 10 miles distance. The Liberator 'flew into cloud' and when emerging, sighted a U-boat at 2 miles distance and dived. The crew released two depth charges from 100ft seven seconds after the U-boat 'had submerged, overshooting by 100ft and exploding 40ft to starboard of swirl. Nothing more seen.'[21]

The RAF established three other Liberator squadrons during this time: 59, 86 and 224. No. 86 Squadron remained in training status in 1942, while 224 Squadron sank two U-boats in 1942, although not without suffering some damage. On 20 October, the crew of Liberator MK. IIIA 'H' from RAF Beaulieu in Hampshire, sighted and attacked surfaced Type VIID *U-216*, a U-boat on its first patrol that had only sunk one Allied vessel. The British crew dropped six depth charges but one of them damaged the Liberator. The crew then benefitted from the extraordinary efforts of the B-24's pilot, David Mackie Sleep, and its flight engineer, George Thomas Lenson. The following describes their actions:

> During the attack an explosion, caused by what appeared to be a hit on the submarine, severely damaged the aircraft. It went into an almost vertical climb but, with great effort, Flying

Officer Sleep recovered control and manoeuvred to observe the result of his attack. It became necessary to jettison the remaining bombs but, to accomplish this they had to be manhandled. Regardless of his own safety, Flight Sergeant Lenson performed the task and, for one and a half hours, he worked on the narrow catwalk with the bomb doors open in order to release the bombs, the catwalk was extremely slippery and Flight Sergeant Lenson had to shed his boots and socks to enable him to obtain a firm grip. On reaching this country Flying Officer Sleep executed an emergency crash landing at night with great skill. On impact, however, the aircraft caught fire, but Flight Sergeant Lenson succeeded in extricating an injured comrade from the burning aircraft. In most trying circumstances, both these members of air crew displayed great courage and devotion to duty.[22]

Although the Liberator caught fire on impact at Predannack airfield in Cornwall, all British crew members survived, while *U-216* sank with all forty-five crew members.[23] Four days later, Liberator 'G' struck again with a different crew. The British found and fatally attacked Type VIIC *U-599*, a U-boat on its first patrol with a rookie commander, with multiple depth charges. None of the forty-four U-boat crew members survived.[24]

No. 59 Squadron, flying from Thorney Island in West Sussex in southern England, attacked several U-boats. On 10 November, Liberator Mk. III 'C', carrying twelve depth charges, found a surfaced boat moving at 68 knots. The British crew observed several Germans near the conning tower. The U-boat attacked the B-24 with 'machine gun fire' from 1,000yd. As the four-engine aircraft passed over the U-boat, the six depth charges 'straddled' it 'whilst still fully surfaced, two falling short, the third bouncing off the after part of [the] submarine, the 4th, 5th, and 6th, falling over [the] U-boat'. The Liberator's rear gunner expended 'about 100 rounds with each gun'. The B-24 ascended for another assault while the U-boat dived. A minute after the first assault, the RAF crew dropped six more depth charges that exploded 25 to 30yd before the conning tower. Oil appeared on the surface and two minutes after the second passing the 'U-boat bows appeared above surface, gradually rising to an angle of about 60°'. The U-boat 'remained in this position' for five minutes while the Liberator circled and fired at the target. Despite the obvious damage though, the U-boat escaped.

The 59 Squadron Liberators attacked only one other U-boat during this month. On the 27th, 'T' discovered a U-boat heading into the mouth of the Bidasoa River, in south-western France, and attacked with six depth charges. However, the resulting explosions did not sink the U-boat. Considering that the squadron conducted over fifty flights that month, managing only two U-boat attacks, it had not been successful. Southern England, as opposed to Iceland, did not offer anti-submarine aircraft the ideal platform from which to launch their patrols.[25]

British B-24 crews did not survive every U-boat encounter this year. No. 59 Squadron Liberator II AL566 disappeared over the Mediterranean with all seven crew members on 15 July. The British later discovered the body of one crew member on the North African coast. Type VIIC *U-561* reported attacks by two Allied aircraft and the downing of one, which they misidentified as a Sunderland, during the time period in which the Liberator went missing.[26]

The Americans also joined in the Allied anti-submarine effort with Liberators. In December 1942, the USAAF's 1st Antisubmarine Squadron arrived in Britain, and conducted two U-boat attacks with their Liberators from St Eval. On 29 December, B-24 'E' dropped twelve 250lb Torpex depth charges on a U-boat twenty-five seconds after submerging. On the last day of the year, B-24 'A' attacked a recently submerged U-boat as well. No historical records indicate that either assault sank a boat, but the British certainly welcomed the additional Liberators.[27]

During this time period, another RAF Coastal Command squadron received another type of American-built four-engine aircraft: the Boeing B-17 Flying Fortress. Although the B-17 would outshine the B-24 in popularity during the American daylight bombing campaign over Europe, the Allies did not employ it in significant numbers in the Battle of the Atlantic, especially when compared with the B-24. The Liberator Mk. I attained a 150 knots per mile patrol speed, while the Fortress flew at 10 knots less. Additionally, in the anti-submarine role, the Liberator hauled 2,000lb of bombs and depth charges while the Fortresses carried 250lb less. The B-24's main advantage though was its endurance: Liberators could patrol for sixteen hours, the Fortress for less than eleven. Allowing the aircraft to loiter over an Atlantic convoy for four more hours provided the B-24s with a distinct advantage in the U-boat war. Nevertheless, B-17s did attack U-boats and achieved some success.[28]

No. 206 Squadron commenced the war flying the ill-suited Anson. Later, Coastal Command replaced the Anson with the Hudson, which the squadron operated until August 1942. The squadron had not sunk any U-boats when flying these two aircraft. In fact, even when flying the much-improved Hudson, the crews carried out only two U-boat assaults in 1941. The following brought more attacks but no fatal ones. However, in September, the unit reequipped with Fortress Mk. IIs, and a month later, on 27 October, a B-17, operating from Britain, sank its first U-boat, and 206 Squadron had its first kill. B-17 'F' located and attacked surfaced Type VIIC *U-627*, a U-boat on its first patrol having sunk no Allied shipping, approximately 300 miles south of Iceland.[29] The U-boat submerged as the aircraft approached and the British crew dropped seven depth charges 25ft ahead of its swirl and 'straddled' the estimated course. The crew noticed 'patches of iridescent oil 100 yards long' after the 'explosions subsided'. They had been successful; *U-627* sank with all forty-members of its crew.[30]

However, B-17 206 Squadron crews faced the same challenge as other aircrews when attempting to attack a surfaced U-boat before it submerged. On 5 October, the crew of B-17 'B' spotted a conning tower but failed to assault due to the 'elapse of time between dive and arrival of aircraft'. However, half an hour later, on a second sighting the crew dropped five depth charges 'ahead of the swirl'. The crew admitted that 'no results were observed' and it was not a fatal attack. On the last day of the month, B-17 'F', flying with a different crew than the one that had sunk *U-627*, attacked another U-boat. At 1345 hours the crew spotted the U-boat surfacing at 5 miles distance. From 1,200ft, the B-17 descended and dropped seven depth charges thirty-five seconds after submerging. The crew spotted no debris and all information indicates that the U-boat survived.[31]

Sometimes crew error, perhaps due to a lack of familiarity with the B-17s, permitted a U-boat to escape. No. 206 Squadron Flying Fortress 'A' discovered a U-boat and dived to attack. The pilot brought the aircraft directly over the target but at the point at which the depth charges should have released, nothing fell from the aircraft. The navigator, according to the squadron's report, 'had set the operate lever at "Safe" instead of at "operate"' and therefore the 'attack failed' because no depth charges released. The Fortress remained in the area for some time without sighting the U-boat again and the crew resigned themselves to passing a warning to a nearby merchantman.[32]

Another RAF Coastal Command squadron transferred to the B-17s, 220, having previously flown Hudsons. However, for nearly the last six months of 1942, the unit only reported one U-boat attack. On 29 November, Fortress Mk. II 'K', flying from Britain, discovered the 'port bow' of a U-boat 5 miles away moving at 5 knots. The U-boat dived and the aircraft attacked with seven depth charges from 30ft. The 'centre' of the stick dropped 'dead ahead of swirl' but the crew witnessed 'no results', even though the Fortress remained in the 'immediate vicinity' for thirty minutes.[33]

The challenge for both Fortress and Liberator squadrons did not revolve around the aircraft or the crews, but rather the bases. At this stage in the war, anti-submarine aircraft launching from only the British Isles failed to operate in the areas most conducive for sinking U-boats. The German U-boat commanders well knew that their prime hunting ground lay within the middle area of the North Atlantic between North America and the British Isles, in part, because they realised that Allied aircraft did not patrol these areas regularly. The poor results of the 206 and 220 Squadron Fortresses directly reflected the wise strategy of Dönitz's U-boat crews.

The British, in recognising all these factors, still placed their greatest hope on the four-engine B-24 Liberators. Nothing better demonstrates their conviction in this regard than their pleadings with the Americans at the watershed Casablanca Conference in January 1943. All the senior British officials who attended, including the Prime Minister and the First Lord of the Admiralty, would beg and cajole their American cousins to provide more of these aircraft. They knew the critical moment had come and they knew what weapon they required to prevail.

Chapter 5

The Casablanca Conference

The Casablanca Conference debates of January 1943 depict the contrasting views of Britain and America in regard to anti-submarine strategy, especially aircraft. The British leaders viewed air power as the critical factor in addressing the U-boat threat, not surface escort vessels. They considered this conference of paramount importance to obtain American promises to provide the most valuable anti-submarine asset that they required: B-24 Liberators. These deliberations also highlight the opposing American position, as stated by Admiral King, that anti-submarine operations did not require aircraft, and that aircraft would be best deployed for other purposes. However, the US President's means of crossing the Atlantic did not strengthen King's position. Franklin D. Roosevelt, a former Assistant Secretary of the Navy, crossed the Atlantic not by ship, his preferred method of travel, but by aircraft, a Boeing 314 Clipper, the first time a sitting president travelled on official business by air. Prime Minister Churchill also travelled to the conference in an American-built plane, a converted B-24.[1]

Before evaluating the Allied leaders' deliberations, Dönitz's opinions provide insight as to the German view of the situation. In November 1942, two months before the President, the Prime Minister and their staffs met at Casablanca, the U-boat commander submitted to German Naval High Command his understanding of the war status. In referring to the successful Allied invasion of North Africa, Dönitz opposed further deployment of U-boats against 'African reinforcement convoys' because 'such a course offers a minimum prospect of success at probably a very high cost and can have no decisive bearing on the subsequent course of enemy operations'. Most critically, this strategy 'would have disastrous effects on the war against shipping in the Atlantic, which U-boat Command has always regarded, and still regards, as the primary task of the U-boat arm'. He considered the U-boat 'war on enemy shipping' as 'the one great contribution that the U-boat arm can make towards winning the war', a fact he believed his enemies shared, because, Dönitz alleged, their 'main preoccupation remains the Battle of the Atlantic and the unceasing drain on his strength which he is incurring in it'.

The admiral asserted that the Atlantic, an area in which the Allies had a preponderance of merchant shipping and lacked comprehensive air cover, must remain the focus. He argued that 'the recent exceptionally high sinkings in the Atlantic arise directly from the enemy's operations in North Africa'. Dönitz contended that 'if sinkings in the Atlantic decrease as the result of the transfer of U-boats from that area to Gibraltar and the Mediterranean, no one will be more pleased than the enemy, and such a course will eventually result not in weakening but rather in strengthening our adversaries'. Dönitz maintained 'that the main weight of the U-boat arm must be concentrated in the Atlantic, that the most important contribution the arm can make to our war effort as a whole is the prosecution of its war on shipping, that the existing favourable conditions must be exploited to the utmost and that any deviation from this principle can only react to the detriment of our whole war effort'.[2]

The German admiral would have been pleased to know the three war goals that the Americans provided to the British in advance of the discussions. First, they argued for a Pacific offensive and, secondly, a 1943 cross-Channel invasion. In their final aim, the only one that directly addressed Germany, they indicated support for a strategic air campaign. The British leadership responded with a recommendation to maintain Mediterranean offensive operations, wait until 1944 for any English Channel invasions, and to limit the emphasis on the Pacific. However, as the debates demonstrated, they required, from the Arsenal of Democracy, more of a specific American-built weapon for the Battle of the Atlantic.[3]

The British lobbied for more Liberators not only in their discussions but also in the appearance of the Prime Minister's war room. The Royal Navy officer, Captain R.P. Pim, who provided Churchill with his daily intelligence briefing, invited Captain Harry C. Butcher, General Dwight D. Eisenhower's naval aide, to visit the Prime Minister's 'villa'. During his visit, the American captain noted the war room charts, which offered 'a clear view of submarine concentrations, convoy movements, and the location of war vessels of the United Nations'. Of all the information displayed, Butcher confessed that for him, 'the most impressive fact in the war room was the number of subs. I tried to count,' he recalled, 'there were easily a hundred, and no telling how many were in ports for servicing'. The American naval officer observed that most of the U-boats operated in the Atlantic with 'a large pack along the northern route from U.S.A. to England'.[4]

The British launched into a discussion of the U-boat menace at the first meeting, at 1030 hours on Thursday, 14 January. American General Marshall opened the meeting with a discussion of resource allocation among the Atlantic and Pacific. American Admiral King then focused primarily on the Pacific theatre and the British general Sir Alan Brooke then followed him. The general wisely complimented the Americans on their knowledge and their performance against the Japanese but quickly narrowed his focus to the one issue of greatest concern to the British. Brooke alleged that the 'the threat to the United Kingdom had been at one time serious' but recent improvements enabled the British to maintain an offensive posture, although the 'greatest danger' remained 'our communications.' He warned and that 'the shortage of shipping' limited 'all offensive operations'. Brooke warned, 'unless we could effectively combat the U-boat menace, we might not be able to win the war'.

After a comprehensive review of a variety of situations throughout the globe, Sir Dudley Pound, the First Sea Lord for the Royal Navy, continued the discussion by arguing that 'in the Atlantic the greatest concerns to the Home Fleet were: first to prevent a break-out of the German naval forces; and, second, to provide protection for convoys to North Russia'.[5] After discussing the supply situation to Russia, de-emphasizing the threat of a German naval surface vessel breakout, acknowledging trade between Imperial Japan and Nazi Germany, the Indian Ocean situation, and the Mediterranean situation, he finally turned to the issue of most concern: the U-boat situation. Pound claimed that the Kriegsmarine possessed 'one hundred and ten submarines in the Atlantic in addition to those in the Mediterranean and off the coast of Norway'. To emphasize the threat to Atlantic convoy, he asserted that U-boat command intended all new U-boats for the Atlantic. The Nazis strategically concentrated three large groups of U-boats, Pound claimed, with one patrolling off the Newfoundland coast, another in the Central Atlantic, and a final one 'off of Southwest Ireland'. At any point, he feared, a convoy could 'blunder' into one of these groups.[6] The First Lord related that U-boats had assaulted two convoys from America but had sunk only two vessels in one convoy and none in the other. The Allies had achieved this success, he maintained, 'by providing air coverage for the convoys with Liberator aircraft', which forced the 'U-boats down during the day. While they were down, the convoys were able to alter their course and, by nightfall, leave the submarines behind.'

Pound then referred to 'an experiment' the British attempted due to the 'shortage of escorts' because of naval operations for Operation Torch, the Allied invasion of North Africa. He stated that, in attempting unescorted operations, the British sent merchant ships to Freetown, a critical West African port. However, the First Lord admitted, the experiment failed, with the unescorted convoys losing 10 per cent, one convoy suffering seventeen vessels sunk out of a total of forty-four ships. In response, he acknowledged, the Freetown convoys had been reinstated. 'Convoys must be sufficiently large to deal with a heavy attack,' he argued. Pound informed his audience that 'our aim must be to get a long-range air protection and additional escort vessels'. And specifically, the Royal Navy leader, in addressing his American colleagues, 'added that it would be desirable to obtain more long-range aircraft protection to escorts from the United States'. 'We must make special efforts to provide adequate protection in the early part of 1943,' he contended, 'in order that we may be able to meet the great demands in the build-up of BOLERO,' the American operation to deliver supplies and materiel to Britain in preparation for the Normandy invasion. However, Pound failed to convince Marshall. The American general acknowledged the 'paramount' importance of the U-boat threat but his plan did not involve more B-24s. Instead, Marshall argued that the Allies needed to direct their attacks against the U-boat's assembly yards and ports.

Sir Charles Portal, Chief of the Air Staff, recognising Marshall's slight, stated 'that the British Chiefs of Staff also felt that the defeat of the submarine menace must be given first priority in the use of air power, particularly in the protection of our line of communications'. Portal discussed the two facets of the aircraft requirement: 'for long range anti-submarine operations not only the provision of suitable aircraft had to be considered but also the bases from which they are to be used'. For this reason, to provide Mid-Atlantic coverage, the British contemplated a Greenland air base. In an attempt to maintain cordiality, he acknowledged the RAF's gratitude 'for the 21 Liberators provided by the U.S.A. for the Bay of Biscay'. In following Marshall's point, Portal argued for attacking three targets to blunt the U-boat threat: '(1) along the sea lanes; (2) against bases in the Bay of Biscay; and (3) against factories in which submarines are built'. He admitted that the 'British now propose making air attacks in sufficient force to destroy the entire port in which the submarines are based rather than confining their attacks to the submarine pens and surrounding installations'. In regard to these attacks though, Portal argued that 'no one can be certain as to how much damage can be done in the port towns themselves and that the method proposed will be in the nature of an experiment, the results of which will not be known for five or six months'.

King, in countering the British argument against Marshall, inquired as 'whether the possibility of concentrating air attacks on the building yards had been considered'. Rebuffing the American, Portal stated 'that the building yards are not sufficiently large to be certain of hitting them at night'. King remained unconvinced, arguing that assembly yards and bases offered the best locations for destroying U-boats and accused the Allied air forces of mere 'sporadic' attacks on these places. The admiral asserted that air assaults should focus on factories that produced U-boat components, U-boat assembly yards, and U-boat bases. Contrary to the British position, attacks at sea should receive the least priority, he maintained. General Henry Arnold, of the USAAF, in supporting his fellow Americans, and advocating for the doomed American goal of winning the war by targeting industrial sites, believed that 'we should attempt to find what component part or parts of submarines constitute a bottleneck and then strike at factories where they are made'. Portal correctly countered that ball bearings represented 'the greatest bottleneck' but the destruction of those factories 'would be tactically impossible', a comment that closed the anti-submarine discussions.[7]

When, later that day, the debates touched upon Japanese submarines, the British took the opportunity to reinforce their main points. King confessed surprise regarding the low Allied losses from Japanese submarines but Pound countered that the submarines represented a far lesser threat because they operated less efficiently than the German ones and 'small escorts' sufficed to 'drive them away'.[8]

Some of the British began to form a negative opinion of King. Lieutenant General Sir Hastings Ismay, the Prime Minister's personal chief of staff, recorded in his memoirs: 'He was tough as nails and carried himself as stiffly as a poker,' and found him 'blunt and stand-offish, almost to the point of rudeness'. Ismay believed that King conveyed intolerance and suspicion for 'all things British'. Japan remained the American admiral's focus and, according to Ismay, 'he resented the idea of American resources being used for any other purpose than to destroy Japanese'.[9]

That night, commencing around 1900 hours, the discussions continued over a dinner meeting with twelve individuals, including Marshall and King on the American side and Pound and Portal on the British. Additionally, President Roosevelt and Prime Minister Churchill attended. No one recorded the evening deliberations but multiple sources mention several discussed subjects. Most critically, Churchill's naval aide, Pim, told Eisenhower's naval aide, Butcher, that Roosevelt 'spent considerable time in the war room the night before, going over all ship movements, analyzing the probabilities of success or failure in the vicious submarine war'.[10]

When briefing the President the following day, Marshall, either not recognising the difference between the Allies or choosing to minimise the substantial points of disagreement, claimed that the Americans and British 'agreed that effective measures must be taken against the Axis submarines'. He reiterated King's position that U-boat assembly locations offered the 'most effective targets' and even, in attempting to describe a far more congenial situation than actually existed, claimed that 'he agreed with the statement,' attributed to Portal, 'that we must keep hammering on one link in the chain, whether it be the factories which manufacture component parts, the submarine assembly yards, submarine bases,' or lastly, what the British argued should be the first focus, 'submarines along the sea lanes'. The Allies could not have been farther apart regarding their anti-submarine strategy.[11]

In opening the anti-submarine discussions on 15 January, Pound argued that air cover remained of prime importance for anti-submarine warfare, and surface escorts of secondary importance. He asserted that the Allies required two requirements 'for dealing with the submarines on the hunting grounds'. First, convoys needed 'as much air cover as possible' and secondly, 'adequate escorts'. He based part of his argument on the fact that the Allies did not have the escort vessels necessary for adequate convoy protection. Pound contended that 'a rough rule of thumb' necessitated three escort vessels for each convoy 'plus one for every ten ships in the convoy'. Therefore, the First Lord of the Admiralty concluded that a forty-ship convoy required seven escort vessels. He acknowledged though, that the Allies never supplied this number of escorts and convoys never received more than six escort vessels. Additional operations that required escort vessels further exacerbated the situation because 'no pool' existed from which additional vessels could be drawn. Furthermore, the convoy escort responsibilities increased with 'new commitments in the Sierra Leone convoys' and the convoys 'from the Dutch West Indies to the United Kingdom and to North Africa'. The Atlantic alone required 'a minimum sixty-five more escort vessels'. Pound demanded that before engaging in any 1943 strategy deliberations, the Allies must 'weigh carefully the requirements in escort Vessels for any operations to be undertaken'. After an operation commenced and escorts were withdrawn from the convoy, he contended that 'four or five months' would pass before the escorts could return to convoy duty. In the meantime, 'the only relief during such a period would be the intake from new construction,' he maintained.

Sir Charles Portal stated unequivocally that 'air had proved the most effective weapon against the U-boat'. While Portal acknowledged air patrol inefficiency in that aircraft flying 'over the U-boat routes to the hunting grounds' resulted in 'only one sighting for 250 hours flying time,' he believed that even if aircraft did not destroy 'a large number of U-boats' the aircraft patrols compelled 'U-boats to remain submerged' and reduced 'their time on the hunting grounds'. He further maintained that another means of attacking U-boats involved 'laying of mines from the air at the exits of the U-boat bases and construction yards.'

Arnold wanted the B-24s for his Western Europe bombing campaign, though. In attempting to blunt the British argument for B-24s, he inquired if flying boats could be employed to patrol 'the hunting grounds and on the routes to them' as a means to 'avoid the use of valuable long-range bombers'. Portal disagreed and maintained his position 'that the long-range bomber' remained 'essential' for convoy duty since flying boats, due to their 'slow speed', could not respond effectively to 'a call for assistance'. Portal also noted that flying boats carried far fewer 'bombs and depth charges' than a Liberator, and they could not now incorporate the surface radar that enabled the B-24s to locate surfaced U-boats. He admitted that the Allies employed a 'considerable number of Catalinas' despite these 'disadvantages' but maintained that 120 to 135 bombers represented the 'minimum requirements' for both 'Atlantic and British Home Waters'. King remained unconvinced. The admiral asserted that the Catalina's endurance extended to 'twenty-four hours if the crew was large enough to provide two watches'. He further argued for the superiority of flying boats since, unlike a land-based aircraft, the flying boats could be based in 'any sheltered water'.

Sir Charles Portal and Sir Dudley Pound both disagreed with the American admiral. 'Catalinas were being used to the maximum,' Portal claimed. Pound then insisted that the 'requirements in long range bombers which had been stated were an absolute minimum, even allowing for the maximum use of flying boats'. Portal then inquired as to whether aircraft assigned to the Pacific Theatre could be redirected for anti-submarine warfare.

King acknowledged that 'the Japanese had not yet made any great use of submarines in the Pacific', thereby necessitating 'only small escorts', but he warned that 'if the Japanese submarines became more active, aircraft' would be required. The admiral claimed that 'total resources available' had been 'insufficient for security everywhere' and acknowledged the 'acute shortage of escort vessels'. Pound, citing the challenge of the Dutch West Indies to the United Kingdom convoys, asserted that on such voyages 'where long range shore based aircraft could not be employed to cover the whole passage,' the Allies would have to deploy 'auxiliary aircraft carriers'. For the North Atlantic, the British admiral 'hoped to establish bases for long range aircraft in Newfoundland to join up with aircraft working from the United Kingdom'. Arnold, seeming to support the British position for more long-range aircraft, admitted that 'Greenland would be of little use' for airbases due 'to the long hours of darkness and the very bad weather'.[12]

On 18 January, the Chiefs of Staff prepared, at the request of Roosevelt and Churchill, a status report regarding the discussions between the American and British military leaders. Brooke conveyed that 'after seven days of argument he felt that definite progress had been made' and 'a document is now being prepared setting forth the general strategic policy for 1943'. Of the eight goals, he related that the first one involved a statement that resources for fighting the U-boat threat would be 'a first charge on the resources of the United Nations and provide security for all of our operations'.[13]

Two days later, the President dined in the Prime Minister's villa, providing the British leader with another opportunity to persuade the Americans. Several attended, including Roosevelt's son, Elliot, who recorded his views. Of all the maps in Churchill's war room, Elliot described the 'quite large picture of the North Atlantic' as 'most fascinating' as it displayed 'all information about every Nazi submarine pack reduced to sliding miniatures: so many lying quiet at L'Orient and Brest, so many more prowling westward, toward our convoys bound for the United Kingdom, so many more in pens along the Channel, so many more lurking in the sea lanes about the Azores, so many more lying off Iceland, or pointing north, toward the Murmansk run each day.' Churchill's staff constantly updated 'the most recent information about ship movements' and Elliot noted 'a sense of mighty suspense about it: would this convoy get through undamaged? How many tons of vital materiel would explode, and scatter, and sink to the ocean floor from that convoy?' In referring to air support, he related the question: 'Would British coastal patrol get a chance at a good bomb-run over this wolf pack?'[14]

On Thursday, 21 January, at 1000 hours, the conference renewed discussion of U-boats. Pound admitted that 'most of the points in the body of the paper' had been discussed previously, but in drawing attention to the British position on anti-submarine warfare, 'he drew particular attention onto paragraph 14 emphasizing the need for adequate air cover' if the Allies intended to operate with a minimum 'number of escorts'. The report's last page listed 'the large number of escorts required', while the 'table in Enclosure 'C' showed the small numbers of escort vessels' that the Allies would produce during the first six months of 1943.

Portal, in support of the First Sea Lord, noted three aircraft categories: 'V.L.R. – Aircraft with a range over 2,000 miles, such as Liberators, and specially prepared Halifaxes with a range of about 2,100 miles which were temporarily assigned to anti-submarine work, L.H. – Aircraft with a range between 1,200 and 2,000 miles' and 'M. R. – Aircraft with a range between 600 and 1,200 miles.' Recognising the British inability to provide long-range aircraft, and the Americans' ability to do so, he 'inquired whether it could be taken that the requirements' of the 'North Atlantic, East Coast U.S. and Canada' demanded 'no commitments for the United Kingdom'. King replied that he did not have 'exact figures, but he had no reason to doubt that this commitment would be fulfilled by the U. S. and Canada entirely'. He agreed that the United States would commit to the Caribbean and South America's east coast. King though, would not commit to the North Atlantic theatre.

Pound, realising King's admission, reminded the attendees 'that in their agreed policy for the conduct of the war in 1943 (C.C.S. 155/1), the Combined Chiefs of Staff had said that the defeat of the U-boat must remain the first charge on the resources of the United Nations'. He acknowledged though, that the Allies' operation to neutralise the Japanese base at Rabaul and Operation Husky, the invasion of Sicily, 'would inevitably detract from the anti-submarine effort'. The British admiral argued that the 'Combined Chiefs of Staff should clearly record their reasons for thus diverging from the anti-submarine effort as a first objective'.

'After an adjournment,' the committee agreed to the following:

1. Intensified bombing of U-boat operating bases should be carried out.
2. Intensified bombing of U-boat constructional yards should be carried out.
3. U.S. and British Naval Staffs should:
   a. Scrutinize the dispositions of all existing destroyers and escort craft;
   b. Allocate as much new construction, or vessels released by new construction, as possible to convoy protection, The above with a view to each nation providing, to the greatest extent possible, half of the present deficiency of sixty-five escorts for the protection of Atlantic convoys
4. U. S. and British Naval Staffs should provide auxiliary escort carriers for working with Atlantic convoys at the earliest practicable moment.

5. Long-distance shore-based air cover should be provided over the following convoy routes as a matter of urgency:
   a. North Atlantic convoys (U.S.–U.K.) – from both sides of the Atlantic
   b. D.W.I. [Dutch West Indies] oil convoys from the West Indies and U.K,
   c. TORCH oil convoys from the West Indies and Gibraltar.
   d. U.K.–Freetown convoys from Northwest and West Africa.
6. Greenland airdromes should be developed for use by L.R. or V L.R. aircraft,
7. Non-ocean-going escorts should be used for HUSKY to the maximum possible extent.[15]

As far as the public face of the conference, the most critical announcement regarded the Allies' policy of 'unconditional surrender'. On 24 January, three days after the last meeting that discussed the U-boat threat, Roosevelt reminded the press that: 'Some of you Britishers know the old story – we had a General called U.S. Grant. His name was Ulysses Simpson Grant' but the president recalled, he also acquired the title '"Unconditional Surrender" Grant'. Roosevelt then announced, 'the elimination of German, Japanese and Italian war power means the unconditional surrender of Germany, Italy and Japan. That means a reasonable assurance of future world peace. It does not mean the destruction of the population of Germany, Italy, or Japan, but it does mean the destruction of the philosophies in those countries which are based on conquest and the subjugation of other people.'

Dönitz, when hearing of the new Allied policy, expressed indignation. 'That meant that in the event of our submitting we should have no rights whatever, but would be wholly at the mercy of our enemies,' the admiral fumed. And, when Soviet Union leader Josef Stalin, promised later in 1943 'that at least four million Germans should be deported for an unspecified number of years to Russia as forced labour', the Russian's statement manifested Dönitz's worst fears. He concluded that 'in view of the enemy's demand for unconditional surrender, it was quite useless for any senior commander of the German Armed Forces, who believed in 1943 or 1944 that the war could no longer be won, to tell Hitler that he must now put an end to the war and make peace; for, to unconditional surrender, which was wholly unacceptable, he could have no alternative proposal to submit to the Head of the State.'

However, Dönitz would have taken some solace if he had known at the time how the proceedings involving the U-boat discussions had concluded. The British failed to convince their Allies, the evidence suggests, for the Americans did not provide substantial numbers of B-24s to the anti-submarine air effort. The addition of three US Navy Liberator squadrons at Dunkeswell, Devon, represented the only significant change in available Liberators from January 1943 to January 1944. However, the conference notes contain persuasive evidence that the British considered the B-24 as the key offensive weapon against the U-boats. Despite the lack of proof of American assistance in this regard, the limited number of B-24 squadrons would deliver an outsized impact for the Allied anti-submarine campaign in 1943.

An event in the middle of January would, no doubt, concern the British all the more. The Nazi Grand Admiral Erich Raeder informed Dönitz that he intended to resign, an action that would elevate the U-boat leader to the position of Commander-in-Chief of all Nazi naval forces. Hitler had lost confidence in surface vessels and now intended to focus the naval efforts on his U-boat force. As Raeder declared: 'If Hitler wished to emphasize that the U-boat Arm was now, in his opinion, of primary importance, the choice of Doenitz would be fully justified.'[16]

The British would now, in 1943, face a renewed U-boat onslaught with a dedicated submariner leading the entire Nazi navy, and would have to oppose this offensive with no substantial increase in the one weapon they desperately needed: the American-built B-24 Liberator.

Chapter 6

The B-24s in the North Atlantic: January–May 1943

Allied aircraft continued their depredations in 1943, but the U-boat war underwent a significant change in this year. In 1942, Allied U-boat sinkings totalled seventy-four, with aircraft contributing to thirty-eight of them. During the first five months of 1943, Allied forces sank eighty-six U-boats, of which Allied aircraft contributed with forty-eight, 56 per cent of the total.[1] However, the aggregate statistics fail to accurately reflect the changing nature of the U-boat war. Only a monthly evaluation provides a proper understanding.

From January to May, the statistics illustrate the increasing impact of Allied aircraft. With only two U-boats sunk at sea by aircraft in January, little can be concluded from the first month of the year. But from February to May, the totals demonstrate a consistent pattern. Allied aircraft destroyed eight of the fifteen U-boats involving at-sea action in February, 53 per cent of the total. In March, Allied aircraft achieved seven of the thirteen U-boats lost, which was 54 per cent. Of the fourteen fatal U-boat at-sea battles in April, Allied aircraft participated in nine of them for 64 per cent. May proved to be decisive. In that month, Allied aircraft contributed to the destruction of twenty-three U-boats out of total of thirty-five destroyed at sea by all other Allied means; 65 per cent of the total. These two months marked the turning point in the Allied campaign against Dönitz's underwater threat as aircraft's lethality had risen to a margin of nearly two-to-one, and now represented the greatest threat to Hitler's U-boats. Furthermore, Allied aircraft would maintain a two-to-one dominance in the at-sea battles until the end of the war.[2] The attacks became so numerous and successful that Dönitz, on 24 May, surrendered the North Atlantic and retreated. It marked the first time that the German admiral had withdrawn from this significant area and the retreat would, as the war progressed, become permanent. Allied air power had begun the long defeat of Dönitz's force.

When considering the statistics for U-boats destroyed by aircraft, several patterns emerge over these five months. Four-engine aircraft – Liberators, Fortresses, Sunderlands and Halifaxes – had significantly increased their contribution as their successes constituted twenty-three (48 per cent) of the sinkings. American-built aircraft dominated with a combination of Liberators, Catalinas, Hudsons, Fortresses and Avengers comprising thirty-seven (77 per cent) of the destroyed U-boats. The B-24s claimed eleven of the forty-eight destroyed during this time, almost a quarter of all sunk, and for the first time in the war achieved a total during a period of the conflict that exceeded the figures for any other Allied aircraft. As to which air force entity dominated, the RAF participated in thirty-two of the sinkings, 66 per cent.

However, despite how 1943 would unfold, as the year dawned one German confidently believed that the U-boats would defeat the Allied forces in the Atlantic. Dönitz recalled that, in response to his new appointment as the Navy's commander, he 'welcomed' it. The German admiral admitted that he 'was fully aware of the grave importance' as well as the 'difficulty of the task' that he had accepted. Yet he claimed to have 'repeatedly suffered during the past war years' while serving the 'continental-mindedness of our political leadership' of the Armed Forces Supreme Headquarters. Britain remained Nazi Germany's 'chief enemy', the admiral asserted, and the German navy 'had not received adequate quantity' of resources to defeat it. 'I intended to try and rectify this,' Dönitz declared.[3]

Dönitz recognised that the British people's existence 'depended upon sea communications'. The 'corner-stone' of Churchill's entire strategy depended on transporting both 'men and materials by sea'. The prevention of this movement 'by every means of sea and air power' continued to be 'perforce our most important object in the war at sea'. The German admiral contended that the U-boat remained the 'most potent weapon we possessed, and an intensification of the U-boat war by every means at my disposal was my most pressing preoccupation'.[4]

B-24s proved to be the most successful of the Allied anti-submarine warplanes to combat Dönitz's aims during this time, as they sank eleven U-boats, nine in the North Atlantic, and from only two squadrons: 86 and 120. Both squadrons flew from Northern Ireland (RAF Ballykelly and Aldergrove), while 120 also operated from Iceland (RAF Reykjavik). No. 86 Squadron remained in training status for January and February, and 120 Squadron sank six of the nine U-boats attributed to RAF B-24 squadrons during this time, with four of those six victories by aircraft departing Iceland. These two squadrons would destroy more U-boats during the war than any other Allied units.

However, January did not begin with great promise for 120 Squadron. The Liberators managed only fifteen days of operations and during those times sighted only two U-boats. On the 10th, Liberator Mk. I 'H' spotted a U-boat 600yd away but it dived too fast and the bomber arrived at the location 'too late to attack'. Sixteen days later, Liberator Mk. I 'W' discovered a surfaced U-boat from 2,000yd but, again, it 'crash dived' and the British crew lost sight of the swirl due to the sun's glare. Forty-five minutes later the pilot saw 'heavy smoke' on the horizon and discovered a likely victim of his missed target, a 'fiercely burning tanker' with 'some wreckage but no signs of life'.

February proved to be more fortunate despite a similar number of days of operational flying, although not all attacks resulted in success as the first fifteen days demonstrate. On the 6th, Liberator Mk. I 'W' took off from Reykjavik at 0539 hours and attacked a U-boat at 1156 hours with six depth charges. The U-boat avoided further attacks by diving 'steeply'. Most likely facing a wolf pack, the crew assaulted another one twelve minutes later with two depth charges. While the British spotted 'oil and scum', the U-boat had escaped. Then, at 1600 hours, the crew targeted another U-boat. This time, with depth charges depleted, they employed their cannon, although the British confessed to 'no hits'. The crew landed at 2136 hours after a frustrating sixteen-hour mission. The same day, Liberator 'O' spotted a surfaced U-boat with 'conning tower awash' but arrived fifty-five seconds after it had disappeared and the crew therefore did not attack.

Still on the 6th, the 120th continued spotting U-boats as B-24 Mk. III 'R' assaulted one with four depth charges. The U-boat 'surfaced twice' after the depth charge explosions before disappearing. The crew found another one three hours later but it disappeared just forty seconds before the B-24 arrived. Again on the 6th, Liberator Mk. III 'X' also found a surfaced U-boat but it dived before an attack could be conducted. The crew then discovered another one and attacked with six depth charges. It disappeared, and they witnessed a 'large gush of bubbles', a 'patch of thick oil', and a twenty foot 'piece of timber', the U-boat bows appeared ninety seconds later and then slipped under the surface. Despite all the visual evidence, the U-boat survived.

On the 8th, Liberator Mk. III 'K' found a U-boat but of the four depth charges selected to fall, only one did and the U-boat slipped away. The next day, B-24 'K' dived on a surfaced U-boat but the German dived quicker. The British crew dropped one depth charge in the swirl but did not spot any evidence of damage. On the 15th, Liberator Mk. III 'R' spotted a conning tower protruding from the surface and bore in but it disappeared before the aircraft arrived and there was no attack.[5]

However, also on the 15th, 120 Squadron Liberator 'S' achieved the first success of the year for the squadron. The crew discovered Type IXC/40 *U-529* over 600 miles south-west of Iceland and they struck with multiple depth charges that sank the U-boat with its forty-eight crew members. The German crew had yet to engage any Allied vessels on this, its first patrol. Six days later, on 21 February, 120 Squadron struck again when Liberator Mk. III 'T' took off from Aldergrove at 0929 hours and rendezvoused with ON 166, a convoy of forty-six merchant vessels, moving at 6 knots. While escorting this North Atlantic convoy, the crew spotted a surfaced U-boat at 2015 hours and the pilot, Squadron Leader D.J. Isted, carefully used clouds to hide his approach. When emerging, the crew now identified not one but two U-boats and Isted commenced his attack. The Liberator dropped six depth charges on the first one 'stem to stern' and the B-24's rear gunner expended 150 rounds for the ninety seconds that the conning tower remained above the surface after the assault. Isted circled the area for fifty minutes until two 'very large oil patches' appeared on the surface. The B-24 landed at Aldergrove at 0333 hours, an eighteen-hour mission. Type VIIC *U-623* lost all forty-six hands on this, its second patrol, and claimed no Allied vessel sinkings during its short career.[6]

Although 120 Squadron delivered one fatal strike in February, it managed none in March. On the 8th, Liberator Mk. III 'O' spotted a 'periscope wake' and assaulted with two depth charges just fifteen seconds after the U-boat disappeared. That same day, Liberator Mk. III 'R' attacked a U-boat, also fifteen seconds after it submerged, with four depth charges and, like the other B-24 crew, noted no evidence of damage. Later, this RAF crew discovered another surfaced U-boat but in this instance the four selected depth charges failed to release. On 11 March, B-24 Mk. III 'H' rendezvoused with convoy HX 288 of fifty-merchant vessels and six escort vessels. While flying astern of the vessels, the crew discovered a surfaced U-boat at 10 miles distance in clear weather. The crew released four depth charges but admitted that 'all over-shot.' However, they later attacked another U-boat with two depth charges twenty seconds after the boat disappeared, but could claim no damage. The crew came upon a third U-boat and, with no depth charges remaining, dived hoping to force the U-boat to submerge, which it did.

No. 86 Squadron commenced patrols in March but both squadrons struggled in the second part of the month, as 120 had struggled in the first part. No. 86 Squadron did not manage any attacks during the first two weeks of the month, and two in the last two weeks, but both failed. On the 17th, B-24 Mk. IIIA 'M' unsuccessfully assaulted a U-boat with four depth charges and on the 29th, 86 Squadron conducted its last attack of the month but Liberator Mk. IIIA 'H''s two depth charges failed to release.

No. 120 Squadron's B-24s engaged in far more battles that month. On the 17th, Liberator Mk. III 'G' descended to attack a surfaced U-boat but it 'crash dived' twelve seconds before the depth charges fell. While the crew witnessed an oil patch, the U-boat did not suffer fatal damage. The B-24 returned to its convoy of forty-four merchant vessels and six escort vessels. Later, with a periscope spotted, the crew initiated another attack but the two remaining depth charges failed to release. That same day, the squadron's Liberator Mk. III 'J' met convoy HX 229, consisting of twenty-seven merchant vessels and three escort vessels moving at 8 knots. The crew later visually spotted a surfaced U-boat at 10 miles distance and when approaching they discovered another one. The first one dived and the pilot attacked the second one with five depth charges eight seconds after it disappeared. The U-boat resurfaced with its bows at a 'steep angle' and slipped down again after a few seconds. The Liberator then found three more U-boats and assaulted the centre one with the only remaining depth charge. However, the British observed no damage from any of these attacks.

The squadron participated in numerous attacks the following day as well. Liberator Mk. III 'E' found a surfaced U-boat and the crew released four depth charges as the U-boat submerged. Liberator Mk. III 'B', upon discovering a surfaced U-boat, descended from 800ft to 50ft and attacked with two depth charges after the U-boat had submerged. The crew later found another one and released four depth charges. One fell 'close to port bow' but the others overshot. Liberator Mk. III 'X' sighted a U-boat but it submerged before the crew could attack. Later, they came upon a second one and dropped four depth charges twenty-three seconds after it submerged. In all cases, the crews reported no evidence of damage.

The next day, B-24 Mk. III 'M' sighted a surfaced U-boat and descended from 900ft when 3 miles away, and released six depth charges with 75ft of the U-boat's stern still on the surface. The crew acknowledged that the first fell 55yd before the swirl and the others 'overshot'. No. 120 Squadron's last attempted attack occurred on 19 March. Liberator Mk.

III 'J' rendezvoused with convoy SC 122, consisting of forty merchant vessels and ten escort vessels. The crew dived on a surfaced U-boat, which dived as well, and the British dropped two depth charges from 200ft thirty seconds after it submerged. Later, the B-24 descended 'in moonlight' on another U-boat but while the target remained on the surface, the aircraft's bomb doors failed to open and the target escaped.[7]

In April, the British Liberators continued their assaults with more success. No. 120 Squadron's B-24s carried out five attacks, two of them fatal. On 5 April, B-24 Mk. III 'N' took off from Reykjavik at 1210 hours and in less than three hours of patrolling the North Atlantic spotted a surfaced U-boat, initiating its attack with the sun to its rear. The British crew released six depth charges and the U-boat disappeared forever under the surface. Type VIIC *U-635* lost all forty-seven hands on its first patrol, with only one Allied vessel sinking to its credit.[8] On 21 April, Liberator Mk. III 'M' arrived over a surfaced U-boat but all four depth charges 'hung up'. The next day, Liberator Mk. I 'H' conducted four attacks, two on the same U-boat, but again none of the depth charges would release. On 23 April, Liberator Mk. III 'J' unsuccessfully assaulted a surfaced U-boat from 100ft. That same day, B-24 Mk. III 'V' took off from Reykjavik at 1354 hours and spotted two surfaced U-boats at 2103 hours. The aircraft descended on the nearest target, one of the long-range Type IXC/40 U-boats, and released four depth charges from 50ft, successfully straddling the target. The Germans fired at the Liberator but caused no damage. The attack failed to sink the U-boat; it continued afloat but 'down by stern'. The aircraft circled and commenced its second attack at 2106 hours, releasing two depth charges again from 50ft. All struck close and the U-boat remained stern down. The crew then estimated that fifty to sixty survivors floated on the surface as the U-boat 'sank vertically, stern first'. Thus ended both *U-189*'s first patrol and the lives of its fifty-four crew members, having sunk no Allied vessels.[9]

No. 86 Squadron experienced one success in April and numerous unsuccessful encounters. On the 6th, Liberator IIIA 'R' took off from Aldergrove at 1047 hours, spotted a U-boat at 1917 hours, and commenced an assault. Unfortunately, on the first pass, only one depth charge dropped but on the second one, four fell. The crew reported no signs of damage. At 2146 hours the British found another U-boat and after this attack they observed a 'dark patch of oil', a temporary grave marker for Type VIIC *U-632* and its forty-eight crew members, who had completed two patrols and sunk three vessels.[10] 'R' returned to base almost five hours later at 0230 hours, having completed a nearly sixteen-hour mission. That same day, Liberator Mk. IIIA 'W' spotted a surfaced U-boat and flew over but the depth charges failed to release. On the second attempt though, they fell and the crew observed, three minutes after the attack, 'large patches of dark oil with greenish streaks'. The crew also later assaulted a second U-boat. However, both U-boats survived. Also on the 6th, Liberator Mk. IIIA 'K' released depth charges on a U-boat with 'no results' seen.

Five days later, B-24 Mk. IIIA 'M' and a surfaced U-boat parlayed with gun fire and the flak discouraged the British crew from engaging. That day Liberator Mk. IIIA 'B''s crew released four depth charges on a U-boat without witnessing any damage and a week later, B-24 Mk. IIIA 'X' successfully overflew a surfaced U-boat, however, the depth charges failed to release and the target disappeared. On the 20th, Liberator Mk. IIIA 'R' did release four depth charges on a U-boat but the crew noted no damage.

In May, 86 Squadron's Liberators engaged numerous U-boats and destroyed two of them. On the 4th, B-24 Mk. V. 'P' 'sighted and attacked' Type IXB *U-109*, which had managed thirteen Allied vessels sunk and one damaged on nine patrols. The British released 'four depth charges' that 'straddled' this highly successful and fully surfaced U-boat. The crew spotted 'two explosions to port and two to starboard just forward of conning tower. As plumes subsided,' the British observed 'much wreckage, consisting of bright coloured planks, top of black cylinder and two white cylinders' and a 'huge oil patch'. All fifty-two crew members perished.

Eight days later, Liberator Mk. III 'B' found Type VIIC *U-456*. This U-boat had sunk six Allied vessels and damaged another on its eleven patrols. The B-24 attacked it with a Fido, an air-dropped acoustic homing torpedo. The U-boat later 'surfaced owing to inability to dive'. The British crew informed the convoy Senior Naval Officer, who directed a destroyer to the scene. The destroyer never found the U-boat or its fifty-two crew members. This attack marked the first successful attack by a Fido.[11]

Besides these two victories, 86 Squadron B-24s fought six other battles in which U-boats avoided a fatal attack. That same day of 'B''s combat, Liberator Mk. III 'N''s crew unsuccessfully battled a U-boat. Instead of departing after the failed attack, the pilot decided to loiter in the area in order to force the submarine to remain submerged, and to thereby allow a lone merchant vessel to escape. As the month progressed, the Liberator Mk. IIIs experienced numerous other failed assaults: 'K' on the 12th, 'G' on the 13th, 'B' on the 16th, 'Z' on the 23rd, and 'J' on the 26th.

In May, 120 Squadron achieved victories against two Type VIIC U-boats. Liberator Mk. I 'P' departed Reykjavik at 0954 hours on the

20th and located a U-boat at 1448 hours. It 'submerged 23 seconds' before the bomber could attack, and therefore there was no attack. At 1710 hours though, the crew sighted a U-boat at 6 miles distance. Two minutes later, the pilot, Squadron Leader J.R.E. Procter, flew over the boat and dropped four 250lb depth charges. They straddled the 'partly submerged' craft, which then submerged, leaving behind an oil patch. Then, at 1924 hours, a U-boat surfaced within 3 miles of the B-24. Proctor 'dived to attack' and the crew commenced machine gun fire as the Germans returned fire. Proctor flew around for another attack, with 180 rounds of cannon fire striking both the conning tower's base and the foredeck. The British aircraft received one hit, 'but no damage'. Proctor then attacked the U-boat for a third time; on this occasion with one 600lb depth charge. Three minutes after this attack, the U-boat floated down by the stern and began to manoeuvre in a circular pattern, leading the Liberator crew to conclude that the boat had suffered significant damage. *U-258* sank with all of its forty-nine crew members, having destroyed one Allied vessel on three patrols.[12]

The second victory transpired eight days later on the 28th when Liberator Mk. III 'E' departed Reykjavik at 1554 hours and almost five hours later, at 2036 hours, spotted a U-boat and dived to assault. The crew released four 250lb depth charges adjacent to the partially submerged submarine. An oil patch subsequently emerged as the only sign of the demise of the U-boat demise, and its forty-six crew members. *U-304* had failed to sink any Allied vessels on its first patrol.[13]

Also in May, besides the before-mentioned victories, 120 Squadron took part in numerous non-fatal attacks. On the 14th, Liberator Mk. III 'J' attacked a surfaced U-boat with one 600lb depth charge and noted no damage. Five days later, on the 19th, the squadron's men witnessed a flurry of activity, but no fatal assaults. Mk. III 'T' assaulted a U-boat with five depth charges in two attacks alone, and with no more ordnance, performed 'mock' attacks on four U-boats. The B-24 and one of the U-boats exchanged gun fire, which forced it to submerge. That same day, Mk. I 'P' dropped four depth charges from 50ft on a U-boat that had submerged twenty seconds before the assault. Mk. I 'O' engaged two surfaced U-boats, and Mk. III 'Y' released a single 600lb bomb on one to no effect. On the 20th, Mk. III 'N' assaulted a recently submerged U-boat with three 250lb depth charges, another with a single 600lb bomb, among a total of five U-boat sightings. The squadron completed the month's unsuccessful attacks on the 28th when Mk. III 'E' released four 250lb depth charges on a partially surfaced U-boat and observed only an oil patch from the fleeing boat.

Despite these setbacks, the Liberators had more than proven their worth during these five months as the most lethal Allied aircraft. Operating from Iceland over the North Atlantic had enabled the B-24s to demonstrate their effectiveness on patrols of greater than a twelve-hour duration, with substantial depth charges and the speed necessary to ambush surfaced U-boats. However, with a shortage of these valuable aircraft, the RAF also employed the shorter-range B-17s, Hudsons, Sunderlands and Hampdens in the North Atlantic during this time, and these aircraft also contributed significantly to the Allied successes during these five months.

Chapter 7

The Allies' Other Aircraft in the North Atlantic: January–May 1943

As the Casablanca Conference demonstrated, if the British had to choose, they would have stocked their Coastal Command squadrons with Liberators. However, with the B-24s in short supply, they resorted to other aircraft to fight in the North Atlantic including Fortresses, Hudsons and Catalinas. The Americans also contributed in this area during this time with aircraft such as Catalinas and their carrier planes. The Allies, especially the British, were determined to wrest control of the North Atlantic from the grasp of Hitler's U-boats.

The four-engine RAF B-17 Fortresses posted numerous successes, as 220 and 206 Squadron crews sank six U-boats during the first five months of 1943, all in the North Atlantic. No. 220 Squadron encountered no U-boats in January, and in February, the Fortresses only attacked only two, but both proved to be successful. On the 3rd, Fortress Mk. II 'N' of 220 Squadron took off from Ballykelly at 0535 hours and at 1106 hours, approximately midway between Ireland and Greenland, with the escorting convoy 29 miles away, its crew sighted a surfaced Type VIIC U-boat 4 miles away. The bomber began its attack from 3,000ft and dropped seven 250lb depth charges from 50ft. The crew spotted 'a purple patch of oil' after the assault. *U-265* sank with all forty-six hands on this, its first patrol having sunk no Allied vessels.[1]

Four days later, on 7 February, another 220 Squadron Fortress struck in the same area. B-17 Mk. II 'J' spotted Type VIIC *U-624* on the surface and used cloud cover to close the distance to 3 miles before commencing an attack through rainy conditions. The crew straddled the target successfully with depth charges and observed the U-boat disappear gradually under the water. Remaining in the area, the British spotted 'a round object' 12ft long and numerous 'pieces of yellow wood' on the surface. Like *U-265*, *U-624* ended its career on its first patrol having sunk four vessels and damaged two others. All forty-five crew members perished.[2]

In March, 220 Squadron did not attack any U-boats with depth charges until the 7th. On that day, Fortress Mk. II 'J' released seven from 80ft, twelve seconds after the U-boat dived. The crew observed some diesel oil and 'darker oil'. On 19 March, Fortress Mk. II 'M' found a surfaced U-boat and dropped four depth charges after it submerged. Fifty seconds after the assault, the U-boat and diesel oil appeared on the surface. The U-boat then submerged again 'with no forward motion'. The B-17 struck again with three depth charges as the conning tower disappeared. Oil appeared for ten minutes but the U-boat escaped. The Fortresses engaged no other U-boats that month and, in fact, none in April until the 16th. On that day, 'J' battled two U-boats. In the first instance, the B-17 encountered two of them and when flying over one, the five depth charges failed to 'release immediately'. Instead, they dropped ineffectually 2,000yd from the swirl. Later that day, in the second instance, the crew released the two remaining depth charges five seconds after the U-boat submerged and they saw no evidence of damage. That same day, Fortress Mk. II 'T' attacked a U-boat with six depth charges and only noted a small oil patch. For the rest of April and for the entire month of May, the squadron's B-17s encountered no further U-boats.[3]

No. 206 Squadron, which would eventually convert to Liberators, would become one of the five most lethal Allied anti-submarine units during the war, and achieved four of its nine fatal attacks during this period. However, these five months began slowly as the B-17s engaged few U-boats in the first two months. The British discovered none in January until the 15th, when Mk. IIA 'G' roared over one. Two depth charges fell short, two hit on target and two 'failed to release'. After the assault, the crew watched the U-boat's 'bow or stern' 'bobbing up and down like a half-filled bottle' until it disappeared. Despite the damage, the U-boat survived. The squadron engaged only one U-boat in February when 'L' found a surfaced one on the 9th that was moving at 12 knots, 5 to 6 miles away. The Fortress Mk. IIA dropped six depth charges, the explosions 'lifted' the U-boat and then, with no forward momentum, it disappeared under the surface and survived.

The squadron's Fortresses encountered their first U-boat in March on the 14th when 'G' attacked one with six depth charges that all fell 'outside lethal range'. Five days later, on 19 March, at 0418 hours, B-17 Mk. IIA 'B' took off from RAF Kinloss in northern Scotland. At 0905 hours it found convoy HX 229, its intended escort, consisting of twenty-four merchant vessels and four escorts, steaming approximately midway between Ireland and Greenland. The British commenced patrolling around the vessels at 30 miles distance. While flying to the rear of the convoy through a squall, at 0924 hours, the crew spotted Type VIIC *U-384*, which had sunk one vessel on its first patrol and on this one, its second, the German crew had fatally torpedoed an Allied vessel three days before. With the cloud and rain as cover, the Fortress commenced its approach and upon reaching the target, released four depth charges that straddled the boat. The crew observed a 'heavy black substance' on the surface and 'large black streaks of oil'. None of the forty-seven-man crew survived. 'B' returned to base at 1614 hours, a twelve-hour mission.[4]

On the 25th, Fortress Mk. IIA 'L' took off into early morning sky from RAF Benbecula, in the Outer Hebrides off Scotland, at 0444 hours. Five hours later, at 0959 hours, the crew discovered surfaced Type VIIC *U-469* south-east of Iceland proceeding at approximately 5 to 6 knots. The B-17 dived and delivered six depth charges from 200ft. The depth charges straddled the U-boat, which partly submerged until the stern appeared on the surface at a 45-degree angle. The crew then initiated a second assault, dropping its last depth charges from 50ft. A large oil patch estimated at 1,000 by 600yd appeared with a 'floating yellow and white debris'. *U-469*, on its first patrol, had not sunk any vessels. All forty-seven crew members perished. The B-17 landed at 1630 hours, another twelve-hour patrol.[5]

Two days later, the same aircraft, with a different crew, struck again. While conducting a patrol 180 miles south-south-east of Iceland, at 1130 hours it spotted long-range Type IXC/40 *U-169* 3 miles away proceeding on the surface at 10 knots. Unlike the previous B-17 encounters that year, this time, the Germans fired back. The pilot, Flying Officer A.C.I. Samuel, took the Flying Fortress down from 2,000ft and the RAF crew observed both 'gun flashes and tracer', though they considered the fire inaccurate and their aircraft received no hits. As the B-17 flew over the U-boat, the crew released six depth charges, with one falling on the starboard side, another on the port side, and the remaining four dropping 'over the port bow'. The tail gunner observed the U-boat to 'heel right' to starboard for fifteen seconds before submerging, and then ten to fifteen seconds later the dying boat's bows emerged at an 'acute angle'. Samuel swung the large aircraft around for a second assault, flew over the U-boat again, and released the remaining depth charges. The tail gunner then observed crew members 'scrambling about the control tower' as it slipped under the surface in twenty to thirty seconds, descending 'almost vertically'. Thus ended *U-169*'s first and only patrol, having sunk no ships. All fifty-four crew members perished.[6]

No. 206 Squadron continued engaging U-boats the following month, with one success. On 7 April, Fortress 'C' found a surfaced U-boat. At 250ft, the pilot 'turned to starboard and dived to the attack'. He had lengthened the 'approach' to 'ensure time for opening' of the 'bomb doors' but when in the 'attacking position' and the 'release button pressed' the bomb doors had not fully opened so that all depth charges 'hung up'. By the time the B-17 swung around for a second attack, the U-boat had been 'submerged for at least 30 seconds' so the captain 'decided not to attack'.

On the 19th, Fortress 'P' discovered a surfaced U-boat and arrived at the attacking position four seconds after it had submerged. However, the depth charges 'failed to release'. The crew tested the bomb gear during the early part of the flight and found it to be 'unserviceable' but had hoped that the 'emergency jettison lever' would permit depth charge release. However, the lever 'also failed to operate after repeated attempts'. On the 22nd, Fortress 'D' attacked a U-boat with six depth charges released twenty-two seconds after it submerged. The crew observed no signs of damage. Two days later, Fortress 'D' commenced its patrol at 1531 hours and, almost two hours later, at 1725 hours, identified a U-boat at periscope depth from 8 miles away. In a prime example of poor timing on the U-boat commander's part, as the B-17 began its descent, the submarine, obviously unaware of the coming onslaught, surfaced. Six Germans emerged in the conning tower once surfaced, and now aware of the approaching hunter, fired two inaccurate bursts. The RAF crew flew over and released six depth charges, which successfully straddled the boat and resulted in multiple explosions that 'seemed to lift' the bows from the surface. The Fortress circled for a second attack and delivered the remaining depth charges, causing the U-boat to slip under by the stern. While the crew noticed twenty-five survivors in the water along with various pieces of wreckage, none of the forty-nine crew members survived. Thus ended Type VIIC *U-710*'s first patrol, not having destroyed any Allied vessels.[7] The same day, Fortress 'C' attacked a U-boat with six depth charges after it had submerged and only observed some 'brown scum and a light grey discolouration'.

No. 206 Squadron participated in two unsuccessful assaults in May. On the 30th, Fortress 'E' spotted a fully surfaced U-boat moving at 18 knots and dived to assault. The U-boat dived as well and the four-engine aircraft arrived at the attacking position forty-five seconds after it submerged. The pilot, nevertheless, released four depth charges but no signs of damage emerged. On the last day of the month, B-17 'A' found a wake at 8 miles distance and then discovered a fully surfaced U-boat moving at 12 to 14 knots. The aircraft dived and released six depth charges. The U-boat 'submerged stern last and at a steep angle' but the British found no evidence of a sinking.[8]

The British-operated American-built Lockheed Hudsons, struck nine U-boats fatally during the first five months of 1943, just one fewer than the Liberators. Seven successes occurred outside the North Atlantic and will be discussed in the following chapter, while two included successful battles in May in the area around Iceland. The 269 Squadron Hudsons, operating from Reykjavik and flying Mk. IIs and Mk. IIIs, initiated numerous attacks that month. On 2 May, 'W' obtained a contact at 8 miles. The pilot used the cloud cover until, at 3½ miles, the Hudson 'broke cloud'. The crew spotted a surfaced U-boat and the aircraft dived. When the Hudson had reached a distance of 2 miles, the U-boat commenced diving and submerged two seconds before the four depth charges fell from 60ft. The British observed extensive oil and a 'rush of bubbles' but the U-boat had escaped. On the 5th, Hudson 'F' dived on a surfaced U-boat and dropped four depth charges from 60ft. The explosions though, did not sink the target. The next day, Hudson 'U' executed an attack on a surfaced U-boat but all four depth charges failed to explode. 'O' assaulted a periscope with depth charges but the crew observed no damage. 'J' visually spotted a conning tower but faced a submerged U-boat when it arrived at attacking position and noticed nothing as a result of four depth charge explosions. 'Z' dived on a rapidly submerging U-boat and released its four depth charges while the conning tower remained visible, but the crew's efforts produced only two oil patches.

On the 9th, 'N' obtained a contact in heavy snow at 4 miles distance and departed the cloud cover at 3 miles to discover a fully surfaced U-boat, which did not submerge. The twin-engine aircraft quickly closed the distance and released four depth charges at the attacking position but only observed a large oil patch for their efforts. On the 17th, 'B' visually sighted and dived on a fully surfaced U-boat and dropped depth charges from 50ft three seconds after it submerged, with only an oil patch as evidence of the attack. 'W' spotted a U-boat at 5 miles and attacked 'from out of sun' and the target initiated a crash dive when the Hudson was just ½ mile away. The depth charges dropped ahead of the swirl and produced only a 'light oil streak'.

However, on that same day, another Hudson achieved great success. 'J' took off from Reykjavik and spotted a fully surfaced Type VIIC U-boat 10 miles away. The crew made this sighting at 3,500ft and determined that the lack of cloud cover necessitated an immediate attack. The pilot,

Sergeant F.H.W. James, flew 'head on' to the U-boat at sea level, 'keeping as close to the water as possible'. When close to the target, he pulled the Hudson up to 50ft and believed that he had taken the German crew 'completely by surprise'. All depth charges released successfully and exploded. The first struck close to the bow, the second close to the starboard side of the conning tower, the third near astern, and number four 'in line'. James circled the U-boat after the attack and the crew observed 'large columns of grey smoke' accompanied by a significant patch of oil and a 'great deal of debris', including 'narrow reddish coloured objects' that 'appeared like wood'. The British aircraft remained in the area for twenty-three minutes before departing. *U-646* sank with all forty-six hands. The U-boat had completed only one patrol and had not sunk any Allied vessels.[9]

Two days later, on the 19th, three 269 Squadron Hudsons assaulted U-boats. 'B' spotted one and dived 'rapidly' but when it arrived in the attacking position it dropped depth charges in the swirl. 'S' found a U-boat 4 miles away but also arrived in time to only attack the swirl with depth charges. Hudson 'M', of the same squadron, had better fortune. It departed Reykjavik and spotted a surfaced U-boat through a cloud gap but the U-boat dived before it could commence its attack. The Hudson crew though, at approximately 300 miles south of Iceland, made another sighting. The captain employed the clouds as cover and manoeuvred the twin-engine aircraft for a stern approach. At this point, the Type VIIC U-boat was cruising 6 miles away straight ahead of the Hudson. The British aircraft dived at a 30-degree angle until it arrived above the conning tower. The crew released depth charges and noticed multiple Germans on the tower but, from the British perspective, as they took no action as a result of the attack, they appeared to be treating the Hudson's actions 'with contempt'. The British circled the stricken boat while firing at the conning tower. The U-boat began 'turning to starboard' while losing a significant amount of oil. After seven minutes, its death throes ended with its disappearance under the water. The Hudson remained for twenty-four minutes and observed a 'long trail of oil' and 'a plank of wood 6 feet long'. *U-273* lost all forty-six hands. It had completed only one patrol and had not sunk any Allied vessels.[10] The final 269 Squadron attack in May came on the 21st when 'R' visually spotted a fully surfaced U-boat and used cloud cover to attack 'out of sun'. The U-boat initiated a dive and the four depth charges fell in the swirl four seconds after it went under. The crew observed an oil patch and 'air bubbles' but the target escaped.

The Catalina, another American-built aircraft, also achieved noteworthy success during this period as this type sank eight U-boats, just once fewer than the Hudson. Three occurred in the North Atlantic. On 14 May, A US Navy VP-84 flying boat released multiple depth charges on Type VIIC *U-640*. All forty-nine crew members perished. This marked the U-boat's first patrol, having sunk no Allied vessels. Eleven days later, on the 25th, another VP-84 Catalina sank Type VIIC *U-467* with the relatively new Fido homing torpedo, which resulted in the loss of all forty-six hands. The U-boat had finished two patrols but had not destroyed any vessels.[11] The Royal Canadian Air Force achieved one sinking during this period with a Catalina, named Canso in Canadian service. On 4 May, 5 Squadron's 'W' attacked *U-209* in the North Atlantic south of Greenland. Depth charges caused significant damage to the Type VIIC U-boat, but it escaped temporarily. However, the damage most likely resulted in its sinking days later because U-boat Command never heard from *U-209* again. All forty-six crew members perished with it. The U-boat had destroyed four Allied vessels.[12]

Sunderlands achieved an impressive record in May this year with five sinkings, one of which occurred in the North Atlantic. No. 423 Squadron Royal Canadian Air Force operated its Sunderlands from Northern Ireland waters at RAF Castle Archdale, and patrolled south of the heavily U-boat trafficked Iceland area. Of the two U-boats encountered this month, only one proved to be a fatal attack. On 12 May, Sunderland Mk. III 'G' took off into the night air at 2243 hours. At 0800 hours, the crew rendezvoused with its convoy of forty-three merchant vessels and eight escort vessels in the Atlantic 500 miles south-west of its base. Thirty minutes later, the crew spotted a fully surfaced U-boat just 10 miles from the convoy. Pilot Flight Lieutenant J. Musgrave headed for the target, using the clouds to cover his approach until he dived on the Type VIIC U-boat, whose crew had not seen the approaching flying boat. However, Musgrave aborted his attack on approach when he determined that the U-boat commander did not intend to dive. Instead, the Canadian pilot called for assistance from a nearly Allied corvette. In the meantime, the Sunderland and the U-boat exchanged fire for twenty minutes. When the corvette arrived and commenced fire, the U-boat dived and the Sunderland now attacked with two depth charges. These charges and those from two surface vessels sank *U-753*. It had destroyed two Allied ships and damaged three on six patrols. All forty-seven crew members perished. The flying boat returned to base at 1424 hours on the 13th, a fourteen-hour mission.[13]

Aircraft from Allied escort carriers contributed to four Type VIIC U-boat sinkings during this time, with the Royal Navy receiving credit for three and the US Navy destroying one. On 25 April, HMS *Biter*'s

811 Squadron Swordfish 'L' discovered one of the most successful of Dönitz's U-boats, Type VIIC *U-203*, in the North Atlantic approximately 300 miles south of Greenland. Under three commanders, this U-boat had destroyed twenty-three Allied vessels and damaged four others. The Swordfish crew directed HMS *Pathfinder* to the location, where the British destroyer delivered multiple depth charge attacks that sank *U-203*. The Royal Navy rescued thirty-eight crew members, while ten died in the attack.[14] On 12 May, another 811 Squadron Swordfish, 'B', destroyed Type VIIC *U-89* in the mid-North Atlantic with depth charges. None of the forty-eight crew members survived. It had sunk four vessels on five patrols.[15] No. 819 Squadron Swordfish 'G' from the HMS *Archer* then used rockets to sink Type VIIC *U-752* in the mid-North Atlantic on 23 May. Twenty-nine crewmen perished but a British destroyer saved thirteen, while *U-91* rescued another four. On eight patrols, its crews had sunk nine Allied vessels and damaged another one.[16]

U-boats downed one Allied naval aircraft on 12 May. A Royal Navy 811 Squadron Swordfish from HMS *Biter* unsuccessfully attacked Type VIIC *U-230* once, and when the pilot approached for a second time, flak apparently fatally damaged the engine and the biplane fell into the water. The subsequent explosion of the Swordfish's bombs resulted in the death of all three crew members.[17]

The US Navy's one sinking also marked the first time that the Allies' breaking of the German Enigma code led to a U-boat destruction's by the service. In fact, such code breaking contributed to all remaining American escort carrier U-boat sinkings in the war. However, the intelligence did not assure success. The code breaking permitted the Americans to know the area where the U-boats operated, but they still had to locate them in that area. This was most often with high-frequency detection finding that narrowed the area by monitoring U-boat radio transmissions. Then, aircraft would need to search the defined area, visually locate the boats and deliver lethal ordnance. On 22 May, in the western North Atlantic, USS *Bogue*'s single-engine aircraft attacked two Type VIIC U-boats: *U-468* and *U-305*. A single Avenger hit *U-468* and two Avengers battled *U-305* but, although damaged, both U-boats escaped despite the intelligence with which the Americans had been provided. On that same day though, two of *Bogue*'s VC-9 Squadron Avengers – T-6 (Lieutenant (jg) W.F. Chamberlain) and T-7 (Lieutenant H.S. Roberts) – discovered the surfaced Type VIIC *U-569* and released multiple depth charges. After several uncontrolled descents and resurfacing, the Germans stabilised the U-boat on the surface, before scuttling it.

The Canadian crew of HMCS *St Laurent* rescued twenty-five crew members but never found the remaining twenty-one men.[18]

A Handley Page Hampden, a dated twin-engine aircraft still operated by some Allied squadrons, managed a single sinking during this time. On 30 April at 0955 hours, 455 Squadron Hampden Mk. I 'X' of the Royal Australian Air Force bore down the runway at RAF Sumburgh in the Shetlands at 0751 hours and, approximately halfway between Iceland and Norway, found surfaced Type VIIC *U-227* on its maiden cruise, having not encountered any Allied vessels. The pilot turned and descended for the attack while U-boat crew, having spotted the aircraft, chose to fire on it and not dive. The Australians flew over the target and released six Torpex depth charges. The explosions lifted the stern 10ft into the air momentarily before it dropped to the surface. The Australians flew over again and dropped two additional depth charges, and after this assault, smoke bellowed from the bows, the stern again lifted from the surface and the U-boat disappeared. The Hampden crew observed thirty men on the surface, along with an oil patch. The aircraft landed at RAF Wick at 1359 hours with six hits from German flak. All forty-nine U-boat crew members perished.[19]

The US Navy achieved one sinking with a land-based, twin-engine aircraft. On 27 April, VB-125 Lockheed Ventura B-6 discovered *U-174*, one of the long-range Type IXC boats, in an area south of Newfoundland, and attacked. The Germans immediately commenced submerging as the American aircraft approached, forcing the crew to release its depth charges from 25ft, just as the U-boat disappeared beneath the surface. The damaged U-boat then appeared on the surface. As the Navy aircraft approached for a second attack, its bows rose to a vertical position and it disappeared. *U-174* sank with all fifty-three hands after a career of three patrols and five Allied merchant vessels sunk.[20]

This period had been devastating to German U-boat forces, and Dönitz considered only one option available. On 24 May, he relayed new orders to his U-boat commanders and retreated from the hunting grounds south of Iceland that had been so fruitful before the Allied aircraft, especially the Liberators, arrived in significant numbers. Dönitz noted that 'we found that the whole of the Atlantic was under strong air patrol, either by long-range four-engine machines or by carrier-borne aircraft from American carriers stationed in the central or southern Atlantic'. He acknowledged 'defeat in the convoy battles of the North Atlantic in May 1943' and therefore ordered many of his U-boats south from the North Atlantic convoy routes, maintaining a small number with active communications in order to force the Allies to deploy significant surface escort vessels. Although he may not have realised the pivotal moment at the time, he related in his memoirs, 'We had lost the Battle of the Atlantic.'[21]

British historian S.W. Roskill's well-known quote aptly explains the defeat, and credits the Liberators for the Allied victory: 'in the early spring of 1943 we had a very narrow escape from defeat in the Atlantic; and that, had we suffered such a defeat, history would have judged that the main cause had been the lack of two more squadrons of very long range aircraft for convoy escort duties'. In fact, the British had succeeded in the North Atlantic with very long-range aircraft from only four squadrons: 120 (Liberators), 86 (Liberators), 206 (Fortresses), and 220 (Fortresses.) When considering that the B-24 destroyed nine in the North Atlantic, and the B-17s six, he could have more accurately stated that the Allies would have suffered defeat without the two B-24 squadrons.[22]

Yet, while Dönitz suffered a significant defeat in the North Atlantic during these five months with twenty-seven U-boats sunk by Allied aircraft, the Allies did not limit his losses to that area. He suffered almost two dozen losses during this same period in other areas such as the South Atlantic, the Bay of Biscay, and the Mediterranean Sea.

Chapter 8

Outside the North Atlantic: January–May 1943

While Dönitz focused on the North Atlantic during the first five months of 1943, he did not limit his U-boats to that area. They prowled the South Atlantic and the Mediterranean as well. However, the Allies responded to this threat by operating aircraft in South America and North Africa, and also invested heavily in scouring the Bay of Biscay area with the intention of intercepting surfaced U-boats departing from, or returning to, their French bases.

With these actions, the Allies began to prove to Dönitz that they could match the global reach of his U-boats with the global reach of their aircraft. The U-boat commanders would learn the necessity of maintaining constant watch while on the surface no matter which sea they crossed. There would be no 'Third Happy Time' for the Third Reich.

With the British focusing their Liberators in the North Atlantic, their B-24s achieved only a single sinking during this time outside the North Atlantic. No. 224 Squadron Liberators patrolled the Bay of Biscay area and west of the Iberian Peninsula while operating from St Eval. For the months of January and February, the pilots' missions proved fruitless as they sighted no U-boats. However, in March, the squadron discovered its first one. B-24 'K' found a fully surfaced U-boat on the 21st, bore in and arrived just above the swirl a mere ten seconds after it submerged. Yet, all depth charges failed to release. Three days later, on the 24th, Liberator 'J' caught a U-boat on the surface and dropped six depth charges 10 to 20ft astern but they failed to deliver a fatal blow to the diving vessel. B-24 'G' spotted a surfaced U-boat 4 to 5 miles away on the 29th and the pilot approached. Just as the U-boat began to disappear under the surface, the British attempted to release four depth charges but all failed to fall. On 4 April, Liberator 'M' found a surfaced U-boat but of the six depth charges set to release, only one dropped on the first attempt. The pilot returned on a second run and all five failed to release again.

On 29 April though, the squadron recorded its first victory. Liberator 'D' departed St Eval at 0519 hours. Less than three hours later, at 2004 hours, the crew spotted a fully surfaced U-boat just 4 miles in front of them. The B-24 then descended quickly from 500ft to 50ft. The Germans, noticing the oncoming threat, dived. The Liberator flew over the recently submerged U-boat twenty-five seconds after it disappeared from the surface and released its depth charges. The crew saw no evidence of sinking or damage though. Over two hours later, at 2243 hours, the crew sighted, 5 miles away, the fully surfaced Type VIIC *U-332*, one of the veteran submarines of the 'Second Happy Time', having sunk multiple Allied vessels off the American coast. On this occasion it had departed from its French base three days before for a hunt in the North Atlantic. This time, the U-boat remained surfaced and the B-24 flew over it at 50ft, dropping six Torpex depth charges. The rear gunner directed 400 rounds of ammunition at the conning tower, where multiple German crew members had gathered. Following the depth charge detonations, a major explosion at the U-boat's stern sent water 100ft into the air. The stern then rose at a 70-degree angle accompanied by a 'large patch of oil,' as the U-boat disappeared. Ten minutes after the explosion, more oil and debris appeared. *U-332* then sank with the loss of all forty-five crew members.[1]

While the British predominantly focused their Liberators on the North Atlantic convoy routes, the Americans commenced operating a B-24 squadron in North Africa and in mid-March, it achieved a sinking shortly after its deployment. On 22 March, Liberator 'T' from the USAAF's 2nd Antisubmarine Squadron flying from Port Lyautey, French Morocco, sighted a surfaced long-range Type IXC U-boat 5 miles away. To maximise the element of surprise, the captain decided to attack out of the sun, and the strategy succeeded. The Liberator released four depth charges from 200ft, resulting in multiple explosions that caused the U-boat to slip from the surface stern first. The Americans noted both wreckage and crew in the water but all fifty-two men perished. *U-524* had commenced its second patrol a week before and had sunk two Allied vessels.[2]

Only one other four-engine Allied aircraft achieved a sinking during this period outside the North Atlantic, namely a British Halifax. On three occasions, all in May, these bombers employed for anti-submarine duty participated in three fatal sinkings. All three of the Halifaxes were with the RAF's 58 Squadron flying from St Eval.[3] However, not all the squadron's attacks proved to be fatal. The squadron observed no U-boats for the first three days of the month but on the 4th, Halifax

'S' discovered a surfaced U-boat and initiated its assault. During their approach a heavy deck gun, a cannon on the bridge, and five machine guns behind the bridge all fired on the four-engine aircraft. The pilot took 'evasive action' and achieved a depth charge straddle just behind the conning tower. The U-boat submerged but the crew did not notice signs of damage on the surface and the boat escaped. Three days later, on the 7th, Halifax 'S' sighted a surfaced U-boat but while flying in for the attack, the U-boat began submerging so the RAF crew released depth charges 100ft forward of the swirl. An hour passed on the patrol and the crew engaged another U-boat, which fired upon them with two machine guns and a cannon. The British released depth charges just behind the conning tower but the U-boat dived and the crew observed no damage.

No. 58 Squadron did not escape without loss. On 7 May, Halifax 'A' began its flight at 0510 hours, and only acknowledged one signal, at 0614 hours. It had engaged Type VIIC *U-228* in battle and the U-boat had destroyed it. All seven crew members perished.[4] Two days later, on 9 May, Halifax 'N' departed St Eval at 0611 hours and the British never heard from it again. The aircraft apparently attacked Type VIIC *U-666* in the Bay of Biscay, delivering minor damage to the U-boat but receiving fatal fire from the Germans. The four-engine plane crashed into the water, resulting in the death of all eight crew members.[5]

Forty-eight hours later, 58 Squadron began to avenge the two losses. On 11 May, Halifax 'D' took off into the dark morning sky at 0305 hours. The crew rendezvoused with their assigned Allied convoy and two hours later, to the west of the Bay of Biscay, spotted a long-range Type IXC/40 U-boat, which dived before any engagement could commence. Later, the British discovered their target, again fully surfaced, and the pilot bore down. As the Halifax roared over the U-boat, multiple depth charges fell from the bomb bay. The boat's stern appeared to rise from the water and then submerged. The crew noted an explosion and the bow then came to the surface before disappearing, leaving behind only a significant oil patch. HMS *Fleetwood*, a Royal Navy sloop, arrived later and attacked with depth charges. The U-boat appeared on the surface and the crew then scuttled it. Eleven of them died but the Royal Navy rescued the remaining forty-five. *U-528* had not engaged any Allied vessels on this, its first patrol.[6]

In the middle of the month, 58 Squadron Halifaxes delivered two fatal attacks. On 15 May, Halifax 'M' took off at 1208 hours and, on the western edge of the Bay of Biscay, discovered a Type VIIC U-boat 10 miles away. The pilot manoeuvred to approach with the sun at his back and then dived towards the target and deposited multiple depth charges.

The U-boat's bow rose until it pointed vertically, where it remained for two minutes until it gradually disappeared. All forty-seven crew members died. *U-266* had sunk four Allied vessels on two patrols.[7] The next day, on 16 May, Halifax 'R', in the Bay of Biscay, spotted a U-boat, one of Dönitz's prized Type XIV *milchkuh*, on the port beam. The RAF pilot 'stalked it out of the sun', attacking it immediately after it submerged. The crew released a single depth charge just 100ft after the swirl, and the remainder in the wake. The Halifax crew noticed oil on the surface and later a Sunderland crew observed debris and a body. None of the fifty-seven crew members survived the attack. *U-463*, constructed for at-sea replenishment and possessing no torpedo tubes, had not achieved any sinkings.[8] No. 58 Squadron conducted another U-boat attack on 30 May, when Halifax 'D' found a surfaced example. The four-engine aircraft bore in 'from ahead', but the boat submerged and no signs of damage emerged on the surface after the depth charges fell on the subsurface target. The squadron's aircraft participated in two other U-boat attacks that are detailed later with the British Sunderlands.[9]

Besides 58 Squadron, another Halifax unit suffered a loss to a U-boat when Type VIIC *U-338* downed one of the four-engine aircraft. On 22 March, 502 Squadron 'B' operating from RAF St Eval, as was 58 Squadron, discovered the surfaced submarine. The German log reports that the aircraft had so surprised the crew that they had insufficient time to submerge and instead fought back with their flak guns. The Halifax managed to fly over the U-boat and drop four depth charges, which caused no damage. However, the German fire brought the four-engine aircraft crashing into the Bay of Biscay. Seven perished, while the Germans rescued one Australian.[10]

The relatively short-ranged twin-engine Hudsons achieved seven of their nine successful sinkings during this time in the Mediterranean and the Atlantic around Gibraltar. On 12 February, flying from Gibraltar, 48 Squadron 'F' Hudson spotted a fully surfaced Type VIIC at 1402 hours in the Atlantic off the Portuguese coast, approximately 150 miles south-west of Lisbon. Descending from 3,500ft to 40ft, the crew released four depth charges that all fell adjacent to the U-boat. Additionally, the rear gunner expended 150 rounds on the two U-boat deck guns. The pilot also opened fire on approach with the Hudson's front guns. During the forty minutes that the twin-engine aircraft remained in the area, the crew noted debris, possibly 'wood splinters', and a significant oil patch. *U-442* had completed one patrol before its sinking and had sunk four vessels; it sank with all forty-eight hands. Britain awarded Flight Officer G.R. Maydew, the Hudson's pilot, a Distinguished Flying Cross for his actions.[11]

A month later, on 4 March, Hudson 'V' of 500 Squadron took off from RAF Bilda on the northern Algerian coast for a western Mediterranean patrol. At 1002 hours, in poor visibility, the crew spotted a fully surfaced U-boat's wake 5 miles away. Three minutes after the sighting, the Hudson's crew dropped three 100lb bombs from a height of 1,500ft, while the Type VIIB U-boat's crew responded with inaccurate 'light machine gun fire'. The Hudson crew fired its guns from both front and turret positions, which apparently silenced the U-boat's deck guns. 'V' then assaulted again, but this time released three 250lb depth charges from 75ft. The U-boat 'immediately began to sink on a level keel'. The British crew noted twenty-five bodies in the water, accompanied by air bubbles and oil. While they dropped two dinghies for the survivors, they apparently sank. In their report, the British crew also expressed surprise that the U-boat commander never attempted to submerge during the attack. *U-83* had sunk five Allied vessels and damaged two others during its career, but under its second commander it had not achieved any successes. There were no survivors of the fifty-man crew.[12]

No. 608 Squadron, also based at Bilda, claimed a U-boat sunk two months later. On 28 May, 'M' Hudson sighted a surfaced Type VIIC U-boat and attacked with a new RAF ordnance, rocket projectiles. The U-boat managed to remain on the surface for nine minutes before sinking., Nine crew survived but forty perished. *U-755* had completed four patrols and had sunk three Allied vessels.[13]

Hudsons operating from Gibraltar also continued their success against Dönitz's boats during this time, and even battled one of his most successful, *U-77*. Launched in November 1940, its crews had managed sixteen cruises, primarily in the Mediterranean, and tallied an impressive sixteen Allied merchant vessels sunk and three damaged. It had even struck the British destroyer HMS *Kimberley* with a torpedo shot to the stern. *U-77* commenced its seventeenth patrol by departing its base, La Spezia, Italy, on 3 March. On the 16th, its crew dispatched the British vessel *Hadleigh*, its seventeenth sinking, and damaged the British *Merchant Prince*. Twelve days later, *U-77* encountered a British Hudson.

At 1607 hours in the Mediterranean, off the south-east Spanish coast, 500 Squadron Hudson 'C' sighted a 'swirl' 15 miles from its position. Flying over the location, the crew did not identify any other signs of a U-boat. However, at 1657 hours, at 3,000ft, just 8 miles from the swirl's location, the British crew noticed a periscope wake. The Hudson dived to that location and released three depth charges along a stern-to-bow course, while the periscope remained visible during the attack.

The RAF aircraft quickly turned to port and gained height as the crew watched the Type VIIC U-boat be 'blown' to the surface, submerge, and then appear on the surface again. The Hudson struck again while the Germans manned the submarine's deck guns. The aircraft passed over the U-boat at 700ft and released two bombs, while a German shell exploded behind the aircraft that resulted in no damage. At 1705 hours, the U-boat ceased moving and remained motionless until 1730 hours, when it commenced forward motion at 4 knots with a zig-zag course and a significant oil slick. At 1754 hours, 233 Squadron's 'L', having received transmissions from 'C' regarding the damaged U-boat, arrived on scene and released depth charges and a single bomb while expending 3,000 rounds of ammunition. The U-boat damaged Hudson 'L' with anti-aircraft fire. 'C' departed at 1820 hours, while 'L' headed for base at 1902 hours. *U-77* made course for the Spanish coast at 5 knots but eventually sank at 0115 hours with thirty-eight crew members perishing and nine surviving when rescued by a Spanish vessel.[14]

The next month, on 6 April, a 233 Squadron Hudson dropped five depth charges on *U-167*, a Type IXC/40 long-range design, in the Atlantic off the north-western African coast. The severe damage forced the commander to head to the Canary Islands, where the crew scuttled the boat. Other U-boats rescued the fifty men and returned them to France. The U-boat had completed one patrol, having sunk an Allied vessel and damaged another one.[15]

A month later, on 7 May, *U-447* had the misfortune to be spotted by not one, but two Hudsons nearly simultaneously in the Atlantic approximately 700 miles west of Gibraltar. At 1843, hours, 233 Squadron's 'I' discovered the surfaced Type VIIC U-boat travelling at 5 knots and attacked two minutes later. The crew released four depth charges 'which fell 50 to 70 ft' to the U-boat's port. At the moment of the attack, 'X' then found *U-447* and commenced its assault with four depth charges, of which one fell to port while the other three fell to starboard. 'I' followed with multiple attacks by gun fire. *U-447* then 'seemed to lose and regain buoyancy and finally submerged stern first' for the last time with all forty-eight crew members on board. The U-boat had completed one patrol and had not sunk any Allied vessels.[16]

British Hudsons did suffer loss during this time. On 24 April, 500 Squadron's 'N' found the surfaced Type VIIC *U-453* in the Mediterranean off the Algerian coast and initiated an assault. While closing the distance, flak hit the twin-engine aircraft, killing the pilot instantly. The navigator assumed control and nursed the damaged British plane to an RAF base in north Africa. Over the base, believing the aircraft too damaged to land, he ordered the crew to abandon the aircraft and all four remaining crew members parachuted safely to the ground.[17]

Of the eight U-boats sunk by twin-engine Catalinas during this time, five of these victories occurred outside the North Atlantic. Unlike the Hudsons, many of these anti-submarine planes battled the German U-boats with American crews. The Americans patrolled the South Atlantic area and on 6 January, VP-83 Catalina P-2 sighted a fully surfaced Type IXC U-boat with some crew swimming. The US Navy crew dropped multiple depth charges on the boat as it dived for the last time. The Catalina dropped a raft and two of the U-boat crew arrived in Brazil on it seven days later; the other fifty-four perished. *U-164* completed one patrol and had sunk three Allied vessels.[18]

When *U-164* sank, another U-boat stalked the same area, commanded by one of the most successful German submarine commanders, Harro Schacht. He commenced his career with *U-507*, a long-range Type IXC boat, in October 1941, and over an eighteenth-month period sank sixteen Allied vessels on four patrols. Schacht began his fifth patrol on 24 November 1942 and destroyed three merchant vessels from 27 December to 8 January. However, five days later, US Catalina P-10 from VP-83 attacked with depth charges and sank *U-507* with all fifty-four hands, including its highly decorated commander.[19]

Two months later, on 8 March, in the same area east of Barbados, another successful German submarine commander prowled the waters. Werner Hartenstein had led his crew since September 1941. During his patrols in the North Atlantic and the Caribbean, he had tallied an impressive nineteen ships sunk and three damaged. But on his fifth patrol, American Catalina P-1 from VP-53 discovered his U-boat, *U-156*, another Type IXC boat, on the surface with its crew sunbathing. The US Navy pilot used the clouds for cover and he ambushed the U-boat with four Torpex bombs released from 100ft. The Navy crew reported that the U-boat shattered into three sections and disappeared. None of the fifty-three crew members survived.[20]

British Catalinas patrolled the mid-Atlantic. No. 202 Squadron's 'J' departed Gibraltar at 1420 hours in the afternoon of 13 February, joined with an Allied convoy off the Portuguese coast at 1718 hours, and discovered a surfaced Type VIIC U-boat at 2240 hours. Unfortunately for the RAF crew, this U-boat submerged before they could initiate an attack. Nevertheless, almost an hour later, at 2330 hours, they made another U-boat sighting and attacked with five depth charges that all fell '57 yards' from its hull. The U-boat submerged and the Catalina returned to its convoy after fifteen minutes, but the attack had been successful.

U-620 sank with all forty-seven hands, ending a career that included two patrols and one damaged Allied vessel.[21]

Three months later, on 30 May, Flight Lieutenant D.W. Eadie lifted 210 Squadron Catalina 'G' from the waters of Pembroke Dock at 0328 hours. At 0955 hours, he caught Type VIIC *U-418* on the surface just outside the Bay of Biscay. Eadie then closed the distance with the U-boat from astern. During the approach, the German deck guns fired on the Catalina, striking it in the bow. The shell exploded in the cockpit, fatally wounding the front gunner, while 'seriously wounding' the second pilot and others. Eadie though, continued on course and dropped four depth charges from 50ft. The U-boat slowed, then stopped. Eadie then nursed the damaged Catalina for over three hours, with petrol streaming from the starboard tank. It made it back to base, where it sank on landing at 1315 hours. The rest of the crew all survived, while none of *U-418*'s forty-eight crew members did, and its career ended on its first patrol with no sinkings.[22]

Sunderlands achieved an impressive record in May with five sinkings by Australian, Canadian and British crews. Four of the lethal attacks occurred in the Bay of Biscay area. Australian Sunderlands fatally attacked two U-boats in this month. The Royal Australian Air Force 461 Squadron's 'M' took off from the waters of RAF Pembroke Dock at 1354 hours on 2 May. At 1915 hours, on the western edge of the Bay of Biscay, the crew spotted *U-465*, a Type VIIC, 10 miles away and cruising at 10 to 12 knots. Using the cloud as cover, Flight Lieutenant E.C. Smith approached the target and when it was a mile away the U-boat crew commenced anti-aircraft fire. Four minutes after the initial sighting, the Sunderland flew over the U-boat and deposited four Torpex depth charges, resulting in significant oil emitting from the port side. Smith turned the Sunderland around, flew over again, and struck with four more Torpex. The U-boat started to settle by the stern as its crew members started leaping into the water. The Australians counted fifteen men in the water but all forty-eight perished. *U-465* had completed four patrols but had not sunk any vessels.[23] Five days later, 'W' of 10 Squadron, RAAF, assaulted Type VIIC *U-663* with two depth charge attacks and it sank the following day. This U-boat had sunk two Allied vessels on three patrols and all forty-nine crew members went down with the boat.[24]

On 31 May, British Sunderlands participated in two fatal sinkings. In one instance, the flying boat delivered a fatal attack on *U-563* after it had first been targeted by 58 Squadron Halifaxes that had departed St Eval. Sunderland 'R' first detected the Type VIIC boat and 'stalked' it through cloud cover before delivering an attack that resulted in damage and a visible oil leak. The Sunderland struck again with its last three depth charges, but the U-boat remained afloat and moving. Sunderland 'J' now arrived and initiated two attacks as the U-boat 'took violent evasive action' with a turn to port on the first assault and a turn to starboard on the next. The second assault resulted in more oil leakage but *U-563* remained defiantly on the surface. Two more Sunderlands now arrived, one with an Australian crew and another with a British one. The Australian attacked and 228 Squadron Sunderland 'X' released four depth charges on its first pass, then came around to release four more on a second assault. The U-boat 'shuddered after the second attack' and the crew witnessed bodies 'thrown' into the air. All forty-nine crew members perished. *U-563* had completed eight patrols, destroyed three merchant vessels, damaged two others, and delivered a fatal torpedo strike against a British destroyer.[25]

On 30 May, 201 Squadron Sunderland 'R' took off from RAF Castle Archdale, Northern Ireland, at 1034 hours and commenced its patrol in the Bay of Biscay area at 1645 hours. Seven hours, later just west of the Bay, the crew found a surfaced Nazi Type VIIC U-boat just 8 miles off their starboard bow. The pilot turned immediately and bore down on the target. Just before the flying boat flew over the U-boat, the German commander attempted to avoid the attack with a 'violent turn to starboard', nevertheless, the four depth charges dropped and exploded. The U-boat maintained speed and course for a minute until the stern disappeared below the surface, and the bows rose at a 'steep angle'. Thirty seconds later, two massive underwater explosions occurred, followed by more explosions in four minutes and a large oil patch. The Sunderland splashed down at 1230 hours on the 31st. *U-440* had not sunk any vessels on its five patrols. All forty-six crew members died.[26]

The Sunderlands did not escape this period without loss. In one of Dönitz's attempts to counter Allied aircraft, he added additional anti-aircraft guns to four U-boats, known as 'flak boats', and he would partially modify three others. The flak boat *U-441* departed Brest on 22 May. Two days later, at 1400 hours, 228 Squadron Sunderland EJ139 took off from RAF Pembroke Dock. The British crew found and attacked *U-441* in the Bay of Biscay and the U-boat successfully shot down the large flying boat, killing all eleven crew members. It was the first success for a flak boat. However, the Sunderland's weapons had damaged the U-boat and caused casualties, forcing it returned to Brest just three days after the attack.[27]

Wellingtons sank two U-boats during the first five months of 1943. In the Mediterranean, at 0945 hours on 19 February, 38 Squadron Wellington 'S' roared down the runway at RAF Berca, Libya, and later, while escorting a convoy of twelve merchant vessels off the North Libyan coast, the rear gunner spotted a submerged U-boat 'directly below', 'in position' to assault the convoy. The British crew attempted to attack but failed. Instead, they directed HMS *Isis*, a British destroyer, and HMS *Hursley*, a British destroyer escort, to the location, where they dropped numerous depth charges. 'S' landed at 1905 hours, after a nine-hour patrol. None of *U-562*'s forty-nine men survived and the Type VIIC U-boat's career ended with six Allied vessels sunk and one damaged.[28]

On 19 February, 172 Squadron Wellington 'B' detected a contact at 4 miles in the Bay of Biscay and 'homed' in on the target as it descended from 1,000ft. When arriving at 500ft and still 2 miles away, the British crew observed a wake, and then a fully surfaced Type VIIC U-boat travelling at 10 knots. Two minutes after initial contact, the Wellington attacked from 50ft. *U-268* turned to port as the British delivered depth charges that caused three explosions. The U-boat slowed to a stop as 'a bright red and orange light flared up' next to the conning tower, 'died away and flared up again, finally disappearing 2–2½ minutes' after the explosions. Three minutes later, the U-boat disappeared, leaving a 25yd diameter oil slick on the surface. The Wellington continued to monitor the area for another ninety minutes but observed no debris. All forty-four hands went down with *U-268*, which was on its first patrol and had sunk four vessels.[29]

The RAF did lose two twin-engine aircraft during this time. On 4 March, 179 Squadron Wellington 'B' discovered surfaced Type VIIC *U-333* in the Bay of Biscay. The British crew employed their Leigh Light, a large external searchlight, on the surprised U-boat crew but apparently released no depth charges. Instead, the aircraft suffered damage from the German guns while passing over, caught fire and crashed. All six crew members perished.[30] Another aircraft employed by the RAF, the outdated Whitley, participated in anti-submarine patrols during this time. They failed to strike any fatal blows but Type VIIC *U-648* downed 'J' of 10 Operational Training Unit in the Bay of Biscay on 17 May, resulting in the loss of all three crew members.[31]

The US Navy achieved its first sinking with the Martin Mariner flying boat on this day. Although it possessed similar characteristics to the Catalina, the Americans used the twin-engine Mariner far less than the Catalina, and it flew primarily in the Caribbean and off the eastern South American coast. On 17 May, two Mariners, P-5 and P-6 of VP-74, discovered one of Dönitz's Type IXC long-range boats, *U-128*, off Brazil and both attacked it. The first aircraft's depth charges brought the U-boat from a submerged position to a surfaced one and the second assault proved to be fatal. When the American destroyers USS *Moffett* and *Jouett* arrived, the Germans decided to scuttle. Three perished in the battle, four died after rescue and fifty-one survived aboard the American ships. *U-128* had sunk twelve vessels and damaged another one on five patrols.[32]

Dönitz had retreated from the North Atlantic. Outside that area in the South Atlantic, the Bay of Biscay, and the waters around Gibraltar, he had suffered nearly a dozen losses to Allied aircraft. Allied aircraft now prowled a wide area searching for his boats. His fortunes would not improve after May as aircraft would continue to discover and destroy his U-boats in rapidly increasing numbers.

Chapter 9

The B-24s: June–July 1943

By 1 June 1943, the Allies had positioned their anti-submarine aircraft well. American and Brazilian units operated off the South American coast, British units flew from Iceland, the United Kingdom, Gibraltar and North Africa. American and British air naval units operated in the central and eastern Atlantic. Dönitz's U-boat commanders had few areas remaining where they could operate safely on the surface. And, with the increasingly effective employment of radar and the Leigh Light, even darkness failed to offer a reprieve. June and July 1943 became one of the worst two-month periods for U-boats in the entire war, with fifty-four of them fatally damaged. Allied aircraft contributed significantly to this number as they participated in thirty-five (65 per cent) of these successes; by all other means, the Allies only sank nineteen.

Of all Allied aircraft, Liberators, destroying ten of Dönitz's boats, led in the destruction of U-boats during this heavy period of anti-submarine aircraft action. The German admiral deployed his U-boats on a variety of missions, including the transport of troops. *U-200*, a long-range Type IXD2 boat, departed Kiel, northern Germany, on 6 June destined for the Indian Ocean. In addition to its crew, the U-boat also carried a detachment from the highly respected Brandenburg division. None would escape the Atlantic. On 24 June, Liberator Mk. I 'H' of 120 Squadron left Reykjavik at 1336 hours. At 1628 hours, the crew spotted a fully surfaced U-boat and descended rapidly. During the approach the Germans fired on the B-24, striking it on the port wing and also the fuselage. The pilot, Flight Lieutenant A.W. Fraser, noticed that these hits had damaged both the aircraft's hydraulics and accumulator. Nevertheless, he pressed on and swept over the U-boat at 50ft, dropping two depth charges. The other two failed to release due to damage from the German guns. The U-boat submerged and the British crew soon noticed air bubbles and significant oil. Then, fifteen German crew members appeared on the surface along with debris. At 1651 hours, the hydraulics became inoperable and the aircraft started losing a considerable amount of fuel, forcing Fraser to return to Iceland. The B-24 arrived above its home base at 1755 hours, released the remaining depth charges and Fraser continued to fly the aircraft despite the lack of hydraulics until 1857 hours. At that point, the pilot lowered both the undercarriage and nose wheels manually. Fraser then ordered the crew and other material to the rear of the aircraft as he had decided to land in a 'tail down attitude'. At 1951 hours, he succeeded with minimal damage. As for *U-200*, it sank with sixty-eight men. It was its first patrol and it had not yet attacked any Allied vessels.[1]

At 0916 hours on 3 July, 224 Squadron Mk. V 'J' took off from St Eval. The Mark V B-24s included Air-to-Surface Vessel radar and while flying over its assigned Bay of Biscay area, the crew made extensive use of this device to scan for any U-boats lurking around the Allied vessels it protected. While maintaining an altitude of 350ft, the crew obtained a radar contact at 10 miles distance 'dead ahead'. On approach, the Liberator crew spotted the U-boat and attacked with anti-submarine bombs at 1405 hours, following with depth charges at 1407 hours. The U-boat slowed and floated 'low' in the sea with 'very little way on'. The crew sighted several crew, including six 'alive and swimming' and another three stationary bodies. However, the B-24's pilot, Squadron Leader P.J. Cundy, was now flying a severely damaged aircraft after the two attacks. Flak had hit the starboard petrol tank, causing fuel to leak out near the starboard inner engine's exhaust. Cundy shut down that engine and feathered it. At 1410 hours, he made the decision to head for base. He transmitted 'engine trouble' and later, 'may be forced to land'. At 1813 hours though, he successfully landed the aircraft. All forty-nine crew of *U-628*, a Type VIIC boat, died in the attack. It had completed four patrols with three Allied vessels sunk, two shared sinkings, and three damaged.[2]

On 25 May, Type IXC/40 *U-535* departed Kiel on its first patrol. U-boat Command though, altered its mission from attacking Allied vessels to refuelling other U-boats on 14 June. After refuelling multiple submarines, *U-535*, in concert with two others, headed for their home base. On 5 July, the three transited the Bay of Biscay on the surface. That morning, 53 Squadron Liberator Mk. V 'G' left Thorney Island and flew over the Bay of Biscay. After completing their patrol with no sightings, the crew commenced their return to England. While on its way home, the crew observed three U-boats in a vic formation. The B-24 dived but German evasive action prevented an attack. During the second attempt, the Liberator's depth charges failed to release. The determined crew then initiated their third assault and dropped six depth charges on *U-535*. The Germans had caused minor damage to the aircraft and injured one crew member, but all returned safely to England. *U-535* though, went down with all fifty-five hands and without sinking any Allied vessels.[3]

Three days later, on 8 July, British Liberator Mk. V 'R' of the RAF's 224 Squadron took off at 0853 hours from St Eval. Four hours later, while cruising at 6,600ft, a waist gunner saw with his naked eye a ship's wake and soon identified its source: a U-boat 8 miles away. The B-24's radar found the U-boat 'almost immediately' after the crew member's sighting. At 1316 hours, the Liberator's captain turned to port, started to descend and headed for the unsuspecting target, which did not initiate any turns as the four-engine aircraft approached. Instead of depth charges or anti-submarine bombs, the crew attacked with two rockets at a distance of 800ft, and then fired a second pair from 600ft, then two more at 500ft while flying at 265mph. The B-24's navigator, while positioned in the front turret, observed a 'splash of entry' located between the conning tower and bow. The front gunner expended thirty rounds, the port waist gunner fired sixty, and both believed they struck the conning tower and the area before it. Allied vessels arrived at the location at 1536 hours and hoisted a 'black pennant', indicating proof of the U-boat's destruction. The Liberator returned to base at 1948 hours, after a nearly eleven-hour mission. *U-514*, a long-range Type IXC boat, lost all fifty-four hands. It had completed four patrols, sunk seven Allied vessels and damaged another one.[4]

American Liberators also began to accumulate an impressive number of U-boat sinkings. On 7 July, USAAF Liberator 'K' from the 1st Antisubmarine Squadron located Type VIIC *U-951* on the surface several hundred miles off the Portuguese coast. Instead of diving, the German commander sought to battle the American aircraft on the surface with gun fire. The Americans released seven bombs that sank the U-boat. Despite a damaged aircraft and injured crew members, the pilot returned successfully to their Moroccan base. *U-951* sank with all forty-six hands on its first patrol, with no sunk ships to its credit.[5]

Unlike *U-951*'s commander, *U-435*'s commander, operating in the same area at the same time, had earned a lethal reputation. Since commanding the U-boat in August 1941, Siegfried Strelow completed eight patrols, sank eleven Allied vessels and damaged another one. For his achievements as a U-boat leader, he had been awarded the prestigious Knight's Cross. Two days after *U-951*'s destruction, Strelow's U-boat proceeded on the surface, while American Liberator 'B' from the same squadron that sank *U-951*, flew at 3,000ft above. B-24's radar detected a contact 18 miles away and the pilot, Lieutenant T.E. Kuenning, commenced an intercept course by manoeuvring the B-24 so that he approached the possible target with the sun to his back. At 8 miles away, the crew visually sighted Strelow's surfaced Type VIIC U-boat and attacked. The Americans dropped four depth charges of 650lb from 50ft. After the explosions, the U-boat immediately started circling, slowing as its stern lost some buoyancy. The U-boat crew had fired prodigiously at the Liberator and struck the plane in the nose area but, undaunted, Kuenning swung around for a second attack run. The German fire improved on this approach, striking the aircraft in numerous locations, and severed both the fuel and hydraulic lines, while also striking the radio. Most consequentially, the bomb-bay door damage prevented its opening and resulted in a failed second attempt. The resourceful crew then managed to open the doors, and Kuenning made his third approach. This time, two depth charges dropped and the U-boat sank by the stern. The B-24 crew suffered only one member slightly wounded but *U-435* sank with all forty-eight hands, including its highly decorated commander.[6]

Three days later, the 1st Antisubmarine Squadron struck again, this time against a 'Second Happy Time' veteran. *U-506*'s commander, Erich Wurdemann, had destroyed fourteen Allied vessels, including American ones, in the Gulf of Mexico during 1942, and had damaged three others. He departed for the South Atlantic on 6 July in *U-506*, a long-range Type IXC boat, and six days later transited the waters on the surface several hundred miles off the Spanish coast as B-24 'C''s radar was scanning the area. The American crew obtained a radar contact and the pilot used the cloud cover to mask his approach while lowering the Liberator's altitude from 5,600ft. Suddenly, the aircraft appeared a mile from the Nazi U-boat at 200ft. The Americans roared over the U-boat and released seven depth charges. After the explosions, the crew saw the submarine separate into two sections and disappear beneath the waves, taking its commander with it. Fifteen Germans escaped the sinking, the Americans released a life raft and, three days later, a British destroyer arrived and saved the six who were still alive. Forty-eight crew perished.[7]

The United States Navy also achieved a sinking during this period with multiple Liberators. On 22 July, a VP-107 PB4Y-1 (the United States Navy's designation for the B-24) was flying off the north-eastern Brazilian coast during a training mission when the crew visually spotted the surfaced Type VIIC *U-598* and delivered two depth charge attacks, which failed to damage the boat. The following day, the U-boat surfaced at 0635 hours, only to be seen by Navy Liberator B-12, which had continued to patrol the area. This aircraft attacked with depth charges, which damaged the U-boat's diving planes, preventing submerging. At 0640 hours, three more Liberators arrived, and two dived to attack. The first one, B-6, went in at such a low altitude that the depth charge explosions resulted in severe damage to the aircraft. The bomber then crashed, killing all those on board. However, B-8 followed and delivered the final, fatal depth charge attack that sank *U-598*. An Allied tug later arrived to rescue two crew members. Forty-three died. The U-boat had completed four patrols, sunk two Allied vessels and damaged another one.[8]

Two U-boats suffered defeat due to Anglo-American co-operation, with B-24s participating in these joint efforts. The first involved Type VIIC *U-558* and its commander, Gunther Krech, one of the most successful German U-boat captains of this time. Krech had sunk twenty-three Allied vessels and damaged another one during ten patrols, including three tankers in one convoy alone, and had served during the 'Second Happy Time' off the American seaboard. On 20 July, in the last days of his command, while his surfaced U-boat transited the Bay of Biscay heading to its base, his crew downed Liberator 'B' of the USAAF's 19th Antisubmarine Squadron, resulting in the loss of all on board.[9] However, that same day, Liberator 'F' from the same squadron detected it, by radar, at 13 miles distance. The pilot altered course for the target when, at 5 miles, the crew obtained visual confirmation that their radar had found a U-boat. Diving from 1,000ft, the B-24 passed over it at 100ft and dropped seven depth charges. The German flak had injured a crew member and also resulted in the loss of an engine. Despite this, the Liberator remained in the area until, at 1226 hours, Halifax 'E' from the RAF's 58 Squadron appeared and the damaged American aircraft headed home. Intense German flak disrupted the first approach but at 1248 hours, with some 'settling' by the stern and the machine gun fire ending, the Halifax crew attempted again. This time eight depth charges fell and the U-boat 'heeled over on the port beam'. Forty to fifty crew, some dead, some swimming, remained after the sinking. Forty-five perished. However, four days later, 224 Squadron Liberator 'R' discovered a dinghy containing five Germans. The British crew dropped two emergency packs and the Canadian destroyer *Athabaskan* rescued the men the following day.[10]

Eight days later, again in the Bay of Biscay, two Liberators – one from the USAAF and another from the RAF – participated in a joint operation against Type VIIC *U-404*. The U-boat had an impressive campaign, sinking fifteen Allied vessels, including fatally torpedoing British destroyer HMS *Veteran*. It also participated in the 'Second Happy Time'. However, Adolf Schonberg replaced Otto von Bulow, the commander that led it during these times, after its sixth and previous patrol. The new leader departed St Nazaire, France, on 24 July and four days later, the crew of 4th Antisubmarine Squadron Liberator 'N' sighted his U-boat on the surface, just 5 miles to starboard. The Liberator descended for the attack, receiving fire from, and delivering fire to, the U-boat. At 100ft, the Americans released eight depth charges and then returned for a second attack, dropping four depth charges from 50ft. With one engine disabled, ammunition low and a gun damaged, the American B-24 could take no further part. Fortunately, Liberator 'W' of the RAF's 224 Squadron then arrived on the scene. The British had been attracted to the area after noticing depth charge explosions 25 miles 'dead ahead'. The pilot, Flight Officer R. Sweeny, proceeded to the location, even though the radar registered no surface contacts. When he arrived, Sweeny observed the USAAF Liberator circling at 600 to 700ft, and so he commenced his attack. The aircraft descended quickly as the Germans fired vigorously at the approaching B-24. The crew dropped seven 250lb Torpex depth charges at 150ft while maintaining a speed of 200mph. Sweeny executed a tight turn to starboard and a crew member informed him that number four engine was on fire. The U-boat disappeared immediately after the depth charge explosions, then reappeared on an 'even keel' but then slipped under the water. The crew observed debris and ten 'bodies in lifebelts bobbing up & down in the water'. *U-404* was never seen again and none of its fifty-one crew members survived.[11]

Sweeny, though, struggled with the damaged Liberator. He continued to circle the area but the 'port outer engine could not be feathered'. Sweeny fought the aircraft to maintain an altitude of 20 to 30ft above the water due to the drag from the non-moving propeller. The crew reported that they 'may be forced to land without further signal' due to 'engine trouble'. Sweeny radioed as to where he could land and the RAF advised him to head for Predannack in southern Cornwall, an airfield closer than the B-24's base. Instead, since the aircraft had by then flown to a point in proximity to their home base of St Eval, Sweeny investigated the 'possibility of landing' there. However, with the airbase closed due to poor visibility, he decided to fly to nearby RAF St Mawgan, where he successfully landed the damaged aircraft at 2115 hours, over nine hours after launching from St Eval.[12]

A U-boat apparently downed one Allied B-24 during this time. US Navy VPB-103 Squadron Liberator B-9, while escorting a convoy off the Canadian coast, encountered surfaced Type VIIC *U-271* and attacked. German flak caused severe damage as the bomber approached, the depth charges fell far from the target, and the aircraft – bellowing fire and smoke – crashed into the water, killing all ten crew members.[13]

An RAF B-17 attained a single at-sea sinking during this time. On 11 June, 206 Squadron Fortress 'R' commenced patrol at 0930 hours and at 1110 hours and from an altitude of 1,500ft, the pilot, Wing Commander R.B. Thomson, discovered a U-boat 7 miles ahead. Upon noticing the four-engine aircraft, the Type VIIC boat increased speed and began turns to port and starboard as the deck guns fired upon the Fortress. The crew initiated their assault and the German fire struck the aircraft in multiple locations. Despite the damage, the Fortress flew over the U-boat and released four depth charges. The bows of the now damaged U-boat rose until reaching 30 degrees, where they remained for ten seconds until the vessel began to disappear under the surface, stern first. The British crew noticed twenty to thirty crew members in the water but had to quickly revert their attention to their now damaged aircraft. Thomson lost the number two engine and then number one started causing issues. The B-17 began losing altitude, forcing Thomson to land in the sea. The Fortress provided little time for the crew to escape as it floated for only ninety seconds before disappearing. The B-17's port dinghy inflated, allowing the crew to escape the water, but they lacked any provisions. Three days later, Catalina 'L' from 190 Squadron landed in the water and the flying boat's crew rescued the crew. *U-417*'s crew suffered a less fortunate fate. All forty-six perished on what was the U-boat's first patrol, with no sinkings to its credit.[14]

During this period, for the first time, a B-17 raid yielded destruction not only of the intended target area, but also of a U-boat as well. On the US Eighth Air Force's first mission to Norway, over 100 Fortresses took off from Britain. Despite the round-trip distance of 1,900 miles, the attack successfully hit Trondheim, resulting in significant destruction to the occupied area. The bombs also struck Type VIIC *U-622*. The Germans raised the wreck in April 1944 but they never repaired it; the Fortress raid had knocked it out of the war. *U-622* had completed five patrols but had not sunk any Allied vessels.[15]

The B-24 squadrons had now established themselves as the most lethal Allied anti-submarine squadrons. Yet their relatively limited supply forced the Allies to employ other aircraft. Nevertheless, some aircraft types experienced their greatest anti-submarine success during these two months, specifically the US Navy's carrier squadrons.

Chapter 10

The United States Navy: June–July 1943

Besides those destroyed by Liberators and Fortresses, other Allied aircraft contributed to thirty-four U-boat sinkings during these two months, with the US Navy participating in a majority of these actions, a total of twenty-two. US Navy carrier aircraft from three escort carriers – *Bogue*, *Core*, and *Santee* – combined to claim eight of those sunk, marking one of the best periods for carrier anti-submarine aviation during the war. Yet, the non-carrier US Navy aircraft participated in even more sinkings over these two months, with fourteen to their credit: Catalinas (six), Mariner (four), B-24s (two), and Venturas (two). The Allies certainly welcomed the carrier aircraft, but the shore-based aircraft continued to dominate the anti-submarine effort.

Second only to the American and British Liberators, US Navy Avengers achieved an impressive number of U-boat sinkings, totalling eight during June and July 1943. On 5 June, in the mid-Atlantic, a VC-9 Wildcat and Avenger from the American escort carrier USS *Bogue* discovered Type VIID *U-217* on the surface. The Wildcat, possessing only machine guns, engaged with a strafing attack that only caused the U-boat to submerge. This forced the depth charge-carrying Avenger to attack a non-surfaced target. The Navy pilot's aim proved accurate and the explosions brought the U-boat to the surface. The Wildcat delivered another strafing attack but the Avenger had delivered a lethal blow – *U-217* disappeared stern first with only a patch of oil remaining on the water. The U-boat had sunk three Allied vessels on three patrols. None of the fifty men survived.[1]

A week later, on 12 June, a U-boat assault well demonstrated the weakness of the Avengers compared with Liberators in delivering fatal attacks. An Avenger and a Wildcat from *Bogue* sighted Type VIID *U-118* moving on the surface in an area south-south-west of the Azores, and commenced their assault. As occurred with *U-217*, the Wildcat attacked initially with a strafing run followed by the Avenger dropping depth charges. *U-118* followed the pattern of submerging but then, perhaps due to damage from the Avenger's ordnance, appeared again on the surface. Two other aircraft, also a Wildcat and Avenger pair, attacked. Then another two Allied aircraft participated until finally an Avenger, the seventh aircraft to engage, delivered the fatal blow with a depth charge attack. The last Avenger pilot released a life raft, which permitted the American destroyer USS *Osmond Ingram* to retrieve sixteen survivors. Forty-three crew members perished. *U-118* had sunk four Allied vessels and damaged another in four patrols. But, more importantly, it had required multiple attacks by seven single-engine aircraft to destroy the U-boat, demonstrating the far greater lethality of four-engine aircraft such as the B-24.[2]

The following day, aircraft from one of *Bogue*'s sister vessels, USS *Core*, attacked a U-boat. And again, the US Navy struggled in the battle. A VC-13 Wildcat and Avenger pair spotted *U-487*, a highly valuable *milchkuh* Type XIV boat, in the same area as the previous attacks, south-south-west of the Azores. Employing cloud cover, the two planes approached undetected until their diving attacks. The Wildcat strafed the deck while the Avenger followed with the release of four depth charges. The explosions damaged the boat, causing it to commence a circular course while leaving a trail of oil. The German gunners though, made effective use of their time. As the Wildcat approached for another run, the machine gun fire destroyed it. An additional Wildcat and Avenger pair arrived and delivered a strafing attack with four more depth charges released. This final assault succeeded and, after attacks by four aircraft, the U-boat disappeared under the surface. Thirty-one crew members went down with the boat, but the destroyer USS *Barker* saved thirty-three. *U-487* had participated in two patrols and had not sunk any Allied vessels.[3]

Twenty-four hours later, on 14 July, the US Navy pilots continued their streak and this time they struck one of the most successful U-boats: *U-160*, a long-range Type IXC. Under its first commander, Georg Lassen, its crew had fatally torpedoed eighteen Allied vessels, including several off the American Atlantic seaboard. When Gerd von Pommer-Esche took command, he continued the boat's impressive record by sinking eight Allied vessels on his first patrol. *U-160* then departed on its sixth patrol on 28 June, and a little over two weeks later encountered Americans again, not in merchant vessels as in 1942, but in naval aircraft. This attack also demonstrated the Navy's attempt to increase the lethality of its airborne ordnance with the Fido acoustic homing torpedo. Catching the U-boat on the surface, a VC-29 Wildcat–Avenger pair from a *Bogue* escort-class carrier, USS *Santee*, engaged. The Wildcat delivered a strafing attack, which again resulted in the U-boat diving before the Avenger had an opportunity to attack. Nevertheless, the Avenger pilot released a Fido before the surface swirl after the U-boat had submerged. The torpedo struck. The Avenger pilot observed an underwater shock explosion and oil. All fifty crew members perished and so ended the career of one of Dönitz's most deadly U-boats.[4]

A day later, another USS *Santee* Wildcat–Avenger pair discovered another surfaced Type IXC U-boat. The Wildcat pilot, the first on the scene, engaged with not one but three strafing runs that, as before, resulted in the U-boat submerging. When the Avenger arrived, the pilot encountered no above-surface signs of the U-boat's presence but commenced his run with the swirl as his target. Dropping a Fido torpedo before the swirl, the Navy pilot recorded an underwater shock wave following by oil. All fifty-four men perished in the attack. *U-509* had participated in four patrols, sinking six Allied vessels and damaging two.[5]

The next day, another US Navy pilot achieved another sinking. Lieutenant R.P. Williams, a VC-13 Avenger pilot from USS *Core*, discovered a surfaced Type IXC, *U-67* and headed towards it. Williams employed cloud cover to mask his aircraft until he attacked with four well-placed depth charges. He observed that the explosions lifted the bow and then the U-boat slipped from the surface, leaving behind oil and debris. This attack ended a U-boat career that had tallied thirteen Allied vessels sunk and five others damaged. Forty-eight men went down with the U-boat but the American destroyer USS *McCormick* saved three who had reached the surface.[6]

A week later, on 23 July, a VC-9 Avenger from USS *Bogue* sighted two U-boats on the surface. These German commanders had rendezvoused so that long-range Type IXC/40 *U-527* could refuel Type VIIC *U-648*. The U-boat commanders' differing reactions to the approaching aircraft demonstrated how one tactic proved to be far safer than the other. *U-648*'s commander dived; *U-527* decided to battle the lone Avenger on the surface. *U-648* escaped; *U-527* did not. The US Navy aircraft released six depth charges and *U-527* started to take on water and disappeared from the surface. The American destroyer USS *Clemson* arrived later and rescued thirteen crew members, including the commander. Forty crew members perished. *U-527* had sunk three Allied vessels on three patrols.[7]

The remarkable two-month hunting success for the US Navy carrier aircraft ended on 30 July when the Americans destroyed their eighth

U-boat during this period, and achieved this victory against one of Dönitz's most successful craft. *U-43*'s three commanders had sunk twenty-three Allied vessels and damaged another. The long-range Type IX boat was transiting the Atlantic south-west of the Azores and a USS *Santee* VC-29 Wildcat–Avenger pair discovered it. They also found Type VIIC *U-403*, for which *U-43* was providing fuel. The Wildcat followed the previous pattern of strafing both U-boats before the Avenger attacked *U-403* with two depth charges. It dived, leaving behind a trail of oil. *U-43*, also dived, but instead of depth charges, the Avenger engaged with a Fido that struck two minutes after release. Oil and debris appeared, and none of the fifty-five crew survived. *U-403* escaped.[8]

US Navy Catalinas served as the sole Allied aircraft in five U-boat sinkings during this period. On four occasions, they initiated the attacks. On 9 July, VP-94 Catalina P-1 discovered Type VIIC *U-590* on the surface off the northern Brazilian coast and sank it with depth bombs. All forty-five crewmen perished. *U-590* had sunk only one Allied vessel on six patrols.[9] On 24 June, VP-84 Catalina 'G' from Reykjavik sighted long-range Type IXC/40 *U-194* on the surface 400 miles off the south-west coast of Iceland. The Americans launched a Fido, which destroyed the U-boat. None of the fifty-four crew members survived on what was *U-194*'s only patrol, it not having sunk any Allied vessels.[10] 20 June, in the same area, another Catalina (P-1), also from VP-84, sank *U-388*, again with a Fido. Thus, ended Type VIIC *U-388*'s single patrol, having sunk no Allied vessels. All forty-seven crew members perished.[11]

On 15 July, an American Catalina joined multiple Royal Navy vessels in a hunt. On that day, *U-135* damaged a British freighter but then caught the attention of three escort vessels: HMS *Rochester*, *Mignonette* and *Balsam*. The Royal Navy pummelled the sea with ninety depth charges until it resurfaced. US Navy Catalina P-6 from VP-92 arrived and attacked *U-135* with machine gun fire; it then swooped over it to deposit four depth bombs. *Balsam* then delivered the final, fatal blow by ramming. Forty-one crew survived as prisoners of war and five perished. *U-135*, a Type VIIC boat, had sunk three Allied ships and damaged another on seven patrols.[12] Six days later, on 21 July, approximately 200 miles from the mouth of the Amazon, a US Catalina crew, P-4 from VP-94, discovered Type VIIC *U-662* on the surface and fatally depth charged the boat. A little over two weeks later, American patrol craft PC-494 rescued two crew members. All the other forty-four men went down with the boat. *U-662* had destroyed three Allied vessels and damaged another.[13]

The US Navy also contributed to winning the U-boat war with another flying boat, the Mariner, which destroyed four U-boats in July, three of the attacks in the Caribbean. On 15 July, a VP-32 Mariner, P-10, escorting in front of an Allied convoy just south of Hispaniola, caught Type VIIC *U-759* on the surface and destroyed it with depth charges. All forty-seven crew died.[14] *U-359*, in the last month of its existence, had already, in company with *U-466*, encountered an Allied aircraft on 3 July off the Portugal coast. There, both U-boats downed an American 480th Group B-24. However, later in the month on 26 July, off the south-west coast of Haiti, a Mariner from VP-32, P-12, destroyed *U-359*. Forty-seven crew perished.[15] *U-759* had sunk only two Allied vessels and *U-359* had not sunk any.[16] Two days later, VP-32 achieved its third victory of the month against one of Dönitz's most formidable U-boats: *U-159*. Under two commanders, this Type IXC had destroyed twenty-three Allied vessels. Its career ended though, when, south of Hispaniola, Mariner P-1 released multiple depth charges on the surfaced submarine and sank it. All fifty-three crew members perished.[17] A US Navy Mariner also attacked a U-boat off the Brazilian cost on 19 July. Friedrich Guggenberger, who had led *U-81* on its successful attack on HMS *Ark Royal*, now commanded Type IXC *U-513*. VP-74 Mariner P-3 found his U-boat on the surface and targeted it with depth charges. Forty-six men perished but seven, including Guggenberger, became prisoners of war.[18]

In one instance, two different Allied flying boats co-operated. On 31 July, a Brazilian Catalina and a VP-74 Mariner attacked *U-199*, a long-range Type IXD2. The Mariner pilot discovered the surfaced U-boat off Rio de Janeiro and released six depth charges that damaged the boat and prevented diving. The American crew then radioed for assistance and a Brazilian Hudson arrived, which strafed the wounded U-boat before a Brazilian Catalina arrived and fatally struck with depth charges. Twelve crew members were rescued while forty-nine died. *U-199* had sunk one Allied vessel on this, its only patrol.[19]

The US Navy also contributed during these two months with the twin-engine Ventura. On 30 July, B-10 from VB-197 spotted Type VIIC *U-591* on the surface off the south-east coast of Brazil. The aircraft attacked with six depth charges and the U-boat sank in just four minutes. Nineteen crew members perished while USS *Saucy*, a corvette, rescued the remaining twenty-eight. *U-591* had sunk five Allied vessels and damaged one on nine patrols.[20]

The US Navy suffered a loss during this time from one of its more unusual aircraft, a blimp. Intended to locate U-boats and request more lethal aircraft to destroy them, in the case of K-74 from Squadron ZP 21, the pilot decided that imminent danger to merchant vessels necessitated an immediate attack. On 19 July, between southern Florida and Cuba, the blimp attacked with multiple depth charges that may have resulted in some minor damage to *U-134*, but the U-boat's anti-aircraft fire shot down the US craft. The American destroyer USS *Dahlgren* rescued ten crew members, while one drowned.[21]

Beyond their impressive contributions with Liberators, the British, along with Australian and even French crews, destroyed eleven more U-boats in these two months. Wellingtons achieved four of these sinkings in June and July, and the first fatal attack occurred against a highly successful U-boat. Under two different commanders, *U-126* had, prior to its sixth patrol, sunk twenty-four Allied vessels and damaged another five. On 20 March, it departed for a patrol off the coast of Freetown, Sierra Leone. While hunting there, the long-range Type IXC fatally torpedoed an Allied tanker and damaged another. Later, it commenced its return journey to France. At midnight on 3 July, the commander of the surfaced U-boat had successfully guided his boat to a location just west of the Bay of Biscay. At 0237 hours, 172 Squadron 'R' obtained a radar contact 13 miles away. The twin-engine aircraft approached at 150ft altitude and, at ¾ mile from the contact, the crew illuminated its Leigh Light. They saw a U-boat with 'decks awash'. At 0244 hours, the British crew roared over the U-boat at 50ft and released six depth charges. The Wellington's rear gunner observed six explosions and expended 500 rounds. The RAF aircraft returned ninety seconds later and the crew noticed nothing on the surface. They remained for nine more minutes before departing, while only noting that 'the sea was rough and there was some haze'. None of *U-126*'s fifty-five crew members survived.[22]

Six days later on 9 July, at 1715 hours, 179 Squadron Wellington 'R' received notice of a U-boat operating approximately 250 miles off the Portuguese coast. The bomber appeared at the noted location thirty-two minutes later, but observed nothing. Then, at 1811 hours, the pilot, Flight Officer E.J. Fisher, sighted a wake and, at 4 miles, a surfaced Type VIIC. Two miles from the target, Fisher dived from 1,300ft. The Wellington's gunner fired during the approach but Fisher recorded that the U-boat 'made no attempt to dive or to engage aircraft although more men were seen in the conning tower'. The British dropped four depth charges from 50ft as the rear gunner expended approximately 150 rounds. The U-boat slowed to a stop and the bows disappeared from the surface as the stern rose 75 degrees out of the water. When the stern 'settled' the crew observed 'two very violent explosions' that spread both debris and oil. All forty-six crew members perished on *U-232*'s first patrol, it not having sunk any Allied vessels.[23]

On 24 July, Type XIV *U-459* found itself facing not one but two Wellingtons, in the western Bay of Biscay. However, the RAF did not escape this combat unharmed as 172 Squadron's 'Q' never returned. Rear Gunner Sergeant A.A. Turner, the only survivor of the six-man crew, provided a first-person account of the battle. He said the Wellington's radar detected a possible target 6 miles away. The pilot, Flight Officer W.H.T. Jennings, approached the contact at 1,000ft and exited the cloud cover when 5 miles from the target. The crew immediately visually identified a surfaced U-boat. Jennings, with the German commander displaying no intention of diving, engaged. He commenced his descent and Turner observed 'pieces of fuselage being shot away' by the U-boat's gunners. He did not know if the depth charges released, but witnessed an explosion in the aircraft and 'next found himself under water kicking away something with his feet'. Turner rose to the 'surface and kicked off his flying boots and swam' to a nearby dinghy. He observed a body, believed to be the second pilot, and then scrambled upon the upside-down dinghy. Turner then sighted the U-boat moving slowly in a circle with black smoke 'pouring from the stern'. The British gunner 'removed his Mae West and coat to wave' at the Germans but the boat did not approach. Turner spotted another dinghy and located a 'knife, leak stoppers and bellows' but lost both his coat and Mae West, and found 'no rations'.

Now though, he had obtained a front-row seat for the next part of the battle as 547 Squadron Wellington 'V' arrived. This crew saw the U-boat 8 miles away 'circling very slowly'. The Wellington 'attacked immediately' and dropped seven Torpex depth charges from an altitude of 50ft while travelling at 210mph. After the explosions, the U-boat 'rolled to starboard' and its crew 'poured' from the conning tower before the U-boat slipped beneath the water. Turner counted twenty-five survivors in 'individual dinghies' while the Wellington crew estimated twenty to thirty. They also noticed, 1½ miles away, a 'dinghy with the sole survivor from an aircraft' and 'dropped supplies' but were 'doubtful if they were recovered'. Turner remained in the dinghy for nine hours before a Polish destroyer, the *Orkan*, retrieved him. Additionally, forty-one German crew members survived, while nineteen perished. *U-459*, developed for a replenishing role, possessed no torpedo tubes and thus had not sunk any Allied vessels.[24]

Five days later, Wellington 'G' from the same squadron, 172, while flying over the western Bay of Biscay, detected a contact at 6½ miles. The nature of the radar contact led the crew to conclude that the U-boat had just commenced surfacing. Just ¾ mile from the target, the twin-engine bomber emerged from the clouds and sighted a fully surfaced

U-boat moving at approximately 10 knots. The Wellington's front gun fired immediately, and the pilot flew over the target at 50ft and released six Torpex depth charges. The crew observed numerous 'plumes' from the depth charges, which momentarily obscured the U-boat. When the plumes subsided, the crew saw nothing. Then, numerous survivors appeared on the surface with life jackets and 'yellow skull caps'. All of Type VIIC *U-614*'s forty-nine crew members perished. The U-boat had conducted three patrols and had only sunk one Allied vessel.[25]

Sunderlands, having served with the RAF's Coastal Command from the start of the war, were still in service in 1943 and carried out two fatal attacks in July. First, on the 13th, 228 Squadron 'N' discovered three fully surfaced U-boats on the western edge of the Bay of Biscay. Type VIIC *U-607* separated from the other two and, now the weaker target, received the British crew's full attention. The flying boat dropped seven depth charges, which destroyed both the bows and the conning tower. The U-boat 'sank immediately', leaving behind twenty-five crew members on the surface. The Sunderland crew released a dinghy, which six men got in. A Luftwaffe Junkers 88 did 'shadow' the flying boat but failed to engage. Forty-five of the U-boat crew perished and seven survived. *U-607* completed five patrols and sank five Allied vessels.[26]

On 30 July, the Allies detected a group of three U-boats transiting the Bay of Biscay together for mutual protection. The British forces would sink all three this day. A Sunderland destroyed one, a Halifax sank another, and Royal Navy sloop vessels, force 'Fisher,' annihilated the third. No. 502 Squadron Halifax 'S' headed for the reported U-boats' location and at 36 miles detected multiple contacts. The pilot 'altered course to investigate' and discovered 'our force "Fisher" steaming at full speed towards the submarines' position'. The force 'instructed' the Halifax to continue to the U-boat positions, 20 miles in front of the surface vessels. When Halifax 'S' arrived, the crew sighted 502 Squadron Halifax 'B' and a Sunderland. After 'B' overshot the three U-boats with three 600lb bombs from 1,000ft, 'S' attacked the port submarine, *U-462*, a highly valuable *milchkuh* Type XIV, with a single 600lb bomb from 3,000ft. The resulting explosion covered the U-boat's 'aft portion' and smoke began rising from the conning tower as the damaged *U-462* 'circled slowly'. Now, the three U-boats 'broke formation'. Then Halifax 'S' struck *U-462* again from 2,000ft. The Germans fired 'intense flak' but the pilot bore in and deposited a bomb that 'exploded 250 ft astern'. As the Halifax completed its attack, a Liberator then assaulted *U-462* and 'wreckage' flew into the air. The B-24 conducted a second assault by flying low over the U-boat and striking it with machine gun fire. The Halifax captain determined to engage a third time as the U-boat circled slowly. On his approach, the U-boat's guns remained silent, but the centre U-boat responded with 'an intense covering fire'. The 'third bomb undershot' by approximately 70ft due to the U-boat's 'evasive action'. Later, *U-462* ceased forward momentum, while '40 men (est.) took to small dinghies'. However, 'almost immediately shells began to fall around' the U-boat as force 'FISHER' closed to within 5 miles. The Halifax captain tried to direct the gun fire but all over- or undershot the U-boat by 500yd. The U-boat sank ten to fifteen seconds after the naval force commenced shelling. Sixty-four crewmen survived the attack and one perished. The U-boat, designed for replenishment purposes, had no torpedo tubes and therefore no sinkings to its credit.[27]

Meanwhile, multiple Allied aircraft had assaulted *U-461*, another *milchkuh* Type XIV boat, without apparently causing serious damage. Then, Sunderland 'U' of the Royal Australian Air Force's 461 Squadron arrived and delivered seven depth charges from 50ft that destroyed the boat. Fifty-three crew perished and the Royal Navy rescued fifteen to be interned as prisoners of war. *U-461*, a replenishment U-boat with no torpedo tubes, thus had no sinkings to its credit during its six patrols.[28]

The third U-boat of this flotilla, *U-504*, a long-range Type IXC, chose to submerge instead of fighting on the surface. While that had saved many a U-boat, this day the strategy failed. HMS *Kite*, *Wild Goose*, *Woodpecker* and *Wren* all steamed to the location, detected the U-boat, and commenced a depth charge assault. Oil, wreckage, clothing and human remains eventually surfaced. *U-504*'s crew all perished, ending a career of seven patrols and sixteen Allied vessels sunk. The British vessels then headed to the location of the other two U-boat sinkings, where their crews retrieved the survivors from the Bay.[29]

During June and July, two Hudsons each fatally assaulted a U-boat. On 5 June, 48 Squadron Hudson 'M' ascended from Gibraltar at 1518 hours. While flying 200 miles west of Gibraltar at 4,000ft, pilot Flight Officer H.W.B. Wright, while scanning the surface with his binoculars, spotted a wake 10 miles away. He turned the twin-engine aircraft to enable a 'down sun' approach. Once Wright had brought the Hudson 'in line' with the surfaced U-boat, he dived. The Germans, apparently seeing the oncoming threat, started to submerge when the British aircraft had closed the distance to one mile, and less than one minute from reaching its target. The Hudson flew over the U-boat and dropped four depth charges, resulting in multiple explosions. The U-boat disappeared while dispersed oil and one body appeared. All fifty crew members went down with the boat. On six patrols, Type VIIC *U-594* had sunk one Allied vessel and damaged another.[30]

On 16 June, Hudson 'T' from 459 Squadron, RAAF, based in North Africa, was flying off the Palestinian coast when it discovered surfaced Type VIIC *U-97* at 4 miles and moving at 8 knots. The Australian pilot descended from 3,000ft and roared over the target while releasing four depth charges. The U-boat turned to port as the sunbathing members of the crew dived into the water. After less than five minutes, the bow rose from the surface, and then the U-boat slipped underwater by the stern. The Royal Navy retrieved twenty-one crew members, while twenty-seven perished in the attack. *U-97* had destroyed sixteen Allied vessels and damaged another in fourteen patrols.[31]

Two other Allied aircraft types achieved a single sinking, including one against two of Dönitz's most successful U-boats. With its first commander, Type VIIC *U-564* had been credited with sinking nineteen Allied vessels and damaging another. These attacks included several during the 'Second Happy Time' off the American seaboard. On 13 June, while travelling across the Bay of Biscay, it had been attacked and damaged by 228 Squadron Sunderland DV967, which *U-564* most likely shot down, resulting in the loss of all eleven crew members.[32] The following day, 10 Operational Training Unit Whitley 'G' spotted the U-boat and further damaged *U-564*, while also receiving extensive damage that forced a ditching. A French fishing boat rescued the British crew and they became prisoners of war when they reached France. The Whitley's final attack had delivered a fatal blow to *U-564*, but a nearby U-boat, *U-185*, saved eighteen crew members while twenty-eight perished.[33]

U-105, a Type IXB long-range boat, had proven to be even more successful. Under three commanders it had sunk twenty-three Allied vessels up to 2 June 1943. On that day, the French Air Force would achieve its sole U-boat sinking. Off the north-western African coast, a French Potez flying boat, while escorting an Allied convoy, struck *U-105* with multiple depth charges. All fifty-three crew members perished.[34]

The British did lose a Catalina during this time after 210 Squadron Catalina 'F' discovered Type XIV *U-642* off the Portuguese coast and attacked. German flak struck the approaching aircraft, which managed to drop depth charges. However, an uncontrollable fire broke out in the flying boat and it had to land in the sea. The U-boat escaped and the Royal Navy rescued eight members of the Catalina's ten-man crew.[35]

By any measure, June and July,1943 had been two devastating months for Dönitz. His U-boats had been struck by Allied aircraft off the South American coast, in the North Atlantic, in the Bay of Biscay and in the Mediterranean. Allied aircraft had not only closed the gap in the mid-Atlantic, they had initiated saturating the Bay of Biscay area that his U-boats needed to traverse to start and end their patrols. The Allied aircraft had dominated the number of U-boat sinkings as well. Unfortunately for the German admiral, these aircraft continued to pummel his U-boats in the next three months of 1943, with the Liberators, once again, in the lead.

A Lockheed Hudson of 269 Squadron, part of Coastal Command, on patrol over the Atlantic. (Historic Military Press)

Type VIIC *U-570* following its surrender to 269 Squadron, Coastal Command, Hudson flown by Squadron Leader James H. Thompson on 27 August 1941. A large proportion of the crew of *U-570* can be seen on the submarine's conning tower in this image, taken as one of the Coastal Command aircraft flew low overhead. (Historic Military Press)

A Fairey Swordfish on the No. 2 elevator of USS *Wasp* in May 1942. (National Museum of the US Navy)

An early war photograph of a Swordfish, K8428, dropping a torpedo. (Historic Military Press)

A US Navy PBY Catalina, 92-P-10, during a patrol over the Caribbean during May 1942. (NARA)

A Royal Navy escort carrier, either HMS *Avenger* or *Biter*, seen as an Atlantic convoy forms up during 1942. (USNHHC)

An unidentified U-boat under attack by a Coastal Command Sunderland. According to the original caption, the image was taken on 25 June 1942. (National Museum of the US Navy)

A US Navy PB4Y Liberator heading over the coast of south-west England at the beginning of a patrol out into the Bay of Biscay during the Battle of the Atlantic. The original caption states: 'It will be 12 hours before the giant plane returns over the English coast, and within the 12 hours may well be included bombing, strafing, and combat with German fighters.' (National Museum of the US Navy)

Members of the crew of a US Consolidated PBY Catalina that sank *U-156* on 8 March 1943, pose for the camera. The original caption states: '[The U-boat was sunk] in West Indies waters by raking deck with machine gun fire and dropping 4 depth bombs from 100'. The U-boat broke in two with terrific explosion and sank. A life raft was dropped for survivors. Pilot, Lieutenant Junior Grade John E. Dryden, Jr., USNR, describes the sinking. The pilot sighted the submarine 8 miles away, and he went into a 45-degree dive. As the submarine sank smoke and debris cascaded 40 feet into the air. The oil slick spread until it was a quarter of a mile wide and three quarters of a mile long.' (National Museum of the US Navy)

An air-to-air shot of some of RAF Coastal Command's 220 Squadron's Flying Fortresses. The aircraft in the centre is FL456. Being flown by the crew of Pilot Officer K. Ramsden, this aircraft spotted and sunk *U-265* while supporting convoy HZ 224on the morning of 3 February 1943. (Historic Military Press)

The Type XB minelaying U-boat *U-117* under attack by Avengers from USS *Card* in the central Atlantic on 7 August 1943. She was sunk in these attacks. (USNHHC)

A US Navy Consolidated PB4Y-1 pictured on patrol circa 1943 or 1944. (USNHHC)

Type VIIC *U-664* under air attack on 9 August 1943. The aircraft in question, flown by Ensign P.M. Rockett USNR, was operating from USS *Card* (CVE-11). (National Museum of the US Navy)

The moment that a Consolidated PB4Y-1 attackeda U-boat in the English Channel on 23 June 1944. Note the wake created by the submarine's Schnorchell (snorkel) bottom left. (National Museum of the US Navy)

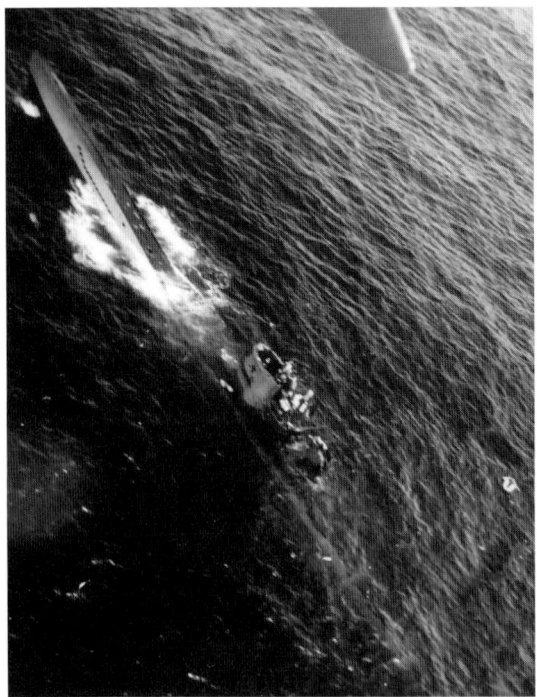

Another view of *U-664* under air attack on 9 August 1943. (National Museum of the US Navy)

Canso 9754, in which Flight Lieutenant Hornell sank *U-1225*. (Historic Military Press)

A US Navy PBY Catalina flying boat pictured during a patrol over the Atlantic, 'on a hunt for Nazi submarines', on 31 August 1943. (National Museum of the US Navy)

Type IXD2 *U-848* under fatal attack by PB4Ys of VB-107 and two B-25s, south-west of Ascension Island, on 5 November 1943. The aircraft delivering the attack shown here was that flown by Lieutenant C.A. Baldwin USNR. (USNHHC)

Another view of *U-848* while under attack. (USNHHC)

U-848 while under attack by PB4Y Liberators of VB-107 and two B-25s, south-west of Ascension Island, on 5 November 1943. (Historic Military Press)

U-848 under attack on 5 November 1943. (Historic Military Press)

A Boeing B-17 Flying Fortress Mk. IIA of 220 Squadron, Coastal Command, based at Benbecula, pictured during a patrol. It is possible that this is FK186, NR-K, seen in May 1943. (Historic Military Press)

A Consolidated PB4Y-1 Liberator flies over the English countryside, bound for its patrol area over the Bay of Biscay, in the summer of 1943. (USNHHC)

The long-range Type IXD2 *U-849* under attack by a PB4Y-1 Liberator of VB-107 near the Congo Estuary on 25 November 1943. The pilot was Lieutenant Junior Grade Vance Dawkins USNR. *U-849* was sunk in these attacks. (USNHCC)

A PB4Y Liberator during an anti-submarine patrol on 22 May 1944. (Historic Military Press)

Aa TseTse Mosquito of 248 Squadron attacking Type VIIC *U-821* near the island of Ouessant, off the Brittany coast, on 10 June 1944. The TseTse Mosquito is more correctly a Mosquito FB Mk. XVIII with an automatic-loading, 6-pounder, 57mm cannon in the nose. *U-821* was sunk during the aerial attacks on this date. (Historic Military Press)

Type IXC/40 *U-1229* under attack by Allied aircraft south of Newfoundland on 20 August 1944. The aircraft in question was from VC-42, operating off USS *Bogue*, and flown by Lieutenant Junior Grade B.C. Sissler. *U-1229* was sunk in these attacks, with the loss of eighteen members of the forty-one-strong crew. (Historic Military Press)

U-1229 under attack by Allied aircraft south of Newfoundland on 20 August 1944. (Historic Military Press)

U-1229 under attack by Allied aircraft south of Newfoundland on 20 August 1944. (Historic Military Press)

Coastal Command Catalina Mk. IVA JX574 of 210 Squadron operating from RAF Sullom Voe during 1944. (Historic Military Press)

Sunderland Mk. V coded WH-B operating from Sullom Voe with 330 (Norwegian) Squadron in 1945. (Danish National Museum)

A night attack on a U-boat by a Coastal Command aircraft. Note the flares dropped at low altitude. (Historic Military Press)

Chapter 11

B-24s: August–October 1943

The Allies' success during the period August to October 1943 proved to be devastating to Dönitz's U-boats. Allied aircraft contributed significantly, with a total of forty-one fatal attacks during these three months, when all Allied forces sank a total of fifty-nine U-boats. Thus, Allied aircraft claimed 69 per cent of all Allied victories. Aircraft continued to serve as the most lethal weapons in the arsenal against Hitler's U-boats.

Again, the Liberator led the pack, participating in fourteen sinkings. The RAF's B-24s dominated the totals among all Allied aircraft for these three months with eleven victories, despite the fact that only nine of the sixty-four Coastal Command squadrons flew Liberators, and of those, four – 59, 86, 120, and 224 – located in the North Atlantic area, participated in ten of the fatal attacks. No. 59 Squadron's B-24s primarily took off and landed at Aldergrove in Northern Ireland, although half of the time in October they were based in Iceland. No. 86 Squadron flew from four bases: Thorney Island in West Sussex, St Eval in Cornwall, and Aldergrove and Ballykelly in Northern Ireland. No. 120 Squadron operated from two bases, Ballykelly and Reykjavik, while 224 Squadron only flew from Beaulieu in Hampshire, southern England.

August proved to be a quiet month for these four units. The 120 Squadron Liberators in Reykjavik did not sight any U-boats, and 86 Squadron noted only a periscope sighting that month. For 59 Squadron, Liberator Mk. V 'K' hit a U-boat on the 1st with two depth charges but while smoke 'emitted abaft' of the conning tower, the target escaped. No. 224 Squadron recorded only one U-boat sighting but did not carry out any attacks.

September remained quiet for all four squadrons except on one day, the 20th, when four 120 Squadron B-24s sighted U-boats. At 1025 hours, B-24 Mk. III 'X' discovered a fully surfaced U-boat and attacked but the 'bomb-doors did not open in time'. Instead, the British crew directed an incoming destroyer to the location. At 1103 hours, the crew sighted another U-boat, which dived quickly. The Liberator attacked the 'swirl' with three 250lb depth charges and a destroyer arrived to continue the battle. The B-24 departed, met convoy ON 202 at 1255 hours and, two hours later, at 1505 hours, discovered two fully surfaced U-boats. The German commanders immediately changed their course upon sighting the bomber and the British relayed to the convoy that, in order to avoid these two U-boats, it should alter course as well. The B-24 and the starboard U-boat fired on each other until a destroyer 5 miles away 'opened fire' and pursued the submarine while the Liberator departed. The British crew reported that they last saw the port U-boat 'at full speed' with Allied destroyers 'in pursuit'. The Liberator crew found another U-boat, but that one submerged immediately.

Three other Liberators engaged U-boats this day. At 1046 hours, Mk. I 'F' assaulted a fully surfaced U-boat with four 250lb depth charges that 'undershot' and dropped a 600lb depth charge on it after it submerged. The crew directed a destroyer to the location before the convoy recalled the Liberator to resume convoy escort. Mk. III 'N' found a fully surfaced U-boat at 2008 hours and assaulted it twice, once with three 250lb depth charges, and on the second attack with two 600lb depth charges. At 2043 hours, Mk. III 'J' 'dived and attacked' a fully surfaced U-boat with three 250lb depth charges but the crew believed that all 'overshot'. Although none of these attacks resulted in fatalities, the next month proved to be more deadly.

The four squadrons struggled during October's first three days. No. 86 Squadron did not find any U-boats and 120 Squadron pilots discovered several but did not make any lethal strikes. On the 1st, Mk. III 'T''s crew sighted three U-boats but bomb door issues prevented any fatal attacks. Mk. III 'X' assaulted a U-boat twice but witnessed no evidence of a sinking, and on the 3rd, 'V' dropped three depth charges on a surfaced U-boat. On 4 October though, 'X', with a different crew than on the 1st, departed Reykjavik at 0933 hours and, while sweeping ahead of convoy ONS 10 south-west of Iceland, received orders to attack a U-boat at a specific position. The crew commenced the hunt and found a fully surfaced target. The aircraft 'dived to attack', fired from its nose gun and dropped three 250lb depth charges. Smoke obscured the U-boat but when it cleared the crew observed the Type VIIC's bows 'rise slowly above the waves', followed by its sinking. Both survivors and wreckage appeared in the area of the attack, but all fifty crew members perished. This marked *U-389*'s only patrol, having not sunk any shipping. 'X' returned to Reykjavik at 2149 hours, a twelve-hour mission.[1]

No. 120 Squadron Liberator 'V', though, did not return from its mission on 4 October. The B-24 took off from Iceland just before 1000 hours for convoy escort. At 1130 hours, the crew reported a surfaced U-boat. While closing on the target, Type IXC/40 *U-539*, both starboard engines erupted in flames. The B-24 missed widely when dropping its depth charges and the aircraft crashed into the Atlantic, killing all nine crew members including the squadron leader, Wing Commander R.M. Longmore.[2]

Four days later, on 8 October, 86 Squadron Mk. III 'R', while escorting convoy Cobra 12 in the mid-North Atlantic, spotted a surfaced U-boat. The German U-boat began diving as the aircraft descended for the attack. The British dropped four depth charges, two of which straddled the U-boat's course 'and the subsequent explosion enveloped the diving swirl'. Unfortunately for the hunters, they reported 'no evidence of damage'. The Liberator continued its aerial escort duties until an hour later, when the aircraft 'returned to the scene of the attack' and at 0954 hours spotted the same Type VIIC U-boat as before. This time, the U-boat commander decided to not dive and the B-24's depth charges 'entered the water alongside the hull'. The British crew reported a 'violent explosion with a white flash and a dirty grey cloud'. When the smoke dissipated, they observed the U-boat's bows protruding in a vertical position above the surface. In the area of the sinking, fifteen men floated among wreckage and oil. A destroyer rescued the lone survivor while all the other forty-eight men died. Thus ended *U-419*'s only patrol, the crew not having engaged any Allied vessels.[3]

That same day, 8 October, Liberators struck again. Type VIIC *U-643* had departed Bergen, Norway, for its first patrol on 14 September and a little over three weeks later it was travelling on the surface in the same area as *U-419* had met its fate. In fact, this U-boat's last day began with the same B-24 that had sunk *U-419*. After its final attack on that boat, 86 Squadron's 'R' resumed its convoy escort position when its crew observed their second U-boat of the day. Out of depth charges, they attacked with machine gun fire while alerting nearby Liberator Mk. V 'Z', also from 86 Squadron, to the location.[4]

'Z' commenced its day in the early morning, taking off from Ballykelly at 0158 hours. It joined its convoy at 0809 hours and a little over three hours later heard from 'R' that they had spotted a surfaced U-boat. 'Z' turned and flew to that location. At 1137 hours, it arrived and *U-643* immediately commenced diving. The Liberator dropped four depth charges but the crew, disappointedly, reported only 'oil and scum'. 'Z' returned to the convoy but then later flew back to the area and discovered 120 Squadron Liberator 'T' involved in a U-boat assault.

No. 120 Squadron's action against this U-boat began with Liberator Mk. III 'G'. It took off from Reykjavik at 0828 hours and at 1203 hours spotted *U-643* and attacked it with one 600lb depth charge. The German commander did not dive. The Liberator turned to attack again and this time the U-boat did submerge, forcing the British crew to drop three 250lb depth charges amidst the swirl. 'G' remained circling in the area until 120 Squadron Mk. III 'T' arrived.

The crew of 'T' reported that they observed 'G/120 circling scene of G/120's attack' and at 1305 hours, they, for the first time, observed *U-643*, which had reappeared on the surface. Liberator 'T' dived immediately and the Germans responded with 'heavy flak', while the British 'replied with nose-gun'. The German fire caused the pilot to engage in 'evasive action', which necessitated aborting the attack run. At 1312 hours though, the RAF crew tried again and this time they dropped four 250lb depth charges but did not observe any damage.

No. 86 Squadron Liberator 'Z' now returned to the battle and made a second attack, dropping its two remaining depth charges on the surfaced boat. No. 120 Squadron's 'T' followed with its second attack at 1315 hours, employing four 250lb depth charges and machine gun fire. After this assault, *U-643*'s forward speed decreased significantly, while the German machine gun fire increased. Then, the U-boat developed a heavy list and the crew commenced 'congregating on the conning-tower', inflating dinghies, and donning life-jackets. 'Z', due to fuel limitations, now departed. Liberator 'T' contacted nearby Allied destroyers and directed them to the stricken boat. Another Liberator arrived, 86 Squadron Mk. V 'L', but the convoy's Senior Naval Officer instructed the crew to not attack. At 1445 hours, as 'T' and 'L' circled, the U-boat suddenly exploded. Fifteen to twenty crew members appeared on the surface and at 1507 hours the three destroyers began rescuing them. Although the crew of Liberator 'T' had begun their day in Iceland, Coastal Command ordered them to land in Northern Ireland, where they arrived at 1205 hours on 9 October, concluding a fifteen-hours and thirty-minute patrol. Allied vessels saved eighteen of *U-643*'s crew, while thirty perished. This ended the U-boat's maiden patrol, with no Allied vessels sunk.[5]

Eight days later, on 16 October, again in the mid-North Atlantic, three British Liberators collaborated in an attack on Type VIIC *U-470*. After being airborne for just over three hours and while escorting convoy ON 206, the crew of 120 Squadron Liberator Mk. III 'E' found the surfaced U-boat and descended for the attack. The Germans responded with 'heavy flak', forcing the pilot to take 'evasive action'. The aircraft experienced a 'lurch', which the British first misidentified as flak damage but they later determined to have been a beam window that had 'blown out' and struck the aircraft's tail. The Liberator's captain 'circled' and commenced a second attack. The B-24 hit the U-boat with machine gun fire and four 250lb depth charges, with the fourth one 'exploding close' to the U-boat's stern. The U-boat remained on the surface 'down by stern'. Meanwhile, 120 Squadron Liberator 'Z"s crew spotted the same U-boat and witnessed 'E"s depth charges 'exploding' near it. 'Z' then attacked with six 250lb depth charges and machine gun fire while receiving German flak fire, and proceeded to attack a second time with two more 250lb depth charges that 'straddled' the U-boat. A third Liberator, 59 Squadron Mk. V 'C', also engaged with two attacks of four depth charges each. The U-boat's bows rose to a 60-degree angle and slipped from the surface by the stern for the last time. Royal Navy destroyers HMS *Vidette* and *Duncan* arrived on the scene and saved two men; the other forty-six perished. *U-470* had not sunk any Allied vessels on this, its first patrol.[6]

The same day, the 16th, two other RAF Liberators attacked another U-boat. This time, the British found one of Dönitz's prized Type IXC/40 boats, built specifically for long-distance operations, in the mid-North Atlantic. For the crew of 86 Squadron Liberator 'L' that had arrived too late to participate in *U-643*'s demise, they would not be tardy this day. The B-24 and its seven-man crew took off at 0252 hours and rendezvoused with its assigned convoy, ONS 20, then found and attacked *U-844*. No. 59 Squadron Lancaster 'S' soon arrived and straddled the surfaced U-boat with four depth charges. The crew witnessed a 'deep red flash' after thirty seconds as *U-844* began to slip under the surface for the last time. Twenty-nine seconds later, the pilot dropped an additional four depth charges before the diving U-boat's swirl, ending *U-844*'s only patrol with no Allied vessels attacked. All fifty-three crew perished. However, the Germans had delivered effective machine gun fire against 'L', destroying two of its four engines and forcing the pilot to ditch in the ocean twenty minutes after the attack. Two of the aircraft's crew died, while the other five suffered injuries but survived.[7]

Again on the 16th, a British Liberator found another of Dönitz's U-boats on the surface approximately 600 miles south-west of Iceland. The crew of 86 Squadron's 'Y' had lifted off from RAF Ballykelly at 0854 hours and found its assigned convoy, ON 206, at 1505 hours. Later, while flying towards another convoy, ONS 20, the British crew spotted the surfaced *U-964*, a Type VIIC. The German flak proved to be challenging this day. The B-24 attacked with three depth charges but the crew could not observe any results. The U-boat's 'intense flak' caused the pilot, Flight Officer G.D. Gamble, to delay another bomb run. After over three hours of shadowing the surfaced U-boat though, at 1910 hours, Gamble determined that, with light fading, he had one last opportunity to strike. The second attack delivered three depth charges in close proximity to the target. The British noted that 'within a few minutes the bows were low in the water and puffs of black smoke' emanating from both sides of the deck. Eventually, the Liberator's crew watched the boat sink 'leaving 35 survivors in dinghies and in the water'. *U-231* rescued three crew members while forty-seven perished. The RAF had sunk *U-964* on its maiden patrol, it not having sunk any Allied vessels.[8]

On the 17th of the month, two Liberators attacked *U-540*, a long-range Type IXC/40 boat. No. 59 Squadron Mk. V 'D', while returning to base, sighted the surfaced submarine and attacked. On the first attempt, the four depth charges 'overshot' but on its second run the first two depth charges successfully 'straddled' the boat. No. 120 Squadron Liberator 'H' arrived almost simultaneously and also delivered multiple attacks. It struck the U-boat first with its 20 mm cannon and then followed with four 250lb depth charges, which also straddled the U-boat. *U-540* lost momentum and appeared 'down by stern'. The 'H' pilot lined up his aircraft and attacked again with cannon and four more 250lb depth charges, which again straddled the target. The crew watched the U-boat 'break in half, the bow and the stern rising out of the water, and she sank'. The British sighted thirty survivors in the water but all fifty-five crew members eventually perished. *U-540*, one of Dönitz's valuable tanker submarines, ended its first and only patrol having sunk no Allied vessels.[9]

On 23 October, 224 Squadron Liberator 'Z' roared into the air from RAF Ballykelly at 0516 hours. At 1038 hours, while escorting its assigned convoy ON 207, the crew spotted the fully surfaced Type VIIC *U-274*. While the Germans fired upon the aircraft, the crew attacked with four rockets and the nose gun and turret. However, as the B-24 circled, they observed no evidence of damage. Next, at 1121 hours, they attacked with two depth charges as the U-boat submerged. The ordnance 'fell 400ft ahead of swirl' and 'slightly to starboard'. With the U-boat now submerged, the RAF crew led British destroyers *Duncan* and *Vidette* to the scene, where they located the German and completed its destruction with attacks by Hedgehogs, a forward-firing mortar launcher. All forty-eight crew members perished. *U-274* sank on its second patrol with no sinkings to its credit. 'Z' landed at 1823 hours, a thirteen-hour mission.[10]

One RAF unit, 200 Squadron, based outside the North Atlantic area in the Gambia region on the western African coast, destroyed a U-boat. *U-468*, a Type VIIC, operated off the western African coast, near Sierra Leone, but did not discover any Allied shipping. On 11 August, Liberator

Mk. V 'D' found it on the surface after an earlier unsuccessful Catalina attack. The Germans remained on the surface and delivered significant fire on the approaching Liberator. Nevertheless, the British dropped numerous depth charges, which destroyed the U-boat. However, the German fire had so damaged the four-engine aircraft that it crashed, killing the entire eight-man British crew. A dinghy dropped by the B-24 permitted seven of the U-boat crew to survive until rescued by a Royal Navy vessel. The remaining forty-four U-boat crew members perished. Ironically, testimony from the survivors led the British Government to award the Liberator pilot, Flying Officer Lloyd Trigg, Britain's highest award, the Victoria Cross.[11]

US Liberators achieved one sinking during this period. In June, VB-105, having recently adopted the Navy's version of the B-24, the PB4Y-1, transferred to Bermuda. On 7 August, the American crew of B-4, while patrolling the central western Atlantic, found Type VIIB *U-84*, homeward-bound, on the surface. Following the traditional tactic of submerging, the U-boat dived upon noticing the four-engine aircraft. The Liberator dived as well and released a Fido torpedo that homed in on the U-boat's sound and destroyed it. All forty-six crew members perished. *U-84*'s sole commander sank six Allied vessels and damaged another one on nine patrols.[12]

USAAF Liberators destroyed one U-boat over these three months. On 29 July, Type VIIC *U-706* departed the Nazi submarine base at La Pallice, France, and four days later, Royal Canadian Air Force 415 Squadron Hampden 'A' discovered it on the surface, just passing the western boundary of the Bay of Biscay. The U-boat crew fired prodigiously at the twin-engine aircraft but, despite the intense flak, the Canadians released six depth charges. Demonstrating the limited capacity of the Hampden, it could not deliver any more ordnance. However, an American crew from the 4th Antisubmarine Squadron flying Liberator 'T' arrived. *U-706* damaged this Allied aircraft with its fire but the B-24 released twelve depth charges that destroyed the submarine. The Americans also released a dinghy. Forty-two crew perished and the frigate HMS *Waveney*, called to the scene, rescued four men who became prisoners of war. *U-706* had sunk three Allied vessels on three patrols.[13]

A Canadian B-24 destroyed one U-boat over these three months. On 19 September, 10 Squadron Liberator 'A' caught Type VIIC *U-341* on the surface near Iceland. The B-24 released six depth charges from 50ft but sustained significant wing damage from the German fire. With the U-boat still afloat, the Liberator swung around and delivered a second assault with four more depth charges that fatally damaged the target.

All fifty crew members perished. *U-341* had not sunk any Allied vessels on two patrols.[14]

Another Allied four-engine land-based aircraft, the British Halifax, achieved one fatal sinking during this period. No. 58 Squadron's report for 27 September for Halifax 'B' states: "B' failed to return. No signals were received from 'B' at all, but H/502 intercepted 'S.O.S'. at 21.40 hours. Signal was faint and call sign 'smothered'. In fact, the Halifax had caught *U-221*, a Type VIIC boat, on the surface west of the Bay of Biscay and attacked it with eight depth charges. All fifty of the U-boat's crew perished. Its commander, Hans Trojer, had successfully destroyed eleven Allied vessels on five patrols. However, the U-boat's gunners severely damaged the four-engine bomber and the pilot had to ditch in the Atlantic waters. Two crew members died in the battle and the destroyer HMS *Mahratta* rescued the remaining six RAF crewmen after eleven days adrift.[15]

Participating in fourteen sinkings, the B-24s led all other Allied aircraft in successful U-boat assaults for these three months. The Liberators did not fight alone. The US Navy's carrier aviation achieved its best period during this time. And, with the other aircraft, the Allies continued to hunt Dönitz's U-boats in multiple seas across the globe.

Chapter 12

United States Navy: August–October 1943

Besides Liberators, the Allies hunted and destroyed U-boats around the world with a variety of aircraft during these three months. However, as in the previous period, US Navy aircraft again dominated among non-B-24 aircraft with a total of twenty U-boat sinkings, the same total for all RAF aircraft during these three months. Uniquely over this time period, of the Navy's total, carrier aircraft contributed the most, by a margin of almost two-to-one. For Dönitz, these battles all proved that aircraft with stars or roundels continued to represent the most lethal threat to his fleet.

With the B-24s participating in fourteen U-boat sinkings, the Avengers followed closely with eleven destroyed during this time period. The Fido acoustic torpedo proved to be one of the Avengers' primary anti-submarine weapons against the U-boats. However, this ordnance suffered from a severe drawback. As a safety measure, the Americans designed the weapon to not attack any targets at a depth of 40ft or higher to prevent any unintended strikes against surface vessels. This limitation severely hampered American naval pilots, who had to force the targeted U-boat to submerge before launching one. The Navy's preference for the acoustic torpedo lay in the fact that naval aircraft could not haul significant ordnance, like B-24s. Thus, Navy pilots had to engage U-boats on the surface with their vulnerable single-engine aircraft hoping that U-boat commanders never learned that remaining surfaced would prove to be the most effective tactic against the Fido.[1]

VC-1 pilots operating from the American escort carrier USS *Card* commenced their U-boat depredations on 3 August when a Wildcat found *U-66*, a long-range Type IXC boat, on the surface, 800 miles off the Brazilian coast in the South Atlantic. The American pilot strafed the boat but the commander refused to dive, apparently believing that he could battle the fighter plane successfully. However, an Avenger then appeared and the U-boat dived, while the Navy pilot dropped two depth charges and a Fido torpedo that failed to locate its target. *U-66* surfaced again but then dived and the American planes departed.[2]

That night *U-66* radioed U-boat Command that the boat required assistance and received instructions to meet *U-117*, one of Dönitz's prized Type XB supply and minelaying boats. They found each other that night, but at 0648 hours on 7 August, the US Navy found them. A VC-1 Avenger pilot from USS *Card*, Lieutenant Sallenger, descended on the two U-boats with the sun at his back and dropped two depth charges, although they caused little or no damage to *U-66*. He remained in the area, shadowing them while calling for assistance. Twenty-five minutes later, that assistance arrived with three additional American aircraft. *U-66* began to submerge and Sallenger renewed his attack with a Fido that failed to locate the U-boat, which escaped. However, his previous attack on *U-66* had sounded the death knell for *U-117*. Sallenger's previous depth charges had so damaged *U-117* that it could not dive. The Americans now had one of Dönitz's largest U-boats on the surface with no subsurface escape ability, and they took full advantage of the opportunity. The Avengers deposited depth charges while the Wildcats engaged with gun fire. The U-boat disappeared from the surface by the stern and the Avengers then attacked with two homing torpedoes.[3] *U-117* had participated in seven patrols with two Allied vessels damaged by its mines. None of the sixty-two-man crew survived.[4]

The following day, on 8 August, *Card* crew members suffered multiple losses. An Avenger–Wildcat pair discovered two Type VIIC U-boats in the process of replenishment, *U-262* and *U-664*. The Wildcat initiated a strafing run but *U-262* shot it down, killing the pilot. The Avenger made one run on *U-262* but failed to release its depth charges. On the second attempt, the depth charges dropped causing damage, but a fire erupted on the Avenger's wing due to the flak. The US Navy pilot landed in the water and two of the three-man crew survived. An American destroyer retrieved them that day. *U-262* escaped but *Card*'s actions against *U-664* had not ended.[5]

Card's pilots struck again after *U-664* almost avenged *U-117*'s sinking when it found itself in an ideal firing position on the American carrier. The U-boat commander fired three torpedoes at the target, which he had mistaken for an Allied tanker. All three missed. The following day, 9 August, three of *Card*'s aircraft – two Avengers and a Wildcat – discovered

U-664 charging its batteries on the surface and they attacked. The first aircraft deposited a 500lb bomb and the Wildcat strafed the target. Now submerging, the third Allied aircraft assaulted with two depth charges. The resulting explosions reversed *U-664*'s momentum from descent to ascent and it appeared once again on the surface. Submerging again only displayed to the German commander the profuse number of leaks in the damaged U-boat, forcing him to ascend. The order to abandon ship given, the U-boat sank at 1420 hours almost exactly two hours after its sighting by American pilots. Lifejackets and rafts were dropped from aircraft and the destroyer USS *Borie* arrived to save forty-four of the crew. Seven perished. A U-boat fired five torpedoes at the American destroyer as it was rescuing the German crew members. Fortunately, all missed. *U-664* had sunk three Allied vessels on two patrols.[6]

Two days later, *Card*'s pilots discovered another of Dönitz's boats. The Wildcat pilot led with a strafing run, a tactic intended to disrupt any German machine gun fire on the following Avenger, which deposited two depth charges. On its second run, the Avenger engaged with a Fido, which fatally hit the U-boat and it released oil to the surface. None of the fifty-four crew members survived the battle. Type IXC/40 *U-525* participated in three patrols and sank one Allied vessel.[7]

USS *Core*'s group, with VC-13, then replaced USS *Card*'s vessels in the mid-Atlantic and on 24 August an Avenger–Wildcat pair spotted the surfaced *U-185*, a long-range Type IXC/40 boat, travelling not only with its crew, but also with fourteen rescued members of *U-604*. Almost two weeks earlier, on 11 August, *U-185* had shot down a US Navy VB-107 Liberator in this area for the loss of all ten crew members.[8] This time, the Americans would prevail. The Avenger pilot dropped two depth charges that sent the U-boat on a fatal descent. Crew members scrambled from the conning tower and the US Navy rescued twenty-two of them, while the remaining twenty-nine went down with the boat, including fourteen *U-604* crew members. August Maus, *U-185*'s commander, had sunk nine Allied vessels and damaged another one on three patrols. The Americans saved him and he became a prisoner of war for the rest of the conflict.[9]

Three days later though, *Card*'s pilots discovered another of Dönitz's long-range boats, a Type IXD2. *U-847*, which served primarily as a supply boat during its career, had resupplied seven U-boats during August alone. On the 27th though, it met American aircraft. Two Wildcats attacked although, as had occurred on multiple occasions, this only resulted in a dive order aboard the U-boat. An Avenger then dropped a Fido which located the submerged target and destroyed the U-boat. None of the sixty-two crew members survived. *U-847* sank no Allied vessels on two patrols.[10]

Two months later, *Card* pilots successfully attacked five U-boats in one month. On 4 October, an Avenger pilot on patrol made a shocking discovery. Below him, on the water's surface, floated four U-boats in the process of replenishment. His urgent report to the escort carrier resulted in three American planes roaring off her deck, while the Avenger pilot now commenced his assault and released a 500lb bomb between Type XIV *milchkuh U-460* and Type VIIC *U-264*. The large *U-460* now dived but the American pilot deposited a 500lb bomb before the U-boat's swirl and sank the boat. Sixty-two crew perished, while two survived.[11] Type VIIC *U-422* had temporarily escaped but when it returned to the surface 5 miles from the previous engagement, another Avenger–Wildcat team attacked and the Avenger's Fido sought out and destroyed it. None of the forty-nine crew members survived.[12]

On 13 October, *Card* pilots encountered a formidable U-boat commander: Freiherr Siegfried von Forstner. He had commenced his career with Type VIIC *U-402* in October 1941 and had achieved remarkable success. This German commander destroyed fourteen Allied vessels and damaged three others, including vessels off the American eastern seaboard during the 'Second Happy Time'; victories that led to the conferring of the prestigious Knight's Cross. Von Forstner had even sunk an American naval vessel, USS *Cythera*, a patrol yacht, off the North Carolina coast. *U-402*'s crew snatched two American survivors from the water and sent them to France as prisoners of war. Von Forstner's crew had also downed an Allied aircraft, 172 Squadron Wellington 'D', on 7 September in the Bay of Biscay, resulting in the loss of all six crew members. A month later though, on 13 October, in the mid-North Atlantic, *U-402* now faced a VC-9 Avenger pilot who had spotted the surfaced U-boat. This incident well highlighted the limitations of the Fido torpedo. Despite the Avenger's presence, the German commander refused to dive, thereby, unknowingly, offering the best defence against the American weapon. The naval pilot requested additional support and a Wildcat then appeared, which caused *U-402*, like so many of its predecessors when so confronted, to dive without recognising the fatal ramifications of the submerge order. The Avenger pilot then released his Fido torpedo, which found its target and sank the U-boat. All fifty hands perished.[13]

On the last day of the month, *Card*'s pilots struck again. An Avenger pilot discovered Type VIIC *U-91* fuelling Type VIIC *U-584*. *U-91*'s commander wisely decided to submerge, while *U-584*'s remained surfaced. Only when two additional Avengers appeared overhead, did *U-584* belatedly commence submerging. These two Avengers then descended on the diving boat and released two Fido torpedoes, which located and struck the U-boat. Explosions preceded the appearance of debris and oil. All fifty-three hands perished. On ten patrols, *U-584* had sunk three Allied vessels and one Allied submarine. *U-91* escaped unharmed.[14]

Escort carrier USS *Block Island*'s pilots delivered one fatal U-boat attack in October. Five days later, on 9 October, *U-220*, a Type XB boat designed for minelaying and at-sea replenishment, released, in the area of St John's, Newfoundland, sixty-six mines, which sank two Allied vessels, the only vessels it would damage during its short career. While crossing the Atlantic on its return to base on 28 October, a VC-1 Avenger–Wildcat pair from *Block Island* sighted the surfaced boat. The Avenger released depth charges that sank it. Of the fifty-six crew members, all hands perished on this, its first patrol, not having engaged any Allied vessels.[15]

VC-13 pilots on USS *Bogue* also achieved one sinking in October. On the 20th, they discovered surfaced *U-378*, a Type VIIC boat, that had sunk only one Allied vessel, but a notable one. A Polish destroyer, the *Orkan*, had served well escorting an Allied convoy across the Atlantic but on 1 October, a *U-378* torpedo fatally struck the small vessel in its rear magazine, causing a catastrophic explosion. The *Orkan* sank in five minutes, taking 179 crew members with her, while forty-four survived as the U-boat slipped away. Nineteen days later though, a *Bogue* Wildcat–Avenger pair spotted *U-378* on the surface and attacked. The Wildcat strafed the boat, followed by an accompanying Avenger, which deposited two depth charges. All forty-eight crew members perished.[16]

While American carrier aviation's accomplishments during this time deserve praise, a discussion of required manpower merits discussion. The three escort aircraft carriers mentioned here – *Bogue*, *Card* and *Core* – constituted three of the forty-five *Bogue*-class vessels constructed by the United States. They operated with 890 men as their standard complement. Three Clemson-class destroyers escorted *Card* as she steamed in the Atlantic during her impressive cruise: USS *Borie*, *Barry* and *Goff*. These ships operated with a standard complement of 106 men, resulting in a total manpower of just over 1,200 crew members. These men supported approximately twenty single-engine aircraft, of which the Avengers, the *Card*'s only aircraft capable of carrying fatal U-boat ordnance, represented just over half the total aircraft. So twelve anti-submarine aircraft required 1,200 men. In comparison, the Table of Equipment and Organization for a United States Army Air Forces B-24 squadron of twelve Liberators showed a required complement of 420 men.

Furthermore, Liberator Mk. IIIs with their 2,240-mile range, operating from the Azores, could have easily reached all eleven of the U-boats fatally attacked by American naval aviation during this period. Nine of these fatal attacks occurred within 700 miles or less from Lagens airfield, while two transpired at over 900 miles. Yet, on 28 May 1943, 120 Squadron Liberator Mk. III 'E' destroyed *U-304* at a location in the North Atlantic over 800 miles from its home base of Reykjavik. B-24s possessed superior range and a superior ordnance load compared with the Avengers, and required one-third the manpower.

The US Navy also achieved five sinkings by shore-based aircraft. Twin-engine Venturas destroyed three Type VIIC U-boats during this time in three different seas. *U-615*, a Type VIIC boat on its fourth patrol having sunk four Allied vessels, received attention from multiple Allied aircraft during its patrol in the southern Caribbean. On 29 July, a twin-engine USAAF B-18 Bolo attacked first, but caused no apparent damage. Three days later, a Liberator released one bomb, while US Navy vessel PC-1196 also attacked. These attacks all damaged the U-boat, and then on 5 August a Mariner from VP-204 assaulted the surfaced boat unsuccessfully. The next day, VP-205 Mariner P-4 caused further damage but the Germans destroyed this aircraft with their anti-aircraft fire, resulting in the loss of all eleven men. Now a third Mariner, P-11 of VP-205, engaged on 6 August and delivered multiple bombs, but *U-615* did not sink. Finally, VB-130 Ventura B-5 attacked with depth charges. *U-615* submerged but quickly rose again. Several other Allied aircraft attacked but the Ventura's assault appeared to have been the death blow as *U-615*, now unable to submerge, then faced the American destroyer USS *Walker*. The U-boat commander had one option remaining, and the boat dived with its commander while leaving forty-three men on the surface for the naval crew to rescue. Four U-boat crew members perished.[17] On 30 July, VB-129 Ventura B-9, flying over the South Atlantic, discovered the surfaced Type VIIC *U-604*, which was on its fifth patrol having sunk five Allied vessels. The Navy pilot released four bombs. The U-boat submerged but had sustained serious damage. On 4 August, a VB-107 Liberator discovered it again accompanied by two other U-boats, *U-185* and *U-172*. While *U-172* submerged, the other two remained surfaced. The B-24 made two successful attacks, and on the third approach, *U-185* shot it down, killing all ten crew members. The damage from the Ventura though, resulted in *U-604*'s scuttling on 11 August.[18] The crew lost fourteen dead, while thirty-one managed to transfer to *U-185*. For these individuals, they experienced only a temporary reprieve. As noted previously, American naval pilots from USS

Core sank that U-boat on 24 August.[19] On 4 October, American Venturas destroyed a third U-boat. VB-128 Ventura 'B' took off from Reykjavik and discovered the surfaced Type VIIC *U-279*, releasing three depth charges while flying at 50ft. All forty-eight crew members perished on what was the U-boat's first patrol, having no sinkings to its credit.[20]

The US Navy achieved two sinkings with its Mariner flying boat. On 3 August, less than 500 miles east of Barbados, a U-boat radioed a message to Germany, and twenty minutes later VP-205 Mariner P-6 radioed, 'Sighted submarine, making attack'. No one received any further communication from either combatant. Most likely, they delivered fatal blows against each other. Seven perished in the flying boat, while forty-seven died in the U-boat. *U-572*, a Type VIIC, had sunk six Allied vessels and damaged another one on nine patrols.[21] Another US Navy Mariner, P-2 of VP-74, successfully attacked Type IXC *U-161* with depth charges on 27 September off the Brazilian coast. All fifty-three perished. *U-161* had sunk seventeen Allied vessels on six patrols.[22]

Other Allied aircraft contributed to the anti-U-boat cause during these months besides the Liberators and those of the US Navy. Sunderland flying boats achieved five sinkings during this time. On 1 August, the RAF 228 Squadron's 'V' took off at 1450 hours from Pembroke Dock. At 2002 hours, the crew spotted surfaced Type VIIC *U-383* just west of the Bay of Biscay and attacked. German fire, described as 'accurate and rapid', forced the pilot, Flight Lieutenant S. White, to engage in 'violent evasive action', which disrupted the attack. On the second attempt, the Sunderland received damage to its starboard aileron and two holes around the front turret. Nevertheless, White flew over the U-boat and released seven depth charges. The resulting explosion 'enveloped' the U-boat as it 'listed heavily to port'. The flak damage sustained by the Sunderland prevented the large flying boat from re-engaging as the crew observed the submariners leaping into the sea. The Sunderland returned to base at 2350 hours, a nine-hour patrol. None of *U-383*'s fifty-two crew members survived. The U-boat had participated in four patrols and damaged on Allied vessel. White received the Distinguished Flying Cross for his actions that day.[23]

That same day, RAAF 10 Squadron Sunderland 'B' discovered surfaced Type VIIC *U-454* in the western Bay of Biscay. The flying boat approached the U-boat and the Germans hit the aircraft multiple times, causing an engine fire, but the Australian pilot maintained his course, traversed the target, released depth charges, and then crashed. Six Australians survived, the other six perished. The depth charge explosions sank the U-boat. Thirty-two died with the boat, while the sloop HMS

Kite rescued fourteen others, who became prisoners of war. *U-454* had participated in ten patrols, damaged two Allied vessels and sunk the Royal Navy destroyer HMS *Matabele*. Two British sailors survived this attack; over 200 did not.[24]

The next day, a British and an Australian Sunderland joined forces to attack *U-106*, one of the long-range Type IXB boats. This U-boat had enjoyed a stellar career under three commanders. Its crew had sunk twenty-one Allied vessels and damaged three others during ten patrols. While crossing the Bay of Biscay on its tenth patrol, a British Wellington damaged it. Although it escaped, the commander decided to rendezvous with German torpedo boats and return to base. While approaching the boats, two Sunderlands – RAF 228 Squadron 'N' and RAAF 461 Squadron 'M' – discovered and attacked the surfaced U-boat together at 2010 hours. The Sunderlands' bombs halted the U-boat's forward momentum, and it commenced sinking by the stern. Thirty minutes after the assault, the U-boat exploded. Twenty-two perished while the torpedo boats retrieved thirty-six men from the water.[25]

Two days later, on 4 August, another Sunderland struck, this time a Canadian one. *U-489*, a highly valuable *milchkuh* Type XIV, floated on the surface 200 miles south-east of Iceland while recharging its batteries. It had been designed by Dönitz as a refueller and not intended for combat, but was armed with anti-aircraft guns. Sunderland Mk. III 'J' from the Royal Canadian Air Force's 423 Squadron slipped from the Northern Ireland waters of RAF Castle Archdale at 0455 hours and at 0910 hours it spotted the U-boat from 4,000ft at 4 miles and descended to 600ft, before attacking at 50ft. At 300yd away, the flying boat sustained significant damage to its aileron controls. Nevertheless, the Canadian pilot, Flight Officer Albert A. Bishop, flew over the stationary U-boat and released six depth charges on target. Now, Bishop faced not only control issues but also a fire in both the 'wing root and the galley'. With ailerons and trimming tab controls unresponsive, he attempted an 'immediate forced landing'. The flying boat 'bounced' twice on the surface but on the third one the 'port wing dropped.' With the wing tip float now in contact with the water, the aircraft cartwheeled. Six of the eleven crew members escaped the burning mass. The surviving British aircrew observed *U-489* sink and its crew climbed into the Sunderland's life rafts. British destroyers HMS *Castleton* and *Orwell* retrieved six Britons and fifty-three Germans. The U-boat crew lost only one member; the Sunderland crew lost five. Thus ended *U-489*'s first patrol. Bishop, who survived this day, received the Distinguished Flying Cross.[26]

Two months later, on 8 October, another Sunderland Mk. III from 423 Squadron spotted a U-boat and sank it. Sunderland 'J' departed RAF Castle Archdale at 1027 hours and met a convoy at 1734 hours, approximately halfway between Iceland and Ireland in the North Atlantic. The Senior Naval Officer ordered the aircraft to 'patrol astern' of the vessels. Emerging from a 'low cloud', at 1936 hours the crew discovered the wake of a fully surfaced Type VIIC boat – *U-610* – just 100yd off its port bow. The four-engine aircraft flew over the U-boat and the rear gunner 'opened fire'. The Germans fired at the Canadian aircraft as the pilot, Flying Officer A.H. Russell, 'banked' the Sunderland 'as soon as possible' while descending from 500 to 100ft to attack from the 'first position obtainable'. The crew attempted to drop four depth charges while passing over the U-boat but only three released, while the fourth 'hung up'. The second and third depth charges successfully 'straddled' the conning tower and the explosion of the second depth charge lifted the boat 15 to 20ft. When the 'plume' from the third depth charge's explosion disappeared, the U-boat had vanished under the surface. Russell swung around for a second run but 'nothing could be seen other than 15 live bodies and much debris floating' amidst an 'oil patch'. The flying boat splashed down in its home waters at 0248 hours on the 9th after a sixteen-hour mission. *U-610* had sunk four Allied vessels and damaged another one on four patrols. All fifty-one crew members perished.[27]

A U-boat did down an Allied Sunderland during this time. On 17 October, RCAF 422 Squadron 'S' found two surfaced U-boats, Type VIICs *U-448* and *U-221*, in the mid-Atlantic. While closing on *U-448*, the pilot dropped the depth charges too early, missed the target and swung around for another attempt. On his second passing, two of the three depth charges fell, causing significant damage to *U-448*, while anti-aircraft fire also struck the Sunderland. The crew managed to fly the aircraft to the convoy, where it landed. Of the Canadian crew, seven survived but four perished. *U-448* escaped, although the damage it had sustained required it to immediately return to base.[28]

Wellingtons achieved four sinkings, one from 344 Squadron, a squadron entirely manned by French pilots and crew.[29] On 18 August, one of its aircraft discovered the surfaced Type VIIC *U-403* in the Atlantic just off the western African coast, near Dakar. Depth charges sank the U-boat with the loss of all forty-nine crew members.[30]

No. 179 Squadron Wellingtons were attributed the other three to be sunk. On 12 September, approximately 100 miles east of Gibraltar in the Mediterranean Sea, two of the unit's Wellingtons spotted the surfaced Type VIIC *U-617*. The British attacked at night, and made effective use of their Leigh Lights. Wellington 'P' had taken off from Gibraltar at 2039 hours on the 11th and arrived at its assigned area at 2157 hours. Fifty minutes past midnight, the crew detected a contact 8½ miles away. The pilot altered course to close in on the target. While flying at 200ft, and less than ¾ mile from the target, the British sighted a U-boat 'silhouette' by 'moonlight'. Once ½ mile away, the crew turned on the Leigh Light and 'illuminated' the fully surfaced *U-617*. The Germans initiated fire on the rapidly approaching aircraft but the Wellington sustained no hits. Flying over the U-boat at an altitude of 30 to 40ft, the crew released six depth charges. The U-boat followed a circular pattern while leaving a trail of oil. From the bomber crew's perspective, the Germans appeared 'unable to steer a definite course'. At 0130 hours though, the crew members apparently completed some repairs so that *U-617* proceeded at 1 knot on a steady course. At 0318 hours, a second Wellington, 'J', from the same squadron arrived, allowing 'P' to return to Gibraltar. It did so at 0445 hours, concluding an eight-hour mission.[31]

'J' had took off at 0223 hours on 12 September and received word at 0258 hours that 'Enemy sub. working for neutral waters position 35.25N 0321W. course 180°' at 2 knots. The British captain set course and detected a contact at 0313 hours, 3½ miles away. The pilot 'at once turned to starboard and began homing onto the contact up-moon and up-wind losing height'. At 1½ miles out, the crew spotted a 'dark object' and when at ½ miles, at 150ft, they activated the Leigh Light. It illuminated the fully surfaced *U-617*, which was travelling at 3 knots. Both antagonists fired upon each other until, at 0315 hours, the Wellington roared over the U-boat at 80ft and dropped six depth charges at a speed of 160 knots. However, German fire mortally wounded the rear gunner during this run, while swinging around to observe the U-boat, the crew noted 'flames in the conning tower'. The crew remained in contact with the rear gunner as he failed to provide any indication of his injuries, but at 0355 hours, they noted that he had died. The Wellington departed at 0400 hours, observing the U-boat ½ mile from the Spanish coast, stern down. The Germans managed to beach the heavily damaged U-boat on the Spanish Moroccan coast. Three Royal Navy vessels and multiple aircraft fired upon it and destroyed it. All forty-nine crew members escaped, and they were held by the Spanish government before their eventual return to Germany. *U-617* had sunk eleven Allied vessels on seven patrols.[32]

On 20 October, 179 Squadron Wellington 'Z' took off from Gibraltar at 1900 hours. Once on patrol, the crew detected a contact at 11 miles away in the Mediterranean off the south-east Spanish coast. The pilot immediately changed course for the target and descended. The crew noticed a wave and at ¼ mile illuminated the Leigh Light, which shone on the fully surfaced *U-431*, travelling at 12 knots. The Type VIIC boat and aircraft traded fire as the bomber approached on its attack run. At 0157 hours the crew dropped six depth charges from 50ft. They next spotted the stricken U-boat at 200yd with no momentum. As the Wellington approached, *U-431* disappeared. The crew remained in the area for two hours but observed nothing. They returned to Gibraltar at 0645 hours. *U-431* lost all fifty-two hands in the sinking, having destroyed twelve Allied vessels and damaged another on fifteen patrols.[33]

Type VIIC *U-566* participated in two battles with Allied aircraft during this period. On 7 August, operating approximately 150 miles from the New Jersey coast, the crew downed two US Navy VB-128 PV-1 Venturas. A Mariner flying boat rescued two of the Americans, while eight perished. *U-566* suffered some damage but successfully returned to base. Its next cruise would unfold far differently. On 24 October, at 2133 hours, 179 Squadron Wellington 'A' rolled down the Gibraltar runway. Over three hours later, at 0106 hours off the northern Portuguese coast, the crew obtained a radar contact at 6 miles distance and the pilot, Sergeant D.M. Cornish, 'homed' in on the target. The second pilot and the navigator believed they had observed some 'bluish lights', so Cornish flew over the target and when directly above the sighting, he recognised a U-boat. Cornish immediately altered course to attack. When within ¼ mile, the crew illuminated the Leigh Light on the target, the front gunner engaged and the U-boat returned fire. Cornish flew over the U-boat and released six depth charges from 50ft, then ascended to 500ft while maintaining radar contact until 2 miles away. The boat remained surfaced and stationary. When the Wellington departed briefly and then returned, no trace of it remained. The crew returned to Gibraltar at 0753 hours. The Germans had scuttled *U-566* and a Spanish trawler rescued all of its forty-nine crew members. On eleven patrols, it had been credited with the sinking of seven Allied ships.[34]

U-boats did successfully fight during this time. On 25 September, 179 Squadron's 'F' departed Gibraltar at 1913 hours. Off the Portuguese coast, the crew found and struck Type VIIC *U-667* with depth charges but sustained anti-aircraft damage from the U-boat. At 2228 hours, British controllers received a 'SOS' message from the aircraft, but never heard anything further from the six-man crew. The following month, on 30 October, 612 Squadron's 'C' took off at 2332 hours from RAF Chivenor. Over the Bay of Biscay, the Wellington's crew found the surfaced Type VIIC *U-415* and guided itself to the target by its Leigh Light. Flying over the boat, they released four depth charges, which exploded and damaged the boat. However, anti-aircraft fire caused the bomber to crash into the sea, killing all six crew.[35]

Catalinas achieved only one sinking during this period. On 20 August, 259 Squadron's 'C', based at Natal, South Africa, discovered the surfaced Type IXD2 *U-197* just south of Madagascar and attacked with six depth charges. The damage prevented the U-boat from submerging, allowing the squadron's Catalina 'N' to arrive and attack it with six more depth charges. The second attack proved to be fatal. All sixty-six hands perished. *U-197* had sunk three Allied vessels and damaged another on its only patrol.[36]

Like the Catalinas, the Hudsons, which had proven so lethal previously, received credit for only one U-boat sinking during this time. Launching from Reykjavik at 0753 hours on 5 October, the crew of 269 Squadron's 'F' sighted the fully surfaced Type VIIC *U-336* at 0900 hours. The Hudson assaulted with rockets, which 'obliterated' the U-boat's bows and conning tower. Twenty seconds after the rockets were fired, the stern 'rose' from the surface until it reached a 45-degree angle, and then it slipped from view. The crew observed an oil patch, within which fifteen bodies floated. The Hudson remained on scene for ninety-three minutes, witnessed nothing, and departed. The crew landed at Iceland at 1512 hours, a seven-hour patrol. All fifty hands died in the attack. *U-336* sank only one Allied vessel on its four patrols.[37]

The Allied battle against the U-boats even extended to the Gulf of Oman. On 16 October, 244 Squadron Bristol Bisley 'O', a twin-engine ground support aircraft based on the Blenheim, took off from RAF Sharjah at 1330 hours. Over the Gulf of Oman, the crew sighted a long-range Type IXC/40 U-boat and released four depth charges. After five minutes, a considerable oil patch appeared. *U-533* had not sunk any Allied vessels on two patrols. Fifty-two men died; the British rescued one survivor after he spent over twenty-four hours on the surface.[38]

Allied aircraft had turned 1943 into a stunning reversal for Dönitz's boats. While Dönitz noted that anti-aircraft armament had resulted in favourable reports by U-boat captains in September, from October onward, 'the number of attacks by aircraft increased, and losses in consequence rose considerably'. The final two months would offer no reprieve. The Allied leadership would attend several critical meetings in December that would indicate how significantly the U-boat war had altered since the dark days at Casablanca in 1942. Dönitz's battle had now transformed into one between aircraft and U-boats, a conflict for which he had no effective strategy or weapons to prevail.[39]

Chapter 13

November–December 1943

During the last two months of 1943 the Allied air campaign continued to succeed, with the Liberators taking the leading role. The B-24s attacked six of the twelve U-boats destroyed by aircraft during this time. Allied forces totalled twenty U-boats destroyed at sea, resulting in aircraft contributing 60 per cent of the total, and Liberators' successes accounting for 30 per cent, nearly one-in-three of all Allied U-boat victories. However, the greatest insight regarding anti-submarine efforts during these months occurred not at sea, but on shore, with the Allied conferences that differed sharply from that in Casablanca in 1942. The Allies' altered attitude towards Dönitz's U-boats, as witnessed at the Sextant and the Eureka conferences, stemmed from the successful U-boat assaults, especially by Allied aircraft. The conferences well demonstrated that 1943 marked the turning point in the U-boat war. The hope with which Dönitz had greeted the new year with his new position and vastly increased influence had been dissipated by Allied aircraft during the long months that followed his promotion.

British Liberators successfully attacked two Nazi Type VIIC U-boats during this time. On 16 November, 86 Squadron Liberator Mk. III 'M' rendezvoused with its assigned convoy in the mid-North Atlantic at 0906 hours, and at 1025 hours the crew spotted *U-280* west of Ireland. The pilot, Flight Officer J.H. Bookless, initiated an 'immediate attack'. On approach, the nose gunner opened fire and scored hits on the conning tower as the U-boat remained on the surface and instituted 'tight turns to port'. German gun fire disabled the outer port engine and the depth charges 'overshot, so the aircraft prepared for a second attack'. Bookless swung the Liberator around and 'three minutes later' the nose gunner struck the conning tower multiple times while 'knocking out the forward gunner'. Yet, the depth charges overshot, with the 'nearest exploding 30ft from the hull'. Bookless remained in the area and 'a few minutes later the U-boat slowly submerged without any forward movement'. The aircraft loitered for over an hour and while the crew witnessed 'no evidence of damage', the attacks did sink *U-280*. The forty-nine crew members went down with the boat, which was on its first patrol having not engaged any Allied vessels.[1]

The following month, on the 13th, in the Bay of Biscay, 53 Squadron Liberator Mk. V 'B' began a 'Square search' hunt in the darkness at 0413 hours after the Allies suspected that a U-boat was operating in the area. The RAF had equipped Mk. V B-24s with radar, but this morning, the aircraft suffered both radar and intercom issues, resulting in only momentary contacts. This irregularity required the crew to use the Leigh Light for verification, an action that immediately brought the aircraft to the attention of *U-391*'s crew and they responded with machine gun fire. The crew 'switched off' the light and the pilot, Squadron Leader G. Crawford, 'manoeuvred to attack up moon'. The U-boat fire ceased, leading the crew to assume that the Germans had 'lost sight of the aircraft'. Crawford ordered the air gunners to hold their fire during approach, and they did not re-engage the U-boat until the German fire commenced again. At that point, the Liberator's gunners 'sprayed' the conning tower as the aircraft roared over the U-boat and 'scored a straddle with six depth charges'. The crew noted 'two bodies, apparently alive' in the water and obtained a momentary 'small, sharp Radar contact', which was 'suggestive' of a U-boat's 'bows or stern at the moment of plunging'. The U-boat flak had not injured any crew members, although they noticed a 'few bullet holes in the aircraft's hull'. All fifty-one crew members went down with the U-boat, which was on its maiden voyage and had not attacked any Allied shipping.[2]

British and American Liberators then co-operated on a U-boat attack. On 9 November off the Spanish Atlantic coast in the Bay of Biscay, a 612 Squadron Wellington 'B' obtained radar contact for Type VIIC *U-966* at 6 miles, and then made visual contact at 4 miles due to 'moonpath'. The crew avoided the use of their Leigh Light to reduce the possibility of detection. They struck with six depth charges and gun fire but the U-boat, while damaged, submerged. *U-966* later surfaced and two US Navy VP-105 Liberators attacked but failed to discharge their depth charges due to flak-damaged bomb bay doors. However, Navy VP-103 Liberator 'E' and VP-110 Liberator 'D' depth charged the boat, followed by Liberator 'D' from the RAF's 311 Squadron, with a Czechoslovakian crew, with a rocket assault. The extensive damage forced the German crew to scuttle the U-boat in Spanish coastal waters on 10 November. Forty-two crew members reached shore by Spanish boats or by swimming, while eight perished. *U-966*'s first patrol ended with no Allied vessels sunk.[3]

NOVEMBER–DECEMBER 1943

American Liberators also achieved solo fatal assaults. Three days later, on 12 November, in the Bay of Biscay, north of the Spanish coast, US Navy VB-103 Liberator 'C' spotted one of the long-range Type IXC boats, *U-508*, led by one of Dönitz's best officers. The U-boat commander, Georg Staats, had sunk fourteen ships on seven patrols and received one of Nazi Germany's highest honours, the Knight's Cross. The American pilot, Lieutenant (jg) Ralph B. Brownell, could not have known his opponent's reputation or skill when approaching the U-boat. In his last radio report, he stated, 'Am over enemy submarine in position ...' Neither the Germans nor the Allies heard from either the U-boat or the aircraft again. The following day, American aircraft searching the area discovered a small oil patch and a larger one separated by 5 miles. It may be presumed that the small oil slick marked the Liberator's final location and the larger oil was *U-508*'s last position. All fifty-seven U-boat crew and all ten on board the B-24 perished.[4]

On 5 November, two VB-107 Liberators co-operated in the destruction of a U-boat. Three hundred miles south-west of Ascension Island in the South Atlantic, a pair of US Navy PB4Ys patrolled the area and one of them spotted surfaced *U-848*, a long-range Type IXD2. The pilot of Liberator B-12 immediately engaged and released depth charges from 75ft. The other B-24, B-4, 200 miles away, arrived after thirty minutes and deposited several depth charges that further damaged the U-boat. Yet, it did not sink or submerge. Two USAAF B-25 Mitchells attacked later but their ordnance, dropped from 4,000ft, missed. The two Liberators from the initial attacks, having returned to base and rearmed, then returned to the scene and collaborated on attacks that destroyed the U-boat. All sixty-three crew members perished on *U-848*'s first patrol, having sunk only one Allied vessel.[5]

A U-boat had been reported off the western African coast on 17 November and VB-107 investigated. US Navy Liberators patrolled the area for a week before locating *U-849*. On 25 November, cloud cover permitted PB4Y-1 B-6 to ambush the U-boat and straddle it with six depth charges. The Americans witnessed the Germans abandon the boat after this attack, then saw it sink by the stern before it exploded. While the aircraft provided a life raft for the survivors, no one sighted them again. All sixty-three crew members perished in the battle. Thus ended *U-849*'s first patrol, having sunk no Allied vessels.[6]

Liberators did not escape this period unscathed. On 20 November, Type VIIC *U-618* shot down 53 Squadron Mk. V 'N' with the loss of all nine crew members. Type VIIC *U-648* downed two Allied aircraft in subsequent days. The crew hit RCAF 422 Squadron Sunderland 'G' on 20 November, causing the aircraft to crash one hour after the battle with the loss of all eleven crew. The following day, the U-boat crew successfully fought 53 Squadron B-24 Mk. V 'A'. During the aircraft's return to base, three engines stopped and the Liberator had to ditch. HMS *Lincolnshire* rescued the pilot, the only survivor of the eight-man crew, the following day. *U-648* did not have long to celebrate these victories. The U-boat transmitted its last report on 21 November and U-boat Command never heard from it again.[7]

A Flying Fortress delivered a fatal attack during this period. The British had finally received permission from the Portuguese government to operate from the Azores in 1943. In October, they prepared Lagens field for full operations, and the next month the Allies sank their first U-boat with an Azores-based aircraft. On 9 November, the pilot, Flight Officer R.P. Drummond of 220 Squadron Mk. II 'J', while flying to his assigned convoy in almost complete darkness, ordered the guns to be tested and immediately the 'front lookout sighted a surfaced' Type VIIC U-boat under the aircraft. The Germans commenced with 'heavy and fairly accurate' fire. The tail gunner replied with 'long bursts' at the conning tower. Drummond turned the plane to port and initiated an attack 'from stem to stern'. The air gunners scored multiple strikes on the conning tower and, as the four-engine aircraft swooped over the U-boat at 40ft, the crew deposited four depth charges. The U-boat ceased momentum after the attack, and appeared 'down by the stern with bows well clear of the water' as it 'developed a forty-five-degree list to port'. Drummond circled again and delivered another assault with three depth charges from 30ft. The explosions engulfed the U-boat and it then 'disappeared stern first'. The British may have seen ten to fifteen survivors. A 'large oil patch' and 'plenty of wreckage' appeared at the U-boat's last-known location. Thirty minutes later the crew saw 'a man swimming amongst the wreckage' and 'climbing a "K" type dinghy'. The RAF crew dropped 'a parachute bag with rations' and reported the sinking to the convoy's Senior Naval Officer, who responded, 'Well done.' None of the fifty-one crew members survived. *U-707* had sunk two Allied vessels on three patrols.[8]

Among the twin-engine aircraft, Wellingtons participated in three fatal sinkings during the last two months of the year. On 31 October, at 0113 hours, 179 Squadron Wellington 'R', flying in the night sky over the western Mediterranean, detected a surface contact at 2½ miles distance with their ASV radar. The pilot, Flying Officer A.H. Ellis, decided to fly over the target to visually confirm its identity and in so doing the crew determined that they had found a U-boat. Six miles later, Ellis turned the aircraft and approached the radar target again. The Wellington flew over the conning tower at 100ft and dropped six depth charges. For the next forty-five seconds, the damaged Type VIIC U-boat remained surfaced and then it disappeared. The British alerted the Royal Navy, whereupon HMS *Fleetwood*, *Bluebell*, and *Poppy* steamed to the area. Hours later, HMS *Witherington* detected the U-boat and a general and ineffective depth charge attack commenced. Later, *Fleetwood*, *Bluebell*, and *Poppy* found *U-340* on the surface and engaged. The U-boat dived deep and escaped the Royal Navy again. However, damage forced the German commander's hand and he surfaced on 2 November, abandoned the boat, scuttled it with charges, and then watched it sink. The crew lost one member, while Spanish trawlers rescued the other forty-seven. However, *Fleetwood*'s crew found the trawlers, boarded them, and transferred the Germans to the British sloop, which transported them to Gibraltar and they became prisoners of war. The British provided the Spanish with 'cigarettes and tobacco', while the Spanish reciprocated with 'fresh sardines'. *U-340* had not sunk any Allied vessels on its three patrols.[9]

In November, 179 Squadron's Wellingtons joined 220 Squadron's Fortresses at Lagens and achieved two sinkings from its Azores detachment. On the 18th, at 2243 hours, Wellington 'F' departed the island of Terceira. At 0202 hours, the pilot, Flight Officer D.F. McRae, rendezvoused with convoy MKS 30 5 miles to starboard in the Atlantic off the Portuguese coast. At 0216 hours, he began a search of the area to which the Allied vessels were heading. At 0340 hours, while at 1,000ft, the Wellington's ASV radar detected a contact 3 miles away off the port side. McRae altered course and, using the existing moonlight, identified the contact as a U-boat and attacked. To achieve 'surprise', he decided to assault without the Leigh Light. The British aircraft flew over the U-boat and dropped four depth charges at 0345 hours. The rear gunner observed multiple plumes from the explosions and *U-211* disappeared. All fifty-four hands perished. *U-211*, a Type VIIC boat, had sunk two Allied vessels on five patrols.[10]

On the 28th, 179 Squadron struck again. Wellington 'H' took off into the night sky from Lagens at 0102 hours. At 0511 hours, approximately 200 miles east of the Azores, its ASV radar detected a contact 3½ miles to starboard. The twin-engine aircraft closed the distance and, when on target, activated its Leigh Light. The pilot then roared over the U-boat and attacked with six depth charges. *U-542*'s forward momentum dropped from 14 knots to zero. It remained motionless for two to three minutes but the British lost sight of it after five minutes. All fifty-six crew members perished in the attack. The long-range Type IXC/40 *U-542* had not sunk any Allied vessels on its only patrol.[11]

The RAF lost a Wellington due to U-boat flak during this time. On 27 November, 172 Squadron 'O', which had departed from Lagens, found surfaced Type VIIC *U-764* in the eastern Atlantic and made two attacking passes. Apparently during the second one, the Germans caused terminal damage to the Wellington, which crashed. Five of the six-man crew perished, with the Germans retrieving one as a prisoner of war.[12]

The Allies also lost two other twin-engine aircraft, specifically Bristol Beaufighters, to anti-aircraft fire from VIIF *U-1062*. Eight RCAF aircraft of 144 and 404 Squadrons found a German minesweeper with a U-boat off the Norwegian coast, and attacked both targets. While four aircraft carried and deployed their torpedoes, all missed their targets. The U-boat's flak destroyed two of the Beaufighters resulting in the deaths of four crew members and *U-1062* escaped with no significant damage.[13]

US Navy carrier aircraft, after an impressive showing in the previous period, destroyed only two U-boats during the last two months of 1943, but one of them had achieved a remarkable record. *U-172*, a long-range Type IXC boat, had sunk twenty-six Allied vessels on six patrols. These successes included a hunt in the Caribbean during the 'Second Happy Time', when it destroyed nine Allied vessels in that area alone. On 12 December, its long death throes began when sighted by a USS *Bogue* VC-19 Squadron Avenger pilot. A 500lb bomb was the first damage it would receive in this battle, but it managed to submerge after this attack. Later that night, it surfaced and USS *G.E. Badger* detected it. As the destroyer closed the distance and fired, the U-boat dived and the Americans initiated a depth charge assault. Another destroyer, USS *DuPont*, joined the hunt but with no other evidence of the U-boat's presence, the Americans departed. Another *Bogue* aircraft spotted oil on the surface and three destroyers commenced another depth charge assault. Finally, at 1016 hours, *U-172* surfaced and started firing at the Navy vessels. The destroyers replied and obliterated the conning tower. Five minutes after surfacing, the highly successful U-boat sank. The Americans rescued forty-six crew members, while thirteen died.[14]

Seven days later, on 20 December, a *Bogue* VC-19 Avenger pilot flying above the mid-Atlantic over 600 miles south-west of the Azores, found another long-range boat, Type IXD2 *U-850*, on the surface and attacked. Yet when in position to release his bomb, the mechanism failed. The pilot remained in the area calling for additional aircraft. When four more appeared, the U-boat crew failed to notice. Two 500lb bombs struck and *U-850* slipped from the surface by the stern. None of the sixty-six crew members survived. Thus ended *U-850*'s short career; it was on its first patrol, with no Allied vessels sunk.[15]

This was all the successful Allied air assaults against Hitler's U-boats for the November to December period. The change in the U-boat war can be measured by the increase in the number of U-boat fatalities, not all of which the Allies could tally. However, the change in the Allies' perspective on the U-boat war can be determined through their own words during the two conferences of this period: Sextant Conference (Cairo, Egypt), in 22–26 November, and the Eureka Conference (Tehran, Iran) 28 November–1 December. The discussions commenced in early November and extended into mid-December.

These gatherings in 1943 stand in stark contrast to the Casablanca Conference the previous year. While the British maintained an unrelenting focus on the U-boat threat in Morocco, in these conferences, the overall issue had dropped from significance. While still mentioned and discussed, the Allies' relentless assaults against the U-boats, especially by aircraft, had shifted the Battle of the Atlantic from Nazi dominance to Allied dominance, as the conference deliberations prove.

Pressure existed for the Allies to find common ground. The Quebec conference held on 11–14 August had failed. To assure success, in preparation for the future meetings, the Combined Chiefs of Staff, representing both American and British leadership, issued a 'Basic Policies' document of 6 November. Of the first five points, none referred to Dönitz's boats. Under the sixth point, 'Basic Undertakings in Support of Over-all Strategic Concept', the Allies outlined eleven subpoints. Of these, U-boats received mention in only the third one, as the Allied leadership agreed to 'maintain vital overseas lines of communication, with particular emphasis on the defeat of the U-boat menace'.[16]

The following day, 7 November, the British issued a memorandum entitled 'Progress Report on the U-Boat War – September–October 1943'. With regard to the 'U-Boat Trend', the British acknowledged that Dönitz had retreated from the North Atlantic in May 1943, but he did manage one foray on 19 September when a pack exceeding fifteen U-boats had hunted in that area with replenishment from supply boats. However, they also described U-boat activity in other areas as 'sporadic', including the Indian Ocean, Brazilian coast, West African coast, Caribbean, American eastern seaboard, and Canadian waters.

The British noted the high effectiveness of anti-submarine aircraft. They mentioned that 'evasive routing', a tactic by which the Allies directed convoys to areas of limited U-boat activity, had succeeded in preventing a pack from intercepting convoys from mid-September to 7 October. The British acknowledged that U-boats managed to engage convoy SC 143 but torpedoed only one merchant vessel and an escort, while the Royal Navy believed that three U-boats had been sunk. U-boats battled two additional convoys during October but sank only one Allied vessel, while the Allies claimed six U-boats sunk. Most critically, the British acknowledged that, in reference to the 'above convoy', the air co-operation was 'very satisfactory and the U-boats suffered severely on each attempt to attack'. With regard to naval operations, the Royal Navy now had three escort carriers operating in the area, and the American carriers in the North Atlantic 'have been most successful'.[17]

They also noted that the U-boats had inaugurated a new policy to avoid Allied aircraft at all costs. For example, the British noticed that U-boat commanders no longer engaged Allied aircraft on the surface. Additionally, U-boats now surfaced for 'a minimum period by night' for the purpose of recharging their batteries. This new practice significantly increased the time necessary to cross such 'transit areas' like the Bay of Biscay, and this served as a powerful compliment to Allied air forces that the Germans had yielded in the battle against aircraft. The U-boat commanders recognised that they could not fight the Allied aircraft.

The British also provided some evaluation of anti-submarine aircraft. They admitted that aircraft sightings in the Bay of Biscay had decreased precipitously, and blamed the lack of Leigh searchlights and the Wellington's 'insufficient range'. The Liberators, although not mentioned, significantly exceeded the Wellingtons in range. The British also called for an augmentation of Leigh Light aircraft, especially in the Very Long Range aircraft, such as the Liberators. And finally, they called for a strategy of 'flooding' by which 'such vigorous and continuous flying' would 'force' German commanders to 'exhaust' their batteries due to constant diving at the appearance of Allied aircraft. The British especially desired to implement this practice in the Bay of Biscay, where the vast majority of U-boats would cross both outbound and inbound on their patrols.

In regards to 'Future Policy', the British asserted that Dönitz's U-boats had returned to the North Atlantic 'in considerable force' and would maintain their presence 'until their losses become unacceptably high'. However, they acknowledged that 'both aircraft and escorts' had 'roughly handled' them. The British did hope that the U-boat losses 'are already approaching the breaking limit' but instead of heralding that moment, they warned that this may result in a new U-boat strategy.

Their primary hope still rested with aircraft. The British stated that when Very Long Range anti-submarine aircraft could commence operating from the Azores, 'we may have great scope for evasive routing' between these islands and Iceland, where they had already established a significant and effective anti-submarine aircraft force with Liberators. They hoped that with the Azores aircraft, the Allies could 'secure the Atlantic trade routes by means of evasion'. Two transatlantic options, both covered by aircraft, would significantly advance the Allied cause.

In this regard, the British, recognising the overall supremacy of aircraft, advocated for sending a 'selected convoy' on the 'most favourable route for air cover, and efficient surface and air escort'. In so doing, they confessed a significant alteration in their approach from the previous year. The British were 'prepared to accept battle with the U-boats' with the 'confidence that we shall be masters of the situation whatever circumstances arise'. They contended that now 'the time has only just arrived when it is considered reasonable to accept the increased risk of encountering U-boats'. The new British position, of such assurance, appeared to encourage engagement battles with the U-boats that had been so feared in years past. 'It is by these means,' they claimed, that 'we hope finally to break the morale of the U-boat service, and encompass its destruction. If successful,' the memorandum concluded, 'it may well prove a decisive factor in the defeat of the German High Command and the armed forces of the Reich.'[18]

The Americans developed a report on 8 November to discuss their perspective on the anti-submarine situation. After devoting some attention to destroyers and destroyer escorts, they concluded that the Allies had some shortcomings. The Americans did not have sufficient numbers of Venturas or Liberators for squadrons of fifteen aircraft. However, while mentioning the far inferior Venturas, the Americans focus remained clearly on the B-24s. They acknowledged, that without additional B-24s, even maintaining twelve Liberators for each of the eight squadrons would be challenging. In concluding this topic, they confessed, 'this plane shortage may adversely affect our ability to meet emergencies'.[19]

In regards to future changes, the Americans noted several improvements to aircraft capability. First, the Allies continued to install rocket projectile equipment for anti-submarine attacks. They had also started installing intercept receivers to detect U-boat radar. The Americans selected a B-24 to first receive such a device for testing. Additionally, limited numbers of aircraft now carried sono-radio buoys and, with regard to the U-boat surface engagements, the Allies now sought, in response to U-boat flak, 'increased forward firing power, additional armor and leak-proof tanks' for their aircraft.[20]

U-boats received no further mention for ten days until an 18 November memorandum, which, in its first point, recommended the Azores Islands facilities be employed not only for 'intensified sea and air operations against the U-boat' but also for 'air ferry operations'. Following this statement, the memorandum discusses the 'Combined Bomber Offensive' and then multiple points regarding Operation Overlord. Twelve subjects comprised the memorandum, of which the U-boats received some of the least attention.[21]

The only other mention of U-boats in the notes demonstrated the radical British change of attitude towards Dönitz's weapons, especially in regard to the upcoming Normandy invasion. They noted several measures would be implemented to allocate more naval vessels for future planned invasions, especially the redistribution of destroyers from the Home Fleet and the Atlantic Fleet. The British even admitted that they would withdraw 'nearly all escorts from the Atlantic and Home Commands' due to the 'diminishing' U-boat danger and 'a possible increase in shipping losses may have to be accepted'. With regard to the British escort carriers, they accepted redeployment from the U-boat duties. The Royal Navy could, if the Allies required 'carrier-borne fighter support', withdraw seven escort carriers from the Atlantic area and re-equip them with RAF fighters for support of the French invasion. This marked an extraordinary retreat from the British position twelve months earlier in Casablanca.[22]

However, what the British offered and what they failed to offer provided the most telling lesson. Churchill would withdraw Royal Navy destroyers for the invasion of Europe. He would further withdraw escort carriers as well. Yet, the British never offered to redeploy any Liberators, or any Coastal Command aircraft. The British well knew which weapon led to victory in the U-boat war and they would not surrender a single one, even for the most critical Allied operation of the European theatre.

The Liberators appear as a focus only once in the notes, and it is the British who, as they had twelve months before at the other African conference, requested more of them, specifically with regard to the Azores. They required three squadrons, of which two would be RAF, and the Allies should create a new US B-24 squadron that would replace the inferior Lockheed Hudsons. In this manner, the British would maintain control of a majority of the squadrons and, if accepted, would bring a new American squadron of Liberators, their preferred anti-submarine aircraft, to the conflict.

The memorandums not only conveyed the British change of attitude, but the meeting minutes also demonstrated the Allied leaders' shift as well. In fact, in the minutes covering multiple days of deliberations at the two conferences, the Allies discussed the U-boat issue on only one occasion. On the meeting of Monday, 6 December, beginning at 1930 hours, at the Villa Kirk in Cairo, with both the President and Prime Minister present after their return from the Eureka Conference in Iran, the two leaders discussed the 'agreed summary of conclusions'. They had some discussion regarding the 'Emergency Return to the Continent', Southeast Asia Command, and Chinese representation. Churchill expressed thanks to the Americans for their support for Operation Anvil, the Allied invasion of southern France, which he contended would assist in the success of Operation Overlord, the Allied invasion of northern France. And then finally, the Prime Minister inquired as to whether the 'draft communique on the U-boat war' had received American approval. Admiral King indicated that it had.[23]

And that would mark the last time that U-boats received mention in the minutes for the Sextant and the Eureka conferences. The Allies discussed the topic only once, and as a topic of among many at that meeting. The papers and the minutes exceed 600 pages but the U-boat menace, while clearly noted, had slipped from significance. It represented a titanic change from the previous year at Casablanca, when the U-boat threat dominated the discussion. In 1944 and 1945, ships would be sunk, U-boats destroyed, aircraft lost, but the Allies, with their aircraft, now had the offensive weaponry to defeat Dönitz. The desperation of Casablanca had dissipated with the Liberators, to the extent that the Allies considered steaming the convoys into known U-boat packs with the confidence that they would prevail. The year 1943 had truly defined the turning point in the U-boat war, and Dönitz and his Führer could only view the future with trepidation as the Allied aircraft continued to hunt their highly vulnerable U-boats in the last two years of the war.

Chapter 14

B-24s: January–May 1944

The U-boat sinkings during the first five months of 1944 demonstrate the radical change in the U-boat war. From 1942 through 1943 Allied aircraft attacked and sank U-boats in multiple theatres, but the area where Allied aircraft found and destroyed U-boats in 1944 had decreased considerably. And so during this period, the Liberator crews, which had dominated the airspace in the North Atlantic, managed only six successes. The B-24s found themselves overshadowed by other Allied aircraft including British Swordfishes, American Avengers, British Wellingtons and the Catalinas.

Coastal Command's poor distribution of B-24 squadrons deserves the primary blame for the Liberators' low numbers. Specifically, the handling of its two most experienced, and most lethal B-24 squadrons, 86 and 120. The RAF continued to employ the 120 Squadron from Iceland in an area where U-boat activity had fallen drastically. In January, the squadron's pilots, despite flying on two-thirds of the days, sighted only two U-boats and did not make any attacks.

The next four months unfolded dismally for these men. In February, 120 Squadron operated on all but four days, with all but two flights originating and landing in Iceland. The Liberators discovered only two U-boats, and in both instances, attacks could not commence before the boats escaped. For March, again flying from Iceland, the B-24s found three U-boats, and made unsuccessful attacks on two of them. In April, now recognising the North Atlantic waters as poor hunting grounds, the RAF moved the squadron to RAF Ballykelly. Still, this new assignment did not result in significant action, with only one failed U-boat attack. Flying from the same base in May provided no change as the B-24s sighted only one U-boat. The RAF had 120 Squadron flying from the wrong bases and over the wrong area.

No. 86 Squadron fared no better. In January, its aircraft flew from Ballykelly and operated off the Irish coast, not discovering a single

U-boat. For February, the squadron originated some flights further south at St Eval. The change in location proved to be a failure; the squadron's Liberators found no U-boats in February. In March, operating from Ballykelly, Reykjavik, and St Eval in areas far west of the Bay of Biscay, north of Scotland, and around Iceland, the B-24s encountered no targets. For April, the RAF decided to move 86 Squadron to Reykjavik, where a majority of its flights originated, but, again, the crews did not encounter any U-boats. Despite the obvious U-boat inactivity in the Icelandic area, 86 Squadron continued to operate from Iceland in May and its crew sighted only one German submarine.

U-boats operated in significant numbers in two areas during this time: the Bay of Biscay and off the Norwegian coast. Both offered ideal hunting grounds as Allied aircraft had the opportunity to strike U-boats, typically surfaced, as they commenced a patrol or returned to port on its conclusion. It should come as no surprise that the only two RAF Liberator victories transpired in one of these areas, namely off Norway. In May, 59 Squadron achieved these two victories. It had operated from Ballykelly in January, February, March and April, patrolling west of Ireland, and had encountered only a single U-boat, which the B-24 attacked unsuccessfully. Coastal Command finally, apparently, recognising the futility of operating in that area, reassigned 59 Squadron to patrol off the Norwegian coast towards late May. Then, the squadron achieved two fatal sinkings in only two weeks of patrolling their new area.

On 24 May, Liberator Mk. V 'S' took off from Ballykelly at 1956 hours. At 0623 hours, 100 miles off the Norwegian coast, the crew visually spotted a surfaced U-boat accompanied by a German surface vessel. The pilot, Squadron Leader B.A. Sisson, patiently awaited an opportunity in the rain squall, and then bore in. Both the U-boat and the surface vessel fired on the B-24, which replied with its own guns on both targets. Sisson flew over the Type VIIC U-boat and released six 250lb depth charges, but two of them failed to drop. The now damaged *U-990* swung to port, leaving a large oil patch behind it, and the surface vessel headed for the stricken U-boat. A little over ninety minutes later, 'S' encountered *U-990* again at 0803 hours and Sisson dived again but the target disappeared underwater when the aircraft arrived and the British crew dropped no ordnance. Their first strike proved to be fatal, though. Fifty-three crew members escaped alive, including nineteen previously rescued from the fatally stricken *U-476*, while twenty perished. *U-990* had sunk one Allied destroyer on four patrols.[1]

On 27 May, Liberator 'S', with a different crew, detected a radar contact at 15 miles. They tracked the target until, at 3 miles, they lost contact.

However, when the B-24 emerged from cloud cover at 200ft, they sighted fully surfaced Type VIIC/41 *U-292*. The British flew 'directly over' the conning tower and released six depth charges. The U-boat's stern submerged quickly, lifting the bows from the surface. A minute later, they observed the U-boat on the surface, stationary, and then it disappeared on 'an even keel'. The British later saw an oil patch. All fifty-one crew members perished. *U-292* had not sunk any Allied vessels on this, its first and only patrol.[2]

The real battle between the Allied Liberators and Hitler's U-boats transpired in the Bay of Biscay region, and west of Ireland, the typical transit route for the submarines departing and returning to the Bay. The failure of Coastal Command to concentrate in these areas cannot be attributed to ignorance. The RAF well knew Dönitz's fondness for his French Atlantic bases, and that the vast majority of U-boats operated from them. Had the British inundated these critical areas with B-24s, its most lethal aircraft, instead of assigning them to non-contested waters, these five months could have unfolded far differently for the Allies. Instead, it assigned one of the most inexperienced Liberator squadrons, 53, and the Nazis delivered a frightful toll on the RAF over the Bay. During these five months, U-boats shot down five B-24s, four from 53 Squadron, and one Halifax, and these units failed to deliver any fatal assaults in these areas.

No. 53 Squadron's history prior to and during this time period foreshadowed the defeats in which it would suffer. First, it had only converted to Leigh Lights in October, which provided precious limited time to train before engaging in the most hotly contested region during the opening months of 1944. Admittedly, the squadron had destroyed two U-boats in the Bay area prior to this period, but the Germans won every battle against the unit during the January–May time period. In some U-boat victories the Liberator escaped without casualties; in others, especially within the Bay, the toll reached far higher. On 6 January at 0643 hours, a Liberator Mk. V being flown by Flight Officer R.D. Hall over the Bay area began pursuing a radar contact 10 miles away. As the range decreased, the crew sighted a fully surfaced U-boat. However, the Germans responded 'immediately' with 'accurate flak' that smashed the 'generator panel, the number 3 engine, the Leigh Light and the intercom'. The U-boat crew could not have aimed better to disable a B-24. Hall admitted that, with this damage, 'the aircraft could not deliver an attack', therefore he returned to base.

That same day, a Liberator Mk. V commanded by Flight Lieutenant Le Maistre obtained a radar contact at 2350 hours, 37 miles away.

When the four-engine aircraft closed the range to 18 miles, the crew spotted the U-boat and swooped over the target at 250ft, dropping four depth charges. The British noted no damage, which was not surprising since the attack had been conducted from such a height, as compared with previous B-24 attacks in which the depth charges fell from as little as 50ft. The crew then obtained a second contact from 2 miles away and the Liberator attacked this target with four depth charges from 250ft with no results observed. However, the German flak hit the bomb bay rear door and 'control surfaces', which, in LeMaistre's opinion, 'compelled' a return to base.

These defeats should have served as warning to both the squadron and the RAF that more of these battles, with far worse conclusions, could occur in the Bay. Additionally, another fact the RAF overlooked was that on one January day, 53 Squadron had encountered the same number of U-boats that both 120 and 86 Squadron had discovered in the entire month of January. However, halfway through the month, the RAF sent 53 Squadron to Ballykelly, away from the Bay, where, of course, the squadron encountered no U-boats while flying above northern waters.

In February, the inexperienced squadron split flights from St Eval and Ballykelly. The St Eval flights, covering the Bay of Biscay, proved to be the most opportune and the most dangerous. Liberator Mk. V 'F' departed St Eval at 2230 hours on the 3rd and at 0811 hours the next day, the crew sent a 'flash report' indicating that they intended to assault a U-boat. The squadron report then stated that the command heard 'nothing further' and that the B-24 'failed to return'. 'F' had discovered and fought Type VIIC *U-763*, on its maiden patrol, and the U-boat's flak had brought down the B-24, which crashed into the Bay with the loss of all nine crew members.[3] The next day, 5 February, Liberator Mk. V 'D' from St Eval found *U-763* and attacked with five 250lb depth charges as the sixth failed to release. Although the crew straddled the U-boat's wake, they observed no damage. However, the British did describe the U-boat's defence as 'intense flak' that, fortunately for this B-24 crew, resulted in only a few tailplane holes. *U-763*'s encounters with Allied aircraft had not finished. While continuing to head east for its French base, the Germans fought off 172 Squadron Wellington 'M'. Later, 502 Squadron Halifax 'R' engaged and the U-boat notched its second aircraft victory as it shot down the four-engine bomber, which crashed into the Bay with the loss of the eight-man crew. After these four days of battle, *U-763* arrived safely at port on the 7th.[4]

During the remainder of the month, despite St Eval's ideal location for operating over the Bay, the squadron's flights focused on the waters west of Ireland, but nevertheless, discovered five U-boats. However, the squadron's aircraft engaged all of these unsuccessfully. On the 10th, B-24 Mk. V 'G' dropped six depth charges from 70ft on a U-boat and then immediately hit another one with two depth charges from 50ft. The crew noticed no damage to the submarines in these assaults. On the 16th, Liberator Mk. V 'U', suddenly obtained a radar contact at 3½ miles distance, seeming to indicate a 'just surfaced' U-boat. The B-24 immediately commenced its approach and descent from 1,500ft. Two miles from the target, the crew spotted the surfaced U-boat. From 100ft, the pilot released six depth charges. Four fell, but despite the successful straddle, the U-boat submerged and escaped. On the 18th and 19th, Mk. V 'S' fought two U-boats. The B-24 released six depth charges on the first one from 150ft but all missed. The crew attacked the second one with two depth charges but did not observe any results. In both instances, the flak 'intensity' resulted in no damage to the aircraft. On the 20th, the crew of Mk. V 'D' engaged what they considered to be two U-boats. The flak shattered the number three engine and injured a crew member, preventing an assault. The pilot struggled to bring the aircraft to base and, due to the U-boat attack, had to land without the nose wheel, which he managed successfully.

In March, the squadron engaged two U-boats, both unsuccessfully. At 0113 hours on the 6th, Mk. V 'V' obtained a radar contact at 17 miles distance and headed for the target. At ¾ mile, the crew activated the Leigh Light and spotted a surfaced U-boat 'under the starboard wing'. Flak hit the aircraft, the pilot swung to starboard and released the depth charges. The explosions failed to significantly damage the U-boat, so the pilot attempted a second run. The Liberator's gunners hit the target but German flak 'disabled the number one engine, forcing a return to base'. The U-boat escaped. On the 11th, west of Ireland, Liberator Mk. V 'C' began obtaining intermittent radar contact at 0413 hours at 11 miles distance. Eventually, the crew visually sighted the U-boat and dropped depth charges, but all fell 50ft from the U-boat. Although the crew observed oil patches, the U-boat had escaped.

Five 53 Squadron Liberators had engaged U-boats in April, and in two instances, U-boats had shot them down. The squadron, now flying exclusively from St Eval, had now focused on the Bay. Still, it had not acquired the necessary experience and struggled to deliver fatal assaults and avoid fatal flak fire. At 2324 hours on the 6th, Mk. V 'N' obtained a radar contact and when the crew activated the Leigh Light at 2337 hours, they sighted not one, but two fully surfaced U-boats. Due to miscommunication between the pilot and navigator, instead of flying over one, the B-24 flew between both targets and received significant flak. The German fire damaged the bomb bay doors and the beam gunner suffered a leg wound. The inoperable bomb bay doors necessitated a return to base without any more attempted attack runs.

On the early morning of the 10th, Mk. V 'A' homed on a radar contact beginning at 0257 hours, and five minutes later it sighted a surfaced U-boat. The pilot, Flying Officer W.J. Irving, bore in but failed to track over the target, so he initiated a second run. This time, all the depth charges failed to release. During the third run, flak hit the bomb bay and damaged 'hydraulics and instruments'. The damage prevented any further offensive action and Irving decided to return to base. However, the crew's problems had not passed. With the hydraulics not functioning, Irving could not operate the flaps or the brakes, and the crew had to lower the wheels manually. To Irving's credit, he landed the wounded four-engine aircraft and none of his crew were injured.

On the 16th, B-24 Mk. V 'H' departed St Eval at 2215 hours. At 0126 hours, the crew reported that they had arrived at their assigned location over the Bay. Then they made another report at 0457 hours, and nothing further. The crew had found Type VIIC *U-993* and on approach, flak had struck the Liberator. The Germans noticed a flaming port engine when it flew over the conning tower. The aircraft released three bombs, which caused no damage, crashed in the Bay of Biscay, with the loss of all eleven crew members.[5] Just sixty minutes after this battle, 53 Squadron Mk. V 'H' roared over Type IXC/40 *U-546* and released six depth charges that caused little damage. However, the U-boat flak downed the B-24 for the loss of all nine crew members, bringing to four the number of 53 Squadron Liberators shot down by U-boats during these five months.[6]

For May, the final month of this period, 53 Squadron continued to patrol the Bay of Biscay and, although the unit lost no B-24s this month, it achieved no sinkings either. The Liberators found only three U-boats in this area despite the effective use of radar and flying at night, a time when U-boats operated on the surface. The only battle fought this month was in the early morning of the 3rd and involved Mk. V 'S'. The crew obtained a radar contact at 0337 hours at 13 miles distance and the pilot approached the target. When at a mile from the contact, two crew members spotted a U-boat and the British assaulted it with six depth charges from 250ft. The dropped ordnance straddled the target's stern. The B-24 monitored the U-boat from 'astern' until it moved in for a second run. This time, the radar contact 'split' and the crew spotted another U-boat, which the British attacked with the two remaining depth charges, again at 250ft. The B-24 escaped with no damage, but it had not delivered a fatal strike to either U-boat. It had been a disappointing five months for 53 Squadron.

The other British Liberator destroyed by U-boats during this period came from 224 Squadron. This group of men would, by the number of U-boat fatalities, become the third most lethal anti-submarine Allied squadron of the war. During the first five months of 1944, these B-24s patrolled the Bay of Biscay regularly from their St Eval base. While the squadron sighted and attacked numerous U-boats during this time, unlike months before and after, they did not destroy any U-boats. The RAF required more than two B-24 squadrons to patrol this area regularly in order to battle U-boats over these target-rich waters. Nevertheless, while the squadron recorded no sinkings, unlike 53 Squadron, the Germans managed to shoot down only one of its Liberators. On 19 March, 'F' departed St Eval at 2105 hours and encountered Type VIIC *U-256* in the Bay. The B-24 approached and was hit by flak. The aircraft crossed the conning tower at 150ft and dropped six depth charges. The Germans noticed fire in the aircraft's bomb bay and one of its starboard engines when it passed over. The Liberator remained airborne for over 1,500ft before crashing. All ten perished. The U-boat suffered no damage.[7]

American Liberators contributed to the Allied cause with two successful attacks in these five months. On 28 January 1944, just over 200 miles west of Ireland and heading towards a convoy it had been assigned to escort, the navigator aboard US Navy VB-103 Liberator 'E' spotted an object that appeared to be a U-boat. The pilot, Lieutenant C.A. Enloe, took notice and agreed. He commenced a turn while descending to attack. At this point the Germans noticed the approaching aircraft and began firing. Enloe flew over the U-boat at 50ft and straddled the target with six depth charges. With a setting of 30ft depth, all exploded and 'lifted most of the sub right out of the water'. The Type VIIC then sank stern first. The Americans, to ensure its destruction, deployed sonobuoys, through which the radioman reported an explosion. Despite remaining in the area for half an hour, the crew did not spot any debris. Nevertheless, the Americans had sunk *U-271*. All fifty-one crew members died. It had not destroyed any Allied vessels on three patrols.[8]

A Liberator also struck in the South Atlantic. On 6 February, 800 miles east of the Brazilian coast, Type IXD2 *U-177*, one of the most successful U-boats, was transiting the South Atlantic on the surface. This U-boat had, with three different commanders, sunk fourteen Allied vessels on three patrols. This day though, it met not merchant vessels but US Navy Liberator VB-107 B-3. As the pilot approached, the Germans fired on the aircraft and the Americans dropped numerous depth charges. As the

U-boat began to sink, crew members jumped into the water. The Liberator returned as the U-boat slipped under the surface and the crew dropped additional depth charges. Fifteen Germans survived, while fifty went down with the boat.[9]

Two other Allied land-based, four-engine aircraft, a RAF Halifax and Flying Fortress, achieved a sinking during this period. On 29 January, 502 Squadron Halifax 'O' took off from RAF St David's in south-west Wales at 1605 hours and flew to the Bay of Biscay. At 2100 hours, the crew's radar detected a target at 7 miles range and the pilot headed to the location. The crew, upon arriving in the area, found a fully surfaced Type VIIC U-boat and attacked it with multiple bombs. Surprisingly, the U-boat did not submerge. The Halifax circled the position but eventually lost contact with the U-boat. All forty-nine crew members died. *U-364* had not attacked any Allied vessels on this, its maiden patrol.[10]

The crew of 172 Squadron Wellington 'B' took off from Lagens, Azores, on 13 March and, approximately 500 miles north of its base, detected a radar contact at 0147 hours. The British pilot headed for the position and at 0151 hours spotted the surfaced Type VIIC *U-575*, attacking it with depth charges. The crew reported that the U-boat remained on the surface and believed that it had been 'disabled'. At 0330 hours though, they lost contact and at 0430 hours, the crew reported what they considered 'patches of oil'. No. 206 Squadron B-17 Mk. II 'R' then arrived and its crew noticed the five marine markers that the Wellington had dropped. At 0740 hours, the Flying Fortress crew spotted *U-575* surfacing. The Germans immediately fired and the pilot initiated evasive action. When the U-boat ceased firing, the British bore in and the U-boat fired again. The B-17 crew deposited four depth charges. The U-boat's fire halted and it disappeared, leaving behind large oil patches. The U-boat, though, had not sunk. B-17 Mk. II 'J' from 220 Squadron arrived at 1130 hours and would deliver one of the two fatal attacks. It flew into the area and sighted an aircraft with four Allied warships. The Fortress then detected a radar contact at 24 miles and headed for that location. The crew spotted a 3 to 4-mile-long oil streak and found an Avenger circling. Believing that the oil streak had developed from a damaged U-boat, the Fortress attacked the U-boat's presumed position with two depth charges dropped from 60ft. The British though, could ascertain no impact of the attack. Then, three Allied warships arrived and commenced a depth charge assault, leading to its eventual sinking. Eighteen crew members perished while thirty-seven survived. *U-575* had sunk nine Allied vessels and damaged another one in ten patrols.[11]

However, the Allies did lose a Fortress to U-boat fire during this time. No. 206 Squadron Fortress 'U' discovered the surfaced Type VIIC *U-270* on 6 January north-east of the Azores and conducted two strafing runs on the target. While approaching for the third attack, fire erupted on the inner starboard engine, causing the B-17 to lose height. The crew ineffectually released four depth charges and the Fortress then crashed into the water. All eight crew members perished. The strafing damage did necessitate *U-270*'s return to port.[12]

For the Allies and their four-engine aircraft, the first five months of 1944 held great potential, but this had not been realised. The areas along the Norwegian coast and in the Bay of Biscay offered the best opportunity for attacking U-boats, and the RAF occasionally assigned B-24 squadrons to these locations. Additionally, their best Liberator squadrons patrolled areas where the U-boats had nearly vacated, causing the British to lose the opportunity of devastating Hitler's U-boats with their highly skilled 120 and 86 Squadrons. Fortunately, though, other Allied air squadrons performed well during these five months.

Chapter 15

Swordfish, Catalinas, Avengers and Wellingtons: January–May 1944

While the Liberators did not dominate this period, a variety of other Allied aircraft did. The Swordfish, with hardly the appearance of a modern aircraft, led the pack with nine successful attacks. Catalinas followed closely with eight sinkings, and Avengers and Wellingtons with six. These five months all proved to be unusual not only because of the B-24's low number of successful missions, but also because the sinkings by aircraft equalled those by all other at-sea means. Allied aircraft contributed to the destruction of forty-seven U-boats, while all other Allied attacks also totalled forty-seven. The first five months of 1944 failed to follow the traditional two-to-one ratio of aircraft dominance seen the previous year.

The Royal Navy's Fleet Air Arm achieved significant success during this period with its Swordfish's nine sinkings, six of which were in the Norwegian waters. On 11 February, escort carrier HMS *Fencer*'s 842 Squadron Swordfish successfully depth charged Type VIIC *U-666* west of Ireland. All fifty-one crew members perished. *U-666* claimed credit for sinking two Allied vessels on four patrols. On 4 March, just north of Norway, an 816 Squadron Swordfish from the carrier HMS *Chaser* severely damaged Type VIIC *U-472*, leaving it vulnerable to the approaching destroyer HMS *Onslaught*. The German commander chose scuttling to outright destruction, and the British removed thirty men from the water while twenty-three men died. *U-472* had not sunk any Allied vessels on its two patrols.[1] On 5 March, just west of the *U-472* battle, *Chaser*'s aircraft struck again. An 816 Squadron Swordfish targeted Type VIIC *U-366* with rockets and all fifty hands went down with the U-boat.

U-366 had not sunk any Allied vessels on its two patrols. A day later, just south-east of the previous two engagements, a Swordfish from the same *Chaser* squadron spotted the surfaced Type VIIC *U-973* and destroyed it with a rocket assault. Fifty-one perished and two survived. *U-973* sank no Allied vessels on its two patrols. On 15 March, west of Ireland, an 825 Squadron Swordfish from HMS *Vindex* spotted the surfaced Type VIIC *U-653* and although it submerged before an attack could commence, the pilot dropped flares and markers on the location. British destroyers *Wren*, *Starling*, *Magpie* and *Wild Goose* all joined and *Starling*'s depth charges most likely destroyed the U-boat. All fifty-one crew members died. *U-653* had sunk four Allied vessels and damaged another one on nine patrols.[2]

In May, Swordfish achieved four U-boat sinkings. On the 1st, an 842 Squadron Swordfish from HMS *Fencer* discovered the surfaced Type VIIC *U-277* approximately 200 miles north of Norway and sunk it with depth charges. None of the fifty crew members survived. *U-277* had not sunk any Allied vessels on seven patrols.[3] The next day, a Swordfish from the same squadron and carrier 300 miles north-east of the Norwegian coast sank another Type VIIC boat, *U-674*, with depth charges. All forty-nine hands perished in the U-boat, which had not sunk any Allied shipping on three patrols.[4] That same day, a little over 100 miles to the south-west of *U-674*'s demise, an 842 Squadron Swordfish from *Fencer* sank Type VIIC *U-959* with depth charges. All fifty-three crew members went down with the boat. It had not sunk any Allied vessels on two patrols.[5] On 6 May in the mid-Atlantic, Type VIIC *U-765* surfaced after a Hedgehog assault by three Royal Navy frigates. No. 825 Squadron Swordfish 'V' from HMS *Vindex* destroyed it with two depth charges. The British rescued eleven crew members while thirty-seven perished. *U-765* had not engaged any Allied vessels on this, its only patrol.[6]

Catalinas flown by American, British and Canadian crews destroyed eight U-boats during this time. British Catalinas participated in the sinkings of four U-boats, with three successful attacks in Norwegian waters, while one RAF squadron, 210, engaged in two of these battles. On 24 February, 210 Squadron Catalina 'M' slipped from the water and took off into the night sky at 2355 hours from RAF Sullom Voe in the Shetland Islands. The crew initiated a radar search until at 0920 hours, off the northern Norwegian coast, they finally obtained a contact 24 miles away. In five minutes, the British closed to 4 miles, at which point the pilot visually identified Type VIIC *U-601* with 'decks awash'. The Catalina flew over the U-boat at 50ft altitude and dropped two depth charges while the submarine fired back unsuccessfully. The British aircrew observed debris and eight to ten survivors, although all fifty-one would die. *U-601* had sunk three Allied vessels on ten patrols. Catalina 'M' splashed down at RAF Sullom Voe at 1555 hours, after a sixteen-hour mission.[7]

On 18 May, Type VIIC *U-241* fought two Catalinas. The first one, 333 (Norwegian) Squadron 'C', suffered significant damage in an unsuccessful depth charge attack but managed to return to base with the loss of one crew member.[8] The second flying boat proved to be more lethal. No. 210 Squadron British Catalina 'S' lifted from the waters of Sullom Voe at 0643 hours. Despite its serviceable radar, the crew first discovered the surfaced *U-241* off the Norwegian coast by visual contact just 5/8 mile away. The U-boat crew, noticing the aircraft simultaneously, commenced firing on the flying boat. The pilot, Flight Officer B. Bastable, initiated evasive action and the front gunner fired at the conning tower. Bastable observed one body drop into the sea and then turned the Catalina towards the target and swooped over the boat, releasing six Torpex depth charges that straddled the target. The U-boat's bows lifted from the water to a 30-degree angle and it disappeared from the surface by the stern. The British crew observed an oil patch and 'many survivors' on the surface. The Catalina returned to its Scottish base at 1155 hours. None of *U-241*'s fifty-one crew members survived. Thus ended its first patrol, having not sunk any Allied vessels.[9]

At 2345 hours on 23 May, Catalina 'V' of 210 Squadron roared from Sullom Voe's waters and commenced its patrol. At 0716 hours the next day off the Norwegian coast, the crew spotted, from 900ft, the surfaced Type VIIC *U-476* 5 miles away moving at 12 knots. The flying boat approached for an assault while the Germans fired back ineffectively. Three minutes after the sighting, the Catalina flew over the boat and released six Torpex depth charges. The U-boat seemed to 'spin round on its tail for almost 360°' before ceasing its forward momentum. The bows rose from the surface and then the U-boat disappeared. A minute later, the U-boat resurfaced as if 'all tanks had been blown'. Then, in less than ten minutes, *U-476* disappeared again. A snowstorm inhibited the crew's ability to report any details as they could not see any debris or survivors. At 1240 hours, 'V' landed back at Sullom Voe. *U-476*, meanwhile, had not yet sunk. Able to remain afloat, two other U-boats – *U-276* and *U-990* – arrived and saved twenty-one men, while thirty-four perished when it submerged for the last time on this, its only patrol having not encountered any Allied vessels.[10]

Catalinas even conducted their predations from South Africa. An Italian submarine that had entered German service, *UIT-22*, traversed the South Atlantic and sustained damage from American aircraft but continued south on its mission. On 11 March, at 0350 hours, 262 Squadron Catalina 'D' took off from RAF Congella, in Durban, South Africa, at 1022 hours and spotted surfaced *UIT-22* off the Cape of Good Hope. The British attacked with gun fire and six depth charges. The U-boat submerged but the twin-engine flying boat remained on scene, although damaged by flak, until Catalina 'P' relieved it at 1045 hours. 'P' flew in circles with 'A' above the oil patch until at 1130 hours, *UIT-22* reappeared. 'A' now attacked with gun fire and depth charges as its predecessor had done. After an explosion, *UIT-22* commenced diving, forcing the Catalina to attack only with gun fire as the U-boat had completely disappeared when the flying boat attained an ideal depth charge release position. Debris and oil floated on the surface and the U-boat never surfaced again, taking forty-three crew members with it. It had not engaged any Allied vessels on this, its first patrol.[11]

American Catalinas fatally attacked three U-boats during these five months. Their first success involved the use of a relatively new anti-submarine technology. The Allies continued improving their ability to locate U-boats and the Magnetic Anomaly Detection (MAD) represented one of the most sophisticated developments. This device, situated in an aircraft's tail boom, permitted the crew to locate a submerged U-boat if the aircraft flew at low altitude and the submarine was at a shallow depth. The Straits of Gibraltar provided the ideal area for MAD use and on 24 February, the Allies employed it successfully for the first time. At 1500 hours, two VP-63 Catalinas detected the submerged Type VIIC *U-761* in the Straits. Two destroyers, HMS *Anthony* and *Wishart*, arrived and informed the Catalinas that they had not found a U-boat. However, their disruption of the surface resulted in the flying boats' crews losing contact with *U-761*. The Catalinas reacquired it at 1557 hours and released retro bombs, munitions that fired rearward to strike a MAD-detected target. A US Navy Ventura (B-46) from VB-127 joined the hunt and all three began circling the area. The British warships arrived and commenced a depth charge attack but the U-boat had already sustained fatal damage from the Catalinas. It surfaced and the crew abandoned the boat. The destroyers fired on the U-boat, while a Catalina attacked with more retro bombs and RAF Ventura 'G' from 202 Squadron followed. After these two aircraft dropped their ordnance and flew over, the U-boat exploded. The British rescued forty-eight crew members; nine perished. *U-761* had not sunk any Allied vessels on two patrols.[12]

Gibraltar remained a dangerous area for Dönitz's U-boats. *U-392*, a Type VIIC, departed Brest, France, on 29 February, intending to patrol the Mediterranean but never arrived at its intended area. On 16 March, two VP-63 Catalinas, P-1 and P-8, discovered the surfaced *U-392* in the Straits of Gibraltar. The aircraft attracted the attention of HMS *Vanoc*, a destroyer, which initiated a Hedgehog assault on the now submerged target. All fifty-two crew members perished. *U-392* had not sunk any Allied vessels on two patrols. Two months later, on 15 May, another U-boat, *U-731*, attempted to slip into the Mediterranean by passing through the Straits. However, VP-63 Catalinas P-1 and P-14 detected the submerged Type VIIC U-boat with their MAD equipment. This detection received further confirmation by propeller sounds heard by a sonobuoy and the two flying boats attacked. The launch of thirty retro bombs brought splintered wood to the surface but no confirmation of destruction. The Americans directed two British vessels – HMS *Kilmarnock*, a sloop, and HMS *Blackfly*, an anti-submarine trawler – to the scene and they targeted the submerged U-boat with Hedgehogs and depth charges. U-boat Command never heard from *U-731* again. All fifty-four crew members perished. It had not sunk any Allied vessels on three patrols.[13]

A Royal Canadian Air Force Canso, the Canadian name for a Catalina, achieved a sinking during this period. On 17 April, a 162 Squadron aircraft spotted the surfaced Type VIIC *U-342* in the North Atlantic south-west of Iceland. The U-boat crew fired extensively but the nose gunner's firing ceased the flak. The pilot released three depth charges and *U-342* disappeared; all fifty-one crew members perished. It had not sunk any Allied vessels on its first and only patrol.[14]

US Navy Avengers only trailed the Catalinas by two during this period as the American torpedo bomber destroyed six U-boats during the opening five months of the year. The Navy delivered its first successful attack of 1944 on long-range Type IXC/40 boat *U-544*. The odyssey of the U-boat's first patrol reflects the extraordinary change that had occurred for Dönitz's craft as compared with the target-rich areas they had prowled earlier in the war. *U-544* commenced its first patrol on 9 November. It laid in wait with other U-boats to ambush convoy ONS 24 but the vessels passed to the north, and all the U-boats failed to encounter a single Allied vessel. In mid-December it then joined other U-boats for another ambush, this time against ON 214. Again, it found no Allied vessels. On 19 December, with five other U-boats, its commander again tried to intercept a convoy, namely HX 270. This time, their intended target passed to the south of their position. Now, the German command ordered *U-544* to meet with two other U-boats to refuel them several hundred miles north-west of the Azores. The Americans, though, had deciphered the message and now knew the location for the intended refuelling, so the escort carrier USS

Guadalcanal steamed into the area with VC-13 on board. Before sunset, on 16 January, the Americans sent out multiple Avengers and two of them found all three U-boats, surfaced. Avenger T-12 dived on *U-544*, attacking it with depth charges and rockets, and the U-boat disappeared from the surface for the last time. It had not encountered any Allied vessels on this, its maiden patrol. All fifty-seven hands perished.[15]

On 11 March, after three days of repairs, the escort carrier USS *Block Island* departed Casablanca and headed for the Atlantic with VC-6 on board. The carrier group's radar detected the surfaced *U-801*, a long-range Type IXC/40 boat, on 15 March and dispatched aircraft. However, the poor weather conditions hid the U-boat from the Navy pilots' prying eyes. The following day, the Germans' fortune faded. Immediately upon rising to the surface, the U-boat found itself directly under an Avenger–Wildcat pair. Following the familiar pattern, the Wildcat strafed, the U-boat dived, and the Avenger dropped a Fido. Yet the U-boat escaped again, though not without damage. The attack wounded or killed at least ten crew members, even though the U-boat remained operational. The German commander transmitted a message for assistance to U-boat Command intending the information for an audience of one, but the Americans detected the message as well. Destroyer USS *Corry* searched the area from which the message originated but discovered nothing. On the 17th though, Allied aircraft succeeded again when an Avenger located it and released a 500lb depth charge. *U-801* submerged but the German commander could not hide the leaking oil that appeared on the surface. Depth charges from *Corry* and the destroyer escort USS *Bronstein* exploded in the area, which brought the U-boat to the surface. With no hope of battling two destroyers while on the surface, the crew abandoned and scuttled the boat. Nine perished while the Americans rescued forty-seven men. *U-801* had not sunk any Allied vessels on two patrols.[16]

U-801's signal to U-boat Command had alerted the Americans to the presence of another U-boat in the area and *Block Island* aircraft continued to search until, on 19 March, a Wildcat sighted Type VIIF *U-1059* on a mission to deliver torpedoes to German U-boats operating in the Indian Ocean. The Navy pilot strafed the boat. Lieutenant Norman T. Dowry, in Avenger T-3, followed and released two depth charges on the target before the plane, damaged by German fire, crashed. Dowry perished, as did another member of the aircrew, but the destroyer USS *Corry* rescued the remaining airman along with eight Germans. Forty-seven U-boat crewmen died in the attack. Thus ended *U-1059*'s only patrol, it not having engaged any Allied vessels.[17]

The battle against *U-288*, a Type VIIC boat, involved three Royal Navy aircraft: a Swordfish, a Wildcat, and an Avenger. The cat-and-mouse hunt commenced on 3 April with an 819 Squadron Swordfish from HMS *Activity*. The pilot, Lieutenant S. Brilliant, observed the U-boat but it dived before he could attack. Brilliant marked the location and continued flying. Later, he returned, sighted the surfaced *U-288* and called for assistance. While awaiting reinforcements, Brilliant remained in visual contact with the U-boat and avoided German fire. An Avenger and a Wildcat from HMS *Tracker* arrived. The Wildcat targeted the U-boat with gun fire, enabling Brilliant to fire rockets and followed by the Avenger dropping depth charges. The U-boat exploded and sank. All forty-nine hands went down with the boat. *U-288* had not sunk any Allied vessels on its two patrols.[18]

U-515, a long-range Type IXC boat, had a sterling career against the Allies with only one commander: Werner Henke. He sank an extraordinary twenty-six Allied vessels on six patrols. Henke departed on 30 March for what would be his last one, and a little over a week later, on 8 April, southeast of the Azores, a USS *Guadalcanal* VC-58 Avenger sighted his surfaced boat and relayed the position back to the American escort carrier. Other Avengers roared off the deck, found the U-boat and released two depth charges. Henke submerged but the following day, an Avenger discovered his U-boat again and assaulted with two more depth charges, forcing him to submerge once more. Four American destroyers now employed Hedgehog assaults and depth charge assaults until the damaged *U-515* appeared for the last time. USS *Chatelain* fired on it and Navy aircraft launched rockets and strafed it. The U-boat slipped under the surface, leaving forty-four men, including Henke, for the Americans to rescue, while sixteen perished.[19]

U-68, another long-range Type IXC boat, had extraordinary success with three different commanders. When the third one took command, Gerhard Seehausen, the U-boat had destroyed twenty-eight Allied vessels. He continued its streak of triumphs with the sinking of four more vessels on its tenth patrol. However, its eleventh would be its last. Seehausen departed the Atlantic base at Lorient, France, on 27 March. On 10 April, three VP-58 American aircraft from the escort carrier USS *Guadalcanal* – one Wildcat (F-4) and two Avengers (T-22 and T-24) – found the surfaced *U-68* by moonlight and assaulted it with depth charges and rockets. The U-boat sank with all fifty-six crew members but one, ending its career with thirty-two Allied vessels destroyed.[20]

Allied naval forces suffered a setback during this time when, on 29 May, a U-boat struck *Block Island*. The submerged long-range Type

IXC/40 *U-549* slipped by the four American destroyer escorts protecting the aircraft carrier and fatally hit the flattop with two torpedoes. Six Wildcats, airborne at the time, attempted to reach the Canary Islands, but failed. Two of the six pilots survived. Six *Block Island* crew members perished as a result of the attack, while the surface vessels rescued the remaining 951 men. However, *U-549* had not finished its depredations. The U-boat severely damaged destroyer escort USS *Barr* before two of the remaining vessels, *Eugene E. Elmore* and *Ahrens* – finally sank *U-549* with depth charges for the loss of all fifty-seven crew members. This battle marked its only engagement with Allied vessels on its two patrols. Although this was the only American escort carrier destroyed by Dönitz's U-boats, the loss well demonstrated the vulnerability of naval vessels to U-boat torpedoes as opposed to Allied land bases.[21]

Wellington crews participated in six U-boat sinkings during the first five months of the year. On 14 January, Wellington 'L' of the RAF's 172 Squadron departed Lagens in the Azores at 1822 hours and commenced its patrol at 2210 hours. Just fifteen minutes later, 500 miles west of the Bay of Biscay, the crew spotted the surfaced Type VIIC *U-231* and assaulted with guns and two groups of three 250lb Torpex depth charges. German returning fire injured the rear gunner and disabled the rear turret. The damage caused by the depth charges proved to be more substantial and the commander, Wolfgang Wenzel, ordered all hands to abandon the fatally stricken U-boat. Believing the situation warranted his own suicide, Wenzel fired a gun into his mouth. However, the attempt failed as the bullet stopped in his neck. Allied destroyers rescued him and forty-two other crew members, who all became prisoners of war. Seven died in the attack. Medical personnel on the USS *Block Island* successfully removed Wenzel's bullet and he survived the suicide attempt.[22] Wenzel had proven to be an unsuccessful commander; on three patrols, he had not sunk any Allied vessels.[23]

While Allied anti-submarine pilots certainly understood the advantages of poor weather in regards to hiding their attack approach, weather that provided little or no visual contact challenged them as well. However, on one day, poor weather aided the hunt. The crew of 612 Squadron Wellington 'O' took off from RAF Limavady, Northern Ireland, on 10 February at 1621 hours and headed north. The crew patrolled to the extent of their defined search area and then turned around and commenced returning to base. Outbound, the crew released twenty-five flame floats to guide their return but the fog and low clouds obstructed their view so that, on their way home, they only sighted five of them. Due to these factors, the Wellington flew at 8 miles north of its intended course. However, since it had departed from its outbound flight path, the crew, when flying at approximately 300 miles north of Northern Ireland, detected a radar contact 12 miles away, and altered course to intercept from an attitude between 700 to 800ft. The weather, though, steadily deteriorated. While they obtained a contact at 8 miles, the crew lost contact for two minutes due to interference. Eight minutes after initial contact, when 7 miles away, they reacquired the target. The crew needed visual contact for a depth charge attack, but instead, when the Wellington closed to 4 miles, the crew encountered cloud cover, and maintained course while at 200 to 300ft. At one mile from the target, still unable to visually identify its target, the pilot, Pilot Officer M.H. Paynter, had no choice but to descend rapidly and when just ½ mile from the contact, he activated the aircraft's searchlight. However, drizzle reflected the light and limited its effectiveness. Then, suddenly at just a mile from the target, the crew spotted a U-boat, and quickly prepared for the attack. Flying over the submarine at 50ft, Paynter released six depth charges that fell parallel to the target. He continued on course until the aircraft emerged from the cloud and rain and circled back to the attack area. The crew spotted the two flame floats that had been released with the depth charges but never sighted the U-boat again. They continued to search and yet did not even sight any significant debris or oil, just some 'oval objects' and 'small orange lights' that the crew believed may have been lifejackets or dinghies. Paynter eventually set course for home and landed back at Limavady at 0310 hours the next day, a nearly twelve-hour patrol.[24] *U-545*, a long-range Type IXC/40 boat, although severely damaged, survived until the following day. Then, *U-714* arrived, and *U-545*'s commander ordered the crew to abandon the boat, and they then scuttled it. One crew member died. Thus ended *U-545*'s first patrol, having shared the credit for the sinking of only one Allied vessel.[25]

On 10 February, north-west of the British Isles, RAF 612 Squadron Wellington 'N' discovered the surfaced Type VIIC *U-283* midway between Scotland and Iceland. On this occasion though, the U-boat prevailed and the German crew shot down the British aircraft for the loss of all six men.[26] However, RCAF 407 Squadron Wellington 'D' would avenge the British crew the next day. Flying Officer P.W. Heron departed Limavady at 2205 hours on the 10th and his crew obtained a radar contact at 0408 hours, 9 miles away. Heron altered course and closed the distance. At ½ mile from the target, he ordered the Leigh Light illuminated and it shone on *U-283* moving at a steady 10 knots. At 2054 hours, just four minutes after initial contact, Heron attacked. The Germans, apparently caught completely by surprise, fired poorly at the approaching aircraft.

Heron then released six depth charges from 60ft. Radar contact had been lost and he returned to the area of the attack in two minutes, but never sighted the U-boat again. The Wellington returned to Northern Ireland at 0825 hours after a nearly ten-hour mission. All forty-nine U-boat crew members perished. *U-283* had been destroyed on its first patrol, having neither sunk nor damaged any Allied vessels.[27]

In May, Type IXC/40 *U-846* battled two Allied aircraft. The U-boat departed Lorient on 29 April, and while crossing the Bay of Biscay on 2 May, downed 58 Squadron Halifax 'H' for the loss of all eight crew members. However, two days later, the crew encountered another Allied aircraft. On 4 May at 2147 hours, RCAF 407 Squadron Wellington 'M' took off into the night sky from RAF Chivenor. While patrolling at 500ft, the crew obtained a radar contact at 7 miles distance. Flight Lieutenant L.J. Bateman changed heading to the target and commencing descending until, at 2 miles away, he took the bomber down to 400ft when the crew sighted the surfaced boat. He now had the option of illuminating the Leigh Light but demurred because the moonlight proved to be sufficient. Bateman descended to 200ft and began his approach as gun fire from the conning tower erupted around the Wellington. The Canadian pilot released six 250lb Torpex depth charges from 150ft. The resulting plumes prevented the crew from observing any indication of U-boat damage. The aircraft now circled the attack location from a distance of 2 miles while maintaining radar contact with the U-boat. When radar contact had been lost, Bateman flew over the attack area and observed an oil patch. He then activated the Leigh Light but the crew did not notice any further evidence. *U-846* had not sunk any Allied vessels and all fifty-seven crew members perished. Bateman received the Distinguished Flying Cross for this mission.[28]

One of the most notorious stories regarding U-boats involves the officers of long-range Type IXD2 *U-852*. They departed Kiel, Germany, on 18 January with the Indian Ocean as their intended destination. On 13 March, in the South Atlantic, south of Liberia, they discovered SS *Peleus* and fatally torpedoed the merchant vessel. Many of the vessel's crew survived by clinging to floating debris. The German commander, Heinz-Wilhelm Eck, contended that the merchant vessel's remains would provide the Allies with evidence of a nearby U-boat. Therefore, the U-boat crew members machine-gunned and threw hand grenades at the survivors and the wreckage. Thirty-eight perished in the attack and the subsequent slaughter; only three survived. Eck then encountered another Allied merchant vessel near Cape Town and sank it as well.

U-852, having transited the western African coast, now turned north and followed the eastern African coast.[29]

The British had tracked *U-852* on its voyage around Cape Horn. Once it reached the range of 621 Squadron, an earnest search commenced, although at the time, the RAF did not realise that they were searching for not only a U-boat, but someone that the British would regard as a war criminal. The attacks would demonstrate the RAF's tenacity, but also the weakness of the Wellingtons as six of these twin-engine aircraft failed to sink this U-boat during two days of attacks. The first Wellington, 'E', took off into darkness from RAF Scuiscuiban, Somalia, on 1 May, at 0105 hours. Over three hours later, at 0421 hours, the crew members spotted a 'suspicious object', which they later identified as a surfaced U-boat. They had found *U-852*. This Wellington struck with six depth charges dropped from 50ft as the U-boat dived. The bomber remained in the area flying in circles, *U-852* reappeared and the Germans began significant anti-aircraft fire, forcing the Wellington to depart. However, the depth charges had struck the U-boat's air induction valve and *U-852* could no longer dive. The race now began as to whether the German commander could escape the range of the Wellingtons before they finished the work that 'E' had begun.

Wellington 'T' engaged next. The crew discovered an 'oil streak', which they followed until discovering *U-852* 'fully surfaced' with a 'wide wake'. They immediately sent a message to Wellington 'U' to assault together but, not then seeing the other aircraft, decided to commence the attack. Its front guns 'jammed' and the pilot swung away before dropping any ordnance. However, at 0630 hours, Wellington 'U' arrived and, despite the 'heavy flak', deposited depth charges. 'T' then approached and this time released five depth charges but the crew believed that the attack did not cause any damage. This crew then returned to Scuiscuiban to retrieve more ordnance.

At 0835 hours, Wellington 'F' spotted the surfaced *U-852*, which was moving at 9 knots, and deposited four depth charges from an altitude of 50ft, while the Germans maintained significant anti-aircraft fire. 'F' then followed with a 'dummy attack' with only machine gun fire and then assaulted a third time with its last depth charges. The Wellington then headed to Scuiscuiban after suffering engine issues and landed at 1335 hours. The U-boat continued travelling on the surface.

'D' took off with the now rearmed 'T' from Scuiscuiban at 1040 hours. At 1255 hours, 'D' spotted *U-852* proceeding at 12 knots and dived on the U-boat with 'T' following. The Wellington 'D' crew intended to receive the

German fire instead of 'T', and when Wellington 'D' had flown directly over the U-boat, Wellington 'T' dropped six depth charges and five of them exploded.[30]

No. 8 Squadron Wellington 'G' delivered the final attack. On 3 May, two days after the first assault on *U-852*, this British crew sighted the U-boat at 1351 hours and approached. The depth charges failed to release. The pilot swung around and approached a second time and, on this assault, the six 250lb depth charges fell. At 1655 hours, the pilot found the U-boat not moving with a significant oil patch and departed for base at 1658 hours. Eck lost any hope of escape. He beached the U-boat, and scuttled it. *U-852* had sunk two Allied vessels on this, its only patrol. The British seized fifty-nine crew members, while seven perished in the battle. The British also retrieved Eck's log and placed him and four of his crew members on trial. The German commander never denied his actions; only that he considered them justified. The British concluded otherwise. A firing squad shot three of the crew, including Eck. The other two Germans received prison terms.[31]

The demise of Type VIIC *U-616* involved primarily surface vessels. The first attack on 16 May in the western Mediterranean saw USS *Hilary P. Jones* mount a depth charge assault. The next day Wellington 'X' of 36 Squadron discovered *U-616*, now damaged, on the surface, off the Algerian coast, and attacked with six more depth charges before the U-boat submerged. When the Allies discovered an oil slick, of 10 miles length, the next morning, they had a trail to pursue. That night, as American destroyers combed the surface after an aircraft sighting, *U-616* appeared and the destroyers fired. The Germans immediately abandoned the boat and the Americans rescued all fifty-three crew members. *U-616* had sunk one Allied destroyer and damaged two vessels on nine patrols.[32]

While Wellingtons delivered numerous fatal strikes during this time, U-boats did down several of the twin-engine aircraft during the first five months of the year. On 31 January, the crew of 304 Squadron Wellington 'B' spotted an aircraft over the Bay of Biscay using their Leigh Light and then heard what they described as depth charge explosions. Most likely, the Polish crew had heard the downing of 172 Squadron Wellington 'K' by Type VIIC *U-608* for the loss of all six crew members.[33] Four months later, on 24 May, Type VIIC *U-736* shot down 612 Squadron's 'L' for the loss of all six crew members.[34] On two January days in the extreme western Mediterranean, Type VIIC *U-343* managed to shoot down not one, but two British Wellingtons. On the 7th, 36 Squadron 'Y' located the surfaced U-boat, attacked unsuccessfully, and fire erupted on the port wing. The crew managed to land in the water. Two perished, while the Polish destroyer *Slazark* rescued four crew members.[35] The next day, early in the morning, 179 Squadron Wellington 'R' appeared and hit the U-boat with depth charges, but on the approach German strikes on the port wing caused it to catch on fire. The twin-engine aircraft plunged into the water. Five died but the British destroyer *Active* rescued the one survivor. *U-343* escaped.[36]

Sunderlands achieved four U-boat sinkings during this time. On 8 January, at 0700 hours, Sunderland 'U' of the RAAF's 10 Squadron slipped from the waters of RAF Mount Batten in Devon. Around 1130 hours, the crew discovered an oil streak but no debris. The Sunderland remained in the area for twenty minutes but after not sighting anything further, continued its patrol. At 1154 hours though, at the western extreme of the Bay of Biscay, the crew spotted, at 12 miles distance, the surfaced Type VIIC *U-426* maintaining 12 knots with its conning tower 'awash'. The Australians informed their base of the sighting and then Flying Officer J.P. Roberts 'immediately altered course' for an assault. *U-426*, apparently damaged, remained on the surface to battle the aircraft and commenced fire on the flying boat, while the Australians responded with evasive action and return fire. The Sunderland flew over the U-boat but its depth charges failed to release on the first pass. Roberts then executed a 'steep turn' and engaged in a second pass, during which all six depth charges fell from a height of 50ft. *U-426* slowed, listed to starboard, and commenced sinking stern first. Roberts attacked again with machine gun fire and the Germans began departing by the conning tower. At noon, six minutes after the initial sighting, the bow rose and the U-boat slipped from the surface by the stern. The Australians counted forty crew members in the water but all fifty-one eventually perished in the attack. *U-426* had sunk one Allied vessel on two patrols. Sunderland 'U' returned to base at 1542 hours after over eight hours in the air.[37]

The same month, on the 28th, Sunderland MK577 from 461 Squadron, RAAF, spotted the surfaced *U-571*, a Type VIIC, approximately 200 miles due west of Ireland, and began an attack. On approach, the Australians received flak from the U-boat, and responded with their guns, which silenced the German weapons. The first pass failed to damage the U-boat as the depth charges missed by a considerable distance, but on the second assault the crew dropped two depth charges, which caused the U-boat to explode. They saw approximately 'thirty survivors and bodies' on the surface with debris. The Sunderland, having apparently been damaged during evasive manoeuvres, turned for base. Two additional Australian aircraft arrived on the scene and released a dinghy.

None of the fifty-two crew members survived. *U-571* had sunk seven Allied vessels and damaged another on ten patrols.[38]

On 10 March, Sunderland 'U' from 422 Squadron, RCAF, took off from RAF St Angelo, Northern Ireland, at 1125 hours and at 1500 hours, while flying at 1,000ft and approximately 400 miles due west of Ireland, a crew member spotted Type VIIC *U-625* 6 miles way. Flight Lieutenant S.W. Butler 'immediately manoeuvred' the flying boat for an assault by descending to 400ft when a mile from the target. The U-boat had started inaccurate fire when the Sunderland was 5 miles away. The Germans then initiated a variety of course changes, including circling and a zig-zag tactic, which prevented the Canadian pilot from acquiring an ideal attack position in the relatively slow flying boat. Finally, Butler 'dived in a steep turn' while descending from 400ft to 30ft. The Germans managed significant fire that pieced the flying boat's hull as the Canadians returned fire. When over the target, the crew released six Torpex depth charges. *U-625* disappeared from the surface and then three minutes later resurfaced with a slow momentum. Eighty-eight minutes later, the Germans abandoned the boat in multiple dinghies. Then at 1740 hours, it disappeared underwater stern first with the bows protruding upwards. All fifty-three crew members perished. *U-625* had sunk four Allied vessels and damaged another one on nine patrols.[39]

On 24 May, a training mission resulted in combat. Sunderland 'R' from 4 Operational Training Unit found surfaced *U-675*, a Type VIIC boat, off the Norwegian coast. The training instructor, Flying Officer Fritzell, had to decide whether to attack with his trainee crew or allow the U-boat to escape. Fritzell decided to engage. The Germans responded with significant gun fire but he successfully dropped numerous depth charges, which sank the U-boat. All fifty-one crew members perished in the attack. *U-675* had not sunk any Allied vessels on this, its only patrol. Fritzell was awarded the Distinguished Flying Cross for this action.[40]

A U-boat downed one Sunderland during these five months. On 24 May off the Norwegian coast, 422 Squadron RCAF's 'R' attacked the surfaced Type VIIC *U-921* with three depth charges and strafing. However, on approach, flak damaged the large flying boat and it plunged into water for the loss of all twelve crew members.[41]

Twin-engine Mosquitoes achieved one victory during this period. On 25 March, multiple 248 Squadron Mosquitoes took off from RAF Portreath in Cornwall to patrol the Bay of Biscay. Approximately 50 miles from St Nazaire, they discovered surfaced Type VIIC *U-976*, a German destroyer and two merchant vessels. Two Mosquitoes, 'L' and 'I', focused on the U-boat. Cannon fire from the British aircraft struck its batteries, released chlorine gas, and the crew abandoned ship. Four perished and the Germans rescued the remainder. *U-976* had not sunk any Allied vessels on its two patrols.[42]

Ventura–U-boat battles produced mixed results for the Allies. On 4 February, in the Mediterranean, south of Cyprus, Type VIIC *U-453* and 'Y' of 17 Squadron, South African Air Force, met. The aircraft made two passes, the first unsuccessfully, and on the second the crew managed to release five depth charges that missed. However, U-boat flak caused a fire in the port engine and the aircraft plunged into the water for the loss of all four crew members. *U-453* slipped away.[43] On 19 May though, *U-960*, a Type VIIC boat, found itself assaulted by RAF Ventura 'V' of 500 Squadron on patrol in the western Mediterranean. The pilot, Warrant Officer E.A.K. Mundy, homed Allied destroyers to an area where a U-boat had been reported. Soon after the vessels arrived, he sighted an emerging periscope, which led to the fully surfaced *U-960* and the destroyers commenced fire. Mundy swooped over the U-boat at 50ft and released three depth charges. Ten seconds after the explosions, the U-boat sank and the Ventura crew sighted men on the surface. The destroyers messaged the RAF crew: 'Our job is over. U/Boat is sunk.' The Allies retrieved twenty men while thirty-one perished in the attack. *U-960* had sunk three Allied vessels and damaged another on five patrols.[44]

Allied forces had also, during this time, continued their depredations on German cities through aerial bombing. These attacks also devastated ports, vessels, and U-boats as well. Dönitz's U-boat crews could no longer view their home bases as safe havens. On 9 January, the 15th Air Force struck Pola, Yugoslavia, and destroyed Type VIIC *U-81*. Two perished. *U-81* had sunk HMS *Ark Royal* in 1941.[45] The 15th Air Force, USAAF, struck Toulon on 11 March and sank two Type VIIC boats, *U-380* – in which one died – and *U-410*. American bombers returned to Toulon on 29 April and destroyed Type VIIC *U-421*.[46]

The RAF also wrecked two U-boats through an aerial laid minefield in north German coastal waters. On 4 February Type IXC/40 *U-854* sank in the Geranium minefield, causing the death of fifty-one crew members, seven being rescued. On 27 April Type IXC/40 *U-803* perished in the same minefield, losing nine killed while the Germans rescued thirty-five. These incidents marked only the second and third time that aerial mines had achieved any success.[47]

Allied aircraft had decimated Dönitz's boats during these five months. His strategy of abandoning the North Atlantic had not succeeded in avoiding the terror from the skies. The situation would not improve in the near future. As the Allies mustered their forces for the Normandy invasion in June, the U-boats would find themselves fatally targeted multiple times, and during that month, the Liberators would once again prove to be the Allies' most lethal aircraft.

Chapter 16

June 1944

The Liberators dominated in June 1944, with ten U-boats terminally damaged. Catalinas sank five, followed by Mosquitoes with two, Sunderlands with two, and Avengers with one. Aircraft contributed to twenty fatal attacks of the twenty-five achieved by all Allied means, for 80 per cent of all successes during this decisive month. The location of the Liberator sinkings reveals the concentration of forces by both Allied and Axis powers. The ten B-24 attacks occurred, with three exceptions, in the English Channel area. As the U-boats prowled in anticipation of the Normandy invasion, the Liberators patrolled the skies above and again found and destroyed those boats attempting to disrupt the invasion for the liberation of Europe.[1]

For the men of U-boat Command, Operation Overlord represented a significant threat. The French western coast bases facilitated Dönitz's U-boats' access to the Atlantic and beyond. Allied forces could threaten U-boats heading that way from northern Germany by patrolling the narrow straits around Denmark. In regards to the Mediterranean U-boat bases, the Allies had, by mid–1943, effectively closed the confines of the Straits of Gibraltar. The Norwegian bases provided some relief but their isolation limited the Germans' ability to supply and refurbish U-boats. And while Dönitz had complained bitterly of the losses his force suffered to Allied aircraft in the Bay of Biscay, the French bases certainly provided far less risk than operating from any other European location. From the closest U-boat base to Normandy, Brest, Hitler's U-boat crews would depart in their attempt to enter the English Channel by its western edge to send both Allied supplies and men to a watery grave.

The Liberator crews made extensive use of radar during this month. Of the twenty B-24 attacks on U-boats this month, the ten fatal ones reveal the greatly expanded detection range that the Liberator crews now possessed. Many of these assaults commenced with radar detection.

The B-24s could patrol at night with the same effectiveness that they searched for U-boats in daylight.

The first B-24 attacks in June all originated with British Liberators flying from St Eval. No. 224 Squadron Liberators would attack seven U-boats this month, four successfully. On 4 June, Liberator 'M' took off from south-west England at 1906 hours with sixteen 250lb depth charges. The B-24 crew finished one patrol over the Bay of Biscay without incident and then initiated a second one during which, at 0306 hours at 20 miles range, they obtained a radar contact. Flight Lieutenant J.W.A. Posnett closed on the target and, when 1½ miles away, the crew spotted a dark patch that they originally suspected to be the U-boat. However, they quickly realised that they had merely observed a stratus cloud shadow. The British then turned on the Leigh Light and Type VIIC *U-256* replied with gun fire. This, of course, attracted the attention of the entire crew, including the second navigator, who sighted the surfaced U-boat by moonlight, ¾ mile away. Posnett turned the Liberator to attack and made two attempts that both failed because the Leigh Light could not penetrate the extensive haze. On the third run, the British released fourteen depth charges from 200ft altitude travelling at 180 knots. The ordnance straddled the U-boat's track. The front gunner had expended twenty rounds, the beam gunner 250, and the rear gunner 500. Although they still had depth charges remaining, the Liberator's fuel situation necessitated a return to England. *U-256* remained on the surface and the B-24's radar continued to maintain contact for 27 miles. 'M' landed at 0615 hours after completing an eleven-hour mission.

U-256 had not sunk, but had been heavily damaged. While returning to Brest on 7 June though, Liberator 'M', under a different crew, may have found it again and attacked. The RAF never heard from this B-24 again and *U-256* may have destroyed the aircraft that had attacked it before. All eleven crew members died. The heavily damaged U-boat entered Brest for emergency repairs and then proceeded to Norway, where the Germans used it for scrap. Its first battle with Liberator 'M' effectively ended its career. *U-256* had sunk one Allied vessel on five patrols.[2]

A day after Allied forces stormed the Normandy beaches, three U-boats travelled on the surface at the English Channel's western entrance. They employed a relatively new German tactic by which the combined fire of three surfaced U-boats would best combat air attacks. They first encountered 53 Squadron, which would attack three U-boats this month, two fatally. In their first action against the unit, these U-boats succeeded in downing Liberator Mk. V 'M' for the loss of all ten men.[3] However, 53 Squadron Liberator Mk. V 'L' demonstrated that aircraft could still deliver successful strikes against surfaced U-boats travelling together. The British crew were patrolling at 500ft when they obtained 'three radar contacts'. Flight Lieutenant J.W. Carmichael, with the radar operator's direction, manoeuvred the B-24 towards one of the contacts 'up moon'. At 0425 hours, thanks to moonlight, the second pilot sighted a 'conning tower at 2 miles'. Carmichael immediately assaulted the target with six 250lb depth charges from 100ft. The Germans did not return fire, leading the British to conclude that the U-boat crew had not sighted the four-engine plane. After the attack, the German flak became 'intense', although no shots struck the aircraft. The crew dropped a marine marker and flame floats as Carmichael turned around 'for a second attack'. When approaching the U-boat, the aircraft received 'flak from three vessels'. The fire caused Carmichael to 'stand off and report the position before attacking again'. The Liberator crew continued monitoring the radar contacts as Carmichael flew in a circular pattern.

Less than an hour after the first assault though, Carmichael decided to attack again when the second pilot spotted a U-boat's wake. The crew, unsure of the U-boat's identity, admitted, 'it may or may not have been the U/Boat previously attacked'. Their radar had located only one contact and they concluded that the other two U-boats had submerged. Their target steered 'north at approximately 15 Kts, trimmed well down and the Liberator approached up moon with the intention of tracking across its bows'. At the last minute though, the U-boat 'turned to port'. Nevertheless, the British roared over the target and dropped six 250lb depth charges from an altitude of 50ft while the rear gunner fired on the U-boat. He observed the first depth charge explode and the 'second, very large explosion followed, which blotted' both the conning tower and 'part of the hull forward of it. The bows then lifted' and 'the whole of the hull visible forward of the explosion showed clear above the water before it settled again'.

The Liberator did suffer damage. 'During the approach very intense and accurate flak had been experienced,' Carmichael admitted. 'No. 3 engine was hit, and a shell exploded in the bomb bay.' The number three engine, having received significant damage, could not function and so the crew feathered it. Although the German gunners had struck the aircraft, no RAF crew members suffered injury. The six depth charges had done their job and Type VIIC *U-629* sank with all fifty-one men. The U-boat had not destroyed any Allied vessels on its ten patrols.[4]

The same day that 53 Squadron Liberator 'L' sank a U-boat, a 224 Squadron Liberator did so as well. On this flight though, one Liberator fatally hit two U-boats. On 7 June, B-24 'G' took off from St Eval at 2214 hours. At 0211 hours and while flying less than 50 miles west of Brest, the crew obtained a radar contact 12 miles away directly in the aircraft's path. The weather proved to be ideal for the hunters with a full moon, visibility at 3 miles and a calm sea. The pilot, Canadian Flying Officer K.O. Moore, changed course slightly so that he could approach the target 'up moon'. The B-24 descended over these 12 miles from 500ft altitude to an attack height of less than 100ft, while Moore effected a slight course change to port and then another to starboard in order to keep the target in the moon path. At 3 miles, the crew visually sighted a fully surfaced U-boat maintaining a speed between 10 and 12 knots. Moore executed one last course adjustment to keep the U-boat in the moon path before the attack. At 2½ miles range, the crew shut down the radar and, due to the sufficient moonlight, decided not to employ the Leigh Light. The Liberator swooped over the U-boat at 50ft, observed eight crew members in the conning tower and released six depth charges. The crew achieved a perfect straddle with three exploding on each side of the conning tower. The six explosions appeared to raise the U-boat from the water, and then it disintegrated. Moore turned the B-24 around and the crew only observed debris and oil. *U-740*, a Type VIIC boat, sank with all fifty-one hands. It had not attacked any Allied shipping on its two patrols.[5]

This RAF Liberator crew then managed another attack. After the first engagement, Moore resumed patrol when at 0240 hours, just thirty minutes after the last battle, the crew obtained another U-boat radar contact at 6 miles range, again approximately 40 miles west of Brest. At 2½ miles from the target, the crew saw a surfaced U-boat travelling at 8 knots. Not having achieved an up-moon path position, Moore turned to port and then approached. As before, the Liberator passed over this Type VIIC U-boat at 50ft and dropped six depth charges. Four seconds after release, four exploded on the U-boat's starboard side while the other two exploded on the port side, resulting in 10ft-high plumes. The B-24 circled the position and observed the U-boat with a heavy list to starboard, and then its bows protruding from the surface at an angle exceeding 45 degrees. The U-boat slipped underwater from this position. Now, with the danger passed, the crew illuminated the Leigh Light and observed crew members in the oil and debris. *U-373* had sunk three Allied vessels on twelve patrols. Four crew members died in the attack, while a German patrol boat rescued forty-seven men.[6] B-24 'G' landed at St Eval at 0709 hours after a highly successful nine-hour patrol with no damage and no casualties. Moore received an immediate Distinguished Service Order after landing. No Allied single-engine or twin-engine aircraft could have conducted these attacks because none of them would have the capacity to hold twelve depth charges. These assaults well demonstrated the Liberator's strengths.[7]

Four days later, on 10 June, another RAF Liberator struck. The attack on *U-821* though, commenced with four Mosquitoes from 248 Squadron. At noon, the four flew in formation when 'T' spotted a U-boat surfacing 1 to 1½ miles away. The Mosquitoes increased altitude, turned to starboard, and dived on the target. They struck with several machine gun and cannon attacks. These assaults resulted in some damage but nothing fatal. No. 206 Squadron had recently converted from Fortresses to Liberators, and one of their new B-24s, 'K', piloted by Flight Lieutenant A.D.S. Dundas, soon arrived. This Liberator had commenced its day from St Eval at 0510 hours, and began to patrol the Channel's western approaches. At 1209 hours, seven hours into their patrol, the crew obtained a radar contact 10 miles to starboard and Dundas altered course to home on the target. At 4 miles away, the British spotted a U-boat moving at around 10 knots. The crew noticed multiple RAF Mosquitoes engaged in 'dummy attacks' as they witnessed 'no shell bursts'. Dundas now approached. At 1220 hours the four-engine bomber flew over Type VIIC *U-821* at 50ft and dropped five depth charges. One exploded on the port side, while the other four exploded on the starboard. Surprisingly, the U-boat maintained speed and its zig-zag course. Dundas then conducted two additional attacks but on both occasions the depth charges failed to release. On the fourth assault, as the B-24 approached, the U-boat 'turned sharply to starboard' but this time, the six depth charges fell and 'perfectly straddled' the target. The U-boat slowed to a halt, its bows swung to port, rose from the surface, and the U-boat slipped underwater stern first among 'bubbles, oil and debris'. The British spotted three crew members in the water. The Liberator returned to St Eval at 1447 hours, a nine-and-a-half-hour patrol. This marked 206 Squadron's only U-boat encounter for the month. On a later patrol, the crew spotted seven empty dinghies. One German crew member survived while fifty men perished. *U-821* had not sunk any Allied vessels on its two patrols.[8]

No. 311 Squadron, one of the Czechoslovakian units, attacked two U-boats and destroyed one in June. On the 24th, B-24 'O' took off from Predannack at 1409 hours. The Czechs discovered surfaced Type VIIC *U-971* at the western approach to the Channel and attacked with both rocket projectiles and depth charges. They then alerted nearby Allied vessels of the now-submerged U-boat. Destroyers HMCS *Haida* and HMS *Eskimo* engaged in a depth charge attack, which forced *U-971* to the surface. The Germans fled the doomed boat as Allied gun fire pummelled and sank it. Two crew members died while the Allied vessels rescued the other fifty-one. *U-971* had not destroyed any Allied vessels on this, its only patrol.⁹

The RAF's 86 Squadron attacked three U-boats in June and destroyed two of them, beginning on the 26th. That day 'N' took off from RAF Tain in northern Scotland at 2045 hours and patrolled off the Norwegian coast. Shortly before midnight, the crew spotted a U-boat and attacked. On the first pass, the depth charges failed to release, but on the second, three fell on the starboard side. Type VIIC/41 *U-317* 'rolled over to Port' and disappeared. The British sighted a significant oil patch and bodies. The pilot, Flight Lieutenant G.W.T. Parker, circled the area but with oil and petrol leaking, he decided to return to base immediately after the attack and landed at RAF Stornoway in north-west Scotland at 1245 hours. All fifty U-boat crew members perished. *U-317* had not sunk any Allied vessels on this, its first and only patrol.[10]

Four days later, on 30 June, 86 Squadron struck again. This time, Liberator Mk. III 'E' took off from Scotland at 0730 hours and, while flying off the Norwegian coast at 2102 hours, a Canadian Catalina reported itself in battle with a surfaced U-boat. Flight Lieutenant N.E.M. Smith immediately set course for the location and at 2115 hours spotted the target, a Type VIIC boat, and attacked with six depth charges that successfully straddled the boat. The U-boat's bows rose from the surface and it slid underwater by the stern, with the British stern, with the British witnessing a significant patch of oil. The Liberator had sustained damage in its number four engine from the U-boat's guns and Smith nursed it back to base, where it landed on 1 July at 0128 hours. All fifty-two crew members went down with the U-boat. Thus ended *U-478*'s maiden patrol, not having sunk any Allied vessels.[11]

At 2100 hours on 29 June, 224 Squadron Liberator 'L' took off from St Eval. At 0101 hours on the 30th, the British crew, while flying over the western area of the Channel, obtained a weak radar contact at 5 miles. This contact remained intermittent until, within 2 miles of the target, the crew lost it entirely. The pilot, Flight Lieutenant J.W. Barling, continued on course and reacquired radar contact at 5 miles distance. He swung the four-engine aircraft around and proceeded straight to the target's location. At 3 miles, Barling turned to starboard and several crew members caught sight of a *schnorkel* off the aircraft's port beam. This device, which protruded from the surface to provide air for submerged U-boat operations, had so impressed Dönitz that he ordered all boats for Atlantic patrols to have it installed.[12] Yet as this British crew demonstrated, Allied radar could detect it and it would prove to be no salvation for the U-boats against Allied air power. Barling altered course to starboard, flew for 5 miles and swung the B-24 completely around. He then proceeded in the moon path with the visual sighting of a surface disturbance straight ahead. He descended to 200ft and 1 mile away the crew activated the Leigh Light and spotted the *schnorkel*, with smoke emitting, moving at approximately 4 knots, and possibly a periscope 6 to 8ft in front of it. The British had intercepted Type VIIC *U-441*, a U-boat that had already quarrelled with Allied aircraft earlier that month. No. 407 Squadron, RCAF, Wellington 'C' had encountered Type VIIC *U-441* on 7 June in company with two other U-boats. *U-441*'s flak brought it down, killing all six Canadians.[13] On this night though, the German commander's faith in the *schnorkel* would deprive his lethal flak crew from intercepting the oncoming RAF onslaught. At 0115 hours, fourteen minutes after the initial radar contact, the B-24 flew over the two objects protruding from the surface and released seven depth charges before the *schnorkel*. The crew had high confidence that they had attained a straddle pattern. Air bubbles and oil appeared less than two minutes after the attack and remained for ten minutes. The B-24 landed at 1041 hours on the 30th. All fifty-one U-boat crew members perished in the attack. *U-441*, a Type VIIC boat, had sunk one Allied vessel during its ten patrols.[14]

However, U-boats did defeat some of the Allied land-based four-engine aircraft that attacked them this month. In addition to those noted previously, U-boats shot down three others of this type. On 7 June in the Bay of Biscay, 224 Squadron Liberator 'B', with 179 Squadron Wellington 'G', attacked three U-boats. None of Dönitz's boats received terminal damage, the Wellington survived, but Type VIIC *U-415* destroyed the B-24 and all ten crew members perished. Also in the Bay of Biscay on 13 June, 53 Squadron Fortress 'U' attacked surfaced Type VIIC *U-270* on two passes but on the third one, although it released multiple depth charges, the German crew struck one of its engines and the aircraft crashed, killing all eight crew members. U-boats fatally struck one other Liberator as well. On 20 June off the Norwegian coast, 86 Squadron Liberator 'N' discovered surfaced Type VIIC *U-771* and roared above it but, for unknown reasons, failed to release any depth charges. Instead, the flak caused the aircraft to plunge into the water after passing over the conning tower. All eight crew members perished.[15]

A few other Allied aircraft also targeted U-boats in June, with Catalinas achieving five sinkings in the area off the Norwegian coast. On 5 May, *U-477* departed Kristiansand, Norway, for its first patrol. Before encountering any Allied vessels, it encountered an Allied aircraft. On 2 June at 1745 hours, Canso 'T' of 162 Squadron, RCAF, departed its base at RAF Wick in northern Scotland and began a patrol of the

Norwegian Sea. Eight hours later, at 0211 hours, while maintaining an altitude of 1,700ft, the crew spotted the surfaced Type VIIC *U-477* 4 miles away travelling at a crisp 15 knots. Flight Lieutenant R.E. MacBride turned the flying boat to port while descending, until at 1,000yd from target, the Catalina's front guns fired on the U-boat's conning tower and the Germans delivered 'intense accurate' machine gun fire in reply. The U-boat swung to starboard as the flying boat continued to descend until it flew over the conning tower and released four depth charges from 'stern to bow'. The depth charges straddled the boat and plumes temporarily obscured the U-boat from the Canadians' view. As the plumes subsided, the U-boat appeared to 'lift bodily', then turned to port and lost almost all momentum. After continuing on an attack heading for fifteen seconds, MacBride turned to port and commenced a second assault with machine gun fire directed at the conning tower. The previous attack had proven to be sufficient, though. The U-boat sank on an even keel until the bows protruded 80 degrees into the air. The Canadians noticed five survivors 'waving' at the Canso. The aircraft remained in the area for three and a half hours and sighted a significant oil patch. The Canadians landed at Wick at 1010 hours, ending a fourteen-hour patrol. None of the U-boat's fifty-one crew members survived.[16]

The same Canadian squadron engaged another U-boat eight days later. *U-980* departed Bergen, Norway, on 3 June for its first patrol but like *U-477*, instead of finding any Allied vessels, an Allied aircraft found it. The Canso crew, while flying at 1,000ft, discovered the Type VIIC boat at 1515 hours and the pilot, Flying Officer L. Sherman, 'immediately turned to starboard' and commenced descending, while both the front and starboard guns engaged from 800yd. The conning tower crew members delivered 'accurate' and 'concentrated' fire at the approaching flying boat. The U-boat manoeuvred so that its stern faced the attacker and at 1522 hours, just seven minutes after the initial sighting, the Canso roared over the conning tower at 50ft and deposited four depth charges. The dropped ordnance straddled the target and the resulting explosions hid the U-boat from view. *U-980* circled slowly with oil leaking from its tanks. At 1532 hours, less than thirty minutes from the battle's commencement, the U-boat disappeared on an even keel. The Canadians did not notice any wreckage, only oil and some survivors. Sherman received an immediate Distinguished Flying Cross for his actions. None of the U-boat's fifty-two crew members survived.[17]

However, another U-boat exacted revenge. On 13 June ten days later, Sherman's eight-man crew took off from Wick for another patrol and after radioing their position, attacked Type VIIC *U-480*. They dropped one bomb off target but the U-boat's anti-aircraft flak ignited a fire in the Canso and it landed in the sea. Sherman disappeared in the water shortly thereafter, while two other Canadians went down with the flying boat. The remaining five died gradually over the next seven days, except for Sergeant J.R. Roberts. A fishing vessel retrieved him and he remained a prisoner of war for the next year, the only survivor of the crew that sank *U-980*.[18]

The RCAF's 162 Squadron fatally attacked a third U-boat this month. *U-715* departed Stavanger, Norway, on 8 June, and five days later, before locating any Allied shipping, the Canadians found it. The Canso, with its eight-man crew, commanded by Wing Commander C.G.W. Chapman, departed Reykjavik and when approximately 140 miles north of the Shetlands, spotted, at a distance of 3 miles, two periscopes moving at a slow 3 knots. Canso 'T' flew towards the target and the crew spotted the conning tower underwater as it flew overhead. The Canadians released four depth charges and believed that at least three exploded. After twenty seconds on the attack course, Chapman swung 'hard to port' and noticed the U-boat rising to the surface. The Canadian officer circled from mile away while maintaining 1,000ft. *U-715*, a Type VIIC, remained on the surface while moving to starboard with almost no visible wake. After moving for 400yd after the assault, it stopped. The bows disappeared beneath the surface, then the conning tower and the stern rose. The Canso crew had a clear view of both the still propellers and the rudder as the German crew began appearing on the surface. Remarkably, the conning tower then surfaced and at least one U-boat crew member manned the guns as Chapman bore in for another assault. As the flying boat flew over the U-boat, the crew heard an explosion and the port engine began leaking oil and 'belching black smoke'. Chapman switched that engine off but, despite the crew's efforts, the propeller failed 'feather'. With the port propeller dragging, Chapman increased the starboard engine to maximum boost. The injured aircraft descended from 1,000ft until it struck 'wave tops' at a speed of 45 knots and landed in the water. The German flak had punctured the Canso's hull in numerous locations and this necessitated a quick abandonment of the sinking flying boat. The Canadians rapidly removed all equipment such as cameras, operational documents and maps. Of the two inflated dinghies, the port one 'exploded', forcing the crew to move to the starboard one 'which had 2 holes in it'. Two members entered the dinghy with the removed gear while the remainder 'hung on' to the sides. The Canadians initiated a rotation system but three men became 'waterlogged' and could not enter the dinghy. Having difficulty keeping the dinghy afloat, they 'jettisoned' all gear. A Liberator arrived but departed. Then 'an hour or so later' the same B-24 appeared and located the crew. A Sunderland followed and a Warwick released an airborne lifeboat, which landed approximately 100 to 150yd from the dinghy. One Canadian, Pilot Officer Waterbury, removed all clothing except for his Mae West life vest, and swam to the lifeboat. After an hour of strenuous labour, he brought it to the survivors. Flight Sergeant Leatherdale though, 'relaxed his hold and was lost'. The seven remaining crew members entered the lifeboat and brought the dinghy on board. The lifeboat had been damaged and only the bows and stern remained above water. A second Warwick arrived and released Lindholme gear at 100yd from the waterlogged lifeboat. Lindholme gear contained a dinghy and four containers of supplies. Unfortunately, while loading a crew member into the new dinghy, they inadvertently punctured it and they reverted back to the lifeboat. A second Lindholme dinghy 'drifted away'. The conditions of two crew members continued to deteriorate due to 'waterlogged immersion suits and general exposure' as they sat in the lifeboat with 'water up' to their armpits. An air-sea rescue boat arrived and all seven crew members transferred to it. The rescue crew immediately commenced artificial respiration on two of the Canso's crew, but they had died. The remaining five arrived at the Military Hospital in Lerwick. The RAF awarded Chapman the Distinguished Service Order while the other four received either the Distinguished Flying Cross or the Distinguished Flying Medal. Of *U-715*'s crew, sixteen lived while thirty-six perished.[19]

The fourth and final successful attack by 162 Squadron came on 24 June. RCAF Canso 'A' departed Reykjavik at noon with its eight-man crew and at 1900 hours, the Canadians spotted the fully surfaced *U-1225*. The pilot, Flight Lieutenant D.E. Hornell, bore in on the target. When the Canso was ¾ mile away, the U-boat's guns began an accurate and severe fire as it closed the distance and the submarine, attempting to evade the flying boat, shifted course by 80 degrees to starboard. The Canso continued on to the target and its front guns started firing when it had reached 1,200yd from the U-boat. German fire hit one of the engines and disabled it. Hornell managed to feather the prop but the engine then fell from the wing. The injured flying boat roared over the U-boat and Hornell delivered a 'perfect straddle' with its depth charges that sank *U-1225*, one of the long-range Type IXC/40 boats. However, for Hornell, his problems had just started. The damage kept the Canso from maintaining lift and he crashed a mile from the U-boat in turbulent water. His base failed to receive his radio report but remarkably, 333 (Norwegian) Squadron Catalina 'D', returning to base, spotted a dinghy with five survivors and two men either injured or dead in RAF uniforms. At 3 miles from the Canso survivors, the Norwegians counted thirty-five to forty 'bodies in water – some appeared to be dead. Others alive'. RAF Sunderland 'W' from 330 Squadron arrived and guided a rescue boat to the survivors. Two of the Canadians – Sergeant Scott and Sergeant St Laurent – had perished and 'their bodies lost at sea'. Hornell then died, his body returned to shore for burial. All the other crew members survived despite eighteen hours of exposure. Hornell received the prestigious Victoria Cross posthumously for his actions, and the other crew members received either the Distinguished Service Order, the Distinguished Flying Cross or the Distinguished Flying Medal. While the British Sunderland crew had found the remaining Canadians, by the time it arrived at the Germans' location they had all disappeared. All fifty-six U-boat crew members perished. *U-1225* had not sunk any Allied vessels on its first and only patrol.[20]

Another Catalina from 333 (Norwegian) Squadron carried out a fatal U-boat strike. On 17 June at 1320 hours, Catalina 'D' lifted off from the waters of Sullom Voe. At 1515 hours, the crew commenced a sweep of the area with 5 miles visibility, which apparently improved because ninety minutes later, at 1643 hours, from a height of 1,000ft, they found the surfaced Type VIIC *U-423*. It was travelling at 12 knots approximately 100 miles off the south-western Norwegian coast at 10 to 15 miles distance. The pilot, Lieutenant C.F. Krafft, descended to 50ft. The Germans responded with some inaccurate flak, the Catalina's front guns jammed, but Krafft pressed on and dropped six depth charges that successfully straddled the boat with three on each side. The U-boat's bows rose from the surface to a 30-degree angle as the stern disappeared and the boat sank six minutes after the attack. The British crew sighted forty survivors among the oil and debris. The Catalina splashed down at its base at 1850 hours. All fifty-three crew members perished on this, *U-423*'s only patrol, having engaged no Allied vessels.[21]

The same Norwegian Squadron, 333, also operated twin-engine Mosquitoes during this time and battled two U-boats. On 16 June, Mosquito 'R' performed a strafing attack on Type VIIC/41 *U-804* and the flak brought it down for the loss of both crew members. The same day though, Mosquito 'H' departed RAF Sumburgh in the Shetlands at 1815 hours and in less than an hour, at 1904 hours, the crew visually spotted a surfaced U-boat 8 miles away moving at 8 knots. Six minutes later, pilot Lieutenant E. Johansen entered a cloud to mask his approach. When exiting this cover, he sighted the U-boat turning to starboard only 2 miles off his port bow. Johansen established his attack approach at 800yd from 1,500ft. Both the U-boat and the aircraft commenced firing. Johansen flew over the U-boat at 100ft, 'stern to bow', and released two depth charges. Both exploded 5ft from the U-boat's starboard side. *U-998* now started moving in a small circle leaving a trail of oil. The U-boat eventually dived, then reappeared with bows at a 90-degree angle, where it remained suspended for five minutes. The Mosquito attacked again with gun fire. The bow's angle decreased to 30 degrees for two minutes, until it slid stern first underwater. Remarkably, *U-998*, a Type VIIC/41 boat, arrived at Bergen the next day. However, the Mosquito's damage proved to be so extensive that the Nazis decommissioned it ten days later. *U-998*'s war career had ended. It had not sunk any Allied vessels on its only patrol.[22]

The Sunderlands, one of the few original Coastal Command types still hunting U-boats, achieved two sinkings this month. On 7 June, 'S' from 201 Squadron patrolled the western edge of the Bay of Biscay before midnight. The British crew probably had little optimism for the night's hunt. With a cloud base of 500ft obscuring the moon, any visual sightings would be challenging. These conditions clearly favoured the U-boats. Nevertheless, at 2355 hours, the crew, from 450ft, obtained a radar contact at 9 miles distance. Flying Officer L.H. Baveystock homed on the target while decreasing to 250ft. The contact remained constant on the approach until, at ½-mile range, it disappeared. Now at 50ft, Baveystock continued flying in the area until the second pilot sighted an 'unmistakable swirl' with 'rising bubbles'. The visual evidence confirmed the U-boat's presence but did not create an ideal attack scenario, so Baveystock continued flying below 500ft awaiting a more opportune occasion. At 0244 hours, the crew acquired radar contact again from 400ft. Baveystock set course for the target, now 11 miles from the flying boat, and descended from 400 to 250ft. Once in the area, the crew released numerous flares, which illuminated a fully surfaced Type VIIC U-boat turning hard to starboard. The U-boat's gun commenced firing with 'red, green and yellow' tracers. Baveystock turned to attack and the Sunderland's front guns and middle upper turret engaged. After six seconds of fire from the flying boat, the U-boat's guns fell silent. Baveystock aimed for the conning tower, with the Sunderland now at 100ft and 200yd from the target. Roaring over the boat, six depth charges fell and straddled the submarine. The crew spied four depth charge plumes. The radar contact then 'disappeared immediately afterwards'. The Sunderland remained in the area for fifty-eight minutes but the crew did not observe anything. Finally, at 0348 hours, almost four hours after the initial radar contact, Baveystock made course for home.

JUNE 1944

All fifty U-boat crew members went down with the boat. This ended *U-955*'s first and only patrol, it not having sunk any Allied vessels.[23]

At 2345 hours that same 7 June, 228 Squadron Sunderland 'R' slipped from the waters of Pembroke Dock at 1830 hours. While flying at around 1,200ft over the Bay of Biscay, the crew discovered a fully surfaced U-boat 7 miles away. The U-boat gunners immediately fired on the large flying boat and the Sunderland's lack of speed became a critical factor in this engagement. As the aircraft moved to attack, the German commander had ample time to submerge before the British could attack. The Sunderland pilot, Flight Lieutenant J. Quinn, with no other options, continued flying hoping his luck would change and, four minutes later, it did. The crew detected a target at 5 miles distance. Quinn circled until he had obtained a 'down moon' position and six minutes after the initial contact, the crew visually spotted a fully surfaced U-boat at 5 miles. The large flying boat flew over the U-boat at 70ft and straddled it with depth charges. The damaged U-boat now began moving in circles and decreased in speed. Eventually, it disappeared under water with just an oil patch remaining on the surface. German forces rescued fourteen crew members while thirty-eight perished. *U-970*, a Type VIIC boat, had not sunk any Allied vessels on its two patrols.[24]

U-boats did shoot down numerous British Sunderlands this month. Two days after 228 Squadron's successful attack on *U-970*, Type VIIC *U-228* fought a Sunderland from the same squadron. On 10 June, ML762 took off from Pembroke Dock at 2010 hours for the last time. It encountered *U-228* in the Bay of Biscay and attacked with six depth charges that dropped off target. After the flying boat flew over the U-boat, flak caused fire on the Sunderland's starboard side. The four-engine aircraft gradually lost height until it crashed into the water. None of the eleven-man crew survived.[25] On 12 June, U-boats downed two Sunderlands. Type VIIC *U-333* shot down 201 Squadron Sunderland 'S', resulting in the deaths of twelve crew members, while Type VIIC *U-993* hit 228 Squadron Sunderland 'U', killing all eleven men.[26]

VC-9 Avengers sank one U-boat, one of the long-range Type IXD2 boats, during June. An Avenger pilot from the escort carrier USS *Solomons*, in the South Atlantic, visually sighted *U-860* but German fire downed the single-engine aircraft, killing all three Americans before the crew could radio the position. Nevertheless, the Americans began a search for the U-boat. Another pilot discovered it, but having no significant ordnance, used the opportunity to home in additional aircraft. Three more naval aircraft arrived and two of them assaulted it with rockets. None of these attacks proved to be fatal. Then, two more Avengers appeared, T-1 flown by Lieutenant (jg) D.E. Weigle and T-32, piloted by Lieutenant (jg) W.F. Chamberlain, who had contributed to the sinking of *U-569* in May 1943. Weigle strafed the U-boat, while Chamberlain swooped over the U-boat at 50ft and dropped two depth charges. The subsequent explosion destroyed both the U-boat and the low-flying attacking aircraft, killing Chamberlain and his two crew members. The US Navy rescued twenty German survivors while forty-four men perished. *U-860* had not sunk any Allied shipping on this, its only patrol.[27]

Dönitz's interpretation of this month though, bordered on delusion. In his war diary, he claimed that the 'old spirit of the arm was once again magnificently displayed', concluding that 'the decision to put in the U-boats had been a right one'. He acknowledged, though, that the 'expense of losses' amounted to 'severe' although not 'intolerable', and confessed that U-boats 'had no decisive effect upon the enemy's build-up' for the Normandy invasion. Instead, he claimed that the attacks had 'hampered' the Allies 'to a considerable extent' and therefore 'lightened the burden of the troops ashore'. He noted that from 6 June until 31 August his U-boats had sunk five escort vessels, twelve merchantmen, and four landing craft while damaging seven other Allied vessels.[28]

By any measure though, June 1944 had been a stunning success for Allied anti-submarine aircraft. With ten fatal attacks, the Liberators alone sank almost as many U-boats as the German vessels sank merchantmen. Allied aircraft destroyed twenty U-boats in June, while U-boats only destroyed twenty-one Allied vessels in June, July and August. Allied forces now began spreading throughout France preparing to capture Dönitz's valuable French U-boat bases. His attempts to disrupt the Normandy landings had clearly failed. With the Mediterranean lost as well, his main operational area had narrowed to the Norwegian Sea, while his opponent's anti-submarine aircraft numbers continued to soar throughout the last six months of 1944, and to saturate his rapidly reduced operational areas.

Chapter 17

July–December 1944

Aircraft continued to dominate the Allied anti-submarine fight. Of the seventy-four U-boats actively destroyed during these six months by all means, aircraft contributed to forty-seven, 62 per cent, almost a two-to-one margin. B-24s engaged in more successful attacks than any other aircraft. On the high seas, Liberators participated in eight, while the next closest aircraft, Sunderlands, contributed to six. A variety of aircraft participated in the remaining at-sea aircraft attacks: Swordfish (three), Avengers (two), Catalinas (two), a Firefly (one), a Fortress (one), and a Halifax (one). B-24s, B-17s and the British Lancasters added to the overall total through air raids on a variety of German U-boat bases. Dönitz's boats found no solace whether at sea or in port as the war entered its final twelve months.

The RAF's 206 Squadron, operating B-24 Mk. VIs, sent out eight aircraft on 15 July and one encountered *U-319*. The U-boat's demise, and that of B-24 'E', remains a mystery, but the primary sources provide a plausible tale. 'E' took off from Leuchars with its ten-man crew at 0550 hours. The squadron's recorder typed in his report that 'nothing further was heard from this aircraft which failed to return'. However, two other Liberator crews provided details when they returned from their patrols. B-24 'B' took off at 1409 hours that day and at 1643 hours, off the southwest Norwegian coast, the crew discovered a dinghy a mile away. They also sighted an occupant inside. The British crew released multiple markers in addition to a food pack, radio and other equipment. However, the occupant 'made no apparent effort to retrieve them'. Of especial note, the B-24 crew discovered 'a very large oil patch' but no wreckage just a mile from the dinghy. They also sighted two nearby aircraft, flew to them and made contact with two Warwicks, aircraft the British employed for search and rescue missions. One Warwick followed the B-24 to the dinghy location and it released an airborne lifeboat that 'landed intact in good position down wind' of the dinghy, and then dropped Lindholme gear in good location as well. Both floated past the dinghy without the occupant stirring. Finally, the Liberator crew released two more emergency packs in proximity to the dinghy and returned to Scotland.

The following day, Liberator 'P' took off from Leuchars at 0606 hours. Six hours later, at 1242 hours, the crew discovered an inverted dinghy. They reported that the dinghy contained 'one live survivor'. The crew reported the position to base and also noticed a Catalina nearby. B-24 'M' lifted off at 1422 hours and sighted a 'dinghy with one survivor' and an airborne lifeboat. A Catalina flew over the dinghy and the Liberator kept returning to the location 'at intervals' until, at the Catalina's crew's request, the B-24 released a marker on the location. At 1843 hours though, the British noted that the dinghy no longer held any occupants. Twenty minutes later, at 1907 hours, the Liberator guided a RAF High Speed Launch to the location. The B-24 departed when the boat arrived. The launch crew found Sergeant Hilton, one of Liberator's 'E' crew members, but he had expired. U-boat Command never heard from *U-319* again and it is presumed that all fifty-one members perished. With no survivors from the battle, the information would suggest, due to the large oil slick, that 'E' destroyed *U-319*, a Type VIIC/41 boat, with depth charges and German flak may have fatally damaged the aircraft as well.[1]

On 17 July, Liberator Mk. III 'U' from 86 Squadron departed Tain at 1426 hours. Seven hours later, the crew found the fully surfaced Type VIIC *U-347* in the Norwegian Sea. The British crew attacked it and sank it. The B-24 crew spotted an oil patch and survivors in the water before it departed. The U-boat crew managed to hit the Liberator multiple times as it approached but the aircraft sustained no serious damage. None of the forty-nine crew members survived. *U-347* had not sunk any Allied vessels on its two patrols.[2]

On 9 August, Liberator Mk. VI 'C' of 53 Squadron took off from St Eval at 1100 hours to search the Bay of Biscay. At one point during the patrol, pilot Wing Commander R.T.F. Gates diverted from his course to investigate radar contacts in the eastern bay and only found Allied vessels. However, while maintaining an altitude of 4,000ft with no cloud cover, calm waters and 5 miles visibility, the crew spotted an oil slick to starboard. Gates altered course and followed the trail of oil, 50ft wide, for a mile. Then, the British spotted a U-boat, underwater in front of the oil. Gates dived immediately and passed once without taking any action. He then released a marker at 100ft altitude on the second pass. On the third run, the crew dropped six Torpex depth charges, which they had specifically 'set to shallow depth'. The charges exploded, sending plumes into the air. As the plumes dissipated, the B-24's rear gunner observed 'large green bubbles in the middle of the disturbance'. More oil rose to the surface ten minutes after the explosions. The crew radioed the position to surface naval vessels and other British aircraft, specifically Sunderlands, arrived as well. They witnessed 'heavy orange coloured grease' and wood, which they contended resembled 'U-boat planking'. HMS *Wren*, a Royal Navy sloop, steamed to the location and rescued all of *U-608*'s fifty-two men. The Type VIIC boat had sunk five Allied vessels and damaged two others on eight patrols.[3]

Five days later, on 14 August, 53 Squadron Liberator 'G' departed St Eval at 2013 hours. For the British, the weather provided ideal hunting conditions: no cloud, moderate sea and clear visibility. While flying at 600ft over the northern Bay of Biscay, the crew detected a radar contact at 7½ miles. As the contact slowly increased, the British radar operator believed that they had discovered a surfacing U-boat. Flight Lieutenant G.G. Potier maintained course to ensure that the operator tracked a steady contact and after ½ mile, Potier, now convinced that the crew had discovered a U-boat, manoeuvred away to prepare his approach. By 2356 hours, Potier had the contact at 11½ miles and bore in. A 'relative drift' caused him to shift the course slightly. The flight lieutenant performed a similar manoeuvre at 3 miles distance. At ¾ mile, the crew illuminated the Leigh Light, which found the surfaced U-boat 'dead ahead' maintaining a crisp 12 to 15 knots. The crew did not realise at that time that they had found Type VIIC *U-618*, a U-boat with a lethal record against Allied aircraft. The U-boat crew had shot down 53 Squadron Liberator 'N' in November 1943, killing all nine crew members, and on 30 July 1944, it had destroyed 172 Squadron Wellington 'J' in the Bay of Biscay, resulting in the death of the six crew members. Now, the experienced German gunners aimed at the approaching Liberator. The B-24's front gunner began targeting the conning tower, while the Germans apparently aimed at the Leigh Light but failed to cause any damage. The four-engine aircraft roared over the surfaced U-boat at 170 to 190ft altitude and dropped six Torpex depth charges. Plumes appeared immediately and flak halted when the Liberator flew over the boat. The radar contact held steady for less than 2 miles until 'it slowly disappeared'. The B-24 returned to the area of attack and illuminated the area twice but saw no trace of the U-boat. More than two hours after the assault, at 0230 hours, a Wellington appeared and illuminated the area. The Liberator crew observed 'oil streaks a quarter to a half mile in length. 'G' landed at 0902 hours, ending a patrol of over nine hours. All sixty-one men on the U-boat perished. *U-618* had sunk three Allied vessels on eight patrols.[4]

U-867, a long-range Type IXC/40 boat, departed Kristiansand on 12 September for its first patrol. It would encounter no Allied shipping but would find itself the target of multiple Allied aircraft. The RAF operational records suggest the first attack was carried out by Mosquitoes from 248 Squadron. Six of them roared down the runway on 18 September between 0623 and 0633 hours and commenced an anti-U-boat patrol along the Norwegian coast. At 0820 hours, they spotted a surfaced U-boat travelling at 6 knots. The six aircraft assaulted it with machine guns and cannon, while two of the Mosquitoes released depth charges that struck near the U-boat's stern. The British pilots noted 'cannon strikes' around the conning tower and that the depth charge explosions appeared to lift the boat. Before departing they observed the U-boat moving to port with a 10 to 15-degree list to port. Most notably, none reported any oil. They all returned to base between 1001 and 1015 hours. *U-867* had survived an attack by six twin-engine Mosquitoes. Against the Liberators, it would not prove to be so fortunate.

Liberator 'H' of 224 Squadron left RAF Milltown, in northern Scotland, at 1755 hours later that same day. While flying along the south-west Norwegian coast at 1942 hours, almost twelve hours after the Mosquito assault, the B-24 crew detected, by radar, a contact at 9½ miles. Flight Lieutenant A.B. Young, altered course to port by 75 degrees to head for the target. At 2½ miles, the second pilot visually spotted a fully surfaced U-boat. The German crew, upon noticing the Liberator, commenced firing their guns but the front gunner silenced them with fire of his own at ½-mile range. Young flew over the U-boat at 75ft and released six 250lb Torpex depth charges. The U-boat resumed fire on the Liberator after the attack until, three minutes after the depth charge explosions, the submarine gradually disappeared with the telltale sign of a 50yd-wide oil patch on the surface. The Liberator landed at base at 0119 hours. *U-867* had not sunk, but the British had severely damaged it.

On 19 September, at 1220 hours, 224 Squadron Liberator 'Q' took off from Milltown and commenced its patrol along the south-west Norwegian coast. At 1625 hours, radar discovered a surface contact at 15 miles range. The radar operator faced several weather issues – moderate seas with a heavy swell, wind at 35 knots – that all decreased the chance of maintaining the contact. Nevertheless, he overcame these problems so that at 8 miles distance, the second pilot made a visual contact, finding *U-867* on the surface, transiting the Norwegian Sea at 6 knots and 'leaving a trail of oil'. Flight Lieutenant H.J. Rayner, swung to starboard for a 'down sun' assault, and the U-boat commander responded by shifting to port, forcing Rayner to alter course accordingly. The U-boat commenced accurate fire and the B-24's front and mid-upper turret replied. The Liberator roared over the damaged boat and dropped six depth charges. The U-boat crew may have been in the process of abandoning the boat when the attack occurred. Although the British crew did not notice anything unusual, photographs indicate two dinghies, one large and one small one, close by the boat. After the attack, the U-boat decreased from 6 knots to zero. And then, five minutes after the depth charge explosions, the U-boat, maintaining an even keel, slipped under the surface. When Rayner flew over the location after the sinking, the crew noticed a large dinghy and forty smaller ones with around fifty men amidst a gradually increasing patch of oil. The B-24 departed three minutes later and landed at 2015 hours, a nearly eight-hour flight. All sixty members of the U-boat crew perished on its first patrol having engaged no Allied vessels.[5]

RAF Liberators and Royal Navy aircraft teamed together for the demise of *U-1060*. On 27 October, four single-engine Fireflies from HMS *Implacable* initially assaulted the surfaced Type VIIF U-boat, losing one to flak. Additional Navy aircraft assaulted a second time and U-boat crew downed another Firefly. Of these four crew members, two died and the Germans captured the other two. The damage though, led the U-boat commander to beach off the Norwegian coast to save the U-boat. With *U-1060* still afloat, the RAF turned to its most lethal anti-submarine aircraft. Early on the morning of the 29th, the Czech crews of 311 Squadron's Mk. V Liberators 'G' 'H' and 'Y' crews received a briefing on the U-boat's location, and at 0400 'H' roared down the Leuchars runway. 'Y' ascended three minutes later and 'G' two minutes after 'that. Liberator 'Y' arrived at the U-boat's location at 0903 hours and during the next thirty-seven minutes delivered seven attacks with sixteen rocket projectiles and four depth charges. 'H' attacked between 0921 hours and 0949 hours with six assaults involving sixteen rocket projectiles and four depth charges. Forty-three U-boat crew members escaped the attack, while fourteen perished. *U-1060*, serving as a transport U-boat between Norway and Germany, never conducted any attacks. 'G', with its nine crew members though, never reached the target. It crashed in northern Scotland, injuring four crew members and killing the remaining five.[6]

On 26 July, *U-863*, a long-range Type IXD2 boat, departed Europe and set a course through the South Atlantic for its final destination in the Indian Ocean. It never arrived. The US Navy first sighted it on 28 September, in the South Atlantic, when VP-211 Mariner P-4 obtained a radar contact and homed on the signal until its crew visually sighted it. The intense flak forced the flying boat to avoid the U-boat and the Americans did not attempt a bomb or depth charge assault. However, the US Navy now knew a U-boat was traversing the area and it sent its PB4Y-1 Liberators the next day. VB-107's B-9 departed its base in Natal, Brazil, and found the surfaced *U-863*. The Liberator flew over the boat and released five depth charges. Another American Liberator, B-7, soon arrived and conducted three depth charge attacks that destroyed the craft. The B-24s released life rafts for the twenty survivors but on later searches the Americans did not find any. All sixty-nine crew perished. *U-863* had not sunk any Allied vessels on its two patrols.[7]

Fortresses participated in one fatal sinking during this time. *U-871*, another long-range Type IXD2 boat, departed Trondheim, Norway, for the Indian Ocean on its first patrol. It travelled as far as the Azores without encountering any Allied vessels. Instead, it would be discovered by a Flying Fortress. On 26 September, B-17 Mk. IIA 'P' of the RAF's 220 Squadron began its day at 1103 hours from its base at Lagens, Azores. The British found an Allied merchant vessel, the *Irish Rose*, stationary, apparently with engine trouble. The crew informed base and then at 1405 hours, they received a radio report from Fortress 'H' of the same squadron indicating that they had discovered a surfaced U-boat. B-17 'P' arrived at the reported location and joined 220 Squadron Mk. IIA Fortresses 'H' and 'F' in the search. They found nothing. Later, at 1544 hours, 'P''s crew spotted a periscope wake. Flight Lieutenant A.F. Wallace tracked the U-boat and, three minutes after the sighting, he flew over the periscope at 50ft and dropped three 250lb Torpex depth charges just as the conning tower began to emerge from the sea. Oil appeared on the surface after the explosions and continued to increase for fifty minutes after the assault, along with assorted debris. The Fortress returned to base at 2023 hours after a nine-hour flight. All sixty-nine crew members went down with *U-871*.[8]

Sunderlands participated in six U-boat sinkings during this period manned by British, Australian and Norwegian crews. The destruction of *U-243* marked a joint effort by Sunderlands and a Liberator, by Australians and Americans. On 8 July at 0531 hours, Sunderland Mk. III 'H' of the RAAF 10 Squadron slipped from the water at RAF Mount Batten. The Australians commenced flying in their patrol area at 0750 hours and on their 'fifth circuit', at 1435 hours, they visually discovered, 6 miles away, the fully surfaced Type VIIC *U-243* moving at 8 knots in the northern area of the Bay of Biscay. The large flying boat 'immediately dived' on the target as Flight Officer W.B. Tilley initiated evasive action, as did the U-boat commander. At 2 miles from target, German fire erupted and the Sunderland's nose gunner responded from 2,000yd, while the turret nose gun commenced fire when at 1,250yd. Both guns effectively silenced the U-boat's fire before the depth charge assault. Tilley swooped over the target at 75ft and released six depth charges. He then immediately swung around and began observing the target from a mile away. *U-243* ceased forward momentum, started to settle by the stern, and developed a list to port. The U-boat's guns commenced firing again but at 1500 hours, less than thirty minutes after the assault, the crew 'launched two large yellow dinghies' and fifteen smaller ones.

Now, two more Allied aircraft arrived. A US Navy Liberator detected *U-243* by radar at 1441 hours, 8 miles away. When the Americans appeared three minutes after the initial contact, they sighted both the Australian Sunderland and the German U-boat. The Navy pilot, Aurelian H. Cooledge Jr, bore in for the attack. He made two runs, with the U-boat and the Liberator firing at each other, but on both occasions, the depth charges failed to release. As Cooledge commenced his third run, he noticed that another Australian Sunderland Mk. III from 10 Squadron RAAF had arrived. 'K' found *U-243* at 1456 hours after the American's two failed runs. This Australian crew initially failed to notice the American B-24 though. Fortunately for both aircraft, Cooledge sighted the Sunderland. He concluded that sufficient distance existed between the two aircraft that he could follow the Australians. This strategy could result in two nearly simultaneous attacks on the now damaged and static U-boat. The Germans first engaged Sunderland 'K' at 2,000yd and the Australians returned fire at 1,500yd. Six depth charges fell from the large flying boat from 50ft. No fire had damaged the Sunderland. However, the Sunderland's depth charges caused plumes to rise, which blocked Cooledge's view on his approach and thrust the four-engine plane higher. As the plumes collapsed, he spotted *U-243* and dropped to around 80ft. This time, all depth charges fell when passing over the target. At 1510 hours, the U-boat slipped under the surface by the stern as the bows rose vertically. The Americans and Australians all reported survivors in the water and dinghies. Sunderland 'K' headed to England at 1514 hours. Sunderland 'H' flew over the men and released a dinghy along with a food pack. It remained until 1622 hours when, due to reaching its fuel limit, the flying boat headed home. The Americans departed at 1705 hours. The destroyer HMCS *Restigouche* arrived and rescued thirty-nine crew members. Eleven perished. *U-243* had not sunk any Allied vessels on its two patrols.[9]

On 11 July, 201 Squadron Sunderland 'P' slipped from the waters at Pembroke Dock at 0435 hours and commenced its patrol at 0700 hours. At 1054 hours, the flying boat's port inner engine started to malfunction and Flight Lieutenant I.F.B. Walters decided to head back to base.

Just over an hour later though, at 1210 hours, the engine resumed normal operation, so Walters continued flying in the assigned patrol area. At 1345 hours in the northern Bay of Biscay, the second pilot visually discovered a wake at a distance of 8½ miles. Walters turned and followed the trail as he descended to attack height. With binoculars, the British sighted both a *schnorkel* and a periscope moving slowly at ¾ knot. 'Aircraft went straight in to attack,' the British reported. Walters lined up the flying boat with the two moving objects and flew over. Five of the six selected depth charges fell, causing multiple 'explosion plumes' and lifting the U-boat's stern momentarily above the surface. Only floating debris appeared. The Sunderland landed in Welsh waters at 1915 hours, a fifteen-hour patrol. All fifty-six U-boat crew members went down with the boat. *U-1222*, a long-range Type IXC/40 boat, had not sunk any Allied vessels on its only patrol.[10]

RAAF 461 Squadron Sunderland 'P' took off into the night sky from Pembroke Dock at 2220 hours on 10 August. At 0225 hours in the eastern Bay of Biscay, the crew detected a contact at 8 miles and pilot Flying Officer I.F. Southall altered course to close the distance. Three minutes later, the Australians spotted the fully surfaced Type VIIC *U-385* and at 0235 hours attacked it with six depth charges. The U-boat's crew fired at the flying boat after the explosions and the Sunderland's rear gunner fired back. Southall flew 1,000yd from the U-boat's stern and noted that the boat had ceased all forward momentum. At 2 miles, the Australians lost visual sight of it and two minutes later they lost radar contact as well. The Sunderland returned to base at 0930 hours, completing an eleven-hour mission. HMS *Starling*, a Royal Navy sloop, acquired radar contact, arrived and completed the destruction with depth charges. Only one crew member perished, with the British rescuing the other forty-two and they became prisoners of war. *U-385* had not sunk any Allied vessels on its two patrols.[11]

The Australians of 461 Squadron struck again this same month. On the 12th, Sunderland 'A' took off from English waters at 2025 hours. While prowling the eastern Bay of Biscay, the flying boat's radar detected a contact 6 miles away. Flying Officer D.A. Little altered course to close the distance and began to descend. At ¾mile from the target, the crew activated their Leigh Light, which illuminated the fully surfaced Type VIIC *U-270*. The U-boat's guns immediately commenced firing and the Sunderland's front guns replied. At ¼ mile, the Germans ceased fire. Little flew over the target and dropped six depth charges from 300ft. The Sunderland continued flying for 2 miles from the U-boat until it lost radar contact. Little then ascended in preparation for another assault.

However, when flying over the location of the attack, the Australians found nothing. Later, the crew heard that Allied surface vessels had arrived, confirmed the U-boat's destruction and had rescued crew members. Sunderland 'A' splashed down at 0958 hours after a patrol of more than eleven hours. A British destroyer rescued all seventy-one crew. *U-270* had sunk one Allied warship on four patrols.[12]

Six days later, on 18 August, 201 Squadron Sunderland 'W', took off from Pembroke Dock at 1305 hours. The flying boat arrived off St Nazaire, its patrol area, at 1705 hours, in the eastern Bay of Biscay. A quick five minutes elapsed before the crew visually spotted, 4 miles away, the telltale sign of a wake. Closing to 3 miles, the British then discovered a periscope. Flight Lieutenant L.H. Baveystock brought the large aircraft above the periscope and released six depth charges from 50ft on both sides of the wake. He then commenced a circle pattern as the crew strained for signs of their attack. They observed a 'large volume of compressed air bubbles' on the surface. These continued for twenty minutes, followed by an oil patch, 'wooden debris, yellow floating material and a great number of German Naval charts'. At 1838 hours, ninety minutes after the assault, Baveystock headed for home, where he landed at 2150 hours, ending a nearly nine-hour patrol. None of the fifty-eight crew members survived. *U-107*, a long-range Type IXB boat, had been one of Dönitz's most successful U-boats, having participated in the 'Second Happy Time' and having sunk thirty-eight Allied vessels and damaged four others on thirteen patrols.[13]

The tale of *U-482* well demonstrated the ability of aircraft to locate U-boats for destruction even if they did not conduct an attack. Sunderland 'G' from the RAF's 330 Squadron departed the waters of Sullom Voe at 1551 hours on 25 November. At 2157 hours, the crew obtained a radar contact at a distance of 6 miles. The pilot descended for an assault but failed to locate the target due to poor visibility. The radar operator transmitted the report and location. The Royal Navy frigate HMS *Ascension* responded to the report and found the U-boat, destroying it with depth charges. All forty-eight crew members were killed in the attack. Type VIIC *U-482* had sunk six Allied vessels and damaged another during two patrols.[14]

Another four-engine aircraft – the Halifax – achieved a single fatal sinking during this period. On 12 August, 502 Squadron 'F' departed RAF St David's at 1221 hours to patrol the Bay of Biscay. At 0533 hours, just off the French coast, the aircraft's radar detected five 'blips' at 11 miles distance with four grouped together and another following behind. Twenty minutes after first contact, the crew spotted two fully surfaced U-boats 'in line abreast' about 100yd apart. The pilot assaulted the one rear

U-boat with five 600lb bombs. Twelve perished while the accompanying U-boat, *U-309*, rescued forty men. Type VIIC *U-981* had not sunk any Allied vessels on three patrols.[15]

Three Wellingtons unsuccessfully engaged U-boats during this time. On 14 August, Type VIIC *U-766* fired on the approaching 'E' of 407 Squadron, RCAF, in the Bay of Biscay, causing a fire in the port engine before it crashed killing all six crew members.[16] That same day, again in the Bay, 172 Squadron Wellington 'K' most likely encountered Type VIIC *U-445* as the RAF never heard from it again. *U-445* claimed the downing of a twin-engine aircraft, which the Germans incorrectly identified as a Beaufighter. All six British crew members perished.[17] On 26 August, again over the Bay, 172 Squadron Wellington 'B' discovered surfaced long-range Type IXC/40 *U-534*. The U-boat crew downed the twin-engine aircraft on its approach when 1,000yd away. Three RAF crew members died and three survived.[18]

The dated biplane Swordfish continued its depredations against Dönitz's U-boats during this time, although these three attacks would mark the last U-boats that the slowest Allied anti-submarine aircraft would sink. HMS *Kite*, a Royal Navy sloop, had participated in five U-boat sinkings. *U-344*, a Type VIIC boat, avenged their sinkings on 21 August, when it fatally torpedoed the British vessel, its only successful attack in three patrols. The torpedo explosion and the subsequent sinking killed 157 crew members. The remaining sixty men suffered due to exposure in the Arctic conditions until the destroyer leader HMS *Keppel* arrived. She found only fourteen survivors, of which five later died aboard her. In the end, only nine *Kite* crew members survived. The following day though, an 825 Squadron Swordfish pilot, Lieutenant Gordon Bennett, from the British carrier HMS *Vindex*, sighted *U-344* on the surface at 3 miles range between Spitsbergen Island and the northern Norwegian coast. He employed his boost to approach as rapidly as possible until he flew over the stern and attacked with three depth charges. Two dropped alongside but Bennett observed one roll down the deck until wire halted its movement and held it steady over the bows. The depth charge, set to explode at 24ft depth, then apparently remained in that position until the U-boat reached that depth and it exploded. The U-boat's stern rose into the air and then disappeared. All fifty crew members perished.[19]

During the next sinking involving a Swordfish, the pilot operated as the initial spotter and the Royal Navy destroyers served as the deliverers of fatal ordnance. On the morning of 2 September, Type VIIC *U-394* cruised on the surface off the northern Norwegian coast on its third patrol, not having sunk any Allied vessels. An 825 Squadron Swordfish from *Vindex* spotted it and dropped a smoke flare where the now submerged U-boat had been. Two Royal Navy destroyers and two sloops arrived, and with one in the rear using its sonar and the three in front firing depth charges, they eventually lost sonar contact and observed debris, oil, bubbles and remains of the crew. All fifty men perished.[20]

The final Swordfish attack occurred on 13 December against Type VIIC *U-365*. Two 813 Squadron aircraft from the escort carrier HMS *Campania* discovered the surfaced U-boat and targeted it with depth charges. All fifty crew members went down with the boat. *U-365* had sunk three Allied vessels and damaged two others on eight patrols. This marked the twenty-first U-boat sinking in which Swordfishes had participated.[21]

The Avengers destroyed two U-boats during this period. The American USS *Wake Island* group was operating off the north-west coast of Africa and on 2 July an Avenger pilot sighted *U-543*, a long-range Type IXC/40 boat, and attacked with depth charges. When the U-boat decided to submerge, he assaulted it a second time with a Fido torpedo, which completed the destruction. All fifty-eight crew members perished. *U-543* had not sunk any Allied vessels on two patrols.[22]

In late 1944, as a desperation measure, the Nazis decided to again land spies on the eastern American coast. *U-1229*, another Type IXC/40 boat, departed Norway on such a mission. However, on 20 August, off the Grand Banks, a VC-42 Avenger from USS *Bogue* sighted the surfaced U-boat and attacked it. The U-boat commander promptly submerged but the American's damage to the boat's battery cells soon forced him to surface. Now, instead of one carrier aircraft, he faced five Avengers, which fired rockets until one deposited a 500lb bomb. The stern rose into the air and the U-boat disappeared underwater. The Americans rescued forty-two men including the spy, whom the Americans quickly identified. Eighteen died. Thus ended *U-1229*'s only patrol, it not having sunk any Allied vessels.[23]

A U-boat did shoot down an Avenger during this time. On 28 September, an aircraft from USS *Tripoli*, operating in the mid-Atlantic and hunting for U-boats based on Enigma intercepts, discovered the surfaced Type XB *U-219*. The pilot reported the contact and that U-boat responded with anti-aircraft fire, upon which the transmission ended. All three American airmen died and *U-219* eluded the escort carrier group to continue to its destination in the Pacific.[24]

The RAF delivered the only successful Catalina attacks against U-boats in this period. On 17 July, 210 Squadron Catalina 'Y' left RAF Sullom Voe at 1345 hours. At 2145 hours, the crew obtained a radar contact at 15 miles range. Flying Officer J.A. Cruickshank turned to the target and closed the distancing while descending from 1,500ft. The crew discovered a stationary U-boat but entered clouds, lost sight of it and instead, when they emerged from the clouds, they spotted a vessel 2 miles away moving at a swift 20 knots. The British assumed that they had found a Royal Navy destroyer and 'fired recognition cartridges', while also flashing the 'letter of the day'. Instead of a friendly response, the vessel started a 'heavy box barrage' and slowly turned to port. The Catalina maintained distance at 2 miles and, after five minutes, determined that they had not discovered an Allied vessel but instead a U-boat. Cruickshank 'went into attack diving' as the flying boat descended from 1,000ft to 50ft. The U-boat maintained a fast 20 knots and its crew fired 'heavy inaccurate flak' at the closing Catalina. When at 1,000yd range, the front British gun fired and succeeded in several hits on the conning tower. As the British aircraft swooped over the U-boat all the depth charges failed to drop. Cruickshank pulled the aircraft into an ascent to 800ft, made a turn to port and initiated a second attack run. The U-boat had now ceased forward momentum and fired 'heavy accurate flak', which struck the flying boat in multiple locations. This fire killed the navigator and 'seriously wounded' Cruickshank. Nevertheless, the Catalina maintained course, flew over the U-boat and dropped six depth charges from 50ft. Immediately entering a 'sea fog', the crew could not assess the results. However, Cruickshank's injuries necessitated that the second pilot, Flight Sergeant J.S. Garnett, fly the damaged flying boat home. This proved to be challenging as the second pilot had little experience, and Cruickshank kept falling unconscious. At 2345 hours, the Catalina radioed base, 'Need ambulance on arrival, Navigator dead, captain injured.' Clearly worried about Garrett's limited experience, the base then inquired at 0145 hours, 'Report pilot's condition and if he can land a/c. Report condition of a/c.' The crew responded. 'Pilot unable land. Has been badly wounded. 2nd pilot safe. Hull damaged, 450 galls petrol.' At 0324 hours, base requested 'Report extent damage, is beaching necessary.' The flying boat crew responded, 'Yes' and at 0405 hours Garrett, with Cruickshank's guidance, successfully landed in the Shetland waters and beached the damaged flying boat. The hospital staff found seventy-two wounds in Cruickshank, but he survived and received the prestigious Victoria Cross. All of Type VIIC *U-361*'s fifty-two crew members perished with the boat. It had not sunk any Allied vessels on three patrols.[25]

No. 210 Squadron sank another U-boat this month. Catalina 'Z' departed Scottish waters at 0635 hours on 18 July, and at 1430 hours received a report of a U-boat at a specified location. The crew commenced sweeping the area with radar, then at 1450 hours, began a square search with 10 miles of visibility. They spotted an object that they originally identified as a vessel but with binoculars they determined they had discovered a U-boat on the surface. The pilot, Flight Officer R.W.G. Vaughn, then bore in to the target. At 3 miles out, anti-aircraft fire commenced and Vaughn soared over the U-boat and released the depth charges, which all exploded. He then swung to port and the crew watched the U-boat sink with thirty-five to forty crew members on the surface. The crew also observed multiple small yellow dinghies, bodies and an oil patch. The crew then focused their attention on the Catalina as the starboard engine had developed a 'serious oil leak' and the port tank had commenced leaking fuel. Vaughn ascended in preparation for 'single engine flying'. The crew also had two wounded members from the flak and identified a leak of 100 gallons per hour. By 1507 hours, they reported to base that they were 'losing oil rapidly' and signalled 'S.O.S.' thirty-one minutes later. At 1640 hours, the British requested 'ambulance on arrival' and that they intended to beach the damaged flying boat on landing. At 2125 hours, Vaughn hit the water and successfully beached the aircraft. All survived. However, none of Type VIIC *U-742*'s fifty-two crew members did. It had not sunk any Allied vessels on two patrols.[26]

U-boats shot down two twin-engine Allied aircraft during this time, a Mosquito and a Catalina. On 2 August, two 333 (Norwegian) Squadron Mosquitoes caught Type VIIC/41 *U-1163* and Type VIIC *U-771* surfaced while moving along the Norwegian coast and attacked. Neither succeeded in damaging either U-boat but *U-1163* fatally hit one of the Mosquitoes, which slammed into the water killing both crew members.[27] On 20 August, in the Indian Ocean, 265 Squadron Catalina 'H' discovered the surfaced long-range Type IXD2 *U-862* and bore in for an assault. While the flying boat flew over the U-boat, no munitions dropped but flak damage caused the Catalina to crash into the water just 30ft away. None of the twelve individuals on board survived.[28]

Allied bomber aircraft also fatally damaged eleven U-boats in port during this period. The US 15th Air Force conducted a bombing raid on Toulon, France, and destroyed Type VIICs *U-586*, *U-642*, and *U-952* on 5 July.[29] Nineteen days later, on 24 July, the RAF's Bomber Command attacked Kiel, Germany, and hit Type VIIC *U-239* and Type VIIC/41 *U-1164*.[30] American bombers struck Bremen on 29 July and fatally damaged Type IXD2 *U-872* (one killed).[31] On 5 July, the 15th Air Force once again targeted Toulon and fatally struck Type VIIC *U-466*.[32] It returned to Toulon on 6 August and hit three Type VIIC U-boats: *U-471*,

U-967 (two died) and *U-969*.³³ The 15th Air Force hit Dönitz's boats again, this time on 24 September in Salanis, Greece. Type VIICs *U-565* and *U-596* (one killed) received such damage that the Germans decided to scuttle both of them.³⁴ Bomber Command struck Bergen, Norway, on 4 October and destroyed Type VIICs *U-228*, *U-437* and *U-993* (two killed), and then hit Wilhelmshaven, Germany, on 15 October and sank Type VIIC *U-777*.³⁵ The Soviets struck Gotenhafen, Germany, on 19 December, and ended the career of Type VIIC *U-262*.³⁶ No. 5 Group, RAF Bomber Command, attacked Oslofjord, Norway, on 28 December and sank Type VIIC *U-735* (Forty-two died; one survived).³⁷ On 31 December, Allied bombs struck Type XXI *U-2530* in Hamburg, Germany.³⁸

The Allied battle against the U-boats included attacks in the Black and Baltic Sea areas. In an air raid on Constanza, Romania, Soviet bombs fatally damaged Type IIBs *U-9*, *U-18* and *U-24* on 20 August. Five days later, before the Soviet army entered the town, the Germans scuttled the boats since the damage to the docks prevented their escape. *U-9* had destroyed eight ships, a submarine, and damaged four other vessels. *U-18* had sunk five Allied vessels and damaged eight others, while *U-24* had sunk seven Allied vessels and damaged two others. In October in the Baltic area, *U-676* claimed to have downed two Soviet aircraft.³⁹

The RAF also achieved a single success with its air-laid minefields during this time. Type XXIII *U-2323* sank on 26 July in northern German coastal waters due to the British minefield Forgetmenot. Two perished, while the Germans rescued twelve men. The U-boat had not taken part in any patrols and thus had not attacked any Allied vessels.⁴⁰

With the close of 1944, Dönitz's position could not have been more dire. With the Allied air forces now prowling along the Third Reich's coasts without interference and his U-boats now confined to ports without the concrete protection they had enjoyed in France, he could only face 1945 with more foreboding that the Allied aircraft would destroy his U-boats on the seas and in their ports. They had no sanctuary remaining.

Chapter 18

1945

The Allied anti-submarine air campaign ended in 1945 within a limited area around Europe. The men who had found the U-boats lurking throughout the globe during the war now found them in waters much closer to Germany. Dönitz's threat had, by 1945, diminished considerably. And yet, he continued to send his U-boats to sea and the Allied aircraft remained vigilant in hunting and destroying them.

Allied aircraft's at-sea dominance over surface vessels in sinking U-boats diminished during the war's last year, though. At sea, all Allied efforts sank sixty-seven U-boats, while aircraft participated in seventeen, a quarter of these, and surface vessels participated in forty-six. However, aircraft also contributed to the destruction of forty-one U-boats in raids by four-engine bombers and single-engine fighter-bombers in and near German ports. With these combined at-sea and in-port destruction totals, aircraft eliminated more U-boats than any other means.

Liberators continued to destroy the majority of U-boats at sea, with nine sunk by American and British forces. RAF Liberators contributed to the sinkings of six U-boats in 1945. In two of these instances, the *schnorkel*, for which U-boat Command had held such high hopes, served as the means by which the Allies were able to target two of them. At 0342 hours on 29 March, 224 Squadron Liberator 'O' lifted into the darkness from RAF Milltown to patrol due north of the Shetlands. This episode demonstrated one of the inherent weaknesses of the *schnorkel*: its visible wake. The B-24 commenced its patrol at 0514 hours and at 0956 hours the British crew spotted the wake. The pilot, Flight Lieutenant M.A. Graham, closed the range and discovered a *schnorkel* at the wake's front. Using the *schnorkel* as the focus for the attack, he bore in and dropped depth charges. The U-boat's stern rose as a result of the explosions, but then fell again. The crew sighted none of the traditional signs of a sinking but U-boat Command never heard from *U-1106* again. All forty-six crew members perished on what was the Type VIIC/41 boat's first patrol, it not having even sighted an Allied vessel.[1]

On 29 April, at 1152 hours, 120 Squadron Liberator 'Q' departed RAF Ballykelly and commenced its patrol at 1256 hours. As with 224 Squadron's attack, once again, a *schnorkel* betrayed the U-boat. At 1312 hours, the B-24's second pilot spotted a wake, then the crew spotted smoke, and finally at 2 miles range, they found a *schnorkel*. The pilot, Flying Officer H.J. Oliver, flew over the object and released four depth charges. All thirty-three crew members perished. Type VIIC/41 *U-1017* had sunk two Allied vessels on two patrols.[2]

On 5 May, 547 Squadron Liberator Mk. VI 'K' obtained a radar contact in the waters east of Denmark, and when closing on the target discovered two surfaced U-boats at a range of 7 miles moving in a 'line astern' formation. Flying Officer A.A. Bruneau selected the rear one. The leading U-boat turned to starboard, while the rear U-boat commenced firing on the B-24 and the aircraft's front turret began shooting back. Bruneau flew over the U-boat and dropped six 250lb depth charges. The U-boat's bows rose from the water to 40 degrees and the submarine then disappeared quickly. 'K' remained in the area for approximately fifteen minutes and the crew noticed debris, oil and bodies. All twenty-four crew members perished. Type VIIC *U-579* had not achieved any sinkings on what was its first patrol. The other U-boat escaped.[3]

Also on 5 May, 86 Squadron Liberator 'G' began patrolling its assigned area at 1313 hours. While flying at 1,000ft above eastern Danish waters, the crew obtained a radar contact at 4½ miles range. The pilot, Warrant Officer J.D. Nicol, homed in on the target and discovered three surfaced U-boats in 'staggered lines astern' 3½ miles in front of the B-24. The crew watched 547 Squadron Liberator Mk. VIII 'E' conduct two unsuccessful attacks on one of them. They believed the second assault may have damaged the boat but they then noticed that flak had hit 'E'. The B-24 crashed into the water, leaving only one crew member out of ten, whom a rescue boat later saved. As Liberator 'G' entered the battle, the first U-boat that had been attacked commenced a dive. The centre one had already submerged, leaving only the third U-boat still fully surfaced. At 1339 hours, the British attacked the remaining one with six 250lb depth charges, which all missed. The front and rear gunners fired successfully to halt the U-boat flak. On the second attack, the British released four 250lb depth charges and the rear gunner observed the U-boat disappearing from the surface by the stern with forty crew members in the water, debris and dinghies. Forty-eight crew members survived; three died. *U-534*, a long-range Type IXC/40 boat, had not sunk any Allied vessels on three patrols.[4]

The same day, 5 May, 86 Squadron Liberator 'Z' soared above Danish waters. At 2140 hours, the British crew obtained a radar contact, and on closing the distance discovered a fully surfaced Type VIIC/41 boat. The pilot, Flight Lieutenant J.T. Lawrence, dived in. When flying over the target though, the depth charges failed to release. As the U-boat commenced submerging, Lawrence made a second attempt, but the depth charges failed to release again. On the third run, the Liberator dropped six 250lb depth charges in the swirl of the now submerged U-boat. Lawrence also executed a fourth attack with more depth charges ahead of the swirl seventy-five seconds after the U-boat disappeared from the surface. Although there were no signs that indicated a successful attack, the depth charges had damaged the U-boat and the German commander chose to scuttle it the next day along the Danish shore. All forty-four crew members survived. *U-1008* had not encountered any Allied vessels on what was its first patrol.[5]

On 6 May, 86 Squadron struck again, this time with Liberator 'G'. It departed Tain at 1324 hours, began its patrol at 1743 hours, and at 1834 hours, in waters just north of Denmark, the British crew obtained two radar contacts. At 2½ miles from the contact, the crew spotted both a *schnorkel* and a periscope. Sixty seconds later, the B-24 flew over the two objects and released six 250lb depth charges. The explosions forced the conning tower to appear on the surface, which then disappeared. The crew later observed debris, oil, and air bubbles. All fifty-eight crew members perished. *U-3523*, a Type XXI that incorporated numerous advances as compared with the most common Type VIIC boat, had not encountered any Allied vessels on its only patrol.[6]

US Navy Liberators participated in the destruction of three U-boats in the last year of the war. On 27 February, just off the south-west English coast, depth charges from VPB-112 PB4Y-1 Liberator 'H' along with Royal Navy depth charges from three vessels – HMS *Labuan*, *Loch Fada*, and *Wild Goose* – all contributed to the sinking of Type VIIC/41 *U-1279*. The forty-eight crew members perished on the U-boat's first patrol, it not having encountered an Allied vessel. On 12 March, a VPB-103 PB4Y-1 Liberator, commanded by Lieutenant R.N. Field, sighted Type VIIC *U-681* in the Irish Sea. The U-boat, having suffered prior damage, could not dive. Field flew over the target and released eight depth charges. The Royal Navy rescued thirty-eight men, while eleven perished. *U-681* had not sunk any Allied vessels on this, its first patrol.[7] On 25 April, VPB-103 struck again. PB4Y-1 Liberator 'K' discovered Type VIIC/41 *U-1107* underwater with its *schnorkel* protruding from the Bay of Biscay surface at 1938 hours. Once the crew had spotted the U-boat, the pilot, Lieutenant D.D. Nott, descended quickly from 800ft and swung to starboard for the attack. Two minutes after the initial sighting, the Liberator dropped two Fidos, which found their target and in the subsequent explosion the U-boat's *schnorkel* flew into the air. All thirty-seven crew members perished. *U-1107* had sunk two Allied vessels on one patrol.[8]

No other Allied four-engine aircraft participated in any successful at-sea U-boat attacks, but Liberators, Fortresses and Halifaxes contributed to defeating Hitler's U-boats during this time with multiple attacks on German harbours and ports. The USAAF and the RAF attacked the numerous vulnerable U-boats as they floated stationary within Germany's waters. The British bombed Wilhelmshaven on 12 January and fatally struck Type VIIC *U-382*.[9] Allied bombers attacked Hamburg on 17 January and destroyed Type XXIs *U-2515* and *U-2523*.[10] On 24 February, Allied forces hit Type XXI *U-3007* (one killed) in an air raid over Bremen and then struck Wilhelmshaven on 4 March, where they ended Type XXI *U-3508*'s career.[11] An air raid by American forces devastated Type VIIC *U-682* at Hamburg. American bombers struck Kiel on 16 March and fatally damaged Type VIIC *U-758*.[12] A 30 March attack by the US 8th Air Force and RAF Bomber Command on Wilhelmshaven, Bremen, and Hamburg, devastated eleven U-boats: Type VIICs *U-72*, *U-96*, *U-348* (two killed), *U-350*, *U-429*, *U-430*, *U-1131*, *U-1197*, Type IXC/40 *U-870*, Type VIIC/41 *U-1167* (one killed), and Type XXIII *U-2340*.[13] The 8th Air Force hit Kiel on 3 April and fatally damaged Type IIC *U-56*, Type IXC/40 *U-1221* (seven killed), and Type XXIs *U-2542*, and *U-3505* (one killed).[14] The following day it struck Kiel again and annihilated three more: Type VIICs *U-237* (one killed), *U-749* and Type XXI *U-3003*.[15] On 8 April, RAF Bomber Command hit Hamburg and destroyed Type XXIs *U-2509* and *U-2514*, while an Allied attack on Kiel that same day sank Type XXI *U-3512*.[16] The following day, the British destroyed Type VIICs *U-677* and *U-982* at Hamburg-Finkenwerder and Allied bombers hit Type IXC/40 *U-1227* and Type XXI *U-2516* at Kiel.[17] The 8th Air Force struck Hamburg-Finkenwerder on 3 May and hit Type VIIC *U-1201*, and two days later struck again and fatally damaged Type VIIC *U-747*.[18]

The Soviets also destroyed U-boats in air attacks. On 24 January the Russians conducted an air raid on Königsberg and hit Type VIIC *U-763*. The Germans decided to scuttle the heavily damaged boat five days later. *U-763* had sunk one Allied vessel on four patrols.[19]

The RAF achieved its highest success with air-laid minefields in 1945. Four U-boats sank when encountering these underwater munitions: *U-3520* (eighty-five lost), Type VIIC *U-923* (forty-eight lost), Type VIIC/41

U-1273 (forty-three lost, eight rescued) and Type XXI *U-3519* (seventy-five killed, three rescued).[20] All the boats struck the mines when close to port and none had ventured on a single patrol nor had any attacked a single Allied vessel.

RAF Mosquitoes participated in the destruction of five U-boats. These assaults though, well demonstrate the aircraft's weakness compared with the four-engine Liberators. While both the British and the Americans had ample examples over the past five years of single, large aircraft sinking U-boats on their own, the Allies persisted with smaller aircraft such as the twin-engine Mosquitoes. The depth charge had been consistently proven as the most effective weapon. However, as the Mosquito possessed a limited load, the British fixed the aircraft with rocket projectiles for anti-submarine attacks. As this example demonstrates, despite all the anti-submarine advances by the Allies, it still required over a dozen Mosquitoes to deliver a lethal attack that one B-24 could have easily delivered.

On 9 April, thirteen 143 Squadron Mosquitoes took off from RAF Banff in north-east Scotland between 1435 hours and 1438 hours on an anti-shipping patrol. However, instead of finding surface vessels, they found U-boats. Mosquito 'S' developed issues with its artificial horizon, so the pilot returned to base at 1710 hours. The remaining twelve continued their mission until, at 1722 hours, the patrol leader visually spotted two wakes 7 miles away and approximately 200yd apart. The Mosquito pilots swung to starboard so that they could attack the targets 'out of sun'. As they approached, the pilots discovered two surfaced U-boats 'in line astern' moving swiftly at between 12 and 15 knots. Six of the Mosquitoes – 'Z', 'X', 'W', 'N', 'Q' and 'J' – targeted the leading U-boat by firing forty-three rocket projectiles and observing six strikes at the conning tower's base, with four more behind the conning tower. The pilots also struck the U-boat with multiple cannon hits along the entire boat. The other five Mosquitoes, 'H', 'D', 'K', 'A', and 'G', with 'J' as well, attacked the second U-boat with forty-four rocket projectiles, with ten observed strikes and cannon hits.[21]

The 143 Squadron Mosquitoes did not fight alone. Four 235 Squadron Mosquitoes – 'H', 'S' 'R' and 'D' – attacked the first U-boat with four cannon strikes. The first U-boat disappeared and then reappeared for ten seconds before it slipped away by the stern with the bow extending 10 degrees above the surface. For these ten seconds that it reappeared, a third Mosquito squadron, 248, which had maintained an orbit over the target, engaged the U-boat down sun. Seven Mosquitoes assaulted it with both rocket projectiles and cannon. After these attacks, the U-boat exploded 'with a terrific flash and sheet of flame' as an 'instantaneous mushroom of greyish white smoke' appeared along with wreckage 'flung into the air' that 'slightly damaged' four Mosquitoes. The second U-boat swung to starboard after the attacks by 143 and 235 Squadrons and submerged, 'leaving a large patch of oil' on the surface, wreckage, and approximately ten to twenty yellow dinghies. The British had destroyed both. They observed survivors in the water and some believed that they heard an explosion from this U-boat as well. All fifty-five of Type IXC/40 *U-804*'s crew perished, along with all forty-five in Type VIIC/41 *U-1065*. *U-804* had sunk a destroyer escort during three patrols, while *U-1065* had not encountered any Allied vessels on this, its only patrol.[22]

Mosquitoes destroyed another U-boat this day. At 1722 hours, 235 Squadron's 'A' discovered a long-range Type IXC/40 boat. A minute later, it attacked the surfaced boat with rocket projectiles that struck amidships and cannon hits on the conning tower and the hull. The U-boat commander decided to not submerge and fight it out on the surface. The Mosquito departed the scene with 'considerable greyish smoke' emitting from the U-boat. *U-843* sank that day in Danish waters carrying forty-four men with it. Twelve survived. *U-843* had sunk one Allied vessel on four patrols.[23]

On 19 April, three RAF Mosquito squadrons – 143, 235 and 248 – attacked three (or four) surfaced U-boats, one of which, Type VIIC *U-251*, U-boat Command never heard from again. At 1631 hours, 143 Squadron Mosquitoes discovered a German surface vessel with three surfaced U-boats trailing behind in line astern. The 'strike leader ordered two sections' to engage the vessel while the remaining Mosquitoes would assault the U-boats. The Mosquitoes' strike on the vessel resulted in a stern explosion, a fire 'burning furiously amidships', and a port list accompanied by 'masses of black smoke', Three 143 Squadron Mosquitoes – 'K', 'Q' and 'E' – hit the first U-boat with twenty-four rocket projectiles and multiple 'cannon strikes'. 'Q' and 'Z' followed with another attack solely by cannon. The U-boat attempted to dive but instead initiated evasive turns. Smoke emerged from the conning tower and the crew inflated eight to ten yellow dinghies. The second U-boat, apparently spared from the attacks, also ceased its forward momentum and the British crews noticed 'several unidentified light coloured objects' in front of the conning tower. 'J' focused on the last U-boat and struck with eight rocket projectiles, of which six hit the U-boat. On its second pass, it opened fire with machine guns and cannon. This U-boat slowed to a halt. Black smoke appeared and the U-boat sank.[24]

The 143 Squadron Mosquitoes did not attack these U-boats alone; the swarm also included those from 248 Squadron. Their pilots claimed that four U-boats, not three, accompanied the merchant vessel. 'G' and 'A' struck the third U-boat with cannon shots and rocket projectiles, while 'S' and 'T' only attacked that U-boat with cannon. These two Mosquitoes also hit the last U-boat with rocket projectiles and cannon.

No. 235 Squadron's Mosquitoes also participated. These eleven aircraft took off from RAF Banff between 1430 hours and 1440 hours. However, when they joined the battle at 1722 hours, apparently only two U-boats remained surfaced. The leader spotted two 'wakes in line astern about 200yd apart'. The formation swung to starboard and manoeuvred to a position abreast of the wakes. The RAF leader ordered 143 Squadron to initiate the attacks and have 235 follow. 'H', 'S' and 'R' assaulted the first U-boat with at least four rocket projectile hits. 'W', 'P', and 'N' all fired rocket projectiles at the second U-boat and observed at least two hits.[25] However, only one of the U-boats sank this day, *U-251*. Thirty-nine of its crew died and only four survived. It had completed six patrols and destroyed two Allied vessels.[26]

On 2 May, nine 143 Squadron Mosquitoes left Banff from 0604 to 0606 hours. At 0853 hours, the pilots spotted a German merchant vessel but the leader told the pilots to maintain patrol and not engage. The leader's intuition proved to be well founded. One minute later they spotted a far more tempting target: two surfaced U-boats at 3 miles distance, line astern, ½ mile apart, moving at 10 knots. At 0855 hours, the leader 'ordered all sections to attack'. Five Mosquitoes – 'Z', 'Q', 'N', 'L' and 'G' – dived on the first U-boat and fired cannon and a total of thirty-eight rocket projectiles. 'T' attacked with cannon alone. This U-boat submerged after the attack began and the British observed air bubbles and maybe oil. Records indicate though, that it escaped.

The second U-boat, *U-2359*, also received attention from the Mosquitoes. 'K' and 'F' targeted this U-boat with sixteen rocket projectiles and cannon, while two others, 'L' and 'Z', also attacked with cannon fire. The 404 Squadron, RCAF, Mosquitoes provided fighter cover for these attacks but did not engage the U-boats. *U-2359* swung to port and halted. It then disappeared from the surface by the stern surrounded by debris and oil. The pilots watched four dinghies inflate and crew members enter them. Other crew members remained in the water. There were only twelve crewmen on board and they all perished. *U-2359*, a Type XXIII boat, never commenced a patrol. In addition to the U-boat attacks, six Mosquitoes from 235 and 248 Squadrons later attacked the merchant vessel. The rocket projectiles and cannon caused the vessel to burn 'furiously' and develop a starboard list.[27]

A U-boat did down a British Mosquito during this time. On 24 March, a 235 Squadron aircraft discovered surfaced Type VIIC *U-249* off the Norwegian coast and attacked. The Germans shot down the aircraft, resulting in the death of the two crew members. The aircraft may have damaged the U-boat as it soon returned to its Norwegian port.[28]

Wellingtons made one successful attack in 1945. On 2 April, 304 (Polish) Squadron Mk. XIV 'Y' left St Eval at 1132 hours. Over three hours later, at 1446 hours, the crew obtained two radar contacts off the south-west Irish coast. The first one appeared at 8 miles range, while the second 'bigger and brighter' one appeared at 6 miles distance. Warrant Officer R. Marczak decided to fly to the closest one but lost contact when 3 miles away. Despite now flying through a rain shower, the navigator, situated in the Wellington's nose, visually spotted two objects in front of the bomber and believed them to be a *schnorkel* and a periscope. As the aircraft closed the distance, the crew sighted both the *schnorkel* and periscope submerging, but the objects provided Marczak with a 'broken wake' by which to guide the Wellington. Six depth charges, dropped from 120ft, fell where the periscope and *schnorkel* had just disappeared. Although the crew did not see any wreckage, Type VIIC/41 *U-321* had been destroyed and all forty-one crew members lost on its first patrol, not having encountered an Allied vessel.[29]

The Warwick achieved its last victory of the war on 24 February. No. 179 Squadron's 'K' took off from southern England at 1715 hours and just inside the western entrance to the Channel, the crew obtained a radar contact 2 miles away directly in the aircraft's path. At 1½ miles, the pilot, Flight Lieutenant A.G. Brownsill, spotted a wake. He then identified a *schnorkel* at 4 to 6ft above the surface, descended to 100ft and followed the wake to the target. The aircraft dropped multiple depth charges as it flew above the submerged U-boat and the crew. By illuminating the surface, the crew spotted debris and oil. The aircraft landed at 0140 hours after a nine-hour flight. Type VIIC *U-927* had not engaged any Allied vessels. All forty-seven crew members perished.[30]

Catalinas claimed two U-boats in 1945. Both instances demonstrate the U-boats' high vulnerability when using a *schnorkel*, despite the German belief that the device helped them to avoid detection. The second Catalina battle, the last involving U-boat and aircraft, will conclude the chapter. In the first instance, the *schnorkel* betrayed the U-boat's presence due to a visual sighting. On 30 April, the crew of VP-63 Catalina 'R', flying above the northern Bay of Biscay, sighted the protruding device and flew toward the visual target. The flying boat's MAD device confirmed the U-boat's presence and the aircraft flew over the *schnorkel* and released twenty-four retro-bombs. The Americans observed debris, oil and bubbles. Type VIIC/41 *U-326* had not encountered any Allied vessels on this, its first and last patrol. All forty-three crew members died.[31]

On 4 May, Avengers and Wildcats achieved their last U-boat sinking of the war. From three Royal Navy escort carriers – HMS *Searcher, Trumpeter,* and *Queen* – twenty-eight Wildcats and seventeen Avengers descended on the German naval base at Kilbotn in northern Norway. The British pilots found Type VIIC *U-711* tied to the supply vessel *Black Watch*. They attacked and sank both of them. Thirty-two of *U-711's* crew died in the assault and eighteen survived. This U-boat had sunk three Allied vessels and damaged another on twelve patrols.[32]

Allied single-engine aircraft also battled U-boats in transit between northern German ports and Norway. On 3 and 4 May, in Gelting Bay, American fighter-bombers discovered several U-boats and attacked Type VIICs *U-393, U-746* and *U-1210*. The crews of *U-393* and *U-746* soon scuttled the heavily damaged boats. *U-1210* (one killed) sank immediately after the assault. None of these boats had sunk or damaged any Allied vessels.[33] RAF single-engine Typhoons also took part in these attacks on these two days. The British attacks led to the demise of four additional U-boats: Type VIIBs *U-52* and *U-101* and Type VIICs *U-236* and *U-276*. In the process, the RAF destroyed two of the most successful U-boats. *U-52* had sunk thirteen Allied vessels and damaged another one, while *U-101* had destroyed twenty-one Allied vessels and damaged another one. *U-236* and *U-276* though, had not any engaged Allied vessels in their careers. However, U-boats achieved one victory against single-engine aircraft. *U-155* shot down a 126 Squadron P-51 Mustang when several of these aircraft attacked a group of four U-boats.[34]

In the second Catalina battle of 1945, the *schnorkel* provided the U-boat's location to an Allied aircraft due to its radar signature. On 7 May, the day of Nazi Germany's surrender, 210 Squadron Catalina 'X' slipped from the waters of RAF Sullom Voe at 0330 hours to commence a mission that would mark the end of the Allied air campaign against Hitler's U-boats. In the darkness over the Norwegian Sea, the British obtained a radar contact at 0443 hours, 2 miles away, and the pilot, Flight Lieutenant K.M. Murray, veered towards the target. Two minutes later, he found abundant evidence of a submerged U-boat: *schnorkel*, periscope, white smoke, and a wake. Sixty seconds later, Murray engaged the completely submerged U-boat. Four depth charges fell from the flying boat and all exploded. The Catalina crew had also dropped a sonobuoy that, for security reasons, they called 'High Tea'. The sonobuoy would confirm whether the depth charges had been fatal. At 0640 hours, the Catalina crew reported to base, 'High Tea negative – large patch of oil' and 'request instruction fuel left for 15 hrs'. Base informed that Murray to remain in the area for two hours and then, if nothing was observed, to return to base immediately. The crew then heard 'noises' from one buoy and at 0820 hours reported that the sonobuoys had found the U-boat: 'High Tea Contact positive – no traces of propeller – hammering noises as of repair'. The British heard similar noises fourteen minutes later from two other buoys and then observed two oil streaks. A Liberator now joined the hunt and released additional sonobuoys but none of these detected the illusive U-boat. At 1030 hours though, the Catalina crew relayed, 'High Tea positive' and 'hammering persists'. At 1410 hours, 210 Squadron Catalina 'S' met Catalina 'X' and also released sonobuoys, and that crew 'reported positive contacts of engine noises and continued hammering'. An additional buoy also detected these sounds. Now though, Catalina 'X''s time had expired and Murray headed for the Shetlands, where he splashed down at 1650 hours. The German commander managed to limp his wounded Type VIIC/41 boat to an area off the Norwegian coast, where he scuttled it. The entire crew survived. *U-320* became the last U-boat fatally damaged by Allied aircraft. This battle, waged by a British crew in an American-built aircraft, appropriately represents the final engagement as RAF crews and American aircraft defeated more U-boats than any other personnel or any other Allied nation aircraft. Thus ended the Allied air campaign against Hitler's U-boats, which spanned five years of lethal battles from 30 January 1940 to 5 May 1945.[35]

Chapter 19

Conclusion

U-boat historians should approach aggregate numbers for the war with care. The battle against Dönitz's boats did not unfold evenly from 1939 to 1945. The conflict changed from year to year, and even from month to month. Only by studying the conflict through different time periods can a historian properly understand the factors that altered the conflict, especially in regards to air power.

At the war's commencement, RAF Coastal Command, the predominant British anti-submarine air force, contained twenty-one squadrons, of which seventeen flew a type of aircraft that would never sink a single U-boat during the entire war. Only four squadrons operated a competent anti-submarine aircraft: three with Sunderlands and one with Hudsons. Despite the military measures employed by the British in the face of the U-boat augmentation, the anti-submarine aircraft initiative had failed. It should surprise no historians that Allied aircraft sank no U-boats in 1939.[1]

Allied aircraft achieved poor improvement in 1940. The RAF had, however, increased the number of Coastal Command squadrons from seventeen to forty-four. Furthermore, British anti-submarine aircraft now flew from certain airfields that would operate some of the most successful Allied anti-submarine squadrons, including St Eval in Cornwall, Thorney Island in southern England, Sullom Voe in northern Scotland, and most critically, the Allies had commenced flying from Iceland. The British had also improved their arsenal of aircraft with additional Sunderland and Hudson squadrons. However, these steps failed to significantly increase their attacks against Hitler's U-boats, and allied aircraft achieved only three U-boat sinkings in 1940. A Sunderland operating from Pembroke Dock sank *U-55* in the northern Bay of Biscay, while a RAAF Sunderland destroyed *U-26* just west of the Bay, and a Royal Navy Swordfish sank *U-64* off the Norwegian coast. Besides the low number, the Allies also failed to destroy U-boats outside a limited area around the British Isles.

Allied aircraft performed dismally again in 1941, with only three sinkings and a capture. An RAF Hudson flying from Iceland contributed significantly to the seizing of *U-505*. A British Catalina from Iceland destroyed *U-452*. A Royal Navy Swordfish from Gibraltar depth charged *U-451* and the actions of Royal Navy Martlets led directly to *U-131*'s demise. The Iceland operations represented the most significant positive development as Allied aircraft from Reykjavik would close the North Atlantic gap and tally impressive records in future years against the U-boats. The most wanting aspect of the 1941 Allied aircraft campaign revolved around the issue of ineffective aircraft. Of the fifty-five Coastal Command squadrons, only six operated very long-range aircraft. Of these, five flew Sunderlands but the other one gave some hope. No. 120 Squadron had begun training with the American-built B-24 Liberator. Nevertheless, by December 1941, the Allied aircraft campaign had failed.

The Allies' fortune began to change in 1942. For the RAF, their twin-engine aircraft – Hudsons, Wellingtons, and Whitleys – tallied the most U-boats with thirteen. Royal Navy Swordfish destroyed three boats. This year also marked the entrance of American air power. The US Navy, predominantly with Catalinas, destroyed nine, while the USAAF sank four. Most critically, the Allies now had two four-engine aircraft active in their arsenal, and RAF Liberators sank three U-boats, while a RAF Fortress destroyed another. In total, Allied aircraft destroyed thirty-seven boats in 1942, more than the totals from 1939, 1940 and 1941 combined.

The year 1942 also marked a positive change when considering the greater geographic reach of Allied aircraft. Dönitz prized his French ports along the Bay of Biscay. The British began to inundate this critical area and sank four of his boats in and around these waters. The RAF also struck U-boats north of Britain, off the Norwegian coast, and in the essential Gibraltar area. The Americans' aircraft destroyed U-boats off the American seaboard, the Canadian seaboard, and even in the Caribbean for the first time. The Royal Canadian Air Force hit U-boats off their coast as well. Also, British aircraft, operating from North African airfields, achieved their first sinkings in the Mediterranean, with seven U-boats destroyed in those waters. Furthermore, the Allies had converted Iceland into a stationary aircraft carrier for U-boat assaults. Both British Hudsons and American Catalinas had sunk boats north and south of that strategic island and, most critically, the large four-engine aircraft began to engage in the Battle of the Atlantic. Of the Liberators' three fatal assaults in 1942, two of the B-24s took off from Iceland and the sole B-17 U-boat sinking occurred south of Iceland. These engagements all demonstrated the Allies'

CONCLUSION

commitment to dominating the gap, the central North Atlantic, which was the preferred hunting ground for Dönitz's U-boat commanders.

The Allies had steadily increased their anti-submarine arsenal and its global breath in 1942. The story of 1943 proves that they had, marking this year as the turning point in the U-boat war. January commenced slowly though. The Allies demonstrated their reach when American Catalinas fatally destroyed U-boats off the Brazilian coast. In February, the Allies sank seven U-boats, of which Fortresses claimed two and a Liberator destroyed another one, all three in the critical central North Atlantic area south of Iceland. A change began in March, though. For the first time, sinkings by B-24s and B-17s exceeded all others. During that month, the four-engine aircraft achieved four of the seven Allied aircraft U-boat sinkings, with three destroyed by Fortresses and one by a Liberator. In April, the pattern continued as Allied aircraft struck tallied that month, with Liberators contributing four of that total and Fortresses one. May 1943 proved to be the most successful month for Allied aircraft to date as they destroyed twenty-four U-boats. Sunderlands struck five, Liberators four, Hudsons four, Catalinas four, Halifax three, Swordfish two, Avengers one and Mariners one.

For the totals of the first five months of 1943, the Liberators provided a striking contribution with eleven, the most of any Allied aircraft. The B-17s followed with six to their credit. Adding the five sunk by Sunderlands and three destroyed by a Halifax, four-engine aircraft managed twenty-five, over half (52 per cent) of the forty-eight credited to Allied aircraft. These successes marked a significant increase from the four U-boats destroyed in all of 1942. Twin-engine aircraft also managed nineteen during this time, while single-engine aircraft sank only four.

Another pattern emerges during this time that would become the dominate one in the Allied air campaign against the U-boats. The primary combination that led to U-boat sinkings involved American-built, British-crewed aircraft. Twenty-six of the forty-eight sinkings during the first five months of 1943 involved American-built, RAF-crewed combinations: Liberators, ten; Fortresses, six; Hudsons, eight, and Catalinas, two. While the British certainly welcomed the contributions from the American, Australians and Canadian airmen, the Allied air campaign became primarily the RAF against the German Navy, with the United States serving its critical role as the Arsenal of Democracy.

While forty-eight fatal sinkings in five months marked a considerable improvement for the Allied anti-submarine aircraft, the performance in June and July 1943 significantly exceeded the first five months. From January to May, the Allied aircraft had averaged over eight sunk per month. In June and July, they averaged eighteen, with thirty-six destroyed in only two months. Dönitz's withdrawal of his U-boats from the mid-Atlantic had not stemmed the tide.

The statistics prove to be even more surprising when assigned by month. Allied aircraft achieved nine sinkings in June and twenty-seven in July, the highest number for any single month thus far in the war. This fact highlights the significant contribution of the Liberators. These aircraft sank the most U-boats in these two months but proved to be especially devastating in July. While only destroying one U-boat in June, the B-24s eliminated nine in July.

The geographic distribution of the sinkings also reflects Dönitz's retreat from the North Atlantic. Allied aircraft only destroyed two U-boats in that area. By reducing the operating area though, the German admiral had increased the possibility of air attacks, and during these two months Allied aircraft pummelled his U-boats in the Bay of Biscay area with twelve sinkings, a third of the overall total achieved in these two months. Additionally, the Allies continued to display their global reach against the underwater threat with fatal sinkings off the Brazilian coast, in the Azores area and off the north-western African coast by US Navy aircraft, and in the Mediterranean by the Royal Australian Air Force.

The next five months varied considerably. In August, Allied aircraft managed sixteen U-boats sunk, with US Navy Avengers contributing to the total with five sinkings, Sunderlands four, B-24s three and the remaining four scattered among three different aircraft types. September unfolded as a light month with only two sinkings but October's successful attacks increased to eighteen. However, in that month, the real story revolved around the RAF Liberators. These crews destroyed eight U-boats, followed by five for the American Avengers, with five sinkings attributed to five other Allied aircraft. In November, Allied aircraft participated in the destruction of nine of Hitler's boats, with B-24s attacking six of them and destroying three in December. Despite the extraordinary action of 1943, the last month ended the year quietly with only three U-boats destroyed. Nevertheless, the year marked a titanic change in the aircraft battle against Dönitz's force. In the war's first four years – 1939, 1940, 1941 and 1942 – Allied aircraft totalled forty-four sinkings. In 1943, Allied aircraft decimated 124 U-boats.

The geographic distribution for the final five months of 1943 again demonstrates the Allied aircraft's global reach. These air crews dominated the Atlantic Ocean, sinking U-boats in the north, central and southern areas. Furthermore, they found and destroyed boats south of Madagascar, in the Mediterranean and the Caribbean. The Allied aircraft crews also continued to successfully target Dönitz's boats as they commenced or ended their patrols crossing the Bay of Biscay.

However, the extraordinary story of these months resides with the battles in the North Atlantic, that area that Dönitz's commanders had prized as the ideal U-boat hunting ground. While he had called for retreat in May, the boats returned to that area in the later part of this year with devastating results. The days of 1942 when they could operate without fear of air assault had long disappeared because the Liberators now ruled these waves. In October 1943, RAF B-24s participated in the destruction of eight U-boats. Dönitz's May retreat had been wise. The loss of over half a dozen boats five months later proved the point.

The US Navy also deserves credit for dominating the central Atlantic region with its carrier aircraft. In August, its pilots destroyed five U-boats and then five more in October. These attacks combined with the British Liberators effectively eliminated two significant areas for safe U-boat activity. And, if Dönitz could not operate in the North and Central Atlantic, he could not imperil the Allies' convoys from the United States.

The year 1943 marks the end of one Allied aircraft's contribution to fatal U-boat sinkings: the Hudson. This twin-engine aircraft had played a vital role in the RAF in the war's early years with twenty-six sinkings, but no Hudsons would fatally assault any U-boats after October 1943. The four-engine aircraft would continue their ascent as the dominant Allied anti-submarine aircraft.

During the first five months of 1944, aircraft contributed to the destruction of forty-seven U-boats, just one fewer than in the last five months of 1943. This period, though, marked one of the few during that, after the B-24's emergence, they did not dominate U-boat sinkings. However, Dönitz had retreated once again from the North Atlantic area south of Iceland, leaving the four-engine aircraft crews few opportunities. Americans B-24s destroyed a U-boat west of Ireland and one east of Brazil, while in May British Liberators sank two U-boats off the Norwegian coast.

Surprisingly during these months, one of the slowest Allied anti-submarine aircraft destroyed the most U-boats: the British Swordfish. These pilots benefitted from Dönitz's redistribution of his boats to the Norwegian coast, where the biplanes, operating from Royal Navy aircraft carriers, destroyed six of the nine that they fatally attacked. The fact that these aircraft performed so well at this late stage of the war bears strong evidence that Dönitz never developed an effective air defence against any aircraft, including the slow, biplane Swordfish.

The U-boats still maintained a wide geographic sway. Allied aircraft targeted the boats in the central Atlantic, off the Cape of Good Hope and even one in the Arabian Sea. However, in 1944, these represented the exceptions, not the rule. Allied aircraft typically discovered the U-boats in an area from north of Norway to west of Gibraltar. For example, US Navy Avengers sank five of the six U-boats during this period in that defined zone, with only one south of Gibraltar, found and destroyed off the north-western African coast.

June 1944 proved to be decisive for the course of the war. Both the Allies and the Germans prepared for an invasion across the Channel and both knew the ramification of success or failure. Dönitz attempted to patrol these waters with his U-boats. He further held numerous ones off the Norwegian coast to determine where they could best assist the Nazi effort. The British expected the U-boats to operate in these areas and deployed anti-submarine aircraft accordingly. Allied aircraft would participate in the destruction of more U-boats in this one month second only to July, 1943, with twenty fatally attacked.

The majority of the attacks occurred in those formerly mentioned areas. The B-24s carried out ten assaults, seven in or at the English Channel's western entrance. Allied aircraft decimated eight U-boats off the Norwegian coast, with only two fatal attacks in the Bay of Biscay and one by US Navy Avengers in the South Atlantic. Dönitz's limited area of operations clearly benefitted Allied aircraft during this month.

In the July through December period of 1944, Allied aircraft participated in forty-seven fatal attacks. This total represents a decline over recent months but the number depicts an even more reduced area of aircraft attacks. Of the forty-seven targeted successfully, twenty-two befell from Allied bombing raids on U-boat ports and one from an aerial mine. Therefore, Allied aircraft actions destroyed only twenty-four at sea, a significant reduction since 1943. This result does not reflect a lessening of Allied pilots and crew, but rather a lack of targets as Dönitz's U-boat numbers fell precipitously while Allied land forces captured his highly coveted French bases.

At sea though, the Liberators continued their domination as they contributed to the sinkings of eight U-boats. The Sunderlands managed six fatal assaults during this time, Swordfish with three, Avengers and Catalinas both with two, and a Fortress received credit for one. In a vast majority of these assaults, aircraft's crews discovered their targets either off the Norwegian coast or within Dönitz's dreaded Bay of Biscay. The three exceptions involve the B-17 battle north-west of the Azores, an American Liberator attack off Brazil, and an American Avenger assault off the north-west African coast.

CONCLUSION

For the war's final year, the Allied aircraft campaign against the U-boats again unfolded as one in which the bombing raids destroyed more U-boats than at-sea assaults. Allied bombers decimated forty-one of Dönitz's fleet, while Allied aircraft participated in the destruction of seventeen on patrol. The German admiral's plans for expanding the war beyond European waters were curtailed during this period as all the fatal attacks occurred well within reach of Western Europe. As the German admiral acknowledged: 'During the last weeks of the war we also suffered heavy losses in our own ports and coastal waters as the result of the ever-increasing pressure of the enemy's air forces on the shrinking area of territory in German hands.'[2]

The Liberators led in the fatal sinkings at sea with nine to their credit, six by the RAF and three by the US Navy. British Mosquitoes successfully targeted five boats off the western Swedish coast, while a British Avenger and a British Catalina each found one along the Norwegian coast, and a US Navy Catalina fatally assaulted a U-boat in Dönitz's treacherous Bay of Biscay. The only outlier involved a Wellington, which attacked a U-boat off the south-west Irish coast.

In the end, Allied aircraft participated in the destruction of 365 U-boats, with 288 at-sea and seventy-seven in port areas, including seven destroyed by aerial mines. Allied vessels contributed to the sinking of 264 U-boats. The aircraft, with all its advantages in speed, detection and extensive patrol area, had proven to be the most lethal weapon against the underwater threat. Their introduction in the North Atlantic theatre, based in Iceland, had clearly altered the Battle of the Atlantic to the Allies' benefit.

The RAF proved to be the main assailant against the U-boats at sea. The British participated in 157 (55 per cent) at-sea battles that led directly to a U-boat's demise. The next closest entity, the US Navy, contributed to seventy-five lethal battles (26 per cent). The RAF and US Navy totals equal 81 per cent of the at-sea successful assaults. While the Royal Navy Fleet Air Arm (twenty-eight), Royal Australian Air Force (thirteen), Royal Canadian Air Force (thirteen), United States Army Air Forces (thirteen), all achieved multiple victories, the Allies fought the air war against the underwater threat primarily with RAF and US Navy aircraft.

Of note, while the US Navy's escort carriers have often received more attention from historians than the non-carrier naval aircraft, the latter participated in more sinkings than the former. Avengers or Avenger–Wildcat pairings contributed to the destruction of thirty-three U-boat, while naval aircraft such as B-24s, Catalinas, Venturas, and Mariners contributed to forty-two. In percentages, carrier-based aircraft receive credit for 44 per cent and non-carrier-based aircraft account for 56 per cent of the US Navy aircraft's contribution to the Allied air campaign against the U-boats.

In regard to which nation supplied the most aircraft that resulted in at-sea U-boat destruction, America led the pack. Of the 288 at-sea Allied victories, American-built aircraft contributed to 182 of these engagements, equaling 63 per cent, almost two of every three victorious battles. The United States' reputation as the Arsenal of Democracy clearly applies to the battle against Dönitz's U-boats.

Of all the aircraft though, none fatally assaulted more U-boats than the American-built B-24 Liberators. These aircraft participated in the sinkings of seventy-four U-boats. No other Allied aircraft's contributions exceed this total: Catalinas (thirty-eight), Avengers (thirty-two), Sunderlands (twenty-six), Wellingtons (twenty-four), Hudsons (twenty-three), Swordfish (twenty-one), Fortresses (eleven), Halifaxes (nine), Mariners (nine), Mosquitoes (seven) and Venturas (six). Whether flown by British, American, Australian or Czechoslovakian crews, these four-engine aircraft had exceeded all others in range, endurance and payload, factors that led directly to their destructive ability. The B-24's contribution deserves even more praise considering that the Allies did not fully employ this weapon against U-boats until 1943. Even then, the RAF's Coastal Command continually begged for more of these aircraft. Knowing how relatively few of these aircraft the Allies deployed compared with other anti-submarine aircraft, one may rightly wonder how more decisively the Allies would have defeated Dönitz's boats with more Liberators.

In April 1939, five months before Hitler would plunge the world into five years of death and destruction, President Roosevelt warned the Nazi Chancellor that in a war 'victor nations, vanquished nations, and neutral nations, will suffer'.[3] The American leader's prediction proved correct in all theatres of war, including the U-boat one. Allied vessels, neutral vessels and U-boats all suffered casualties from Dönitz's strategy. In the U-boat–aircraft battles, the U-boats suffered far more. U-boats claimed ninety-seven aircraft shot down, resulting in 393 Allied fatalities. However, Allied aircraft contributed to the destruction of 365 U-boats, resulting in the loss of 12,089 of Hitler's U-boat crew members, with the American-built B-24s the most decisive and lethal weapon in the Allies' anti-submarine arsenal.

Endnotes

Chapter 1: The Second Happy Time

1. *Peace and War: United States Foreign Policy, 1931–1941* (United States: US Government Printing Office, 1943), 455–56.
2. Dan ver der Vat, *The Atlantic Campaign: The Great Struggle at Sea, 1939–1945* (Bury St Edmonds, Suffolk: Hodder and Stoughton, 1988), 237.
3. Ibid., 126.
4. Ibid., 236.
5. Karl Doenitz, *The Memoirs of Karl Doenitz: Ten Years and Twenty Days* (Yorkshire: Frontline Books, 2019), 198. Peter Sharpe, *U-Boat Fact File: Detailed Service Histories of the Submarines Operated by the Kriegsmarine 1935–1945* (Lancaster: Midland Publishing Limited, 1998), 46. Mark Lardas, *Battle of the Atlantic 1939–41: RAF Coastal Command's hardest fight against the U-boats* (Oxford: Osprey Publishing, 2020), 26.
6. Doenitz, 198.
7. Roger Jordan, *The World's Merchant Fleets 1939: The Particulars and Wartime Fates of 6,000 Ships* (London: Chatham Publishing, 1999), 148.
8. Michael Gannon, *Operation Drumbeat: The Dramatic True Story of Germany's First U-Boat Attacks Along the American Coast in World War II* (New York: Harper and Row Publishers, 1990), 213. Kenneth Wynn, *U-Boat Operations of the Second World War: Volume 1: Career Histories, U1–U510* (Annapolis, Maryland: Naval Institute Press, 1997), 99. Jordan, 494. Homer H. Hickam, Jr. *Torpedo Junction: U-Boat War off America's East Coast, 1942* (Annapolis, Maryland: Naval Institute Press, 1989), 9.
9. Doenitz, 201–202.
10. Robert J. Cressman, *The Official Chronology of the U.S. Navy in World War II* (Naval Historical Centre, 1999), 142.
11. Sharpe, 47.

12. Cressman, 144. Sharpe, 32–33.
13. Sharpe, 113–114.
14. Doenitz, 207.
15. Sharpe, 105.
16. Jordan, 580.
17. Sharpe, 96. Paul Kemp, *U-Boats Destroyed: German Submarine Losses in the World Wars* (Annapolis, Maryland: Naval Institute Press, 1997), 159. Axel Niestle, *German U-Boat Losses During World War II* (London: Frontline Books, 2014), 138.
18. *Dictionary of American Naval Fighting Ships, Volume 3* (Washington: Naval History Division, 1968), 485.
19. Cressman, 152, 158. Sharpe, 132.
20. Cressman, 165. Sharpe, 92.
21. Cressman, 165, 169, 167, 168.
22. Sharpe, 54. Wynn, 1:119.
23. Kenneth Wynn, *U-Boat Operations of the Second World War, Volume 2: Career Histories, U511–UIT25* (Annapolis: Naval Institute Press, 1998), 150–151. Cressman, 165.
24. Wynn, 2:99. Cressman, 181.
25. Sharpe, 114. Cressman, 177. Wynn, 2:28.
26. Cressman, 177. Wynn, 1:123, 118.
27. Cressman, 181. Wynn, 1:123.
28. Cressman, 207.
29. Ibid., 202.
30. Sharpe, 121. Niestle, 72. Kemp, 85.
31. Cressman 208, Jordan, 587.
32. Cressman, 208, 210, 215.
33. Jordan, 579. Cressman, 215.
34. van der Vat, 266.
35. Clay Blair, *Hitler's U-Boat War: The Hunters 1939–1942* (London: Butler and Tanner, Limited, 2000), 468.
36. van de Vat, 266.
37. Ibid., 268.
38. Ibid., 269–272.
39. Doenitz, 223.
40. Cressman, 164.Rainer Busch, *Der U-Boot-Kreig 1939–1945* (Berlin: Mittler & Sohn, 1999), 45. Kemp, 79. Niestle, 78.
41. Niestle, 122.
42. Ibid., 120, 81.
43. Ibid., 71. Sharpe, 119. Busch, 53.
44. Niestle, 86.

45. Alan C. Carey, *Sighted Sub: The United States Navy's Air Campaign Against the U-Boat* (Philadelphia: Casemate Publishers, 2019), 13–14
46. John Derrig, *Wrong Made Right: U-166*, 80.
47. Sharpe, 84. Busch, 49. Kemp, 82. Niestle, 56.

Chapter 2: 1939–1941

1. Randolph S. Churchill, ed., *Into Battle: Speeches by the Right Hon. Winston S. Churchill P.C., M.P.* (London: Cassell and Company, Ltd, 1941), 58.
2. Ibid., 82.
3. Karl Doenitz, *The Memoirs of Karl Doenitz: Ten Years and Twenty Days* (Annapolis, Maryland: Frontline Books, 2012), 123.
4. S.W. Roskill, *The War at Sea, 1939–1945 Volume 1: The Defensive* (Uckfield, East Sussex: The Naval and Military Press Limited, 1954), 34. Peter Padfield, *Donitz: The Last Fuhrer* (New York: Harper and Row, 1984), 175. Stephen Budiansky, *Blackett's War: The Men Who Defeated the Nazi U-Boats and Brought Science to the Art of Warfare* (New York: Alfred A. Knopf, 2013), 89–91
5. While Allied forces failed to sink any U-boats in 1939, the U-boats also failed to destroy any Allied aircraft. Two Skuas from the *Ark Royal* crashed due to their bomb explosions during an unsuccessful attack on *U-30*, but these two downings, as not caused by German fire, are not credited to the U-boats as Allied aircraft shot down. Kenneth Wynn, *U-Boat Operations of the Second World War Volume 1: Career Histories, U1–U510* (Annapolis, Maryland: Naval Institute Press, 1997), 21.
6. Roskill, 38–39. Niestle, 40. Andrew Hendrie, *The Cinderella Service: RAF Coastal Command 1939–1945* (Great Britain: Pen and Sword Books Limited, 2006), 201. Mark Lardas, *Battle of the Atlantic 1939–41: RAF Coastal Command's hardest fight against the U-boats* (Oxford: Osprey Publishing, 2020), 10. Daniel J. March, *British Warplanes of World War II* (London: Aerospace Publishing Limited, 1988), 15. David Wragg, *RAF Handbook 1939–1945* (Gloucetsershire: Sutton Publishing, 2007), 278.
7. Wragg, 278.
8. Rene J. Francillon, *Lockheed Aircraft Since 1913* (Annapolis, Maryland: Naval Institute Press, 1987), 147, 158. Daniel J. March, ed. *British Warplanes of World War II* (London: Aerospace Publishing, 1998), 197. Wragg, 278.
9. Roger Jordan, *The World's Merchant Fleets 1939: The Particulars and Wartime Fates of 6,000 Ships* (London: Chatham Publishing, 1999),

215, 187. Peter Sharpe, *U-Boat Fact File: Detailed Service Histories of the Submarines Operated by the Kriegsmarine 1935–1945* (Lancaster: Midland Publishing Limited, 1998), 29.
10. Operational Records, 228 Squadron, January 1940 (Appendix, 11). Wynn, 1:39–40. Axel Niestle, *German U-Boat Losses During World War II* (London: Frontline Books, 2014), 40.
11. John D.R. Rawlings, *Coastal, Support and Special Squadrons of the RAF and their Aircraft* (London: Jane's Publishing Company Limited, 1982), 155.
12. Operational Records, 10 Squadron, RAAF, July 1940. Niestle, 29.
13. Paul Kemp, *U-Boats Destroyed: German Submarine Losses in the World Wars* (Annapolis, Maryland: Naval Institute Press, 1997), 65. Axel Niestle, *German U-Boat Losses During World War II* (London: Frontline Books, 2014), 117. *Jane's Fighting Aircraft of World War II* (New York: Crescent Books, 1998), 120–121
14. Roskill, 339,609. Hendrie, 80.
15. Operational Records, 269 Squadron, August 1941. Niestle, 70.
16. Niestle, 70
17. Operational Records, 269 Squadron, August 1941.
18. Wragg, 278. March, 62.
19. Operational Records, 209 Squadron, 25 August 1941. Niestle, 66.
20. Operational Records, 209 Squadron, September 1941.
21. Sholto Douglas, *Years of Command: the second volume of the autobiography of Sholto Douglas, Marshal of the Royal Air Force, Lord Douglas of Kirtleside* (London: 1966), 246. Operational Records, October, 1941.
22. Niestle, 65. Kemp, 77. Ray Sturtivant, *The Squadrons of the Fleet Air Arm* (Great Britain: Air Britain Historians Limited, 1984), 206.
23. Konstam, 26. William T. Y'Blood, *Hunter Killer: U.S. Navy Escort Carriers in Gallant Battle Against the Nazi U-Boat Menace* (New York: Bantam Books, 1992), 6–7.
24. Niestle, 120. Kemp, 76. Sturtivant, 167.
25. Sturtivant, 167. Maurice Cocker, *Aircraft-Carrying Ships of the Royal Navy* (Great Britain: The History Press Limited, 2008), 47–48. Kenneth Wynn, *U-Boat Operations of the Second World War Volume 2: Career Histories, U511–UIT25* (Annapolis, Maryland: Naval Institute Press, 1997), 148.

Chapter 3: 1942

1. As quoted in Ronald W. Clark, *Tizard* (London: Methuen and Company Limited, 1965), 309.
2. Ibid., 310–312.

3. Budiansky, *Blackett's War: The Men Who Defeated the Nazi U-Boats and brought science to the Art of Warfare* (New York: Alfred A. Knopf, 2013), 202.
4. Operational Records, 233 Squadron, May 1942. Axel Niestle, *German U-Boat Losses During World War II* (London: Frontline Books, 2014), 71.
5. Operational Records, 233 Squadron, November 1942. Norman Franks and Eric Zimmerman, *U-Boat versus Aircraft: The Dramatic Story behind U-boat claims in Gun Action with Aircraft in World War II* (London: Grub Street, 1998), 13, 14.
6. Operational Records, 500 Squadron, November 1942. Niestle, 61.
7. Operational Records 233 Squadron, November 1942. Operational Records 500 Squadron, November 1942. Niestle, 50, 74. I have not included Hudson 500/S in the list of Allied aircraft shot down by U-boats since the downing resulted from the explosion of the aircraft's depth charges.
8. Operational Records, 608 Squadron, November 1942. Operational Records, 500 Squadron, November 1942. Niestle, 73. Peter Sharpe, *U-Boat Fact File: Detailed Service Histories of the Submarines Operated by the Kriegsmarine 1935–1945* (Lancaster: Midland Publishing Limited, 1998), 123.
9. Operational Records, 500 Squadron, November 1942. Niestle, 54. I have not included the downing of 53 Squadron Hudson 'L' that occurred in the Caribbean during an unsuccessful attack on *U-505* since the damage that caused the aircraft crash resulted from the depth charge explosion and not anti-aircraft fire. Franks and Zimmerman, 15. Operational Records, 53 Squadron, November 1942.
10. Operational Records, 500 Squadron, December 1942. I did not include the supposed downing of Catalina 'Z' of 330 Squadron by *U-606* on 21 September 1942 due to lack of primary source information. Wynn, 75.
11. Operational Records, 269 Squadron, October 1942. Monthly Anti-Submarine Report, November 1942, 30. Niestle, 75. Kenneth Wynn, *U-Boat Operations of the Second World War Volume 1: Career Histories, U1–U150* (Annapolis, Maryland: Naval Institute Press, 1997), 87. Sharpe, 127.
12. Niestle, 86, 79, 124. Paul Kemp, *U-Boats Destroyed: German Submarine Losses in the World Wars* (Annapolis, Maryland: Naval Institute Press, 1997), 85. Kenneth Wynn, *U-Boat Operations of the Second World War Volume 2: Career Histories, U1–U150* (Annapolis, Maryland: Naval Institute Press, 1997), 11, 113, 151.
13. Niestle, 146.

14. Monthly Anti-Submarine Report, November 1942, 35.
15. Niestle, 44.
16. Franks and Zimmerman, 12–13.
17. Karl Doenitz, *The Memoirs of Karl Doenitz: Ten Years and Twenty Days* (Annapolis, Maryland: Frontline Books, 2012), 285.
18. Roger Jordan, *The World's Merchant Fleets 1939: The Particulars and Wartime Fates of 6,000 Ships* (London: Chatham Publishing, 1999), 400.
19. Operational Records, 172 Squadron, July 1942. Niestle, 122. Mark Lardas, *Battle of the Atlantic 1939–41: RAF Coastal Command's hardest fight against the U-boats* (Oxford: Osprey Publishing, 2020), 10. Sharpe, 195. John D.R. Rawlings, *Coastal, Support and Special Squadrons of the RAF and their Aircraft* (London: Jane's Publishing Company Limited, 1982), 122–123. Jonathan Falconer, *RAF Airfields of World War 2* (Surrey: Midland Publishing, 2014), 64. Daniel J. March, ed., *British Warplanes of World War II* (London: Aerospace Publishing, 1998), 230. *Jane's Fighting Aircraft of World War II* (New York: Crescent Books, 1998), 146. David Wragg, *RAF Handbook 1939–1945* (Gloucetsershire: Sutton Publishing, 2007), 278.
20. Operational Records, 311 Squadron, September 1942. Niestle, 121. Rawlings, 199.
21. Operational Records, 179 Squadron, October 1942. Niestle, 61.
22. Operational Records, 502 Squadron, July 1942. Operational Records, 61 Squadron, July 1942. Niestle, 86. Sharpe, 141. Rawlings, 227. James J. Halley, *The Squadrons of the Royal Air Force and Commonwealth 1916–1988* (Tonbridge, Kent: Air-Britain Limited, 1988), 126.
23. Operational Records, 77 Squadron, September 1942. Niestle, 82. Rawlings, 77.
24. Niestle, 50. Wynn, 1:184.
25. Operational Records, 47 Squadron, October 1942. Niestle, 69. Regarding *U-568*, which Allied forces destroyed during this period, some sources contend that Flight Sergeant Nash in Blenheim 'S' contributed to its sinking in the Mediterranean. Although the operational records for 203 Squadron on 27 May 1942 note an attack on a U-boat with four 250lb bombs at 1015 hours, the crew claimed no evidence of damage. It would appear that the three British vessels – destroyer HMS *Hero* and escort destroyers *Eridge* and *Hurworth* – deserve full credit for the victory at 0500 hours on 28 May.
26. Niestle, 65.
27. Niestle, 71, 72, 78, 124. Wynn, 9. Ray Sturtivant, *The Squadrons of the Fleet Air Arm* (Great Britain: Air Britain Historians Limited, 1984), 222.

28. Wynn, 1:55.
29. Niestle, 78, 81, 123. Kit C. Carter and Robert Mueller, ed., *U.S. Army Air Forces in World War II* (Washington, DC: Centre for Air Force History, 1991), 25, 46.
30. S.W. Roskill, *The War at Sea, 1939–1945 Volume 2: The Defensive* (Uckfield, East Sussex: The Naval and Military Press Limited, 1954), 217. Doenitz, 296–297.
31. Roskill, Volume II, 218, 474. Doenitz, 296–297.

Chapter 4: The B-24 Arrives

1. Karl Doenitz, *The Memoirs of Karl Doenitz: Ten Years and Twenty Days* (Annapolis, Maryland: Frontline Books, 2012), 285.
2. Mark Lardas, *Battle of the Atlantic 1939–41: RAF Coastal Command's hardest fight against the U-boats* (Oxford: Osprey Publishing, 2020), 11.
3. Alan C. Carey, *U.S. Navy PB4Y-1 (B-24) Liberator Squadrons in Great Britain during World War II* (Atglen, Pennsylvania: Schiffer Miltary History, 2003), 12. David Wragg, RAF Handbook 1939–1945 (Gloucestershire: Sutton Publishing, 2007), 278. Lardas, 10.
4. Axel Niestle, *German U-Boat Losses During World War II* (London: Frontline Books, 2014), 303.
5. John D.R. Rawlings, *Coastal, Support and Special Squadrons of the RAF and their Aircraft* (London: Jane's Publishing Company Limited, 1982), 103. Jonathan Falconer, *RAF Airfields of World War 2* (Surrey: Midland Publishing, 2014), 155–156. Operational Records, 120 Squadron, June 1941.
6. Operational Records, 120 Squadron, October 1941. This may have been *U-203*.
7. Operational Records, 120 Squadron, December 1941.
8. Roger Jordan, *The World's Merchant Fleets 1939: The Particulars and Wartime Fates of 6,000 Ships* (London: Chatham Publishing, 1999), 469. Operational Records, 120 Squadron, January 1942.
9. Operational Records, 120 Squadron, February 1942.
10. Operational Records, 120 Squadron, April 1942.
11. Operational Records, 120 Squadron, June 1942.
12. Operational Records, 120 Squadron, July 1942.
13. Operational Records, 120 Squadron, August 1942.
14. Andrew Hendrie, *The Cinderella Service: RAF Coastal Command 1939–1945* (Great Britain: Pen and Sword Books Limited, 2006), 96. Doenitz, 245.

15. Operational Records, 120 Squadron, December 1942. Monthly Anti-Submarine Report, November, 1942, 29. Niestle, 73. Peter Sharpe, *U-Boat Fact File: Detailed Service Histories of the Submarines Operated by the Kriegsmarine 1935–1945* (Lancaster: Midland Publishing Limited, 1998), 123. Paul Kemp, *U-Boats Destroyed: German Submarine Losses in the World Wars* (Annapolis, Maryland: Naval Institute Press, 1997), 92.
16. Niestle, 74. Sharpe, 125.
17. Operational Records, 120 Squadron, December 1942.
18. *Foreign Relations of the United States: The Conferences at Washington, 1941–1942, and Casablanca, 1943*. (Washington: United States Government Printing Office, 1968), 195–199.
19. Operational Records, 120 Squadron, December 1942.
20. Operational Records, 120 Squadron, December 1942.
21. Operational Records, 120 Squadron, December 1942.
22. As quoted in Colin Pateman, *Fuel, Fire and Fear: RAF Flight Engineers at War* (Croydon: Fonthill Media Limited, 2018), 184.
23. Niestle, 114. Kenneth Wynn, *U-Boat Operations of the Second World War Volume 1: Career Histories, U1–U150* (Annapolis, Maryland: Naval Institute Press, 1997), 158–159. Sharpe, 65. Imperial War Museum, CH 7708. Rawlings, 152.
24. Niestle, 73.
25. Operational Records, 59 Squadron, November 1942.
26. Norman Franks and Eric Zimmerman, *U-Boat versus Aircraft: The Dramatic Story behind U-boat claims in Gun Action with Aircraft in World War II* (London: Grub Street, 1998), 10–11.
27. Mauer Mauer, ed. *World War II Combat Squadrons of the United States Air Force: The Official Military Record of Every Active Squadron* (Woodbury: Platinum Press, 1992), 3. Max Schoenfeld, *Stalking the U-Boat: USAAF Offensive Antisubmarine Operations in World War II* (Washington: Smithsonian Institution Press, 1995), 44–45.
28. David Wragg, *RAF Handbook 1939–1945* (Gloucestershire: Sutton Publishing, 2007), 278.
29. Sharpe, 128.
30. Operational Records, 206 Squadron, September 1942. Operational Records, 206 Squadron, October 1942. Niestle, 76. Rawlings, 137.
31. Operational Records, 206 Squadron, October 1942.
32. Operational Records, 206 Squadron, October 1942.
33. Operational Records, 220 Squadron, November 1942. Rawlings, 149.

Chapter 5: The Casablanca Conference1.

1. Denis Richards, *Portal of Hungerford: The Life of Marshal of the Royal Air Force Viscount Portal of Hungerford KG, GCB, OM, DSO, MC* (London: Butler and Tanner Limited, 1978), 256.
2. Karl Doenitz, *The Memoirs of Karl Doenitz: Ten Years and Twenty Days* (Annapolis, Maryland: Frontline Books, 2012), 284.
3. Thomas B. Buell, *Master of Sea Power: A Biography of Fleet Admiral Ernest J. King* (Boston: Little, Brown and Company, 1980), 252.
4. Harry C. Butcher, *My Three Years With Eisenhower: The Personal Diary of Captain Harry C. Butcher, USNR Naval Aide to General Eisenhower, 1942 to 1945* (New York: Simon and Schuster, 1946), 238.
5. *Foreign Relations of the United States: The Conferences at Washington, 1941–1942, and Casablanca, 1943.* (Washington: United States Government Printing Office, 1968), 541.
6. Ibid., 543.
7. Ibid., 546.
8. Ibid., 556.
9. Buell, 257.
10. Butcher, 557. Elliot Roosevelt also described the meeting but focused on the discussions regarding the French leader, Charles De Gaulle. Elliot Roosevelt, *As He Saw It* (New York: Duell, Sloan and Pearce, 1946), 66–71.
11. *Foreign Relations of the United States*, 561.
12. *Casablanca Conference, January 1943, Papers and Minutes of Meetings* (Office, US Secretary, Office of the Combined Chiefs of Staff, 1943), 195–199.
13. *Foreign Relations of the United States*, 628.
14. Roosevelt, 104. Elliot further wrote: 'That winter, of course, the Battle of the North Atlantic would reach its height; and the suspense that was engendered in the tiny pins and miniatures of that Admiralty map was a global suspense, with the answer to world history caught up in its resolution.'
15. *Foreign Relations of the United States*, 669. *Casablanca Conference*, 277–279.
16. Doenitz, 299.

Chapter 6: The B-24s in the North Atlantic: January–May 1943

1. Axel Niestle, *German U-Boat Losses During World War II* (London: Frontline Books, 2014), 199.

2. Ibid., 199.
3. Karl Doenitz, *The Memoirs of Karl Doenitz: Ten Years and Twenty Days* (Yorkshire: Frontline Books, 2019), 309–310.
4. Ibid., 342.
5. Operational Records, 120 Squadron, February 1943. John D.R. Rawlings, *Coastal Support and Special Squadrons of the RAF and their Aircraft* (London: Jane's Publishing Company, 1982), 103.
6. Operational Records, 120 Squadron, February 1943. Niestle, 76, 127. While Sharpe and Wynn claim that *U-529*'s demise is uncertain, I was persuaded by Niestle's argument via email correspondence regarding photographic evidence and the original post-war U-boat assessment that Liberator 'S' of the RAF's 120 Squadron sank *U-529*. Unfortunately, the 120 Squadron Operational Records for this attack are missing. Niestle, 127. Kenneth Wynn, *U-Boat Operations of the Second World War, Volume 2: Career Histories, U511–UIT25* (Annapolis: Naval Institute Press, 1998), 90–91. Peter Sharpe, *U-Boat Fact File: Detailed Service Histories of the Submarines Operated by the Kriegsmarine 1935–1945* (Leicester: Midland Publishing, 1998), 110.
7. Operational Records, 120 Squadron, March 1943. Operational Records, 86 Squadron, March 1943.
8. Operational Records, 120 Squadron, April 1943. Niestle, 77. Wynn, 2:98.
9. Operational Records, 120 Squadron, April 1943. Niestle, 126. Kenneth Wynn, *U-Boat Operations of the Second World War, Volume 1: Career Histories, U1–U510* (Annapolis: Naval Institute Press, 1997), 141.
10. Operational Records, 86 Squadron, April 1943. Niestle, 76. Wynn, 2:96–97.
11. Operational Records, 86 Squadron, May 1943. Niestle, 118, 66. Paul Kemp, *U-Boats Destroyed: German Submarine Losses in the World Wars* (Annapolis, Maryland: Naval Institute Press, 1997), 116. Wynn, 1:303–304.
12. Operational Records, 120 Squadron, May, 1943. Niestle, 50. Wynn, 1:181–182.
13. Operational Records, 120 Squadron, May, 1943. Niestle, 53. Wynn, 1:207.

Chapter 7: The Allies' Other Aircraft in the North Atlantic: January–May 1943.

1. Operational Records, 220 Squadron, February 1943. Axel Niestle, *German U-Boat Losses During World War II* (London: Frontline Books, 2014), 51. Kenneth Wynn, *U-Boat Operations of the Second World War,*

Volume 1: Career Histories, U1–U510 (Annapolis: Naval Institute Press, 1997), 188.
2. Operational Records, 220 Squadron, February 1943. Niestle, 76. Kenneth Wynn, *U-Boat Operations of the Second World War, Volume 2: Career Histories, U511–UIT25* (Annapolis: Naval Institute Press, 1998), 91.
3. Operational Records, 220 Squadron, March 1943. Operational Records, 220 Squadron, April 1943.
4. Operational Records, 206 Squadron, April 1943. Niestle, 59. Wynn, 1:256–257.
5. Operational Records, 206 Squadron, April 1943. Niestle, 67. Wynn, 1:312.
6. Operational Records, 206 Squadron, April 1943. Niestle, 125. Wynn, 1:129. Peter Sharpe, *U-Boat Fact File: Detailed Service Histories of the Submarines Operated by the Kriegsmarine 1935–1945* (Leicester: Midland Publishing, 1998), 157.
7. Operational Records, 206 Squadron, May 1943. Niestle, 82. Wynn, 2:132. There is speculation that on 12 May, *U-311* shot down a Fortress from 206 Squadron. However, that squadron reported no losses for the entire month and, in fact, reported no flying on that date.
8. Operational Records, 206 Squadron, May 1943.
9. Operational Records, 269 Squadron, May 1943. Niestle, 78. Wynn, 2:105.
10. Operational Records, 269 Squadron, May 1943. Niestle, 51. Wynn, 1:192–193.
11. Niestle 66, 77. Wynn, 1:311.
12. Niestle, 46. Wynn, 1:153–154.
13. Operational Records, 423 Squadron, Royal Canadian Air Force, May 1943. Niestle, 86. Wynn, 2:150–151. The only other U-boat encounter occurred on the 23rd when Sunderland 'A"s crew spotted a conning tower at 5 miles and dropped four depth charges fifteen seconds after the periscope disappeared, but witnessed no significant evidence of damage. John D.R. Rawlings, *Coastal Support and Special Squadrons of the RAF and their Aircraft* (London: Jane's Publishing Company, 1982), 211.
14. Niestle, 45. Wynn, 1:149–151.
15. Niestle, 44. Wynn, 1:67–68.
16. Niestle, 86. Wynn, 2:148–150.
17. Wynn, 1:168. Norman Franks and Eric Zimmerman, *U-Boat versus Aircraft: The Dramatic Story behind U-boat claims in Gun Action with Aircraft in World War II* (London: Grub Street, 1998), 125.

18. William T. Y'Blood, *Hunter Killer: U.S. Navy Escort Carriers in Gallant Battle Against the Nazi U-Boat Menace* (New York: Bantam Books, 1992), 48–49. Niestle, 70. Wynn, 2:44–45.
19. Operational Records, 455 Squadron, Royal Australian Air Force, April 1943. Niestle, 47. Wynn, 1:165–166.
20. Niestle, 122. Wynn, 1:132.
21. Karl Doenitz, *The Memoirs of Karl Doenitz: Ten Years and Twenty Days* (Yorkshire: Frontline Books, 2019), 341.
22. Ibid., 333.

Chapter 8: Outside the North Atlantic: January–May 1943

1. Operational Records, 224 Squadron, April 1943. Axel Niestle, *German U-Boat Losses During World War II* (London: Frontline Books, 2014), 54. Kenneth Wynn, *U-Boat Operations of the Second World War, Volume 1: Career Histories, U1–U510* (Annapolis: Naval Institute Press, 1997), 221–222.
2. Niestle, 124. Paul Kemp, *U-Boats Destroyed: German Submarine Losses in the World Wars* (Annapolis: Naval Institute Press, 1997), 107. Kenneth Wynn, *U-Boat Operations of the Second World War, Volume 2: Career Histories, U511–UIT25* (Annapolis: Naval Institute Press, 1998), 13. Mauer Mauer, ed. *World War II Combat Squadrons of the United States Air Force: The Official Military Record of Every Active Squadron* (Woodbury: Platinum Press, 1992), 10.
3. John D.R. Rawlings. *Coastal Support and Special Squadrons of the RAF and their Aircraft* (London: Jane's Publishing Company, 1982), 75.
4. Norman Franks and Eric Zimmerman, *U-Boat versus Aircraft: The Dramatic Story behind U-boat claims in Gun Action with Aircraft in World War II* (London: Grub Street, 1998), 27–28. Wynn, 1:166.
5. Wynn, 2:118.
6. Operational Records, 58 Squadron, May 1943. Niestle, 127. Wynn, 2:16.
7. Operational Records, 58 Squadron, May 1943. Niestle, 51. Wynn, 1:188.
8. Operational Records, 58 Squadron, May 1943. Niestle, 146. Wynn, 308–309.
9. Operational Records, 58 Squadron, May 1943.
10. Franks and Zimmerman, 22–23.
11. Operational Records, 48 Squadron, February 1943. Niestle, 64.
12. Operational Records, 500 Squadron, March 1943. Niestle, 40. Wynn, 1:294–295. Peter Sharpe, *U-Boat Fact File: Detailed Service Histories*

of the Submarines Operated by the Kriegsmarine 1935–1945 (Leicester: Midland Publishing, 1998), 37.
13. Operational Records, 608 Squadron, May 1943. Niestle, 86. Wynn, 2:152.
14. Operational Records, 500 Squadron, March 1943. Niestle, 43. Wynn, 1:59.
15. Operational Records, 233 Squadron, April 1943. Niestle, 125. Wynn, 1:127–128.
16. Operational Records, 233 Squadron, May 1943. Niestle, 65. Wynn, 1:297.
17. Operational Records, 500 Squadron, April 1943. Franks and Zimmerman, 24–25.
18. Niestle, 121. Sharpe, 56. Ragnar J. Ragnarsson, *US Navy PBY Catalina Units of the Atlantic War* (Oxford: Osprey Publishing, 2006), 57. Wynn, 1:126.
19. Niestle, 123. Ragnarsson, 58. Wynn, 1:325–326.
20. Niestle, 120. Wynn, 1:121.
21. Operational Records, 202 Squadron, February 1943. Niestle, 75. Wynn, 2:88.
22. Operational Records, 210 Squadron, May 1943. Niestle, 62. Wynn, 1:278.
23. Operational Records, 461 Squadron, Royal Australian Air Force, May 1943. Niestle, 66. Wynn, 1:309.
24. Operational Records, 10 Squadron, Royal Australian Air Force, May 1943. Niestle, 79. Wynn, 2:116
25. Operational Records, 58 Squadron, May 1943. Operational Records, 10 RAAF, May, 1943. Operational Records, 228 Squadron, May 1943. Niestle, 69. Wynn, 2:37–38.
26. Operational Records, 201 Squadron, May 1943. Niestle, 64. Wynn, 1:292–293.
27. Operational Records, 228 Squadron, May 1943. Wynn, 1:293. Franks and Zimmerman, 34.
28. Operational Records, 38 Squadron, February 1943. Niestle, 69. Wynn, 2:36–37.
29. Operational Records, 172 Squadron, February 1943. Niestle, 51. Wynn, 1:190. Some sources count the combat between Wellington 'N' and *U-613* on 30 April/1 May as shot down but since the aircraft successfully returned to base I have not counted it as a downing by a U-boat: From RAF Chivenor, Wellington 'N' took to the air at 10:55 pm on 30 April. While flying at an altitude of 1,200ft, the crew obtained a contact at 6½ miles away. The pilot closed on the target

while descending and at ¾ mile, while at 550ft, the crew activated the Leigh Light and found the surfaced *U-613*. The British dropped six depth charges from 75ft and all exploded two on the port side and four on the starboard side. While flying in the area subsequently, the crew sighted 'bubbles' but no other signs and *U-613* had escaped serious damage on its return to La Pallice, France, where it arrived on 6 May. However, an hour after the battle, the British, recounting a 'shudder' that the two-engine plane experienced when over the U-boat, now realised that U-boat gun fire had damaged the hydraulic system. When touching down at base at 4:52 am, the 'port leg' collapsed, resulting in a crash landing. Yet, none of the six crew members sustained any injuries. Operational Records, 172 Squadron, May 1943. Wynn, 2:81.

30. Franks and Zimmerman, 21–22.
31. Ibid., 31.
32. Niestle, 120. Wynn 1:104–105.

Chapter 9: B-24s: June–July 1943

1. Operational Records, 120 Squadron, June 1943. Axel Niestle, *German U-Boat Losses During World War II* (London: Frontline Books, 2014), 138. Kenneth Wynn, *U-Boat Operations of the Second World War, Volume 1: Career Histories, U1–U510* (Annapolis: Naval Institute Press, 1997), 146.
2. Operational Records, 224 Squadron, July 1943. Niestle, 76. Kenneth Wynn, *U-Boat Operations of the Second World War, Volume 2: Career Histories, U511–UIT25* (Annapolis: Naval Institute Press, 1998), 93–94.
3. Operational Records, 53 Squadron, July 1943. Niestle, 128. Wynn, 2:19.
4. Operational Records, 224 Squadron, July 1943. Niestle, 124. Wynn, 2:5–6.
5. Niestle, 91. Wynn, 2:187.
6. Niestle, 64, 222. I have accepted Niestle's contention that the original post-war attributions regarding the sinkings of *U-232* and *U-425* were misattributed and that British Wellington 'R' of the RAF 179 Squadron destroyed *U-435*, while American Liberator 'B' of the 1st Antisubmarine squadron sank U-232. Max Schoenfeld, *Stalking the U-Boat: USAAF Offensive Antisubmarine Operations in World War II* (Washington: Smithsonian Press, 1995), 96. Wynn, 1:286–288.
7. Schoenfeld, 100–101. Niestle, 123.
8. Niestle, 73.

9. Based on typical crew numbers, I am estimating a loss of ten crew members.
10. Operational Records, 58 Squadron, July 1943. Niestle, 69. Wynn, 2:34.
11. Niestle, 61. Wynn, 1:266–267.
12. Operational Records, 224 Squadron, July 1943.
13. Michael D. Roberts, *Dictionary of Naval Aviation Squadrons: The History of VP, VPB, VP(HL) and VP(AM) Squadrons*, 2 vols. (Washington, DC: Naval Historical Centre, 2000), 2:507–508. Norman Franks and Eric Zimmerman, *U-Boat versus Aircraft: The Dramatic Story behind U-boat claims in Gun Action with Aircraft in World War II* (London: Grub Street, 1998), 130.
14. Operational Records, 206 Squadron, June 1943. Niestle, 62.
15. Niestle, 76. Wynn, 1:278. Kit Carter and Robert Mueller, *Combat Chronology 1941–1945* (Washington, DC: Centre for Air Force History, 1991), 163. Wynn, 2:90.

Chapter 10: United States Navy: June–July 1943

1. Samuel Eliot Morison, *The Atlantic Battle Won: May 1943–May 1945* (Edison: Castle Books, 2001), 111–112. Axel Niestle, *German U-Boat Losses During World War II* (London: Frontline Books, 2014), 114.
2. Niestle, 142. Kenneth Wynn, *U-Boat Operations of the Second World War, Volume 1: Career Histories, U1–U510* (Annapolis: Naval Institute Press, 1997), 96–97.
3. Niestle, 146. Wynn, 1:318–319.
4. Niestle, 121. Wynn, 1:123–124.
5. Niestle, 123. Wynn, 1:326–327.
6. Niestle, 119. Wynn, 1:48–49.
7. Niestle, 127. Kenneth Wynn, *U-Boat Operations of the Second World War, Volume 2: Career Histories, U511–UIT25* (Annapolis: Naval Institute Press, 1998), 15–16.
8. Wynn, 1: 29–31. Niestle, 116.
9. Niestle, 72. Wynn, 2:60–61.
10. Niestle, 126. Wynn, 1:143.
11. Niestle, 59. Wynn, 1:259.
12. Niestle, 45. Wynn, 1:110–111.
13. Niestle, 79. Wynn, 2:115.
14. Morison, 191–192. Niestle, 86. Wynn, 2:155.
15. Niestle, 57. Norman Franks and Eric Zimmerman, *U-Boat versus Aircraft: The Dramatic Story behind U-boat claims in Gun Action with Aircraft in World War II* (London: Grub Street, 1998), 49.

16. Niestle, 86, 59. Wynn, 1:237–238. Wynn, 2:155.
17. Niestle, 121. Wynn, 1:122–123.
18. Niestle, 123. Wynn, 2:4–5.
19. Morison, 219. Niestle, 138. Wynn, 1:146.
20. Niestle, 72. Wynn, 2:61–62.
21. Franks and Zimmerman, 133.
22. Operational Records, 172 Squadron, July 1943. Niestle, 119. Wynn, 1:104.
23. Operational Records, 179 Squadron, July 1943. Niestle, 47. Wynn, 1:169–170.
24. Operational Records, 172 Squadron, July 1943. Niestle, 145. Wynn, 1:306.
25. Operational Records, 172 Squadron, July 1943. Niestle, 75. Wynn, 2:82.
26. Niestle, 74. Wynn, 2:76–77.
27. Operational Records, 502 Squadron, July 1943. Niestle, 145. Wynn, 1:308.
28. Operational Records, 461 Royal Australian Air Force Squadron, July 1943. Niestle, 145. Wynn, 1:307–308.
29. Niestle, 122. Wynn, 1:322–323.
30. Operational Records, 48 Squadron, June 1943. Niestle, 73. Wynn, 2:65.
31. Operational Records, 459 Squadron, June 1943. Niestle, 45. Wynn 1:77–78.
32. Operational Records, 228 Squadron, June 1943.
33. Niestle, 70. Wynn, 2:38–40. Some sources list a 307 Squadron Mosquito downing by *U-155* on 14 June in the Bay of Biscay but as that aircraft successfully returned to base and did not crash land, it has not been included in the total number of Allied aircraft shot down by U-boats. Franks and Zimmerman, 45.
34. Niestle, 117. Wynn, 1:85–86.
35. Franks and Zimmerman, 51–54.

Chapter 11: B-24s: August–October 1943

1. Operational Records, 120 Squadron, October 1943. Axel Niestle, *German U-Boat Losses During World War II* (London: Frontline Books, 2014), 59. Kenneth Wynn, *U-Boat Operations of the Second World War, Volume 1: Career Histories, U1–U510* (Annapolis: Naval Institute Press, 1997), 259.
2. Operational Records, 120 Squadron, October 1943. Norman Franks and Eric Zimmerman, *U-Boat versus Aircraft: The Dramatic Story behind*

U-boat claims in Gun Action with Aircraft in World War II (London: Grub Street, 1998), 90–91.
3. Operational Records, 86 Squadron, October 1943. Niestle, 62. Wynn, 1:278.
4. Niestle, 62.
5. Niestle, 77. Kenneth Wynn, *U-Boat Operations of the Second World War, Volume 2: Career Histories, U511–UIT25* (Annapolis: Naval Institute Press, 1998), 103–104.
6. Operational Records, 59 Squadron, October 1943. Operational Records, 120 Squadron, October, 1943. Niestle, 67. Paul Kemp, *U-Boats Destroyed: German Submarine Losses in the World Wars* (Annapolis, Maryland: Naval Institute Press, 1997), 150. Wynn, 1:312.
7. Operational Records, 86 Squadron, October 1943. Operational Records, 59 Squadron, 1943. Niestle, 130. Kemp, 151.Wynn, 2:170.
8. Operational Records, 86 Squadron, October 1943. Niestle, 92. Wynn 2:195.
9. Operational Records, 59 Squadron, October 1943, Operational Records, 120 Squadron, October, 1943. Niestle, 128. Wynn, 2:22.
10. Operational Records, 224 Squadron, October 1943. Niestle, 51. Kemp, 152–153. Wynn, 1:193.
11. Niestle, 66. Wynn, 1:311–312.
12. Alan C. Carey, *Sighted Sub: The United States Navy's Air Campaign against the U-Boat* (Oxford: Casemate, 2019), 34. Niestle, 41. Wynn, 1:63–64.
13. Niestle, 82. Wynn, 2:130.
14. Niestle, 55. Wynn, 1:228.
15. Niestle, 46. Wynn, 1:161–163.

Chapter 12: United States Navy: August–October 1943

1. Frederick J Milford, 'Part Four: WW II development of homing torpedoes 1940–1946', *The Submarine Review* (April 1997) as republished on https://web.archive.org/web/20060224092332 and www.navytorpedo.com/html/legacy/USNT4.htm.
2. Samuel Eliot Morison, *The Atlantic Battle Won: May 1943–May 1945* (Edison: Castle Books, 2001), 122–123.
3. Paul Kemp, *U-Boats Destroyed: German Submarine Losses in the World Wars* (Annapolis, Maryland: Naval Institute Press, 1997), 140. Axel Niestle, *German U-Boat Losses During World War II* (London: Frontline Books, 2014), 142. Kenneth Wynn, *U-Boat Operations of the Second World War, Volume 1: Career Histories, U1–U510* (Annapolis: Naval Institute Press, 1997), 95–96.

4. Niestle, 142. Wynn, 1:95–96.
5. Norman Franks and Eric Zimmerman, *U-Boat versus Aircraft: The Dramatic Story behind U-boat claims in Gun Action with Aircraft in World War II* (London: Grub Street, 1998), 67–69. Kenneth Wynn, *U-Boat Operations of the Second World War, Volume 2: Career Histories, U511–UIT25* (Annapolis: Naval Institute Press, 1998), 116.
6. Niestle, 79. Morison, 123.
7. Morison, 114. Niestle, 127. Wynn, 2:14.
8. Franks and Zimmerman, 142–143.
9. Niestle, 126. Busch, 58. Wynn, 2:138–139. Morison, 127. Alan C. Carey, *Sighted Sub, Sank Same: The United States Navy's Air Campaign against the U-Boat* (Oxford: Casemate, 2019), 149.
10. Niestle, 138. Wynn, 2:171. Carey, 150.
11. Niestle, 145. Wynn, 1:306–307. Carey, 151.
12. Niestle, 62. Wynn, 1:279–280.
13. Niestle, 61. Wynn, 1:263–265. William T. Y'Blood, *Hunter Killer: U.S. Navy Escort Carriers in Gallant Battle Against the Nazi U-Boat Menace* (New York: Bantam Books, 1992), 111–112.
14. Y'Blood, 116. Niestle, 72. Wynn, 2:55–57.
15. Niestle, 142. Wynn, 1:161.
16. Niestle, 58. Wynn, 1:250–252.
17. Morison, 197. Niestle, 75. Wynn, 2:82–84.
18. Niestle, 74. Franks and Zimmerman, 142–143. Wynn, 2:73–74.
19. Niestle, 74.
20. Niestle, 52. Franks and Zimmerman, 136-137. Wynn, 1:196.
21. Niestle, 70. Wynn, 2:48–49.
22. Niestle, 121. Wynn, 1:124–125.
23. Niestle, 59. Wynn, 1:255–256.
24. Niestle, 66. Wynn, 1:301–302.
25. Niestle, 117. Wynn, 1:87–88.
26. Larry Milberry and Hugh Halliday, *The Royal Canadian Air Force At War 1939–1945* (Toronto: CANAV Books, 1990), 345. Niestle, 146. Wynn, 1:319–320.
27. Operational Records, 423 Squadron, October 1943. Niestle, 74. Wynn, 2:79–80.
28. Franks and Zimmerman, 93–95.
29. Some sources contend that 221 Squadron Wellington 'M' participated in the sinking of *U-372* on 4 August 1942. The operational records provide no support for such a contention. The report indicates that the Wellington crew spotted a British destroyer at the location and that the Royal Navy crew reported a U-boat sunk.

30. Operational Records, 344 Squadron, October 1943. Niestle, 61. Wynn, 1:265–266.
31. Operational Records, 179 Squadron, September 1943.
32. Operational Records, 179 Squadron, September 1943. Niestle, 75. Wynn, 2:123.
33. Niestle, 63. Wynn, 1:283–284.
34. Operational Records, 172 Squadron, October 1943. Niestle, 70. Wynn, 2:41–42.
35. Operational Records, 179 Squadron, October 1943. Operational Records, 612 Squadron, October 1943. Franks and Zimmerman, 88–89, 93–94.
36. Niestle, 137. Wynn, 1:144–145.
37. Operational Records, 269 Squadron, October 1943. Niestle, 55. Wynn, 1:225–226.
38. Operational Records, 244 Squadron, October 1943. Niestle, 127. Wynn, 2:18–19.
39. Karl Doenitz, *The Memoirs of Karl Doenitz: Ten Years and Twenty Days* (Yorkshire: Frontline Books, 2019), 415.

Chapter 13: November–December 1943

1. Operational Records, 86 Squadron, November 1943. Axel Niestle, *German U-Boat Losses During World War II* (London: Frontline Books, 2014), 52. Kenneth Wynn, *U-Boat Operations of the Second World War, Volume 1: Career Histories, U1–U510* (Annapolis: Naval Institute Press, 1997), 196–197.
2. Operational Records, 53 Squadron, December 1943. Niestle, 59. Wynn, 1:260.
3. Operational Records, 612 Squadron, November 1943. Operational Records, 311 Squadron, November 1943. Niestle, 92. Paul Kemp, *U-Boats Destroyed: German Submarine Losses in the World Wars* (Annapolis, Maryland: Naval Institute Press, 1997), 157. Kenneth Wynn, *U-Boat Operations of the Second World War, Volume 2: Career Histories, U511–UIT25* (Annapolis: Naval Institute Press, 1998), 196–197.
4. Niestle, 123. Alan C. Carey, *U.S. Navy PB4Y-1 (B-24) Liberator Squadrons in Great Britain during World War II* (Atglen: Schiffer Military History, 2003), 46–47, 143. Kemp, 157. Wynn, 1:326.
5. Niestle, 138. Wynn, 2:171. Samuel Eliot Morrison, *The Battle of the Atlantic 1939–1943* (Edison: Castle Books, 2001), 225.
6. Niestle, 138. Kemp, 159. Wynn, 2:172.

7. Niestle, 78. Wynn, 2: 105–106. Norman Franks and Eric Zimmerman, *U-Boat versus Aircraft: The Dramatic Story behind U-boat claims in Gun Action with Aircraft in World War II* (London: Grub Street, 1998), 97–98.
8. Operational Records, 220 Squadron, November 1943. Niestle, 82. Wynn, 2:130–131.
9. Operational Records, 179 Squadron, October 1943. Niestle, 55. Wynn, 1:166–167.
10. Operational Records 179 Squadron, November 1943. Niestle, 46. Wynn, 1:154–155.
11. Operational Records 179 Squadron, November 1943. Niestle, 128. Wynn, 2:23.
12. Franks and Zimmerman, 99.
13. Franks and Zimmerman, 100.
14. Niestle, 122. Morrison, 169–171. Wynn, 1:130–131.
15. Niestle, 138. Morrison, 170–171. Wynn, 2:172.
16. *Sextant Conference, November–December, 1943 Papers and Minutes of Meetings Sextant and Eureka Conferences* (Office, US Secretary, Office of the Command Chiefs of Staff, 1943), 51–52.
17. Ibid., 87.
18. Ibid., 89–91.
19. Ibid., 82.
20. Ibid., 84.
21. Ibid., 110.
22. Ibid., 330.
23. Ibid., 406.

Chapter 14: B-24s: January–May 1944

1. Operational Records, 59 Squadron, May 1944. Axel Niestle, *German U-Boat Losses During World War II* (London: Frontline Books, 2014), 94. Kenneth Wynn, *U-Boat Operations of the Second World War, Volume 2: Career Histories, U511–UIT25* (Annapolis: Naval Institute Press, 1998), 207.
2. Operational Records, 59 Squadron, May 1944. Niestle, 100. Kenneth Wynn, *U-Boat Operations of the Second World War, Volume 1: Career Histories, U1–U510* (Annapolis: Naval Institute Press, 1997), 201.
3. Operational Records, 53 Squadron, February 1944. Norman Franks and Eric Zimmerman, *U-Boat versus Aircraft: The Dramatic Story behind U-boat claims in Gun Action with Aircraft in World War II* (London: Grub Street, 1998), 108.

4. Operational Records, 502 Squadron, February 1944. Franks and Zimmerman, 109.
5. Operational Records, 53 Squadron, April 1944. Franks and Zimmerman, 117–118.
6. *U-737* battled 120 Squadron 'B' and although heavily damaged, the B-24 returned to base and executed a belly landing. Since it landed at base, I have not included the aircraft as one downed by U-boats. Operational Records, 53 Squadron, April 1944. Franks and Zimmerman, 117–118.
7. Operational Records, 224 Squadron, March 1944. Franks and Zimmerman, 113–114.
8. Alan C. Carey, *U.S. Navy PB4Y-1 (B-24) Liberator Squadrons in Great Britain during World War II* (Atglen: Schiffer Military History, 2003), 59–60. Niestle, 51. Wynn, 1:192. Paul Kemp, *U-Boats Destroyed: German Submarine Losses in the World Wars* (Annapolis, Maryland: Naval Institute Press, 1997), 51. Alan C. Carey, *Sighted Sub: The United States Navy's Air Campaign against the U-Boat* (Oxford: Casemate, 2019), 128–130.
9. Carey, *Sighted Sub*, 109. Niestle, 137. Wynn, 1: 133–134.
10. Operational Records, 502 Squadron, January 1944. Niestle, 57. Wynn, 1:240.
11. Operational Records, 172 Squadron, March 1944. Operational Records, 206 Squadron, March, 1944. Operational Records, 220 Squadron, March, 1944. Niestle, 71. Wynn, 2: 50–52. An Avenger may also be involved in the sinking but sources conflict on this issue.
12. Franks and Zimmerman, 102.

Chapter 15: Swordfish, Catalinas, Avengers and Wellingtons: January–May 1944

1. Axel Niestle, *German U-Boat Losses During World War II* (London: Frontline Books, 2014), 67. Kenneth Wynn, *U-Boat Operations of the Second World War, Volume 1: Career Histories, U1–U510* (Annapolis: Naval Institute Press, 1997), 313.
2. Niestle, 78. Kenneth Wynn, *U-Boat Operations of the Second World War, Volume 2: Career Histories, U511–UIT25* (Annapolis: Naval Institute Press, 1998), 109–110.
3. Niestle, 52. Wynn, 1:195.
4. Niestle, 80. Wynn, 2:122–123.
5. Niestle, 91. Wynn, 2:193.

6. Niestle, 87. Wynn, 2:159.
7. Operational Records, 210 Squadron, February 1944. Niestle. 73. Wynn, 2:70–71.
8. Since the Catalina returned to base, I have not considered it as having been shot down by a U-boat.
9. Operational Records, 210 Squadron, May 1944. Niestle, 48. Wynn, 1:172–173.
10. Operational Records, 210 Squadron, May 1944. Niestle, 67. Wynn, 1:314.
11. Operational Records, 262 Squadron, March 1944. James J. Halley, *The Squadrons of the Royal Air Force and Commonwealth 1918–1988* (Tonbridge: Air-Britain, 1988), 328.
12. Operational Records, 202 Squadron, February 1944. Roscoe Creed, *PBY: The Flying Catalina* (Annapolis: Naval Institute Press, 1985), 212–213. Niestle, 87. Wynn, 2:156.
13. Creed, 214. Niestle, 60. Wynn, 2:139–140.
14. Operational Records, 162 Squadron, April 1944. Niestle, 55. Creed, 257. Wynn, 1:229.
15. Daniel V. Gallery, *Clear the Decks!* (New York: William Morrow and Company, 1951), 85–90. Wynn, 2:24. Samuel Eliot Morison, *The Atlantic Battle Won: May 194 –May 1945* (Edison: Castle Books, 2001), 281–282. Niestle, 128.
16. Morison, 279–280. William T. Y'Blood, *Hunter Killer: U.S. Navy Escort Carriers in Gallant Battle Against the Nazi U-Boat Menace* (New York: Bantam Books, 1992), 155–159. Niestle, 129. Wynn, 2:164.
17. Y'Blood, 159–160. Morison, 280, 284–287. Wynn, 2:221–222. Niestle, 115.
18. Niestle, 53. Wynn, 1:200.
19. Niestle, 124. Wynn, 2:6–7.
20. Niestle, 115. Wynn, 1:49–50. The information regarding *U-66*'s demise, which Allied forces sank during this time, does not support the claim that Allied aircraft contributed to its sinking. The evidence is overwhelming that American destroyers are solely responsible. Therefore *U-66*'s sinking has not been included while previous secondary studies have contended otherwise. Y'Blood, 181-88. Niestle, 119. Wynn, 1:46–48.
21. Niestle, 129. Wynn, 2:26–27.
22. Clay Blair, *Hitler's U-Boat War: The Hunted 1942–1945* (New York: Random House, 1998), 491.
23. Operational Records, 172 Squadron, January 1944. Wynn, 1:169. Niestle, 47.

24. Operational Records, 612 Squadron, February 1944.
25. Operational Records, 612 Squadron, February 1944. Niestle, 128. Wynn, 2:24.
26. Norman Franks and Eric Zimmerman, *U-Boat versus Aircraft: The Dramatic Story behind U-boat claims in Gun Action with Aircraft in World War II* (London: Grub Street, 1998), 110.
27. Operational Records, 407 Royal Canadian Air Force Squadron, February 1944. Niestle, 52. Wynn, 1:198.
28. Operational Records, 407 Royal Canadian Air Force Squadron, May 1944. Niestle, 131. Wynn, 2:171.
29. Roger Jordan, *The World's Merchant Fleets 1939: The Particulars and Wartime Fates of 6,000 Ships*. (Annapolis: Naval Institute Press, 1999), 527.
30. Operational Records, 621 Squadron, May 1944.
31. Operational Records, 8 Squadron, May 1944. Niestle, 138. Wynn, 2:172–173.
32. Operational Records, 36 Squadron, May 1944. Niestle, 75. Wynn, 2:84–85.
33. Operational Records, 304 Squadron, January 1944. Operational Records, 172 Squadron, January 1944. *U-608* War Diary as confirmed by Alex Niestle.
34. Some sources list 407 Squadron Wellington 'H' as having been downed by *U-256* but the same sources agree that the aircraft crashed due to pilot error since the U-boat did not fire on the Wellington as it prepared its approach. Therefore, it has not been included in the list of aircraft shot down by U-boats. Franks and Zimmerman, 112.
35. Franks and Zimmerman, 103–104.
36. Ibid., 104–105.
37. Operational Records, 10 Royal Australian Air Force, January 1944. Niestle, 63. Wynn, 1:281–282.
38. Operational Records, 461 Royal Australian Air Force, January 1944. Niestle, 70. Wynn, 2:46–48.
39. Operational Records, 422 Royal Canadian Air Force, March 1944. Niestle, 76. Wynn, 2:91–92.
40. *The London Gazette*, 30 June 1944. Niestle, 80. Wynn, 2:123.
41. Franks and Zimmerman, 121–122.
42. Operational Records, 248 Squadron, March 1944. Niestle, 93. Wynn, 2:201.
43. Franks and Zimmerman, 107.
44. Operational Records, 500 Squadron, May 1944. Niestle, 92. Wynn, 2:193–194. Some sources contend that Wellington 'M' from 36

Squadron participated in the sinking but the operational records, in regards to this aircraft, state: 'Whilst investigating contact picked up on way to patrol area, experienced concentrated flak from U/Boat proceeding on the surface, course 090, est. speed 8 knots. No attack made, made second run in but U/Boat crash dived. Markers dropped in position, est. 3 miles north of sighting. 465 etc. sent to Base, automatic homing carried out. Forced to return to early – engine trouble. Landed La Senia. Weather very bad – low cloud U/B sunk 27 hours later.' This does not place the Wellington in the area for the Ventura's attack.

45. Niestle, 43. Wynn, 1:60–61.
46. Niestle, 49, 61, 62. Wynn, 1:252–253, 272–273, 279.
47. Niestle, 130–131. Wynn, 2:165.

Chapter 16: June 1944

1. Axel Niestle, *German U-Boat Losses During World War II* (London: Frontline Books, 2014), 199.
2. Operational Records, 224 Squadron, June 1944. Niestle, 50. Kenneth Wynn, *U-Boat Operations of the Second World War, Volume 1: Career Histories, U1–U510* (Annapolis: Naval Institute Press, 1997), 179–180.
3. Operational Records, Norman Franks and Eric Zimmerman, *U-Boat versus Aircraft: The Dramatic Story behind U-boat claims in Gun Action with Aircraft in World War II* (London: Grub Street, 1998), 148–152. Operational Records, 53 Squadron, June 1944.
4. Operational Records, 53 Squadron, June 1944. Paul Kemp, *U-Boats Destroyed: German Submarine Losses in the World Wars* (Annapolis, Maryland: Naval Institute Press, 1997), 194. Niestle, 76. Kenneth Wynn, *U-Boat Operations of the Second World War, Volume 2: Career Histories, U511–UIT25* (Annapolis: Naval Institute Press, 1998), 94–95,
5. Operational Records, 224 Squadron, June 1944. Niestle, 84. Wynn, 2:144.
6. Kemp, 195.
7. Operational Records, 224 Squadron, June 1944. Niestle, 58. Wynn, 1:245–247.
8. Operational Records, 248 Squadron, June 1944. Operational Records, 206 Squadron, June 1944. Niestle, 89. Wynn, 2:166–167.
9. Operational Records, 311 Squadron, June 1944. Niestle, 93. Wynn, 2:200.
10. Operational Records, 86 Squadron, June 1944. Niestle, 100. Wynn, 1:216.

11. Operational Records, 86 Squadron, June 1944. Niestle, 68. Wynn, 1:315.
12. Karl Doenitz, *The Memoirs of Karl Doenitz: Ten Years and Twenty Days* (Yorkshire: Frontline Books, 2019), 424.
13. Franks and Zimmerman, 150–151.
14. Operational Records, 224 Squadron, June 1944. Niestle, 64. Wynn, 1:293–294.
15. Franks and Zimmerman, 148–150.
16. Operational Records, 162 Squadron, June 1944. Niestle, 67. Wynn, 1:315.
17. Operational Records, 162 Squadron, June 1944. Niestle, 93. Wynn, 2:202–203.
18. Franks and Zimmerman, 158–160.
19. Operational Records, 162 Squadron, June 1944. Niestle, 82. Wynn, 2:135–136.
20. Operational Records, 162 Squadron, June 1944. Operational Records, 333 Squadron, June 1944. Operational Records, 330 Squadron, June 1944. Niestle, 133. Wynn, 2:236.
21. Operational Records, 333 Squadron, June 1944. Niestle, 63. Wynn, 1:280.
22. Operational Records, 333 Squadron, June 1944. Niestle, 103. Wynn, 2:211.
23. Operational Records, 201 Squadron, June 1944. Niestle, 91. Wynn, 2:190.
24. Operational Records, 228 Squadron, June 1944. Niestle, 92. Wynn, 2:199.
25. Franks and Zimmerman, 153–154. Operational Records, 228 Squadron, June 1944.
26. Franks and Zimmerman, 156–157.
27. Niestle, 139. Wynn, 2:175–176. Samuel Eliot Morrison, *The Battle of the Atlantic 1939–1943* (Edison: Castle Books, 2001), 291, 295. Alan C. Carey, *Sighted Sub, Sank Same: The United States Navy's Air Campaign against the U-Boat* (Oxford: Casemate, 2019), 178. I did not include the second Avenger as downed by the U-boat since the depth charge explosion caused the crash. Some sources suggest that Allied aircraft participated in the famous capture of *U-505*. I found no evidence supporting that conclusion. Allied surface vessels deserve full credit for its capture. As Morison notes, Destroyer Escort *Chatelain*'s crew had obtained the sonar contact that led to the attack on *U-505*. The only Allied aircraft pilots airborne at the time flying in two Wildcats 'merely confirmed' what the destroyer escort's crew already knew.
28. Doenitz, 422–423.

Chapter 17: July–December 1944

1. Operational Records, 206 Squadron, July 1944. Axel Niestle, *German U-Boat Losses During World War II* (London: Frontline Books, 2014), 100. Kenneth Wynn, *U-Boat Operations of the Second World War, Volume 1: Career Histories, U1–U510* (Annapolis: Naval Institute Press, 1997), 217.
2. Operational Records, 86 Squadron, July 1944. Niestle, 56. Wynn, 1:230.
3. Operational Records, 53 Squadron, August 1944. Niestle, 74. Kenneth Wynn, *U-Boat Operations of the Second World War, Volume 2: Career Histories, U511–UIT25* (Annapolis: Naval Institute Press, 1998), 77–79.
4. Operational Records, 53 Squadron, August 1944. Niestle, 75. Norman Franks and Eric Zimmerman, *U-Boat versus Aircraft: The Dramatic Story behind U-boat claims in Gun Action with Aircraft in World War II* (London: Grub Street, 1998), 97, 173. Wynn, 2:86–87.
5. Operational Records, 224 Squadron, September 1944. Niestle, 131. Wynn, 2:178–179.
6. Operational Records, 311 Squadron, October 1944. Niestle, 115. Wynn, 2: 222. John D.R. Rawlings, *Coastal Support and Special Squadrons of the RAF and their Aircraft* (London: Jane's Publishing Company, 1982), 200.
7. Alan C. Carey, *Sighted Sub, Sank Same: The United States Navy's Air Campaign against the U-Boat* (Oxford: Casemate, 2019), 110. 110. Niestle, 139. Wynn, 2:177.
8. Operational Records, 220 Squadron, September 1944. Niestle, 139. Wynn, 2:180.
9. Operational Records, 10 Royal Australian Air Force Squadron, July 1944. Alan C. Carey, *U.S. Navy PB4Y-1 (B-24) Liberator Squadrons in Great Britain during World War II* (Atglen: Schiffer Military History, 2003), 80–81. Niestle, 48. Wynn, 1:173.
10. Operational Records, 201st Squadron, July, 1944. Niestle, 133. Wynn, 2:235.
11. Operational Records, 461st Royal Australian Air Force Squadron, August, 1944. Niestle, 59. Wynn, 1:257.
12. Operational Records, 461 Royal Australian Air Force Squadron August, 1944. Niestle, 51. Wynn, 1: 191–192. Rawlings, 224.
13. Operational Records, 201 Squadron, August 1944. Niestle, 117. Wynn, 1:88–90.
14. Operational Records, 330 Squadron, November 1944. Niestle, 68. Wynn, 1:317.

15. Operational Records, 502 Squadron, August 1944. Niestle, 93. Wynn, 2:203.
16. Franks and Zimmerman, 176.
17. Ibid., 176.
18. Ibid., 178–179.
19. Niestle, 55. Wynn, 1:229–230. Paul Kemp, *U-Boats Destroyed: German Submarine Losses in the World Wars* (Annapolis: Naval Institute Press, 1997), 214–215.
20. Niestle, 60. Wynn, 1:261.
21. Niestle, 57. Wynn, 1:240–241.
22. Niestle, 128. Wynn, 2:23–24. Samuel Eliot Morrison, *The Atlantic Battle Won: May 1943–May 1945* (Edison: Castle Books, 2001), 299.
23. Morison, 326–327. Niestle, 134. Wynn, 2:237.
24. Morison, 296–297. Carey, *Sighted Sub*, 185.
25. Operational Records, 210 Squadron, July 1944. Roscoe Creed, *PBY: The Flying Catalina* (Annapolis: Naval Institute Press, 1985), 249. Niestle, 57.
26. Operational Records, 210 Squadron, July 1944. Niestle, 84.
27. Franks and Zimmerman, 174–175.
28. Ibid., 166–167.
29. Niestle, 72, 77, 91. Wynn, 2:57–58, 102–103, 187–188.
30. Niestle, 48, 108. Wynn, 1:172. Wynn, 2:228.
31. Niestle, 139. Wynn, 2:180.
32. Niestle, 66. Wynn, 1:310.
33. Niestle, 67, 92. Wynn, 1:312–313. Wynn, 2:197, 199.
34. Niestle, 70, 73. Wynn, 2:40–41, 66–67.
35. Niestle, 47, 64, 95, 88. Wynn, 1:166–167, 289–290. Wynn, 2:208–209, 162.
36. Niestle, 50. Wynn, 1:184–186.
37. Niestle, 84. Wynn, 2:141.
38. Niestle, 159. Wynn, 2:260.
39. Niestle, 32–33. Wynn, 1:11–12, 16–17. *U-481* may have downed a Soviet aircraft in the Baltic area on 30 July 1944 but I found no source information to verify this event.
40. Niestle, 172. Wynn, 2:245.

Chapter 18: 1945

1. Operational Records, 224 Squadron, March 1945. Kenneth Wynn, *U-Boat Operations of the Second World War, Volume 2: Career Histories, U511–UIT25* (Annapolis: Naval Institute Press, 1998), 225.

2. Operational Records, 120 Squadron, April 1945. Axel Niestle, *German U-Boat Losses During World War II* (London: Frontline Books, 2014), 105. Wynn, 2:225.
3. Operational Records, 547 Squadron, May 1945. Niestle, 71. Wynn, 2:54.
4. Operational Records, 86 Squadron, May 1945. Niestle, 127. Wynn, 2:19.
5. Operational Records, 86 Squadron, May 1945. Niestle, 104. Wynn, 2:215.
6. Operational Records, 86 Squadron, May 1945. Niestle, 168. Wynn, 2:274.
7. Niestle, 129, 81. Wynn, 2:125.
8. Niestle, 107. Some sources contend that this was *U-326*. Niestle's argument convinced me that it was *U-1107*. Alan C. Carey, *U.S. Navy PB4Y-1 (B-24) Liberator Squadrons in Great Britain during World War II* (Atglen: Schiffer Military History, 2003), 114–115. Michael D. Roberts, *Dictionary of American Naval Aviation Squadrons: The History of VP, VPB, VP(HL) and VP(AM) Squadrons*, 2 vols. (Washington, DC: Naval Historical Centre, 2000), 2:510. Wynn, 2:225.
9. Niestle, 59. Kenneth Wynn, *U-Boat Operations of the Second World War, Volume 1: Career Histories, U1–U510* (Annapolis: Naval Institute Press, 1997), 254–255.
10. Niestle, 158, 159. Wynn, 2:257, 259.
11. Niestle, 162, 167. Wynn, 2:264, 271.
12. Niestle, 81, 86. Wynn, 2:125, 153–155.
13. Niestle, 43, 44, 56, 63, 96, 97, 132, 108, 174. Wynn, 1:54, 230–231, 283. Wynn, 2:226, 232, 179–180, 229, 248.
14. Niestle, 34, 133, 160, 166. Wynn, 1:40. Wynn, 2:235, 262, 271.
15. Niestle, 48, 85, 162. Wynn, 1:171. Wynn, 2:147, 263.
16. Niestle, 158, 167. Wynn, 2:256, 257, 272.
17. Niestle, 80, 94, 133, 158. Wynn, 2:123, 203, 236–237, 257.
18. Niestle, 97, 85. Wynn, 2:233, 147.
19. Niestle, 87. Wynn, 2:157–158.
20. Niestle, 167, 90, 109, 167. Wynn, 2:273, 185, 240, 273.
21. Operational Records, 143 Squadron, April 1945.
22. Operational Records, 235 Squadron, April 1945. Niestle, 130, 107. Wynn, 2:165, 224.
23. Operational Records, 235 Squadron, April 1945. Niestle, 130. Wynn, 2:169–170.
24. Operational Records, 143 Squadron, April 1945.
25. Operational Records, 235 Squadron, April 1945.

26. Operational Records, 248 Squadron, April 1945. Niestle, 49. No references in the 333 Operational Records indicate any involvement in these attacks. Wynn, 1:176.
27. Niestle, 175. Wynn, 2:252. No references in the 333 Operational Records indicate any involvement in these attacks.
28. Operational Records, 235 Squadron, March 1945. Norman Franks and Eric Zimmerman, *U-Boat versus Aircraft: The Dramatic Story behind U-boat claims in Gun Action with Aircraft in World War II* (London: Grub Street, 1998), 180.
29. Operational Records, 304 Squadron, March 1945. Niestle, 101. Wynn, 1:218.
30. Operational Records, 179 Squadron, February 1945. Niestle, 91. Wynn, 2:186.
31. Niestle, 101. Wynn, 1:219.
32. Niestle, 82. Wynn, 1:132–134.
33. Niestle, 60, 85, 98.
34. Niestle, 40, 41, 48, 51. Operational Records, 126 Squadron, May 1945. Franks, Zimmerman, 180–181.
35. Operational Records, 210 Squadron, May 1945. Niestle, 101. Wynn, 1:218.

Chapter 19: Conclusion

1. Andrew Hendrie, *The Cinderella Service: RAF Coastal Command 1939–1945* (Barnslay, South Yorkshire: Pen and Sword Aviation, 2006), 201.
2. Karl Doenitz, *The Memoirs of Karl Doenitz: Ten Years and Twenty Days* (Yorkshire: Frontline Books, 2019), 427.
3. *Peace and War: United States Foreign Policy, 1931–1941* (United States: US Government Printing Office, 1943), 455–56.

Bibliography

Unpublished Sources

Royal Air Force Operational Records, National Archives, AIR-27 Record Group
    10th Squadron (Royal Australian Air Force)
    10th Squadron
    36th Squadron
    38th Squadron
    47th Squadron
    48th Squadron
    53rd Squadron
    58th Squadron
    59th Squadron
    61st Squadron
    77th Squadron
    86th Squadron
    113th Squadron
    120th Squadron
    143rd Squadron
    159th Squadron
    162nd Squadron (Royal Canadian Air Force)
    172nd Squadron
    200th Squadron
    201st Squadron
    202nd Squadron
    203rd Squadron
    204th Squadron
    206th Squadron
    209th Squadron
    210th Squadron

220th Squadron
221st Squadron
224th Squadron
228th Squadron
233rd Squadron
235th Squadron
244th Squadron
248th Squadron
259th Squadron
265th Squadron
269th Squadron
304th Squadron
307th Squadron
311th Squadron
330th Squadron
333rd Squadron
344th Squadron
407th Squadron
422nd Squadron (Royal Canadian Air Force)
423rd Squadron
455th Squadron (Royal Australian Air Force)
459th Squadron (Royal Australian Air Force)
461st Squadron (Royal Australian Air Force)
500th Squadron
502nd Squadron
547th Squadron
608th Squadron
612th Squadron
621st Squadron

Internet

U-boat.net

Published Sources

Armstrong, Anne. *Unconditional Surrender: The Impact of the Casablanca Policy upon World War II.* New Brunswick: Rutgers University Press, 1961.

Ashworth, Chris. *RAF Coastal Command 1936-1969.* Somerset: Patrick Stephens, 1992.

Barber, Mark. *The British Fleet Air Arm in World War II*. Oxford: Osprey Publishing, 2008.

Bishop, Chris. *Kriegsmarine U-Boats 1939-1945*. London: Amber Books, 2006.

Blair, Clay. *Hitler's U-Boat War: The Hunters 1939-1942*. London: Butler and Tanner, 2001.

Blair, Clay. *Hitler's U-Boat War: The Hunted 1942-1945*. New York: Random House, 1998.

Blue, Allan G. The B-24 Liberator. New York: Charles Scribner's and Sons, 1976.

Bowman, Martin W. *Battlefield Bombers: Deep Sea Attack*. Barnsley, South Yorkshire: Pen and Sword Aviation, 2014.

Bowman, Martin W. *Deep Sea Hunters: RAF Coastal Command and the War Against the U-Boats and the German Navy 1939 – 1945*. Barnsley: Pen and Sword Aviation, 2014.

Bridgman, Leonard. *Jane's all the World's Aircraft 1945-6*. New York: Arco Publishing, 1970.

Brodhurst, Robin. *Churchill's Anchor: The Biography of Admiral of the Fleet Sir Dudley Pound*. Barnsley: Pen and Sword Maritime, 2015.

Budiansky, Stephen. *Blackett's War: The Men Who Defeated the Nazi U-Boats and Brought Science to the Art of Warfare*. New York: Alfred A. Knopf, 2013.

Buell, Thomas B. *Master of Sea Power: A Biography of Fleet Admiral Ernest J. King*. Boston: Little, Brown and Company, 1980.

Busch, Rainer and Hans-Joachim Roll. *German U-Boat Commanders of World War II*. London: Greenhill books, 1999.

Butcher, Harry C. *My Three Years with Eisenhower: The Personal Diary of Captain Harry C. Butche, USNR Naval Aide to General Eisenhower, 1942 to 1945*. New York: Simon and Schuster, 1946.

Carey, Alan C. *Consolidated-Vultee PB4Y-2 Privateer*. Atglen: Schiffer Military History, 2005.

Carey, Alan C. *Galloping Ghosts of the Brazilian Coast*. New York: iUniverse, Inc. 2004.

Carey, Alan C. *Sighted Sub, Sank Same: The United States Navy's Air Campaign against the U-Boat*. Oxford: Casemate, 2019.

Carey, Alan C. *U.S. Navy PB4Y-1 (B-24) Liberator Squadrons in Great Britain during World War II*. Atglen: Schiffer Military History, 2003.

Carter, Kit and Robert Mueller. *Combat Chronology 1941-1945*. Washington, DC: Center for Air Force History, 1991.

Churchill, Randolph S., ed. *Into Battle: Speeches by the Right Hon. Winston Churchill P.C., M.P.* London: Cassell and Company, 1941.

Clark, Ronald W. *Tizard*. Gillingham: Blackmore, 1965.
Cocker, Maurice. *Aircraft-Carrying Ships of the Royal Navy*. Gloucestershire: The History Press, 2008.
Colledge, J.J. *Ships of the Royal Navy: The Complete Record of all Fighting Ships of the Royal Navy from the 15th Century to the Present*. Barnsley: Seaforth Publishing, 2020.
Creed, Roscoe. *PBY: The Flying Catalina*. Annapolis, Maryland: Naval Institute Press, 1985.
Derrig, John. *Wrong Made Right: U-166*. Privately Published.
Doenitz, Karl. *Ten Years and Twenty Days*. Yorkshire: Frontline Books, 2012.
Dorr, Robert F. *B-24 Liberator Units of the Fifteenth Air Force*. Oxford: Osprey Publishing, 2000.
Douglas, Sholto. *Years of Command*, Volume 2. London: Collins, 1966.
Eather, Steve. *The Australian Flying Corps*. Weston Creek: Aerospace Publications, 1995.
Falconer, Jonathan. *RAF Airfields of World War 2*. Hersham: Midland Publishing, 2012.
Faulkner, Marcus and Christopher Bell, ed. *Decision in the Atlantic: The Allies and the Longest Campaign of the Second World War*. Lexington: University Press of Kentucky, 2019.
Foreign Relations of the United States: The Conferences at Washington, 1941-1942, and Casablanca, 1943. Washington: United States Government Printing Office, 1968.
Francillon, Rene J. *Lockheed Aircraft Since 1913*. Annapolis, Maryland: Naval Institute Press, 1987.
Franks, Norman. *Conflict over the Bay*. London: William Kimber, 1986.
Franks, Norman. *Search, Find and Kill: Coastal Command's U-boat Successes*. Huddersfield: Aston Publications, 1990.
Franks, Norman and Eric Zimmerman. *U-Boat versus Aircraft: The Dramatic Story behind U-boat claims in Gun Action with Aircraft in World War II*. London: Grub Street, 1998.
Gallery, Daniel V. *Clear the Decks!* New York: William Morrow and Company, 1951.
Gannon, Michael. *Operation Drumbeat: The Dramatic True Story of Germany's First U-Boat Attacks Along the American Coast in World War II*. New York: Harper and Row, 1990.
Hague, Arnold. *The Allied Convoy System 1939-1945: Its Organization, Defence and Operation*. St. Catherine's: Vanwell Publishing, 2000.
Halley, James J. *The Squadrons of the Royal Air Force and Commonwealth 1918-1988*. Tonbridge: Air-Britain, 1988.

Heiferman, Ronald Ian. *The Cairo Conference of 1943: Roosevelt, Churchill, Chiang Kai-shek and Madame Chiang*. Jefferson: McFarland, 2011.

Hendrie, Andrew. *Flying Catalinas: The Consolidated PBY Catalina in World War Two*. Barnsley, South Yorkshire: Pen and Sword Aviation, 2012.

Hendrie, Andrew. *The Cinderella Service: RAF Coastal Command 1939–1945*. Barnslay, South Yorkshire: Pen and Sword Aviation, 2006.

Hickam, Jr., Homer H. *Torpedo Junction: The U-Boat War off America's East Coast 1942*. Annapolis: Naval Institute Press, 1989.

Ismay, Hastings Lionel. *The Memoirs of General Lord Ismay*. New York: Viking Press, 1960.

Jane's Fighting Aircraft of World War II. New York: Crescent Books, 1998.

Jay, Alwyn. *Endurance: A History of RAAF Aircrew Participation in Liberator Operations of RAF Coastal Command 1941-1945*. Maryborough: Banner Books, 1996.

Johnsen, Frederick A. *Bombers in Blue: PB4Y-2 Privateers and PB4Y-1 Liberators*. Tacoma: Bomber Books, 1979.

Jordan, Roger. *The World's Merchant Fleets 1939: The Particulars and Wartime Fates of 6,000 Ships*. Annapolis: Naval Institute Press, 1999.

Kelshall, Gaylord. *The U-Boat War in the Caribbean*. Annapolis: Naval Institute Press, 1994.

Kemp, Paul. *Decision at Sea: The Convoy Escorts*. New York: Elsevier-Dutton, 1978.

Kemp, Paul. *U-Boats Destroyed: German Submarine Losses in the World Wars*. Annapolis, Maryland: Naval Institute Press, 1997.

Konstam, Angus. *British Aircraft Carriers 1939-45*. Oxford: Osprey Publishing, 2010.

Konstam, Angus. *British Escort Carriers 1941-45*. Oxford: Osprey Publishing, 2019.

Lake, Jon. *Sunderland Squadrons of World War 2*. Oxford: Osprey Publishing, 2000.

Lardas, Mark. *Battle of the Atlantic 1939-41: RAF Coastal Command's hardest fight against the U-boats*. Oxford: Osprey Publishing, 2020.

Lardas, Mark. *Battle of the Atlantic 1942-45: The climax of World War II's greatest naval campaign*. Oxford: Osprey Publishing, 2021.

Leach, Joe. *RAAF Flying Boats at War: The Way It Was*. Australia: Australian Military History Publications, 1999.

March, Daniel J. ed. *British Warplanes of World War II*. London: Aerospace Publishing, 1998.

Mauer, Mauer, ed. *World War II Combat Squadrons of the United States Air Force: The Official Military Record of Every Active Squadron*. Woodbury: Platinum Press, 1992.

Milberry, Larry and Hugh Halliday. *The Royal Canadian Air Force At War 1939-1945*. Toronto: CANAV Books, 1990.

Miller, James. *The Northern Isles At War: The North Atlantic Front*. Edinburgh: Birlinn, 2003.

Milner, Marc. *The U-Boat Hunters: The Royal Canadian Navy and the Offensive against Germany's Submarines*. Toronto: University of Toronto Press, 1994.

Morgan, Daniel and Bruce Taylor. *U-Boat Attack Logs: A Complete Record of Warship Sinkings from Original Sources 1939-1945*. Barnesley, South Yorkshire: Seaforth Publishing, 2011.

Morison, Samuel Eliot. *The Battle of the Atlantic 1939-1943*. Edison: Castle Books, 2001.

Morison, Samuel Eliot. *The Atlantic Battle Won: May 1943 - May 1945*. Edison: Castle Books, 2001.

Nesbit, Roy Conyers. *Coastal Command in Action 1939-1945*. Gloucestershire: Sutton Publishing, 1997.

Niestle, Axel. *German U-Boat Losses During World War II: Details of Destruction*. London: Frontline Books, 2014.

O'Leary, Michael. *Consolidated B-24 Liberator*. Oxford: Osprey Publishing, 2002.

Padfield, Peter. *Donitz: The Last Fuhrer*. New York: Harper and Row, 1984.

Pateman, Colin. *Fuel, Fire and Fear: RAF Flight Engineers At War*. Croydon: Fronthill, 2018.

Poolman, Kenneth. *The Sea Hunters: Escort Carriers v. U-Boats, 1941-1945*. London: Arms and Armour Press, 1982.

Ragnarsson, Ragnar J. *US Navy PBY Catalina Units of the Atlantic War*. Oxford: Osprey Publishing, 2006.

Rainer, Busch. *Der U-Boot-Krieg 1939-1945*. Berlin: Verlag E.S. Mittler and Sohn, 1999.

Rawlings, John D.R. *Coastal Support and Special Squadrons of the RAF and their Aircraft*. London: Jane's Publishing Company, 1982.

Richards, Denis. *Portal of Hungerford: The Life of Marshal of the Royal Air Force Viscount Portal of Hungerford KG, GCB, OM, DSO, MC*. London: Bulter and Tanner, 1978.

Richards, Denis. *Royal Air Force 1939-1945, Volume 1: The Fight at Odds*. London: Her Majesty's Stationery Office, 1953.

Robertson, Bruce. *British Military Aircraft Serials 1878-1987*. Leicester: Oxford University Press, 1987.

Roskill, S.W. *The War At Sea 1939-1945. Volume I: The Defensive*. East Sussex: The Naval and Military Press, 2004.

Roskill, S.W. *The War At Sea 1939-1945. Volume II: The Period of Balance*. East Sussex: The Naval and Military Press, 2004.

Roskill, S.W. *The War At Sea 1939-1945. Volume III: The Offensive, Part 1*. London: Her Majesty's Stationery Office, 1960.

Rohwer, Jurgen. *Critical Convoy Battles of WWII: Crisis in the North Atlantic, March 1943*. Mechanicsburg: Stackpole, 1977.

Rohwer, J. and G. Hummelchen. *Chronology of the War at Sea 1939-1945*. Annapolis: Naval Institute Press, 1992.

Roosevelt, Elliot. *As He Saw It*. New York: Duell, Sloan and Pearce, 1946.

Roskill, S.W. *The War At Sea 1939-1945, Volume 1: The Defensive*. East Sussex: The Naval and Military Press, 2004.

Runyan, Timothy J. and Jan. M. Copes. *To Die Gallantly: The Battle of the Atlantic*. Oxford: Westview Press, 1994.

Sainsbury, Keith. *The Turning Point: Roosevelt, Stalin, Churchill, and Chiang-Kai-Shek, 1943 The Moscow, Cairo, and Tehran Conferences*. Oxford: Oxford University Press, 1985.

Schoenfeld, Max. *Stalking the U-Boat: USAAF Offensive Antisubmarine Operations in World War II*. Washington: Smithsonian Press, 1995.

Sharpe, Peter. *U-Boat Fact File: Detailed Service Histories of the Submarines Operated by the Kriegsmarine 1935-1945*. Leicester: Midland Publishing, 1998.

Showell, Jak P. Mallmann. *Donitz, U-boats, Convoys: The British Version of His Memoirs from the Admiralty's Secret Anti-Submarine Reports*. Barnsley, South Yorkshire: Frontline Books, 2013.

Showell, Jak P. Mallmann. *Hitler's U-Boat Bases*. Annapolis: Naval Institute Press, 2002.

Simons, Graham M. *Consolidated B-24 Liberator*. Barsley: Pen and Sword Aviation, 2012.

Slader, John. *The Red Duster at War: A History of the Merchant Navy During the Second World War*. London: William Kimber and Company, 1988.

Smith, Kevin. *Conflict over Convoys: Anglo-American logistics diplomacy in the Second World War*. Cambridge: Cambridge University Press, 1996.

Stille, Mark. *US Navy Escort Carriers 1942-45*. Oxford: Osprey Publishing, 2017.

Stitt, Robert M. *Boeing B-17 Fortress in RAF Coastal Command Service*. Poland: Stratus, 2019.

Sturtivant, Ray. *British Naval Aviation: The Fleet Air Arm, 1917-1990*. Annapolis: Naval Institute Press, 1990.

Sturtivant, Ray. *The Squadrons of the Fleet Air Arm*. Tonbridge: Air-Britain, 1984.

Syrett, David. *The Defeat of the German U-Boats: The Battle of the Atlantic.* Columbia: University of South Carolina Press, 1994.

Van der Vat, Dan. *The Atlantic Campaign: The Great Struggle at Sea 1939-1945.* London: Hodder and Stoughton, 1988.

Vause, Jordan. *Wolf: U-Boat Commanders in World War II.* Annapolis: Naval Institute Press, 1997.

Vintras, R.E. *The Portuguese Connection: The Secret History of the Azores Base.* London: Bachman and Turner, 1974.

Williams, Andrew. *The Battle of the Atlantic: Hitler's Gray Wolves of the Sea and the Allies' Desperate Struggle to Defeat Them.* New York: Basic Books, 2003.

Wragg, David. *RAF Handbook 1939-1945.* Gloucesershire: Sutton Publishing, 2007.

Wragg, David. *Fleet Air Arm Handbook 1939-1945.* Cheltenham: The History Press, 2019.

Kenneth Wynn, *U-Boat Operations of the Second World War, Volume 1: Career Histories, U1-U510.* Annapolis: Naval Institute Press, 1997.

Kenneth Wynn, *U-Boat Operations of the Second World War, Volume 2: Career Histories, U511-UIT25.* Annapolis: Naval Institute Press, 1998.

Y'Blood, William T. *Hunter Killer: U.S. Navy Escort Carriers in Gallant Battle Against the Nazi U-Boat Menace.* New York: Bantam Books, 1992.

Index

3 Operational Training Unit 172
10 Operational Training Unit 94, 110

Africa 28
Albert F. Paul 7
Alcoa Shipper 9
Alexandra Hoegh 4
Allan Jackson 4
Allegheny 7
Amazon River 108
Arabian Sea 218
Arabutan 7
Armstrong Whitworth Whitley 35–6, 114, 214
Arnold, Henry 57, 59, 60
Aruba 2
Atlas 8
Avro Anson 17, 50
Avro Lancaster 36, 189
Azalea City 6
Azores 33, 41, 60, 105–6, 108, 130, 140–1, 145–6, 157, 163, 165–6, 194, 216, 218

Baltic Sea 202
Barbados 91
Barling, J.W. 180
Barnegat 7
Bastable, B. 161
Bateman, L.J. 168

Battle of the Atlantic 25, 28, 50, 54, 84, 143, 214, 219
Baveystock, L.H. 186, 197
Bay of Biscay 2, 19, 33–6, 56, 84, 85, 87, 88, 92–95, 98, 101, 110–12, 114–15, 123–4, 128, 131–2, 135, 138–9, 144, 150–7, 166, 168, 170–1, 175, 176, 181, 186–7, 190–1, 194, 196–8, 205, 210, 213–14, 216–19
Belinda 10
Bennett, Gordon 198
Bergen, Norway 119, 182, 186, 202
Bidasoa River 49
Bidwell 8
Bigalk, Gerhard 35
Bishop, Albert A. 132
Black Sea 202
Black Watch 211
Blackett, Patrick 28
Boeing 314 Clipper 53
Boeing B-17 Fortress 50–1, 66, 73, 75–8, 84, 103, 105, 140, 156–7, 179, 181, 189, 194, 206, 214–15, 218, 220
Bookless, J.H. 137
Brazil 94, 217–18
Brandenburg division 97
Bremen, Germany 201, 206
Brest, France 60, 93, 162, 175–6, 178
Brilliant, S. 165

Bristol Beaufighter 41, 142
Bristol Bisley 136
Bristol Blenheim 136
Brooke, Alan 55, 60
Brooks, E.J. 18–19
Brownell, Ralph B. 139
Brownsill, A.G. 210
Bruneau, A.A. 204
Buarque 6
Bülow, Otto von 7
Butcher, Harry C. 54, 57
Butler, S.W. 172
Byron D. Benson 8

Cairo, Egypt 143, 147
Canada 41, 61
Canary Islands 90, 166
Cape Canaveral, Florida 5
Cape of Good Hope 162, 218
Cape Hatteras, North Carolina 3–4, 8–9
Cape Horn 169
Cape Town 168
Caribbean 10, 33, 61, 91, 94, 109, 142–3, 214, 216
Caribsea 7
Carmichael, J.W. 177
Casablanca 53, 136–7, 146
Casablanca Conference 52–3, 75, 143, 147
Catahoula 8
Cayru 7
Chamberlain, W.F. 82, 188
Chapman, C.G.W. 183–4
China Arrow 5
Churchill, Winston 1, 15–16, 20, 53–4, 57, 60, 66, 146–7
Cities Service Empire 5
Cities Service Toledo 9
City of Atlanta 3
City of New York 7

Claudius, Herbert C. 12
Cobra 12 119
Collamer 6
Comol Rico 8
Consolidated B-24 Liberator 28, 41–50, 53–5, 59, 61, 63, 66–73, 75, 83–44, 86, 97–102, 105–6, 110, 112, 115, 117–125, 127, 129, 130–1, 137–9, 144–7, 149–156, 159, 174–181, 184, 189–195, 203–7, 212, 214–220
Consolidated PBY Catalina 20–3, 32–3, 41, 59, 66, 75, 79–81, 85, 91–2, 94, 103, 105, 108–9, 114, 123, 136, 149, 159–163, 175, 180–3, 185, 189–90, 199–20, 210–12, 214–15, 218–220
Constanza, Romania 202
Cooledge, Aurelian H. 195
Cornish, D.M. 135
Cornwall 35, 43, 117, 172, 213
Crawford, G. 138
Cruickshank, J.A. 200
Cuba 9, 110
Cundy, P.J. 98
Cyclops 3
Cyprus 173

Dakar 133
Danzig Bay 37
David H. Atwater 8
Dayrose 4
de Havilland Mosquito 172, 175, 179, 185–6, 192, 201, 207–10, 219–20
Degen, Horst 12
Delaware River 5
Delplata 5
Denmark 175, 204–5
Devon 34, 171

INDEX

Distinguished Flying Cross 131–2, 168, 172, 182, 184–5
Distinguished Flying Medal 184–5
Distinguished Service Order 178, 184–5
Dönitz, Karl 2–4, 10, 13, 16, 33, 36, 38–41, 45, 53–4, 62–3, 65–6, 83–5, 93–4, 97, 108–9, 114, 117, 121–2, 124–7, 132, 136–7, 139, 143, 146–7, 163, 166, 173, 175, 180–1, 188–9, 197–8, 202–3, 213–220
Douglas A-20 Havoc 12, 38
Douglas B-18 Bolo 38, 130
Douglas Digby 32
Douglas, Sholto 23
Dowry, Norman T. 164
Drummond, R.P. 140
Dundas, A.D.S. 179
Dunkeswell 63
Durbanm South Africa 162
Dutch West Indies 58–9, 62

Eadie, D.W. 92
Eck, Heinz-Wilheim 169, 170
Eisenhower, Dwight D. 54, 57
Elizabeth Massey 5
Ellis, A.H. 140,-1
Elsa Essberger 42, 43
Empire Gem 4
Empire Woodcock 6
English Channel 54, 60, 175–6, 180, 210, 218
Enloe, C.A. 155
Esparta 8
Esso Baton Rouge 7
Eureka Conference 137, 143, 147

Fairey Albacore 31, 38
Fairey Firefly 189, 193

Fairey Swordfish 20–1, 23, 31, 37, 82, 149, 159–60, 165, 189, 198–9, 213–15, 217–8, 220
Fido acoustic torpedo 71, 81, 107, 125–6, 128, 164, 199, 206
Field, R.N. 205
First Happy Time 2
Fisher, E.J. 110
Fleet Air Arm 802 Squadron 24
Fleet Air Arm 811 Squadron 82
Fleet Air Arm 815 Squadron 37
Fleet Air Arm 816 Squadron 159
Fleet Air Arm 819 Squadron 82, 165
Fleet Air Arm 825 Squadron 160, 198–9
Fleet Air Arm 842 Squadron 159–60
Florida 8
Florida Keys 9
Focke-Wulf Fw 200 Condor 42
Forgetmenot (minefield) 202
Forward 5
France 28
Fraser, A.W. 97–8
Freetown, Sierra Leone 56, 62, 110
French Air Force 114
French Guiana 38
Frances Salman 4
Francis E. Powell 4
Friar Rock 4
Frisco 4
Fritzell, Flying Officer 172

Gamble, G.D. 121–2
Garnett, J.S. 200
Gates, R.T.F. 190
Gelting Bay 211
Georgia 7
German Naval High Command 33, 53, 145
Germany 28, 62

Gibraltar 23, 29–31, 33–4, 54, 61, 88, 90–1, 95, 97, 113, 133–5, 141, 162, 214, 218
Gitana 5
Glenagill 44
Gotenhafen, Germany 202
Graham, M.A. 203
Grand Banks 199
Grant, Ulysses S. 62
Greenland 60, 62, 75, 77, 81–2
Grumman Martlet 21, 24, 31, 214
Grumman TBF Avenger 66, 82, 105–8, 125–9, 149, 156, 159, 163–5, 175, 187, 189, 199, 211, 215–16, 218–220
Grumman F4F Wildcat 21, 24, 105–8, 126–9, 164–6, 211, 219
Guggenberger, Friedrich 109
Gulf King 10
Gulf of Mexico 9, 100
Gulf of Oman 136
Gulfamerica 8
Gulftrade 7

Hadleigh 89
Hagan 9
Halifax, Nova Scotia 2
Hall, R.D. 151
Hamburg, Germany 202, 206
Hampton Roads 9
Hampton Roads, Virginia 8
Hampshire 48, 117
Handley Page Halifax 41, 61, 66, 86–8, 92, 101, 112–13, 124, 151–2, 156, 168, 189, 197, 206, 215, 220
Handley Page Hampden 73, 83, 123
Hardegen, Reinhard 2, 3, 7
Harms, Otto 33
Harris, Arthur 27
Hartenstein, Werner 91

Hawker Hurricane 31
Hawker Typhoon 211
Heidel, Warren 18
Heincke, Hans-Dieter 12
Heinkel He 115 42, 43
Hendrie, Andrew 45
Henke, Werner 165
Heron, P.W. 167, 168
Hessler, Gunther 45
Heyse, Ulrich 5
Hispaniola 109
Hitler, Adolf 1, 2,4, 62–3, 220
Hilton, Sergeant 190
HMCS *Athabascan* 101
HMCS *Haida* 179
HMCS *Oakville* 33
HMCS *Restigouche* 195
HMCS *Skeena* 9
HMCS *St Laurent* 83
HMCS *Wetaskiwin* 9
HMS *Active* 171
HMS *Activity* 165
HMS *Anthony* 162
HMS *Archer* 82
HMS *Ark Royal* 23–4, 109, 173
HMS *Ascension* 197
HMS *Audacity* 23–4, 35
HMS *Avenger* 37–8
HMS *Biter* 81–2
HMS *Blackfly* 163
HMS *Bluebell* 141
HMS *Campania* 199
HMS *Castleton* 32, 132
HMS *Chaser* 159–60
HMS *Courageous* 24
HMS *Dulverton* 37
HMS *Duncan* 121–2
HMS *Eagle* 38
HMS *Eskimo* 179
HMS *Fencer* 159–60
HMS *Fleetwood* 87, 141

HMS *Fowey* 18
HMS *Hero* 37
HMS *Hursley* 94
HMS *Hurworth* 37
HMS *Impacable* 193
HMS *Isis* 94
HMS *Keppel* 198
HMS *Kilmarnock* 163
HMS *Kimberley* 89
HMS *Kite* 113, 132, 198
HMS *Labuan* 205
HMS *Le Tiger* 12
HMS *Lincolnshire* 140
HMS *Loch Fada* 205
HMS *Magpie* 160
HMS *Mahratta* 124
HMS *Marne* 33
HMS *Matabele* 132
HMS *Myosotis* 12
HMS *Newark* 32
HMS *Onslaw* 38
HMS *Orwell* 132
HMS *Pakenham* 37
HMS *Pathfinder* 82
HMS *Petard* 37
HMS *Poppy* 141
HMS *Queen* 211
HMS *Rochester* 19
HMS *Searcher* 211
HMS *Starling* 160, 196
HMS *Tracker* 165
HMS *Trumpeter* 211
HMS *Vanoc* 163
HMS *Veteran* 101
HMS *Victorious* 38
HMS *Vidette* 121–2
HMS *Vindex* 160, 198–9
HMS *Warspite* 20
HMS *Waveney* 123
HMS *Wild Goose* 113, 160, 205
HMS *Wishart* 162

HMS *Woodpecker* 113
HMS *Wren* 113, 160, 191
Hoffman, Eberhard 34–5
Honduras 8
Hopgood, R.B. 33
Hornell, D.E. 184–5
HX 178 6
HX 217 46
HX 229 69, 77
HX 288 68
HX 270 163

Iberian Peninsula 85
Iceland 32, 51, 60, 66–8, 73, 77, 79, 80–1, 83, 97–8, 117–20, 123, 132–3, 149–50, 167, 213–15, 217, 219
IndiaArrow 5
Indian Ocean 143, 164, 168, 193–4, 201
Ireland 75, 77, 83, 133, 137, 150–1, 153, 159–60, 171–2, 217
Irish Rose 194
Irish Sea 205
Irving, W.J. 154
Ismay, Hastings 57
Isted, D.J. 68
Italy 62

Jacksonville, Florida 8
James, F.H.W. 80
Japan 57, 62
Jennings, W.H.T. 111
Johansen, E. 185–6
John D. Gill 7

Kals, Ernst 4
Kerimiai 18
Key West 2
Kiel, Germany 97–8, 168, 201, 206
Kilbotn, Norway 211

King, Ernest 10–11, 53, 55–9, 61, 147
Kittys Brock 9
Knight's Cross 35, 99, 128, 139
Königsberg, Germany 206
Krafft, C.F. 185
Krech, Gunther 101
Kristiansand, Norway 181, 192
KS 520 12
Kuenning, T.E. 100

L'Orient 60
La Pallice, France 123
La Spezia, Italy 89
Lady Hawkins 4
Lagens, Azores 130, 140–1, 156, 166, 194
Lake Osweya 6
Lapwing 5
Lassen, Georg 106
Lawrence, J.T. 205
Le Maistre, Flight Lieutenant 151–2
Leatherdale, Flight Sergeant 184
Leif 6
Leigh Light 97, 110, 134–5, 138, 141, 144, 151, 153, 167–8, 170, 176, 181, 191, 196
Lenson, George Thomas 48–9
Lerwick, Scotland 184
Liberia 168
Lindemann, Frederick 28
Lisbon, Portugal 88
Little, D.A. 196
Lockheed Hudson P-8 11–12, 17, 20–1, 23, 29–32, 38, 50–1, 66, 73, 75, 79, 80–1, 88–91, 113–14, 136, 146, 213–5, 217, 219, 220
Lockheed Ventura 83, 105, 109, 130–1, 145, 162, 173, 220

Longmore, R.M. 119
Lorient, France 165, 168
Louisiana 9

MacBride, R.E. 182
Madagascar 136, 216
Magnetic Anomaly Detection 162–3, 211
Marczak, R. 210
Marshall, George C. 55–7
Martin PBM Mariner 12, 32, 109
M.F. Elliot 9
Maison Blanche 31
Major Wheeler 5
Mamura 5
Margot 9
Marore 6
Marshall, George C. 10, 55–6, 58
Martin PBM Mariner 94, 105, 108, 130–1, 135, 193, 215, 219–20
Maus, August 127
Maydew, G.R. 88
McRae, D.F. 141
Mediterranean 3, 23, 29, 37–8, 50, 54–5, 84–5, 88–90, 93, 115, 133–4, 140, 162–3, 170, 173, 175, 188, 214, 216
Menominee 7
Merchant Prince 89
Miraflores 6
MKS 30 141
Moore, K.O. 178
Morison, Samuel Eliot 11, 13
Morocco 143
Mundy, E.A.K. 173
Murmansk 60
Murray, K.M. 211–12
Musgrave, J. 81

Natal, South Africa 136
Newfoundland 2, 11–12, 32, 55, 60

INDEX

New Jersey 4, 7
New York 2, 8
Nicol, J.D. 204
Norfolk, Virginia 7
Normandy 176, 188
North American P-51 Mustang 211
North Atlantic 33, 61
Northern Ireland 42, 45, 48, 66, 81, 93, 117, 120, 166–8, 172
Norlavore 6
Norness 3
Norvana 4
North American B-25 Mitchell 139
North Carolina 3–4, 7–8
Norway 55, 83, 103, 150, 159–60, 176, 193, 199, 218
Norwegian Sea 182, 188, 190, 192, 211
Nott, D.D. 206
Nottinghamshire 36
Nova Scotia 3

Ocana 7
Oklahoma 7
Olinda 6
Oliver, H.J. 204
Olympic 4
ON 166 68
ON 206 120
ON 207 122
ON 214 163
ONS 10 118
ONS 20 121
ONS 24 163
ONS 120 44
ONS 136 45
ONS 206 121
Ontario 7
Operation Anvil 147
Operation Bolero 56
Operation Husky 61–2

Operation Overlord 146–7, 175
Operation Paukenschlag 2
Operation Torch 55, 62
Oran 31
Orkan 111, 129
Oslofjoid, Norway 202
Ostermann, Johannes 12
Outer Hebrides 77

Pan Massachusetts 5
Panama Canal 38
Parker, G.W.T. 180
Paynter, M.H. 167
Peleus 168
Port Lyautey, French Morocco 86
Poske, Hans-Geog Friedrich 5
Posnett, J.W.A. 176
Potez 114
Pearl Harbor 1, 2
Peisander 9
Piening, Adolf 7
Pim, R.P. 54, 57
Plow City 9
Pola, Yugoslavia 173
Portal, Charles 47, 56–9, 61
Potier, G.G. 191
Pound, Dudley 55–60
Privet II 37
Procter, J.R.E. 72

Quaet-Faslem, Jürgen 30
Quebec Conference 143
Quinn, J. 187

Rabaul 61
Rayner, H.J. 192–3
Royal Australian Air Force 83, 213, 216, 219
RAAF 10 Squadron 19, 92, 131, 171, 194–5
RAAF 455 Squadron 83

265

RAAF 459 Squadron 114
RAAF 461 Squadron 92, 113, 132, 171, 196
Raeder, Erich 63
RAF 29, 32, 34, 37, 44, 66, 73, 94, 101–2, 111, 122, 138, 142, 151–2, 173, 177, 181, 184, 199, 202, 206–7, 211–14, 217, 219
RAF 8 Squadron 170
RAF 36 Squadron 170
RAF 47 Squadron 37
RAF 48 Squadron 88, 113
RAF 53 Squadron 98, 138–40, 151–5, 176–7, 181, 190–1
RAF 58 Squadron 37, 86–8, 92, 101, 124, 168
RAF 59 Squadron 48–50, 117, 121–2, 150
RAF 61 Squadron 36
RAF 77 Squadron 36
RAF 86 Squadron 48, 66, 69–71, 84, 117–21, 137, 149–50, 152, 157, 180–1, 190, 204–5
RAF 120 Squadron 42–8, 66–72, 84, 97, 117–22, 130, 149, 152, 157, 204, 214
RAF 126 Squadron 211
RAF 143 Squadron 207–9
RAF 172 Squadron 34, 94, 110–11, 128, 142, 152, 156, 166, 170, 191, 198
RAF 179 Squadron 35, 94, 110, 129, 133–135, 140–41, 171, 181, 210
RAF 190 Squadron 103
RAF 200 Squadron 122
RAF 201 Squadron 93, 186–7, 195, 197
RAF 202 Squadron 91, 162
RAF 204 Squadron 19

RAF 206 Squadron 50–2, 75–6, 78, 84, 103, 156–7, 179, 189
RAF 209 Squadron 22–3
RAF 210 Squadron 19, 92, 114, 160–1, 199, 200, 211, 212
RAF 220 Squadron 51–2, 75–6, 84, 140–1, 156, 194
RAF 224 Squadron 48, 85, 98–9, 101–2, 117, 122, 155, 176–7, 180–1, 192, 203–4
RAF 228 Squadron 18–9, 93, 98, 112, 114, 131–2, 187
RAF 233 Squadron 29, 90
RAF 235 Squadron 207–10
RAF 244 Squadron 136
RAF 248 Squadron 172, 179, 192, 207–9
RAF 262 Squadron 162
RAF 265 Squadron 201
RAF 269 Squadron 21, 32, 79, 80, 136
RAF 304 Squadron 170, 210
RAF 311 Squadron 34, 138, 179, 193
RAF 330 Squadron 33, 185, 197
RAF 333 Squadron 161, 184, 185, 201
RAF 344 Squadron 133
RAF 500 Squadron 29–31, 89, 90, 173
RAF 502 Squadron 35, 88, 112, 124, 152, 156, 197
RAF 547 Squadron 111, 204
RAF 608 Squadron 30, 89
RAF 612 Squadron 135, 138, 166–7, 170
RAF 621 Squadron 169
RAF Aldergrove 66, 68, 70, 117
RAF Ballykelly 43–4, 48, 66, 75, 117, 119, 121–2, 149–50, 152, 204
RAF Banff 207, 209
RAF Beaulieu 48, 117

INDEX

RAF Benbecula 77
RAF Berca 93
RAF Bilda 89
RAF Bomber Command 17, 20, 27–8, 41, 201, 202, 206
RAF Castle Archdale 81, 93, 132–3
RAF Chivenor 34, 135, 168
RAF Coastal Command 17, 20–1, 23, 27, 32, 35, 41, 44, 112, 117, 120, 146, 149, 150, 151, 213, 214, 220
RAF Fighter Command 17, 20
RAF Kinloss 76
RAF Leuchars 190
RAF Limavady 166
RAF Milltown 192, 203
RAF Mount Batten 171, 194
RAF Nutts Corner 42
RAF Pembroke Dock 18–9, 92–3, 131, 187, 195–7, 213
RAF Portreath 172
RAF Predannack 43, 102, 179
RAF Reykjavik 66–7, 70–2, 117
RAF Scuiscuiban, Somalia 169
RAF St Angelo 172
RAF St David's 156, 197
RAF St Eval 35–6, 42, 50, 85–8, 92, 99, 102, 117, 150, 152–5, 176, 177–9, 190–1, 210, 213
RAF St Mawgan 102
RAF Stornoway 180
RAF Sullom Voe 160–1, 185, 197, 199, 211, 213
RAF Sumburgh 83, 185
RAF Syerston 36
RAF Tain 180, 190
RAF Talbenny 34
RAF Thorney Island 49, 98, 117, 213
RAF Wick 83, 181–2
Royal Canadian Air Force 29, 32, 81, 214, 219

RCAF 5 Squadron 81
RCAF 10 Squadron 32, 123
RCAF 113 Squadron 12, 32
RCAF 145 Squadron 32
RCAF 162 Squadron 163, 181, 183–4
RCAF 404 Squadron 209
RCAF 407 Squadron 167–8, 181, 198
RCAF 415 Squadron 123
RCAF 422 Squadron 133, 139, 172
RCAF 423 Squadron 81, 132–3
Rehwinkel, Ernst-August 6
R.P. Resor 6
Republic 5
Reykjavik, Iceland 22, 45–7, 79–80, 97, 108, 118, 120, 130–1, 136, 150, 183–4, 214
Rio Blanco 8
Robert E. Lee 12
Roberts, H.S. 82
Roberts, J.P. 171
Roberts, J.R. 183
Rochester 4
Roosevelt, Elliot 60
Roosevelt, Franklin D. 1, 53, 57–8, 60, 62, 220
Rosenstiel, Jürgen von 34
Roskill, S.W. 39, 84
Rostin, Erwin 12
Royal Navy 24, 29, 144, 146, 165, 193, 198–200, 205, 213–14, 219
Royal Navy Fleet Air Arm 23, 31, 38, 159, 219
Russell, A.H. 133

SAAF 17 Squadron 173
Salanis, Greece 202
Sallenger, Lieutenant 126
Samuel, A.C.I 77

San Antonio 10
San Gil 5
Saro London 17
SC 122 70
Schacht, Harro 91
Schonberg, Adolf 101
Schultze, Heinz-Otto 5, 6
Scotland 76–7, 150, 167, 180–1, 190–2, 193, 207, 213
Scott, Sergeant 185
Seatrain Texas 4
Second Battle of Narvik 20
Second Happy Time 2, 11, 13, 25, 28, 32, 86, 100–1, 114, 128, 142, 197
Seehausen, Gerhard 165
Sextant Conference 137, 143, 147
Sherman, L. 182–3
Shetland Islands 83, 160, 183, 185, 200, 203, 212
Sicily 61
Sierra Leone 122
Sisson, B.A. 150
Short Sunderland 17–20, 45, 50, 66, 73, 81–8, 92–3, 112, 114, 131–3, 139, 171–2, 175, 184–7, 189, 191, 194–7, 213–6, 218, 220
Skatefellingur 32
Skottland 9
Slazark 171
Sleep, David Mackie 48–9
Smith, E.C. 92
Smith, N.E.M. 180
South America 38, 61, 85
Southall, I.F. 196
Spitsbergen Island 198
St John's, Newfoundland 4, 129
St Laurent, Sergeant 185
St Lawrence 3
St Nazaire, France 102, 172, 197
Staats, Georg 139

Stalin, Josef 62
Straits of Gibraltar 162–3, 175
Stavanger, Norway 183
Strelow, Siegfried 99–100
Suhren, Lieutenant-Commander 44
Supermarine Stranraer 17
Supermarine Walrus 31–2
Suriname 38
Svalbard 37
Sweeny, R. 102
Sydney, Nova Scotia 2

Tafaouri 31
Tamaulipas 8
Tehran, Iran 143
Terceira 141
Thomson, R.B. 103
Tiger 7
Tilley, W.B. 194–5
Tizard, Henry 27–8
Tolten 7
Topp, Erich 4, 8
Torpex depth charge 34, 36–7, 46, 50, 83, 86, 91, 102, 111–12, 161, 168, 190–1, 194
Toulon, France 173, 201
Trigg, Lloyd 123
Trinidad 2
Trojer, Hans 124
Trondheim, Norway 103, 194
Turner, A.A. 111

U-9 202
U-18 202
U-24 202
U-26 19, 213
U-43 108
U-52 211
U-55 18, 213
U-56 206
U-64 20, 213

INDEX

U-66 4, 125–6
U-67 107
U-68 165
U-72 206
U-73 31–2, 38
U-77 89–90
U-81 23, 37, 109, 173
U-83 89
U-84 123
U-85 12–3
U-89 82
U-91 82, 128–9
U-94 7, 33
U-96 6, 206
U-97 114
U-101 211
U-103 5
U-105 114
U-106 4, 9, 132
U-107 5, 197
U-109 71
U-117 126
U-118 105, 106
U-123 2–4, 7–8
U-125 4
U-126 110
U-128 5, 95
U-130 4
U-131 24, 214
U-134 110
U-135 108
U-153 12
U-154 8
U-155 7, 38, 211
U-156 5, 91
U-157 9, 12
U-158 7, 9, 12
U-159 109
U-160 7, 8, 106
U-161 131
U-164 91

U-165 34
U-166 12–13
U-167 90
U-169 77–8
U-172 130, 142
U-174 83
U-177 155
U-185 114, 127, 130
U-189 70
U-194 108
U-197 136
U-199 109
U-200 97–8
U-203 82
U-209 81
U-211 141
U-215 12
U-216 48–9
U-217 105–6
U-219 199
U-220 129
U-221 124, 133
U-227 83
U-228 87, 187, 202
U-231 122, 166
U-232 110
U-236 211
U-237 206
U-239 201
U-241 161
U-243 194–5
U-249 210
U-251 208–9
U-256 155, 176
U-258 72
U-259 29
U-261 37
U-262 126, 202
U-264 128
U-265 75–6
U-266 88

U-268 94
U-270 157, 181, 196–7
U-271 102, 155
U-273 80
U-274 122
U-276 161, 211
U-277 160
U-279 131
U-283 167
U-280 137–8
U-283 168
U-288 165
U-292 151
U-304 72, 130
U-305 82
U-309 198
U-317 180
U-319 189–90
U-320 212
U-321 210
U-326 211
U-331 31
U-332 7, 86
U-333 94, 187
U-336 136
U-338 88
U-340 141
U-341 123–4
U-342 163
U-343 170–1
U-344 198
U-347 190
U-348 206
U-350 206
U-352 12
U-359 109
U-361 200
U-365 199
U-366 159
U-373 178
U-378 129

U-380 173
U-382 206
U-383 131
U-384 77
U-385 196
U-388 108
U-389 118
U-391 138
U-392 162–3
U-393 211
U-394 198
U-402 128
U-403 108, 133
U-404 6–9, 101–2
U-410 173
U-411 29
U-412 35
U-415 135, 181
U-417 103
U-418 92
U-419 119
U-421 173
U-422 128
U-423 185
U-426 171
U-429 206
U-430 206
U-431 135
U-432 5
U-435 99–100
U-437 202
U-440 93
U-441 93, 181
U-442 88
U-445 198
U-446 37
U-447 90
U-448 133
U-451 23, 214
U-452 22, 214
U-453 90, 173

INDEX

U-454 132
U-456 71
U-459 111
U-460 128
U-461 113
U-462 112–3
U-463 88, 119
U-464 32, 33
U-465 92
U-466 109, 201
U-467 81
U-468 82, 122
U-469 77
U-470 120–1
U-471 201
U-472 159
U-476 150, 161
U-477 181–2
U-478 180
U-480 182
U-482 197
U-487 106
U-489 132
U-502 9, 34
U-503 12, 32
U-504 5, 113
U-505 214
U-506 100
U-507 91
U-508 139
U-509 107
U-512 38
U-513 109
U-514 99
U-515 165
U-517 38
U-524 86
U-527 107
U-528 87
U-529 68
U-533 136

U-534 198, 204
U-535 98–9
U-539 119
U-540 122
U-542 141–2
U-543 199
U-544 163–4
U-545 167
U-546 154
U-549 166
U-552 4, 7–8
U-558 101
U-559 37
U-561 50
U-562 94
U-563 92
U-564 6, 45, 114
U-565 29, 202
U-566 135
U-569 82, 188
U-570 21
U-571 171–2
U-572 131
U-573 29
U-575 156
U-576 12
U-578 6
U-579 204
U-584 128–9
U-586 201
U-588 7, 9
U-589 37
U-590 108
U-591 109
U-594 114
U-595 30
U-596 202
U-597 46
U-598 100–1
U-599 49
U-601 160–1

U-604 127, 130
U-605 29
U-606 33
U-607 112
U-608 170, 191
U-610 133
U-611 46, 47
U-614 112
U-615 130
U-616 170
U-617 133–4
U-618 139, 191
U-619 32
U-620 92
U-622 103
U-623 68
U-624 75–6
U-625 172
U-627 51
U-628 98
U-629 177
U-632 70
U-635 70
U-640 81
U-642 114, 201
U-643 120–1
U-646 80
U-648 94, 107, 140
U-652 37
U-653 6, 9, 160
U-654 38
U-656 8, 9, 11–12, 32
U-662 108
U-663 92
U-664 126–7
U-666 87, 159
U-667 135
U-674 160
U-675 172
U-677 206
U-681 205

U-682 206
U-701 12, 32
U-705 36
U-706 123
U-707 140
U-710 78
U-711 211
U-714 167
U-715 183–4
U-731 163
U-735 202
U-736 170
U-740 178
U-742 201
U-746 211
U-747 206
U-749 206
U-751 24, 35–6
U-752 82
U-753 7, 81
U-754 7, 12, 32
U-755 89
U-758 206
U-759 109
U-761 162
U-763 152, 206
U-764 142
U-765 160
U-766 198
U-771 181, 201
U-777 202
U-801 164
U-803 173
U-804 185, 208
U-821 179
U-843 208
U-844 121
U-846 168
U-847 128
U-848 139
U-849 139

INDEX

U-850 142–3
U-852 168–70
U-854 173
U-860 187–8
U-863 193–4
U-867 192
U-870 206
U-871 194
U-872 201
U-921 172
U-923 206
U-927 210
U-951 99
U-952 201
U-955 187
U-960 173
U-964 121–2
U-966 138
U-967 202
U-969 202
U-970 187
U-971 179–80
U-973 160
U-976 172–3
U-980 182–3
U-981 198
U-982 206
U-990 150, 161
U-993 154, 187, 202
U-998 186
U-1008 205
U-1017 204
U-1059 164
U-1062 142
U-1060 193
U-1065 208
U-1106 203
U-1107 205–6
U-1131 206
U-1163 201
U-1164 201

U-1167 206
U-1197 206
U-1201 206
U-1210 211
U-1221 206
U-1222 196
U-1225 184–5
U-1227 206
U-1229 199
U-1273 207
U-1279 205
U-2323 202
U-2340 206
U-2359 209
U-2509 206
U-2514 206
U-2515 206
U-2516 206
U-2523 206
U-2530 202
U-2542 206
U-3003 206
U-3007 206
U-3505 206
U-3508 206
U-3512 206
U-3519 207
U-3520 206
U-3523 205
UIT-22 161–2
U-Boat Command 11, 36, 45, 53, 98, 140, 163–4, 175, 190, 203, 208
Ulysses 8
United Kingdom 58, 60, 62, 97
United States Army Air Forces 27, 29, 38, 101, 129, 206, 214, 219
USAAF 1st Antisubmarine Squadron 50, 99–100
USAAF 2nd Antisubmarine Squadron 86

USAAF 4th Antisubmarine Squadron 102, 123
USAAF 8th Air Force 206
USAAF 15th Air Force 173, 201–2
USAAF 19th Antisubmarine Squadron 101
USAAF 45th Squadron 38
USAAF 59th Squadron 12
USAAF 99th Squadron 38
USAAF 396th Squadron 12
US Eighth Air Force 103
USN 24, 27, 29, 32, 63, 94, 100, 105–6, 109, 193–195, 205, 214, 216, 217, 218, 219
USN VB-103 Squadron 139, 155
USN VB-105 Squadron 123, 138
USN VB-107 Squadron 127, 130, 139, 155, 194
USN VB-125 Squadron 83
USN VB-127 Squadron 162
USN VB-128 Squadron 131, 135
USN VB-130 Squadron 130
USN VB-197 Squadron 109
USN VC-1 Squadron 125
USN VC-6 Squadron 107, 164
USN VC-9 Squadron 82, 105, 128, 187
USN VC-13 Squadron 129, 164
USN VC-19 Squadron 142
USN VC-29 Squadron 107
USN VC-42 Squadron 199
USN VC-58 Squadron 165
USN VP-32 Squadron 109
USN VP-53 Squadron 91
USN VP-58 Squadron 165
USN VP-63 Squadron 162–3, 210
USN VP-73 Squadron 33
USN VP-74 Squadron 12, 94, 109, 131
USN VP-82 Squadron 11–2
USN VP-83 Squadron 91
USN VP-84 Squadron 81
USN VP-92 Squadron 33
USN VP-94 Squadron 108
USN VP-103 Squadron 138
USN VP-107 Squadron 100
USN VP-110 Squadron 138
USN VP-204 Squadron 130
USN VP-205 Squadron 130
USN VP-211 Squadron 193
USN VPB-103 Squadron 102, 205
USN VPB-112 Squadron 205
USN ZP 21 Squadron 109
USCGC *Legare* 8
USCGC *Nike* 5
USCGC *Thetis* 12
USS *Ahrens* 166
USS *Barker* 106
USS *Barr* 166
USS *Barry* 129
USS *Block Island* 129, 164–6
USS *Bogue* 82, 105–6, 129, 142, 199
USS *Borie* 129
USS *Bronstein* 164
USS *Card* 125–7, 129
USS *Chatelain* 165
USS *Clemson* 107
USS *Core* 105–7, 127, 129, 131
USS *Corry* 164
USS *Cythera* 128
USS *Dahlgren* 110
USS *Dupont* 142
USS *Ellis* 38
USS *Eugene E. Elmore* 166
USS *Gannet* 9
USS *G.E. Badger* 142
USS *Goff* 129
USS *Guadalcanal* 164–5
USS *Hamilton* 8
USS *Herbert* 8
USS *Hilary P. Jones* 170
USS *Jacob Jones* 6

USS *Jouett* 95
USS *Lea* 33
USS *Manley* 8
USS *Mayo* 7
USS *McCormick* 107
USS *Moffett* 95
USS *Noa* 8
USS *Osmond Ingram* 106
USS PC-566 12
USS PC-494 108
USS PC-1196 130
USS *Reuben James* 4
USS *Roe* 4
USS *Roper* 12
USS *Santee* 105, 107–8
USS *Saucy* 109
USS *Solomons* 187
USS *Tripoli* 199
USS *Wake Island* 199
USS *Walker* 130

Vaclite 18
Varanger 4
Vaughn, R.W.G. 201
Venore 4
Vickers Vildebeest 17
Vickers Warwick 184, 210
Vickers Wellesley 37
Vickers Wellington 34–5, 93–4, 110–12, 128, 132–5, 138, 140–2, 144, 149, 152, 156, 159, 166–71, 181, 189, 191, 198, 210, 214, 219, 220
Victoria Cross 123, 185, 200

Victolite 6
Virginia 7, 8
Vogel, Victor 9
von Bulow, Otto 101
von Forstner, Freiherr Siegfried 128
von Pommer-Esche, Gerd 106
von Puttkamer, Captain 4
Vought OS2U Kingfisher 12, 32

Wales 18, 34, 156
Wallace, A.F. 194
Walters, I.F.B. 195–6
War Shipping Administration 10
Waterbury, Pilot Officer 184
W.C. Fairbanks 4
W.D. Anderson 5
W.L. Steed 5
Weigle, D.E. 188
Wenzel, Wolfgang 166
West Ivis 4
West Notus 9
West Sussex 49, 117
White, S. 131
Wilhelmshaven, Germany 202, 206
Williams, R.P. 107
Winter, Werner 5
Wright, H.W.B. 113
Wurdemann, Erich 100

Young, A.B. 192

Zapp, Richard 4
Zarian 19